LIVERPOOL LABOUR

To Julie, and Louis, Catherine and Naomi

Liverpool Labour

**SOCIAL AND POLITICAL INFLUENCES
ON THE DEVELOPMENT OF THE
LABOUR PARTY IN LIVERPOOL, 1900–1939**

Sam Davies

KEELEUNIVERSITY**PRESS**

First published in 1996 by
Keele University Press
Keele, Staffordshire

© Sam Davies

Composed by KUP
Printed on acid-free paper
by Hartnolls, Bodmin
Cornwall, England

ISBN 1 85331 161 8

Contents

List of abbreviations

AEU	Amalgamated Engineering Union
AMWU	Amalgamated Marine Workers' Union
ASW	Amalgamated Society of Woodworkers
AUBTW	Amalgamated Union of Building Trade Workers
CIO	Congress of Industrial Organizations
ETU	Electrical Trades' Union
ILP	Independent Labour Party
LLRC	Liverpool Labour Representation Committee
LRC	Labour Representation Committee
LTC	Liverpool Trades Council (up to 1921)
LTCLP	Liverpool Trades Council and Labour Party (from 1921)
MEA	Municipal Employees' Association
NAFTA	National Amalgamated Furnishing Trades' Associations
NASFU	National Amalgamated Seamen and Firemen's Union (up to 1893)
NATSOPA	National Society of Operative Printers and Assistants
NAUL	National Amalgamated Union of Labour
NSFU	National Sailors' and Firemen's Union (after 1893)
NUC	National Union of Clerks
NUDAW	National Union of Distributive and Allied Workers
NUDL	National Union of Dock Labourers
NUGMW	National Union of General and Municipal Workers
NUR	National Union of Railwaymen
NUS	National Union of Seamen
NUSEC	National Union of Societies for Equal Citizenship
NUVB	National Union of Vehicle Builders
NUWM	National Unemployed Workers' Movement
RCA	Railway Clerks' Association
SDF	Social Democratic Federation
TGWU	Transport and General Workers' Union
UPW	Union of Post Office Workers
WCA	Women's Citizens Association
WMCA	Working Men's Conservative Association

List of tables

List of appendices

List of figures

List of illustrations

Preface and acknowledgements

This book had its origins in a collaborative research project, entitled *Economy, Society and Class in Twentieth-Century Liverpool*, which was initiated by a group of historians and social scientists at Liverpool Polytechnic (now Liverpool John Moores University) and the University of Liverpool. After I had been appointed as a research assistant on the project, I spent two years at the Polytechnic laying down the groundwork for my thesis on the Labour Party in Liverpool. The demands of a full-time lecturing post, and also a decision by project members to concentrate on producing collaborative work, meant that my thesis was shelved for a while. Two books (*Merseyside in Crisis* and *Genuinely Seeking Work*[1]) and a number of short reports were produced collectively, and it was only in 1991 that I turned my full attention back to the development of the Liverpool Labour Party.

No doubt I would have put different emphases in this book if it had been completed at an earlier stage. Nevertheless, the questions that I started off with have remained essentially the same. Why was the Labour Party so weak in Liverpool before World War II? How did the socio-economic and political context of Liverpool affect the development of the party? How exceptional was Liverpool in British terms? What can the Liverpool experience tell us about the nature of working-class politics? The basic structure and analytical approach that I adopted to answer these questions has also remained largely intact. In the interdisciplinary spirit of the original project of which it was a part, this book is not a history of the Liverpool Labour Party. Rather, it is an analysis of certain relationships in the economy, society and politics of a locality as they affected the Labour Party. These include relationships between occupation, religion and gender, and political mobilization; between class, class consciousness, culture and political practice; and between the structure and organization of working-class political forces, and the political system those forces had to work within.

Inevitably, given the long gestation period of this work, I owe a great deal to the assistance and encouragement of a very large number of colleagues and friends. One of the greatest pleasures for me in seeing this work in print will be that I will be able to acknowledge all these helpers, and to thank them for their efforts.

My first thanks must go to the founders of the original research project, Nev Kirk, Tony Lane, Adrian Mellor, Martyn Nightingale, and Ron Noon. They provided an analytical and theoretical framework which informed my research from the beginning. Other members of the project helped me enormously, especially Linda Grant and Andy Shallice. Nev Kirk, Tony Lane and Martyn Nightingale also acted as the supervisors of my thesis, and without the benefit of their expertise, advice and encouragement, I would never have completed it.

At various stages of its production, drafts of this book have also been read and commented on by John Belchem, Robbie Gray, John Herson, David Howell, Marion Price, and John Walton. All offered valuable suggestions, corrected errors, and pointed out new avenues of enquiry. Further good advice and assistance came from Karen Hunt (on women and the Labour Party), and Phil Cubbin (on maps and diagrams).

I have also benefitted from presenting various aspects of this book in seminar papers to the Social Studies Department of Liverpool Polytechnic, the Extra-Mural Department of Liverpool University, the Historic Society of Lancashire and Cheshire, the Department of Economics and Economic History at Manchester Metropolitan University, and the History Department of the University of Pittsburgh. I also presented papers to conferences at Warwick University, Wayne State University, Detroit, and (twice) to the North-West Labour History Society. The feed-back I received from all these audiences was invaluable, but I was particularly helped and encouraged by the comments of Eric Taplin and Mike Power in Liverpool, Pat Ayers in Manchester, Joe White in Pittsburgh, and Carol Morgan in Detroit. In the end, of course, I am responsible for the arguments and interpretations put forward in the book.

The staff of various libraries have helped enormously in facilitating the research for this book. Janet Smith and the staff of the Local History Section of Liverpool City Library were most patient and efficient. The staff of the Marx Memorial Library in London, of the Modern Records Centre at Warwick University, and of Hull University Library were also most helpful. The Inter-Library Loans Unit, and Jim Ainsworth and the library staff of Liverpool John Moores University, provided great assistance in tracking down secondary sources. My thanks also to Eric Taplin, Marij van Helmond, Lorraine Knowles, Clare Bates, Karen Kelly and Cyril Taylor, for their help with illustrations.

Eric Taplin, Dave Kermode and Dave McEvoy, successive Heads of my Department/School, all provided encouragement to continue my research, and financial and institutional support whenever possible.

For the most part, I have carried out the physical process of typing the words of this book, but at a critical stage Sue Barlow provided rapid and efficient assistance in transferring the whole text from one word-processing system to another. My colleague, Bob Morley, deserves special thanks for providing coffee and an adequate printer to run off my thesis. In the final stages of seeing the book into print, Lucia Crothall, Nicola

Pike, and the staff of Keele University Press have provided great expertise and patience.

Finally, the arrival of my children provided me with the greatest inspiration of all to complete this book. Their mother gave me advice, toleration, and encouragement throughout its writing. Without the four of them, there would not have been a book, and for this reason I dedicate it to them.

References

1. M. Nightingale (ed), *Merseyide in Crisis* (Manchester Free Press, Manchester: 1980); S. Davies, *et al.*, *Genuinely Seeking Work: Mass Unemployment on Merseyside in the 1930s* (Liverpress, Liverpool: 1992).

Introduction

Liverpool – 'The last place God made'?

For many socialists and trade-unionists, Liverpool Labour's time had come in the immediate aftermath of the First World War. Nationally and internationally, labour was on the offensive. Locally, the great gains in union organization following the 1911 transport strike had been consolidated in the war years, culminating in a widespread and confident industrial militancy in 1919. The Liverpool Labour Party, which had made limited progress before the war, registered substantial gains in the local elections of November 1919. It seemed that the great proletarian city of Liverpool was on the brink of becoming a Labour stronghold at last.

May Day 1920 was intended to be the occasion to celebrate Liverpool Labour's coming of age. The local Trades Council felt confident enough to mount a major demonstration.[1] However, May Day, a Saturday, was marked by heavy rain, and the march to Sheil Park called by the Trades Council attracted only 1,200 supporters. For the speeches in the park, the crowd grew to perhaps 2,000 at most. A call for workers throughout the city to stop work for the day in sympathy with the celebrations was also largely ignored. Trades Council members were quoted as saying the event was 'not a success'. One prominent labour organizer in the city, Mrs Mary Bamber, put it more strongly. In her judgement: 'Liverpool was the last place God made so far as industrial solidarity was concerned.'

Meanwhile, across the Irish Sea from Liverpool, Irish Catholics were engaged in a war of independence against British rule. For Liverpool Catholics, most of whom were of Irish descent, and many Liverpool Protestants too, this was as important a conflict as the struggle between capital and labour. The unhappy scene in Sheil Park took a further twist when, at four o'clock, uninvited guests tried to join the May Day celebrations: some 2,000 supporters of Sinn Fein, led by a local Irish Nationalist councillor, P. J. Kelly, arrived unexpectedly. There followed an embarrassing hour or so, with the Nationalist contingent kicking their heels at one side of the park, while the Labour crowds clung tenaciously to their platforms. Eventually, as the Labour supporters began to drift away, one of the vacated platforms was conceded. Nationalist speeches followed in support of the Sinn Fein hunger strikers being held in Worm-

17

1 'Bloody Sunday', 13 August 1911. Part of the vast crowd assembled on St George's Plateau in the centre of Liverpool during the transport strike. This was a turning point in the unionization of the Liverpool working class, but political mobilization was still a long way off, as the events of May Day 1920 were to demonstrate.

wood Scrubs and Mountjoy prisons. The Trades Council organizers were nowhere to be seen by now. It seemed that Liverpool Labour's time might not have come after all.

The farcical events of May Day 1920 could be seen as symbolizing the Labour Party's weakness in Liverpool between the wars. Working-class support for Labour was not as great as some expected. At the same time, religious sectarianism and ethnic division appeared to loom large, as an unwelcome distraction as far as Labour was concerned. The local press, hostile to both Labour and the Irish Nationalists, took some pleasure in highlighting the failure of the celebrations and the evident political divisions revealed.

May Day 1920 was a false dawn, as this book will show. The recent image of Liverpool as a Labour Party bastion, and a hot-bed of political militancy, bears little resemblance to its earlier history. In fact, a number of important changes can be identified in the labour movement in Liverpool in the last quarter of the twentieth century. The decline of the local economy was the backdrop to a steady process of decay in areas of trade-union organization and strength. On the other hand, economic crisis was accompanied by a leftward shift in the local Labour Party. At the same time, the city tended towards an increasing political exceptionalism. As the Labour Party declined nationally in electoral terms in the 1970s and 1980s, so Labour became stronger in Liverpool. Equally, as the national party became more moderate, so Liverpool's political militancy appeared more exceptional.

This pattern, however, represented a reversal of earlier trends. For much of this century, Liverpool was exceptional, certainly, but only in that Labour was so weak compared with the national picture. Equally, militancy in Liverpool was associated traditionally with trade-union rather than party political struggles.

Liverpool as the exception

Earlier commentary emphasized Liverpool Labour's failure to conform to the rule. 'Liverpool has unusual political traditions,' began one analysis; 'Liverpool political alignments have never been, and are not yet, completely normal', started another.[2] A third concluded that 'Liverpool was a Conservative city' and that 'Liverpool working men' were 'good rioters but lousy socialists'.[3] Contemporary opinion concurred. Ramsay Mac-Donald's comment in 1910 that 'Liverpool is rotten and we had better recognize it'[4] was echoed in the critical conclusions reached by the national party when it investigated the Liverpool organization in 1930, 1939, 1953 and 1961. The local party itself offered a similarly bleak analysis. Its annual report for 1922, for instance, having noted Liverpool's 'good industrial organisation' compared with other towns, stated: 'Politically, however, our position is not all that could be desired, and our ill-luck at the Municipal Elections is much to be deplored. We realise that a great deal must be done in the way of educating the electors, particularly those of the working classes.'[5] The electoral record of the party appears to have confirmed its weakness. In parliamentary elections, Labour's progress locally seemed slow. Its first victory only came in 1923, and the majority of Liverpool seats only fell to Labour for the first time in 1945. In municipal elections Labour fared even worse, only belatedly winning control of the council for the first time in 1955.

Explanations for this failure have varied, but they have all tended to suggest that there was something unusual about the nature of the working class in Liverpool, and, in turn, about the relationship between that class and the party itself. The commonest argument has been to link the existence of a clear divide along religious lines within the working class with Labour's failure. Sectarian and nationalist issues, it has been argued, cut through the bonds of class loyalty, and made it harder for Labour to appeal to the working class as a whole. A number of local studies have already emphasized this argument.[6]

Analyses of the Labour Party and the working class at a national level have also tended to echo this line of reasoning. Eric Hobsbawm, for instance, has highlighted the distinctiveness of Liverpool's labour history, and especially the significance of nationality: 'Here, as Marx himself had realised, there was a force which did deeply split the British working class, at least potentially, as witness the political history of Merseyside.'[7] Others have evinced a similar view. Ross McKibbin, for example, has stated (for the pre-1914 period) that 'given the political and religious peculiarities of Merseyside, it was impossible to establish efficient organization'. Chris Cook, in a passing reference, has suggested that 'sectarian politics undoubtedly weakened Labour's chances' in Liverpool in the late 1930s. David Howell, finally, has asserted, with reference to the 1945 election, that 'traditional religious divisions tended to freeze voting behaviour and prevent Labour annexation of the expected share of working-class support' in Liverpool.[8]

It would be mistaken to deny the influence of religious sectarianism on Liverpool politics, but some studies have already suggested that there may have been other factors which contributed to the problems of the Labour Party in Liverpool. Structural features of the local economy and resultant patterns of employment, for instance, produced other forms of differentiation within the working class. Occupational divisions may have been related to social and cultural expressions of difference, and to spatial patterns of distinctive localities or neighbourhoods. These distinctions may have been germane to the relationship between the party and the working class. Joan Smith, for instance, has argued that both the 'beliefs that workers started with' and the 'industrial and social worlds they inhabited' were relevant to the very different impact that religious sectarianism had on Glasgow and Liverpool.[9]

The main themes, scope, and structure of this book

This book contributes to the debate on the Liverpool Labour Party and the Liverpool working class, and to a wider debate on the nature of the working class and politics in twentieth-century Britain. In particular, it addresses three simple questions. First, how weak was the Labour Party in Liverpool? This book will show that the failure of the party has been exaggerated previously. This is primarily because anomalies in the system of municipal politics, which disadvantaged Labour quite plainly in Liverpool, if not nationally, have never been systematically explored before. The party's poor electoral record was to some extent a reflection of the failings of the electoral system itself. Labour was weak in Liverpool, but not as weak as sometimes assumed.

The second key question addressed in this book is, what were the causes of Labour's failure in Liverpool? It will be argued that a mono-causal explanation of Liverpool working-class politics is not adequate. Differentiation by religion was important, but so were differences of occupation, skill, and gender, in explaining the relationship between party and class in Liverpool. Equally, though, the socio-economic and political influences on

20

the party were not the whole story. How it reacted to the circumstances in which it found itself was also relevant. This book will show that, overall, the local party did not cope well with the difficult problems it faced. At least in part, then, its failure was self-induced.

The third crucial question raised in this study is, to what extent was Liverpool an exception in national terms? The answer given here must be qualified. There were distinctive features of the Liverpool case, of course. However, an exceptionalist approach to the development of working-class politics is rejected here; that is, one which assumes a normal pattern of growth, to be contrasted with occasional exceptions which deviate from the pattern.[10] The Liverpool Labour Party, then, has to be understood in the context of the real historical circumstances that shaped it, as well as being seen as part of a wider historical process.

The spatial limits of this book are precise: it is concerned with Liverpool, not Merseyside. The significance of this distinction will become apparent as the analysis develops. The focus is on the county borough of Liverpool and its internal and external boundaries as defined between the reorganizations of 1894–5 and 1953–4.[11] Economic, social and political change will be traced against the fixed backdrop of the ward boundaries that persisted through this period.

The temporal limits of the study are less precise. Ideally, it would be focused on the period between 1918 and 1939, for two major reasons. First, because the general discontinuities of the two world wars provide an obvious starting and ending point, but also, more specifically, because the municipal system of politics, on which much of the analysis turns, took a particular form in the inter-war period quite distinct from the previous and subsequent periods. Second, because the inter-war period marked a fairly distinct phase in the development of the Labour Party as a whole, when it became a truly national party, but before it reached its monolithic status as the near-equal of the Tory Party. It is also precisely in this period that the weakness of Labour in Liverpool contrasted most strongly with the gains made nationally. However, the ideal and the real seldom match perfectly in historical chronology. Economic, social and cultural patterns never fit in neatly with political events, and in this study it is clear that such patterns had their roots in an earlier, pre-1918 Liverpool. There are also questions of the availability of evidence, which dictate that some of the analysis can only be carried out for the pre-1918 period. Thus, this book is concerned with the Labour Party in Liverpool up to 1939, focusing mainly, but not exclusively, on the inter-war period. As already stated, the book is not a history of the Labour Party in Liverpool. For the most part, the approach is thematic rather than chronological. However, a summary of events in Liverpool Labour history is provided at the end, which readers can refer to between pages 399 and 410.

The book is structured as follows. Part One is concerned mainly with the Labour Party and local politics. Thus, Chapter One will examine in detail the historiography of the development of the Labour Party and its relationship to the British working class, both in Liverpool and in other local studies. Chapter Two will assess Labour's failure in Liverpool, particularly in terms of the poor structure and organization of the party, and the weakness of its links with the wider working class.

Part Two focuses on electoral politics and the Labour Party. Chapter Three will evaluate the Labour Party's record in Liverpool in terms of electoral results at the municipal level, and Chapter Four will go on to explore the idiosyncrasies of the inter-war municipal electoral system and their contribution to Labour's poor performance locally. Chapter Five will analyse Labour's failure in parliamentary elections in Liverpool, and will contrast the municipal and parliamentary records. Chapter Six will examine the Labour Party's response to the problems of the electoral system between the wars, both locally and nationally.

In Part Three, the relationship between the party and the local working class is examined in depth. Chapter Seven will consider one type of differentiation within the working class – gender – and assess its significance in terms of the development of the local party. Chapter Eight will analyse the major economic and social characteristics of the different areas of the city, focusing initially on two key factors – religion and occupation – but also broadening out the analysis to include questions of neighbourhoods and working-class culture. It will then turn to assessing the differential success of Labour in different parts of the city, identifying areas of particular strength and weakness in terms of election results, and synthesizing the relationship between the political and social/cultural patterns revealed. Finally, the book will conclude by drawing together all the elements of the argument that explain the development of Liverpool Labour.

References

1.   *Liverpool Daily Post*, 3 May 1920. All further references to the events of May Day 1920 are from this same source. Labour stood 18 candidates in the 1919 elections, of whom 10 won, all being net gains for the party. This brought their total representation to 22 out of 147 seats on the council.

2.   R. Baxter, 'The Liverpool Labour Party, 1918–1963' (unpublished D.Phil. thesis, University of Oxford, 1969), p. 1; D. A. Roberts, 'Religion and Politics in Liverpool since 1900' (unpublished M.Sc. thesis, University of London, 1965), p. 3.

3.   J. Smith, 'Labour tradition in Glasgow and Liverpool', *History Workshop*, 17 (1984), p. 50.

4.   Quoted in R. McKibbin, *The Evolution of the Labour Party, 1910–1924* (Oxford University Press, London: 1974), p. 14.

5.   LTCLP, AGM, Minutes (5 April 1922).

6.   P. J. Waller, *Democracy and Sectarianism: A Political and Social History of Liverpool, 1868–1939* (Liverpool University Press, Liverpool: 1981).

7.   E. J. Hobsbawm, 'The forward march of labour halted?', *Marxism Today* (September 1978), pp. 281–3.

8. McKibbin, *The Evolution of the Labour Party*, p. 5; C. Cook, 'Liberals, Labour and local elections', in G. Peele and C. Cook (eds), *The Politics of Reappraisal, 1918–1939* (Macmillan, London: 1975), p. 188.; D. Howell, *British Social Democracy: A Study in Development and Decay* (2nd edn., Croom Helm, London: 1980), p. 131.

9. Smith, 'Labour tradition in Glasgow and Liverpool', p. 50.

10. There is a voluminous literature concerned with the notion of 'exceptionalism' in relation to the case of the US working class. See, for instance, S. Wilentz, 'Against exceptionalism: class consciousness and the American labor movement, 1790–1920', *International Labor and Working-Class History*, 26 (1984), pp. 1–24, and the various responses to Wilentz in the same edition; see also A. R. Zolberg, 'How many exceptionalisms?', in I. Katznelson and A. R. Zolberg (eds), *Working Class Formation: Nineteenth-Century Patterns in Western Europe and the United States* (Princeton University Press, Princeton: 1986).

11. For an illustration of these boundaries, see Figure 4.1 below, p.98.

PART ONE

The Labour Party and local politics

1 Local studies of Labour politics: 'How many exceptionalisms?'

If capitalism is of a piece, why is the working class it called into life so disparate? [1]

It is significant that in the late twentieth century it should be an American, Aristide Zolberg, who considers the question posed above a crucial one to be dealt with in the study of working-class history. It is also perhaps unsurprising, given that the working class of the United States has always been notable for its diversity. For historians in the USA, the problem has always been how best to encompass the variety of working-class experience. Ever-shifting, ever-changing, formed by successive waves of migration, scattered over a vast and varied terrain, politically divided, the American working class has never been amenable to simple generalizations.

By contrast, for British labour historians the relative homogeneity of the working class has often been taken for granted, especially in the period with which this book deals. The notion that the British working class – particularly in the years between the last decade of the nineteenth century and the end of the third quarter of the twentieth – was characterized by a high degree of social, cultural and political cohesion, has been highly influential. Diverse historical perspectives have yielded similar results. Henry Pelling could write: 'It is in these years of the late nineteenth and early twentieth centuries that we can most safely speak of a comparatively homogeneous "working class".' [2] Speaking of the same period, Eric Hobsbawm could say that the working class:

> was drawn more closely together, by a growing class consciousness, by political demands which united all strata and sections. ... by a common lifestyle and pattern ... This common 'style' ... of British proletarian life began to emerge just about a century ago ... local differences did not run counter to the sense of a single class consciousness. [3]

It is arguable that the widely held view that the British working class was relatively homogeneous in this period was sustained primarily by the examination of a set of institutions, most notably the Labour Party and the trade unions, which were presumed to represent the class, rather than by any detailed examination of the class itself. For as long as the 'forward march of labour' continued, the historical focus could remain on mainly national, and often narrowly institutional, studies of the Labour Party and the Trades Union Congress and its affiliated unions.

For earlier periods in the history of the working class, such an unproblematic approach was less pervasive. E. P. Thompson's pioneering work on the 'making of the English working class' was highly influential in dealing with the diversity of early class formation and the complex relationship between class and class consciousness.[4] The Chartist period was examined increasingly through a proliferation of local and regional studies, marked by their attention to the diverse strands that made up the Chartist movement.[5] For the later nineteenth century, as well, the focus was increasingly on the heterogeneous nature of the working class, most clearly expressed in the concentration on the theory of the labour aristocracy.[6]

It is really only in the last two decades that the twentieth-century history of the British working class has begun to be re-evaluated, and in a way which has increasingly shifted attention to the study of the social and cultural features of the class itself. Why should this be so? Of central importance has been the contemporary crisis of those institutions, the Labour Party and the trade-union movement, which for so long had been seen as embodying the working class. It may seem now that these institutions never successfully fulfilled such a grandiose function, but it was only when the 'forward march' was demonstrably 'halted' that the blinkers were finally removed.

However, this re-evaluation has taken a number of directions, some of them highly contested. In discovering diversity, for some historians at least, the very concept of class itself has become irrelevant. If empirical study reveals more and more complexity, difference and division, then why struggle to encompass these differences within any unifying concept such as class? In particular, the 'moment of culture' has been for some the opportunity to cut loose from old theoretical moorings and go where no historian has been before, into a post-modern world of discourse analysis.[7]

This is not the course followed in this book. The intention here is to explore the relationship between the specific features of a local economy that shaped a working class, the differentiation by levels of skill, ethnicity, religion and gender that were manifested in that class, and how that differentiation impacted upon the cultural and political practices of the working class. In doing so, it is assumed that variations in the forms of working-class life, culture and politics in no sense invalidate the very concept of class itself, but rather that such variations are to be expected in any description and explanation of a local working class. The idea that mature working classes must assume a homogeneous form, or that they must conform to some single model of class formation, is simply not tenable. Classes are never 'made' in any final or definitive sense, but rather they are constantly in the process of being made, and it is the description and explanation of the empirical circumstances of that 'making' that is aimed at here. The essentialist assumption that a class must, by its very nature, aspire to a particular form of class consciousness, and that any failure to do so must be regarded as an exception, is also rejected.

As the comparative study of working-class formation by Zolberg suggests, there are only so many exceptionalisms that can be tolerated before a single model of class formation has to be rejected. To quote from that study: 'Since differentiation was a key aspect of the process that governed the formation of the western working class, variety was a constitutive element of its eventual character.'[8] Zolberg's essay forms part of a collection which compares different national working classes one with another, but as he also makes clear:

> ... although national economic and political configurations will be treated as indivisible wholes for the purposes of the present analysis, constructs such as these hide as much as they reveal ... *sectoral and regional variations in economic and political organization within each of the countries under consideration were sometimes as wide as variations between countries.*[9] [My emphasis]

In other words, both within and between national economies, capitalism is of a piece, yet it calls into life a disparate working class. This is the assumption that underlies the analysis of this book. To begin that analysis, it is necessary to survey the interpretations of earlier studies of Labour politics in Liverpool. After that, it will be useful to look at other local studies, both in Britain and internationally, to see how they might offer helpful comparisons and contrasts with a Liverpool study. These are the subjects of the rest of this chapter.

Previous interpretations of the Labour Party and the Liverpool working class

As far as comparable local studies are concerned, there have been several concerned with the Liverpool labour movement that need to be considered. Until relatively recently, most of these studies were concerned primarily with the institutions of the labour movement, and paid little attention to wider questions of the relationship between these institutions and the local working class. Chronological narratives such as those by Drinkwater, Hamling, Maddock and Walsh supplied much empirical detail on the developments among local trade unions, the Trades Council and the Labour Party up to the inter-war period, without providing a great deal of analysis of the dynamics of working-class politics in the area.[10] D. A. Roberts also produced a chronological account of the relationship between religion and politics in Liverpool, which outlined a straight-forward argument that Liverpool politics was always exceptional due to the 'pervading influence of Ireland'.[11] Having run through the various local and national election campaigns between 1900 and 1950, high-lighting the sectarian issues as they affected local results, he concluded that only by 1950 had sectarianism ceased to be of any great significance:

> The old, ill-educated and highly bigoted voter of the past was fast disappearing ... From 1950 to 1964, when Liverpool's Parliamentary representation finally reverted to the pattern of other large industrial cities, sectarian bitterness, despite certain resurgencies [sic] declined even further.[12]

The argument that Liverpool was an exception in terms of the development of labour politics is plainly stated. It is less clear, however, precisely how religious differences became so influential in Liverpool, or, for that matter, why they become less significant over time. At the heart of Roberts' argument is an assumption that religion is an essentially irrational force intervening in a supposed modern, democratic political sphere. This irrationality, he implies, was implanted in Liverpool by the accident of Irish migration, to be gradually eroded over time by some inexorable process of education and modernization, so that it gradually faded away as a determinant of political action. It is significant also that Roberts poses his questions very much in terms of religion, rather than ethnicity or nationality, therefore reducing the meaning of sectarian division primarily to that of conflicting denominational beliefs. The social and political context of sectarianism is, therefore, seriously undervalued in his account.

By comparison with these narrative studies, Robert Baxter subsequently provided a more analytical approach to the history of the Liverpool Labour Party.[13] Clearly informed by contemporary debates in the field of political sociology, Baxter went beyond the conventional narrative history of the party in the first part of his thesis, to attempt to analyse the internal dynamics of the party. Thus, there was in his thesis some interesting analysis of the religious, residential and occupational background of Labour councillors, showing how the Catholic influence within the party grew from the 1920s, and also how councillors were increasingly drawn from higher socio-economic categories in the post-1945 era.[14]

Baxter also elaborated on the connection between religious sectarian-ism and party politics by introducing the notion of 'boss politics' into his analysis of Liverpool. This was based on a very vague comparison with city politics in the United States, where political 'machines', based on ethnic identification and cutting across class boundaries, have been his-torically significant. For Baxter, similar machines along sectarian lines were created in Liverpool by powerful bosses of both the Tory and Labour

30

Parties. Within the Labour Party this tradition, initiated by a Catholic caucus in the inter-war period, was transmuted after 1945 into factional conflict between a non-sectarian, right-wing machine and radical opponents, as sectarian issues died away.[15]

While there were superficial similarities between local politics in Liverpool between the wars and some US cities, there were also crucial differences. In particular, the much greater autonomy of the city authority in the United States, the clearer political identification of office-holders in the American system, the much earlier advent of working-class suffrage, and the highly pronounced residential segregation along ethnic lines in many American cities, meant that political machines wielding real local power could be created.[16] By comparison, any such British machines could only be pale shadows of their American counterparts. Liverpool was similar in that there was a degree of ethnic residential segregation, but it was not alone in this in Britain. Moreover, the phenomenon of power being concentrated in the hands of bosses was hardly unique to the Liverpool Labour Party in this period. Ernest Bevin and Walter Citrine in the TUC, and Herbert Morrison in the London Labour Party, are notable examples of powerful leaders, if not bosses, in the labour movement at this time.

Where Baxter's comparison with American boss politics may be more fruitful is in considering the nature of Liverpool Toryism in this period. The popular Toryism organized along sectarian lines by Archibald Salvidge through the Liverpool Working Men's Conservative Association (WMCA) amounted to an effective, and perhaps unique, political machine of sorts. Even contemporaries made the comparison with the United States, Lloyd George describing Salvidge as 'the nearest to a Tammany boss that we have in this country'.[17] However, if the WMCA was effective in delivering working-class votes for the Tories, it was hardly effective in delivering material rewards for its working-class supporters. Nor was it a machine that truly cut across class boundaries. The WMCA, as its very name suggested, remained organizationally quite separate from the thoroughly bourgeois wing of the local party, the Constitutional Association. If anything, the WMCA was a miracle of political ideology, rather than a machine of the US type that offered real rewards to distinct ethnic groups.

In the end, Baxter's argument becomes another version of the exceptionalism of the Liverpool case, caused primarily by religious division within the working class. He states:

> Liverpool has unusual traditions ... *the city developed a social life radically different from other English industrial towns* ... In common with many cities in the United States of America, which have large Irish immigrant communities, Liverpool developed a political power structure that was *not entirely in accordance with liberal democratic theory, and was out of line with the normal practice of British political parties.*[18] [My emphasis]

While Roberts blamed the 'ill-educated' voter, Baxter extended the blame for Liverpool's failure to match up to 'liberal democratic theory' to the 'politically illiterate working men of the city centre'.[19]

A later attempt to provide a 'political and social history' of Liverpool was that of P. J. Waller. Again chronological in approach, and packed with empirical detail, Waller's work did not fully achieve the stated aim of its subtitle, as its primary focus was the political history of the city. In fact his work had a quite specific purpose, to explain the success of Toryism in Liverpool, despite the 'grim circumstances in which much of the population lived and worked'.[20]

This is not to say that Waller entirely failed to consider aspects of the social history of the city. In particular, he did note the unusual structure of the local economy and its impact on the local working class. The heavy reliance on dock-related activity, and the predominance of casual and unskilled labour, resulted in 'irregular wages and irregular ways'.[21] However, this observation is never used in any analytical sense to explain the peculiarities of Liverpool politics, and for the most part Waller's work is a detailed account of how Tory democracy and religious sectarianism worked their spell over local political life.

The most interesting local study of the Liverpool working class carried out to date has been that by Joan Smith, who compares the situation with that in Glasgow.[22] Smith attempts to explain how differences of religion within, and the unusual occupational structure of, the working class were translated into political action. In doing so, she explicitly rejects the exceptionalist view of Liverpool that has dominated the earlier studies quoted above. Liverpool may have been different, but for Smith this is not simply an aberration, but something that has to be explained by the real political activities of a working class shaped by a particular set of historical circumstances. Her work does not assume that the 'generation of a labour or a socialist tradition is an unproblematic and "natural" occurrence'.[23] As she reiterates later: '… there is no necessary or inevitable route between the development of class conflict and the development of socialism'.[24]

The comparison between Liverpool and Glasgow is an intriguing one, as sectarian division was a feature of both cities, and yet their political traditions appeared to be very different, with socialist politics seeming to have a much greater purchase in Glasgow than in Liverpool. Smith gives two main reasons for the varying significance of sectarianism in the two cities. The first was related to occupational structure. From the 1870s, Glasgow became the shipbuilding centre of the British economy, and Protestant workers were predominantly engaged in skilled trades, while Catholics were confined to unskilled sectors. Thus there was no direct competition between Catholic and Protestant workers in the labour market. By contrast, competition between Catholics and Protestants was endemic in the predominantly unskilled labour market of Liverpool.[25]

The second reason for the greater influence of sectarianism in Liverpool was related to patterns of residential segregation. Catholics were mostly scattered through the central areas of Glasgow, whereas they were strongly concentrated in the Scotland Road area of Liverpool. Segregation reinforced sectarianism in Liverpool, while in Glasgow there was 'very little successful anti-Catholic agitation'.[26]

However, these occupational and residential factors were only part of the story for Smith. Her analysis goes on to look at the origins and nature of working-class consciousness. She argues that there were differences in what she calls the 'commonsense' thought of the two towns. This commonsense thought, which dominated working-class consciousness, took different forms in Liverpool and Glasgow. The term is adopted from her reading of Gramsci, and is:

> … a construction out of many contradictory ideological strands … that accepts many dominant beliefs, and that can encompass many contradictory ideas at once … [contrasted with 'goodsense', which] … is the beginning of a critical awareness that may lead to class consciousness.[27]

She argues that there were significant variations in commonsense thought in different localities up to this period. Local social and cultural structures had a strong influence on political life, only to be overwhelmed by a nationally constructed commonsense in the late 1920s and 1930s.[28]

The implications of this assumed change in the inter-war period are presumably that a much more homogeneous working-class politics would have been evident from then on. In pre-1914 Glasgow, however, the working class was the inheritor of a commonsense dominated by a progressive radical liberal and reform tradition. Once the economic and political basis of this tradition began to disintegrate in the years leading up to 1914, it became a platform for the building of a 'radical, even revolutionary world view'.[29] In Liverpool, by contrast, liberalism was weak, and the commonsense of the working class was dominated by Tory democracy and Irish nationalism. Liverpool Tory democracy was unique in emphasizing anti-Catholicism and nationalism, while at the same time incorporating some working-class beliefs, especially temperance and, Smith claims, collectivism. [30]

The final key step in Smith's argument is concerned with those 'private associations' which made up, and reinforced, the commonsense of the working class. In Glasgow, Smith argues, the dominant private associations were the friendly societies, the co-operative movement, temperance societies, and craft trade unions. These were all congruent with liberal beliefs of self-help and independence, and strongly associated with the skilled sections of the working class.[31] In Liverpool, conversely, these self-help organizations were largely absent. Instead, the WMCA, the Orange Order, and more extreme Protestant organizations on the one side, and the Catholic church on the other, provided the 'private associations'.[32]

The most impressive feature of Smith's study is her detailed elaboration of these various social, cultural and political organizations, on both sides of the sectarian divide, which were influential among the Liverpool working class in reinforcing sectional and sectarian attitudes.[33] However, there are still some problematic areas in her overall analysis. Her utilization of Gramscian concepts such as 'commonsense' and 'goodsense' in exploring differences in working-class consciousness is interesting, but ultimately it is arguable how novel it really is. Stripped of the typically allusive terminology of Gramsci's *Prison Notebooks*[34] Smith's interpretation seems to amount to little more than a reworking of the classic false consciousness/revolutionary consciousness dichotomy of the more reductionist interpretations of Marxist theory. The working class moves along a trajectory from commonsense to goodsense to 'the beginning of a critical awareness that may lead to class consciousness' and 'real socialist understandings of the world'. The process appears more or less an automatic one. The misfortune for the Liverpool working class, in Smith's analysis, is that it started from the wrong place, saddled with an inferior commonsense, and therefore inevitably failed compared with its Glasgow counterpart.

In the end, like many of the other studies mentioned above, Smith repeats the by now familiar condemnation of the Liverpool working class for its obstinate failure to match up to some imputed model. She concludes:

> Glasgow was a skilled workers' city without ghettos: its working men and women by and large rejected sectarianism and embraced socialism. In Liverpool this never happened before the Second World War. In Glasgow it was possible to believe in the gradual development of socialism as working men left Liberalism behind and moved to Labour, and some to revolutionary socialism; in Liverpool the only hope was industrial riot in which the dominant organizations of the city were temporarily put to one side. Glasgow working men were good socialists but lousy rioters; Liverpool working men were quite the reverse.[35]

The 'ill-educated' (Roberts), 'politically illiterate' (Baxter) Liverpool workers were also 'lousy' socialists. Once local differences were supposedly overwhelmed in the late 1920s and a nationally constructed commonsense prevailed, Liverpool again becomes the exception, as conservatism continued to dominate the city down to the 1950s.[36]

As already stated in the introduction, the exceptionalist framework itself is one which is rejected in this book. It is also the case, however, that the evidence used to sustain Smith's argument is open to a slightly different interpretation. Without seeking to minimize the real and obvious differences between the Liverpool and Glasgow labour movements, it can be argued that Smith has perhaps exaggerated those differences.

For instance, while the sectarian organizations of Liverpool are given so much prominence in her work, other aspects of working-class activity are rather underplayed. Most notably, the development of trade-unionism, particularly in the period between 1889 and 1914 when general unions were finally established in Liverpool, is barely mentioned, and then only to be dismissed as merely an outburst of syndicalist feeling which ultimately failed to restructure 'political and social life'.[37] This judgement contrasts with another study of the syndicalism of this period in Liverpool, that of R. J. Holton.

Holton shows how an undercurrent of syndicalist feeling was particularly influential in the industrial unrest of the years 1910–14 on Merseyside. He summarizes syndicalist beliefs as follows:

> They stressed Direct Action rather than State-sponsored legislation as the main agency of social emancipation. In the industrial sphere, this meant a reappraisal of trade union methods away from craft sectionalism and conciliatory bargaining policies, towards an all-embracing industrial unionism, using the sympathetic strike and general strike as weapons of class conflict … Politically, syndicalism in Britain involved a rejection of gradualist social reform through Parliament based on electoral politics.[38]

These beliefs lay far outside the ambit of the radical liberal and reform tradition, no doubt, but they were also far removed from the stranglehold of popular Toryism and religious sectarianism. Syndicalism was by no means dominant in Liverpool at this time, as Holton concedes. Nor does he deny the importance of sectarian feeling in Liverpool. Nevertheless, the influence of syndicalist ideas on the strike wave of this period, on both the leadership and the rank and file of several waterfront unions, and on a variety of left-wing campaigns and initiatives in the area, is convincingly outlined by Holton. Moreover, international connections, particularly with the Wobblies of the United States, Spanish anarcho-syndicalists, and Irish trade-unionists, were an important element of the movement, placing it somewhat outside of the mainstream of British labour politics. The Liverpool of organizations like the International Club, the Revolutionary Industrialists, the Clarion Club, the Liverpool Marxian Socialist Society, the Liverpool Anarcho-Communist Group, the Liverpool Communist Sunday School, the Industrial Syndicalist Education League, and the Communist Club, seems a world away from the narrow, sectarian Liverpool of Smith's account.

There were other aspects of Liverpool working-class activity that are understated by Smith. For instance, she downplays the significance of the co-operative movement in Liverpool, seeing it as being restricted to a relatively small group of semi-skilled workers, and excluding the casual poor. This judgement is certainly open to question, given recent research into co-operation in Liverpool.[39] This shows that while the movement was at first confined mainly to the better-off sections of the working class, it changed markedly from the early twentieth century, encouraging significant expansion into the dockside areas of the city. [40]

The Irish nationalist strand within the Catholic working class of Liverpool is also passed over by Smith as essentially a diversion from the real British issue of building a labour movement. As Holton shows, the Irish and syndicalist traditions converged in the influence of James Larkin on the labour movement on Merseyside. This influence may have been resented by the pragmatic leadership of James Sexton in the Dockers' Union, but it was by no means regarded as insubstantial, or diversionary, by many waterfront workers, especially during the Dublin lock-out of 1913.[41] For a much earlier period, John Belchem has shown how Irish migrants brought radical traditions and organizational abilities to local trade-unionism.[42]

Andrew Shallice also makes the point that it is a 'grindingly English' perspective to see the failure of the labour movement of Liverpool as being due to the primacy of ethnicity, 'as a force to disunite and which "pervaded" the Liverpool Labour Party'. As Shallice shows in his study of Labourism and Irish nationalism between the wars, the nationalist tradition in Liverpool had more than one face. There was a right-wing face, which by the 1930s dominated the Labour group on the council. But there was also a radical face, most notably displayed in the strike of Liverpool dockers in 1920 organized by the Irish Workers' Vigilance Committee to press for the release of Sinn Fein internees.[43]

On the other hand, the significance of Tory democracy in Smith's work is perhaps overplayed. She claims that:

> The ruling Liverpool Tory party had adopted the Belfast cry of 'Social reform but no Socialism', and integrated whole sections of the Protestant working class into its ranks on an explicit programme of municipal reform and an implicit programme of power-sharing, through the Conservative Working Men's Association and jobs for the Protestant boys. Token accommodations to the nationalist leadership of the local Catholic Irish community (particularly on housing questions) were also part of the pattern of Liverpool politics before the First World War and after.[44]

Her comment, quoted earlier, that collectivism was part of the Liverpool Tory appeal to working-class voters, overplays the nature of this appeal even more. This claim appears to be based mainly on a speech by a local Tory MP, and leading Orangeman, Watson Rutherford, in 1908, in which he pointed the way to 'corporate, municipal and state enterprise', deplored 'gross disparity in the distribution of wealth', and advocated nationalization of the railways. However, it should be noted that these sentiments were delivered in the unusual context of a speech to the Fabian Society, and moreover to a London, rather than a Liverpool, audience. It is also notable that they came from a notoriously maverick Tory. Rutherford is described by Waller, whose appreciation of the subtlest distinctions in Liverpool conservatism is unequalled, as a politician 'intent on promotion', whose 'talent for publicity was the mark of a soloist', and who 'welcomed every other wind to blow votes his way'. Even Smith herself elsewhere admits Rutherford's views were 'eccentric', and yet goes on to quote copiously from this speech to argue that Rutherford's views 'could be contained within Liverpool's Tory Democracy'.[45]

Other aspects of Smith's view of Tory democracy are questionable. The suggestion of an implicit programme of jobs for Protestants is unsubstantiated and, even if true, was limited by the relatively small scale of employment open to direct control or influence by councillors. The wards of Liverpool were not the wards of New York or Chicago. Conversely, the concessions on housing to the Irish can hardly be described as token. Of the 11,393 persons housed in corporation tenements between 1869 and 1916, virtually all had been rehoused after slum clearance in the wards in which they had previously lived. Almost all of these tenements were situated in strongly Catholic wards of the city.[46] What this suggests is that the relationship between Toryism and the electorate, both Catholic and Protestant, is far more complex than Smith's analysis suggests. Finally, it should be noted that on two occasions, in the first decade of this century, and again in the 1930s, Tory democracy was deserted by the Protestant working class in the north end of the city – in the Netherfield/St Domingo area – for a more explicit Protestant Party. Sectarianism, pure and simple, was what was required there, not municipal reform.

A final point should be made about the previous writings on Liverpool and the Labour Party, which is particularly relevant in the context of the concerns of Part Two of this book. The system of electoral politics that held sway in Liverpool, and its possible impact on the fortunes of the Labour Party, has not been considered in any systematic fashion in any of the works mentioned above. Baxter does mention the fact that ward boundaries in the early 1950s put Labour at a disadvantage in municipal elections, leading to the redistribution of 1953.[47] However, the implications of this observation, and its possible effects in earlier decades, are not pursued. Waller also makes passing references to limitations in the franchise, to ward boundary redistribution, and to the election of aldermen in the council chamber, but the political effect of these factors is not considered in any detail.[48] As will be shown later, this issue is one that repays further attention in explaining Labour's failure in Liverpool.

Interpretations of the Labour Party and the working class in other British local studies

Turning now to other studies of the Labour Party and the working class, it is the case that only comparatively recently has attention been focused on local variation. The national and institutional approach held sway to a great extent previously. There were some general studies of individual boroughs, such as those of F. Bealey *et al.* for Newcastle-under-Lyme,

G. W. Jones for Wolverhampton, or W. Hampton for Sheffield, which worked very much within the tradition of political science.[49] These were concerned primarily with the institutions of local democracy, looking at the nature of political parties and the sociology of electors and elected. As such, they dealt with the Labour Party only as one of a number of competing parties, and they did not deal directly with questions of working-class consciousness. However, they did provide some attempt to analyse the socio-economic characteristics of different areas in the boroughs, and how these related to political allegiances. They also provided details of local election results, which are surprisingly hard to find before 1945.

As for explaining the Labour Party's performance in these three very different boroughs, there is little analysis. Labour's domination of Sheffield from 1926 is hardly considered at all by Hampton, being seen as more or less inevitable, given the proletarian nature of the city, and particularly the prevalence of skilled workers.[50] In Wolverhampton, Jones sees Labour's moderate growth in the inter-war period as primarily stemming from extensions of the franchise and of the city boundaries. For the surge of support for Labour from 1945 he offers no explanation at all, except that Labour's opponents lacked positive, constructive policies.[51]

For Newcastle-under-Lyme, Bealey *et al.* provide a much more interesting analysis of Labour's performance. They show how the party was poorly organized and had little popular support until it suddenly expanded from the summer of 1942 onwards. This rapid growth is attributed to the impact of the war, and to considerable improvements in party organization, and was reflected very clearly in municipal election results. Up to 1939, Labour had limited success on the local council, but after 1945 it increased its support dramatically, taking control of the council in 1946. By contrast, however, in parliamentary elections Newcastle was a safe Labour seat from 1922 onwards. This is explained as being due primarily to the defection of Sir Josiah Wedgwood from the Liberals to Labour in 1919. As a popular sitting MP, with particularly strong support among the North Staffordshire miners, he maintained a personal vote that had little to do with either local party policy or organization. In fact, the miners' support, for an MP who retained many of his Liberal beliefs and was an untypical Labour MP, was essentially a continuation of the strongly Liberal and Nonconformist attitudes held by them previously.[52] Bealey makes little of this fact, but it raises a number of interesting issues of relevance to this book.

First, winning a constituency at the parliamentary level did not necessarily reflect the underlying strength of the local party, or even support for Labour policies. A superficial examination of the electoral record would suggest that Newcastle was an area of Labour strength from the early 1920s, yet it is quite clear from Bealey's study that this was not the case at least until 1942. Comparisons between different areas based on electoral records are therefore to be treated with caution, unless they are backed up by a deeper analysis of the local factors affecting election performance.

Comparisons between one-seat towns, such as Newcastle, and multi-seat cities, such as Liverpool, are even more problematic. A personal vote could determine the whole picture in Newcastle, but could hardly be expected to have occurred simultaneously in all eleven seats in Liverpool.

Second, the sharp divergence between municipal and parliamentary performance by Labour in Newcastle may have been entirely due to the Wedgwood factor. However, it might also be related to differences in the system of electoral politics at the two levels. As will be shown later, there were significant differences in the two systems, especially between 1918 and 1939, which were likely to disadvantage Labour, particularly at the municipal level. Whether this played any part in explaining the divergence in Newcastle is not calculable from the evidence that Bealey provides, but it remains a possibility. The fact that the divergence does not continue after 1945 only increases the possibility, as differences in the franchise in particular were removed from that date.

Third, developments in the 1950s in Newcastle-under-Lyme make the connection between party organization and popular support at elections seem even more tenuous. The sudden growth of the Labour Party from 1942 was only sustained until the early 1950s – in fact Bealey states that a 'well-organized mass Labour Party' only existed in Newcastle for the four years during the period 1947–50 [53] – and yet Labour remained relatively strong in the borough, at both the municipal and parliamentary level, up to the 1960s. The fact that Labour held the Newcastle seat continuously from 1922 seems almost fortuitous, rather than a reflection of real commitment to Labour by the local working class. Simplistic comparisons with other areas are again thrown into question. Labour's electoral record in Liverpool over the same period seems far less impressive, and yet it is arguable whether this mirrors real differences in party organization and working-class commitment to Labour.

More recently, there has been a flood of new material produced on the history of local Labour parties from the early years of this century up to 1939, covering areas or towns as varied as the East End of London, Leicester, Coventry, Preston, Nelson, Lancaster, and Edinburgh.[54] Naturally, these works differ widely in their theoretical and methodological frameworks, but they share in common a commitment to analysing the development of local politics in the context of the specific socio-economic features of the locality. In most of these studies, the occupational structure of the area and the varying experiences of work are seen as important, but not as the only, influences on working-class life, culture and politics. Other influences, such as gender differentiation, ethnicity, and ideological and political structures and practices, are emphasized to varying degrees.

What this body of work signifies most clearly is that the consensus that predominated previously on the supposed homogeneity of the British working class in this period has been considerably modified. Rather than seeing areas of Labour weakness as being in some way exceptions to the rule, most of these studies are now centrally concerned with answering a key question: why did the strength of working-class support for Labour vary so widely between different localities? The answers to this question do not simply come down to differences in economic structure, but constitute a complex range which can be derived from the works listed above.

Bill Lancaster, in his interesting study of Leicester working-class politics, expresses one approach:

> ... a thorough understanding of the structure of the working class has to be achieved in order to grasp the complexities of the relationship between material forces and the Labour movement. Thus close attention has to be paid to the world of work ... Important as this theme is, too great a reliance upon its explanatory powers leads to a somewhat mechanistic analysis of working-class political action ... This point can be underlined if we pose the question, why do apparently similar communities, with similar economic structures, produce radically different forms of working-class political action? The key to answering such a question lies in grasping the unique world of working-class culture and political traditions that exist in specific places. In short, working-class communities possess both a structure and a nature.[55]

Having established the central importance of the hosiery and footwear industries in structuring the Leicester working class, Lancaster shows how successive changes in the organization of production in these industries produced political responses that were eventually to give rise to a strong Labour tradition. However, this process was by no means a mechanistic one, as the tradition of out-work, which came increasingly under attack from the 1880s, was deeply embedded in working-class life, and was associated with an artisan rather than a factory culture, and a radical liberalism in politics. Such cultural and political traditions did not disappear overnight with the rise of Independent Labour Party (ILP) politics, and they left their imprint on the style of Labourism that developed in the area. The strong ILP support that was built up in the area, and the fact that a national figure like Ramsay MacDonald was the local MP, might have made Leicester seem unremarkable among early Labour strongholds, but Lancaster shows otherwise:

> ... on the one side the party with MacDonald at the helm appeared to prefigure the future process of bureaucratizing and centralizing Labour politics; on the other the Leicester movement manifests itself as a product of a specific local political tradition deeply entrenched in, and taking direction from, issues rooted in the local community.[56]

A rather different approach is offered by Michael Savage in his study of working-class politics in Preston. Both the concepts of culture and community, so important in Lancaster's study, are explicitly rejected by

40

Savage. Instead he attempts to show that the basis of practical politics, as opposed to formal politics, has its roots in working-class interests, which flow from the necessity of workers attempting to reduce their material insecurity within capitalism.[57] Savage identifies three major types of practical struggles, which he labels 'mutualist', 'economistic', and 'statist'.[58] This 'practical' politics is closely linked to the social structure, and varies widely at the local level. While he shows that differences in skill levels may be crucial in determining these variations, he is at pains to stress that these are not the only determinants, arguing that gender and neighbourhood relationships, for instance, can also be influential.[59]

In the second half of his study, Savage tries to show how practical politics evolved in Preston between 1880 and 1940. He establishes the basis of the local economy, mainly cotton-weaving and spinning, and shows how decline in these two sectors affected various groups of workers – in particular the mainly male spinners and male overlookers in weaving, and the mainly female weavers – in different ways from the 1880s.[60] The decline of the spinning sector, especially, led to economistic struggles, which, when they reached the formal political agenda, Savage argues, were skilfully latched on to by local Conservatives. Thus, working-class support for Toryism, based on claims of advancing the regeneration of the local economy, reached its peak by the 1880s and 1890s. Savage argues that this working-class Toryism had nothing to do with any deferential attitudes, nor was it in any sense irrational. Rather, it was the logical result of 'workers pursuing their interests in a particular economistic way'.[61]

In turn, Savage argues that the shift away from Conservatism and towards ILP politics from around the turn of the century did not reflect any decline in the economistic attitudes of the local working class. Instead, it was the result of the increasing failure of the Conservatives to meet working-class demands. A new economistic Labourism came to the fore, but also one which was strongly patriarchal in nature. The local labour movement was dominated by male workers, employed mainly in trades which had been increasingly opened up to women workers, such as the élite sections of weaving. By contrast, those workers whose patriarchal position at work remained untouched, such as overlookers, were far less committed to Labourism.[62]

According to Savage, an economistic and patriarchal Labourism reached its peak in the early 1920s, fuelled by fears raised by the widespread use of women workers during the First World War. Its neighbourhood base remained weak, however. This was a crucial weakness, Savage argues, as what he describes as 'women's issues' came to the fore in the early 1920s. As these issues were exploited quite successfully by the Tories initially, so Labour declined. However, changes in the Labour Party organization by 1924–5 led to a diminution of trade-union influence and a growth of neighbourhood involvement through ward parties and women's sections. This gave rise to growing Labour support based on new statist policies, focused on local state services. These policies also have to be seen in the context of relatively high employment, when male workers felt less threatened by female labour.[63]

Finally, the growth of unemployment from 1929 dealt a fatal blow to this popular statist Labourism, as female labour again began to be perceived as a threat by male workers. Women's involvement in the party declined rapidly, and there was a shift to policies based on national state measures to reduce unemployment. The dynamism of the late 1920s faded, and Labour's support in Preston fell away for the duration of the 1930s.[64]

It is difficult within the confines of this brief survey to do justice to the full complexity of Savage's argument, or to the range of evidence that he employs. Some points relevant to this book need to be made, however. First, Savage makes a strong case for the necessity of local studies of Labour and, unlike some of the other works already mentioned, he also argues that the local dimension remained important right through to 1939. He provides an analysis of the changes in Labour's support in Preston which is almost entirely determined by local, rather than national factors. Even when he concedes that national patterns of support for Labour can be distinguished in the inter-war period, he nevertheless asserts that these should be seen as the result of 'commonly found local effects in many different parts of the country'.[65]

Savage pursues this point further by arguing that the transition to neighbourhood-based politics and away from trade-union-orientated struggles, which he identifies in Preston, was repeated elsewhere. It is this which explains the national pattern of Labour support in the 1920s better than more conventional analyses based on the ebb and flow of trade-union fortunes.[66] It is arguable that Savage overstates this point, and that perhaps it is a combination of both factors that were at work in these years. However, it is interesting that similar changes can be identified in the very different context of Liverpool, as will be shown in Chapter Seven.

A second point to be considered in Savage's work is his rejection of the notion that working-class consciousness or culture might influence political attitudes. He gives three reasons for this rejection. First, he argues that it is impossible to establish exactly the nature of working-class consciousness in any particular historical period. Second, he claims that political decisions are determined more by considerations of strategy and tactics than by moral beliefs or social attitudes. Third, Savage argues that people have a variety of beliefs about different areas of their lives, and that there is no necessary coherence to these various beliefs.[67]

There is an element of truth in all three of these reasons, but, nevertheless, they cannot be accepted as a guide to work in other localities. That it is difficult to reconstruct working-class culture is undeniable – witness the debate among historians over culturalism and structuralism over a decade ago.[68] However, only the most die-hard structuralist would still argue that E. P. Thompson's reconstruction of the experience of the English working class, for all its faults, was entirely worthless. Savage's other two points are essentially concerned with the complexity of the relationship between material life, culture and consciousness. Again, this complexity is undeniable, but is not a sufficient reason for abandoning the attempt to explain it. Certainly, attempts to elevate culture to the point of being the sole determinant of working-class politics, while at the same time rejecting any material basis, is unacceptable. But the wholesale jettisoning of the concepts of consciousness and culture is not justified, and they will be employed where relevant later in this book.

The third and final point about Savage's work is that his attempt to link different political practices to differences in occupation and skill-level, but also to other forms of differentiation in the working-class, most notably that of gender, serves as a model for other studies. Whatever reservations there may be about particular aspects of Savage's study, his rejection of any mono-causal explanation of working-class politics has to be endorsed, and coincides with much of the approach employed in this analysis of Liverpool.

Local studies of working-class politics in international perspective

The final part of this introductory survey points towards local studies of working-class formation and development in international perspective. The main focus here will be on studies of the American working class, as these have been particularly plentiful over the past decade or so. However, some mention should also be made of similar work being done on continental Europe. Even limiting the field to English-language studies, there has been a number of recent works exploring local aspects of working-class history across Europe, and this is plainly a growing area of historical research.[69]

To take one example, L. R. Berlanstein's study of Parisian working people in the late nineteenth and early twentieth centuries is an interesting analysis of their economic and social structure, and political responses.[70] Structural change is highlighted, creating a new group of factory workers on the outskirts of the city, as opposed to an older working class concentrated in workshop production in the centre. At the same time, two other main groups could be distinguished, in the service sector and in white-collar occupations. Despite the rather differing work experience of these groups, and the social and cultural differences that Berlanstein examines, the late nineteenth century nevertheless saw some political and industrial convergence. Economic crisis, and attempts by management to reduce workers' control over the labour process, brought increased industrial conflict, first in the older central industries, but also involving what were later to become the highly militant factory workers, and even white-collar workers. The syndicalist tradition and the centrality of questions of control, so often associated with the French labour movement, were seen in both factory and workshop. At the same time, an earlier political radicalism, decisively influenced by the experience of the 1871 Commune, was also to give way to a moderate socialism both in the city and the outlying industrial districts.[71]

Berlanstein's work illustrates the complexity of the internal composition of a local working class, and how structural change can rapidly and radically alter its composition. It also demonstrates that differentiation in the working class, in this case mainly by occupation and skill-level, can lead to distinct social and cultural differences, and yet not necessarily to permanent political or industrial division. For the purposes of this book, the point to be drawn from Berlanstein's study is this: the relationship between the differences within a class, and the historical expression of those differences, is neither automatic, nor unchanging. A similar conclusion flows from some of the American examples outlined below.

Given the earlier comments about the heterogeneous nature of the American working class, it is perhaps not surprising that labour history in the USA has recently provided a number of examples of highly impressive, and instructive, local studies. These have ranged widely in both geographical and chronological terms.[72] It is impossible to explore the full range of historical issues raised by this body of work within the confines of this brief survey. Nevertheless, there are some interesting points of comparison. Most strikingly, the scale and complexity of the racial and ethnic divisions within local working classes that are dealt with in some of these works seems, by comparison with the British experience, overwhelming.

Amy Bridges' study of *antebellum* New York, for example, shows the complex ethnic and occupational differentiation of the city wards by the mid-nineteenth century. A hierarchy of occupational groups could be discerned, ranging from artisans at the upper end of the scale, down through factory workers of various types, and finally to the lowest-paid groups such as teamsters, longshoremen, labourers and domestic servants. Within this pattern, ethnic differentiation was marked, with American-born workers more common at the top of the social scale, Germans and English/Scots concentrated in the middle, and the Irish nearer the bottom. In turn, the wards were differentiated: the West Side wards were predominantly artisanal, and mainly native-born, most notably the ninth ward; along the East River, shipbuilding and ironworking was significant, and the Germans were concentrated, for instance in the eleventh ward; in the South Side were many of the docks, warehouses and factories, and many of the Irish, such as in the first ward.[73]

Bridges stresses that this differentiation of the New York working class was not as clear-cut at this early date as it was to become later. Nevertheless, its effects were marked. Moreover, Bridges shows how ethnically and occupationally distinct neighbourhoods developed a complex set of social institutions, including voluntary fire companies, militia companies, and gangs, which increasingly defined this differentiation. The gangs defended their 'turf' in the working-class areas of the city, and even their names were redolent of a close-knit, and often ethnic, community: the Bowery Boys, Kerryonians, American Guards, Orangemen.[74] Yet Bridges also shows how this apparently rigidly divided working class was eventually brought to a degree of political unity through the creation of the Democratic political machine. 'The true home of the working classes' created a ward machinery which connected to the working-class community and, initially, especially the immigrant groups. This was by no means an independent workers' party, of course.[75] On the other hand, though, Bridges shows how this machine politics arose in the context of the decline of an older political order, brought on by what she calls a social revolution caused by industrialization. Combined with the fact of white male working-class enfranchisement, this created pressures from below on the boss and the machine. As she says:

> ... machine politics is not properly understood as the 'institutionalization' of working-class ethics, ethnic solidarity, or neighbourhood loyalties, nor can it be accounted for by describing it as an admirably designed mechanism for social control (though it may well be true that machine politics bears some relationship to each of these values).[76]

Bridges describes machine politics as a 'peculiarly American urban polity', and points to many other examples from the literature of the American working class where cases of distinct ethnic and occupational differentiation gave rise to specific forms of this polity.[77] Turning to a later period, also, the extent of differentiation in the working class seems decisive. Lizabeth Cohen's study of Chicago between the wars provides a case in point.

Cohen draws a fascinating picture of a city with five working-class areas distinguished by their ethnic and occupational characteristics. In the south-east was an area dominated by employment in the steelworks, and occupied by numerous different immigrant groups from southern and eastern Europe. Centred on the Back of the Yards district was an area dominated by the meat-packing plants, again with a complex mix of immigrant groups. In the west and north-west were the older immigrant neighbourhoods, many of whose residents worked in garment trades and light industries. To the south-west lay an area dominated by the huge plants of Western Electric and International Harvester, again ethnically mixed. Finally, there was the south-side black belt, where 90 per cent of Chicago's black population lived, and who worked in factories and mills across the city.[78]

Cohen stresses the 'centrality of ethnicity to workers' sense of community', which was underpinned by an enormous range of ethnic institutions concerned with social welfare, charity work, religion, banking and recreation.[79] Ethnic and racial conflict in various key industries was widespread, and seemed to preclude any prospect of class-wide solidarity, most notably in the crushing industrial defeats of the steel strike of 1919 and the packinghouse disputes in the early 1920s. Political unity was equally elusive, with high levels of working-class abstention in elections, and minimal workers' involvement in party politics.[80]

Yet, within a decade the picture was transformed, according to Cohen. Many of Chicago's workers were radicalized in campaigns among the unemployed in the early 1930s, and some were influenced by the Communist Party, which was heavily involved in these campaigns. By the mid-1930s many more workers were enthusiastic supporters of the Democratic Party and the New Deal, while many more again were unionized in a great wave of rank-and-file industrial struggle led by the new and militant Congress of Industrial Organizations (CIO). By the early 1940s many workers in the steel mills, the packinghouses and at International Harvester had gained union recognition and improved contracts. Moreover, Cohen shows how the ethnic and racial divisions of a decade earlier were effectively defused, even though the cultural bases of those divisions remained proudly in place, a process actively encouraged by the CIO in constructing what she calls a 'culture' of unity. The situation was not to last long before the post-1945 cold war freeze set in, but the brief moment of working-class unity was nevertheless impressive.[81]

From the perspective of this study of Liverpool, the key point to be drawn from Bridges' and Cohen's work, and from many of the other studies cited above, is the high degree of differentiation in the working class shown in these American cities. By comparison, the ethnic and religious divisions of Liverpool seem relatively insignificant. But what is also instructive is that even these stark American divisions were capable of being broken down, albeit temporarily. To identify deep-rooted structural differences within a class, and to show the social and cultural effects of these differences, does not preclude the possibility of their potential for political and industrial division being reduced. Structures do not automatically determine historical outcomes.

On the other hand, another instructive aspect of these American works is that they highlight the necessity of analysing the whole ensemble of economic, social, cultural and political relations that were specific to each city. Bridges makes this point well, in showing how machine politics, while a 'peculiarly American urban polity', took specific forms in the different cities she surveys. Cohen, however, never makes any comparisons with contemporary developments elsewhere, claiming that working-class politics during the 1930s showed only minor variations between different cities and regions.[82] This debatable claim is never substantiated, and others have identified it as one possible weakness in her study. Bruce Nelson, for instance, has argued that the progress of the CIO took different forms elsewhere, especially in the port cities that are the focus of his research, and that there was not a 'single pattern of ideological development'.[83]

At the same time, Bridges is careful to stress that American cities were never 'self-contained arenas of political activity'.[84] State and national governments, and national political trends and organizations, always impinged on the local polity. This is something that needs especially to be kept in mind in any twentieth-century British study, as local government was even less autonomous in relation to the central state, and labour's own organizations, most notably in national trade unions and the Labour Party, also tended to be more centralized than their American counterparts.

Summary remarks

To conclude this opening chapter it will be useful to recapitulate the main aims and assumptions of this book. The book is intended as a contribution to the growing body of work analysing the local dimension of working-class history. It is informed by several basic assumptions. First, that working classes are never homogeneous, and that local differences are always present. Second, that specific local features of differentiation in the working class are never fixed, but vary according to changes in local economic and social structures. Third, that structural differences within a local working class do not lead automatically or simply to pre-determined historical forms of political consciousness. Fourth, that the whole ensemble of economic, social, cultural and political features of a local working class have to be considered to explain its history. Finally, that the locality can never be seen as a self-contained entity, but rather as being linked to regional and national developments.

What will be shown in the rest of this book is that local economic structures were decisive in forming a Liverpool working class that was distinctively differentiated by occupation. Other forms of differentiation, such as those of religion and gender, were also significant in affecting the way in which the social, cultural and political features of this class developed historically.

What will also be demonstrated is that the local political system itself was important in limiting and shaping the political development of Labour in Liverpool, and may have tended to magnify the scale of Labour's failure. At the same time, the party's own limitations contributed to its lack of political progress. With this in mind, the analysis will start by examining the structure and organization of the Liverpool Labour Party, which is the subject of the next chapter.

References

1. A. R. Zolberg, 'How many exceptionalisms?', in I. Katznelson and A. R. Zolberg (eds), *Working Class Formation: Nineteenth-Century Patterns in Western Europe and the United States* (Princeton University Press, Princeton: 1986), p. 397.
2. H. Pelling, *A History of British Trade Unionism* (3rd edn., Penguin Press, Harmondsworth: 1976), p. 89.

3. E. J. Hobsbawm, 'The forward march of labour halted?', in *Marxism Today* (September 1978), pp. 281–2.

4. See, for instance, E. P. Thompson, *The Making of the English Working Class* (Penguin, Harmondsworth: 1968); 'The moral economy of the English crowd in the eighteenth century', in *Past & Present* 50, (1971); 'Patrician society, plebeian culture', *Journal of Social History* 7, (1974).

5. See, for instance, the various articles in A. Briggs (ed.), *Chartist Studies* (Macmillan, London: 1959); J. Epstein and D. Thompson (eds), *The Chartist Experience: Studies in Working-Class Radicalism and Culture, 1830–1860* (Macmillan, London: 1982).

6. See, for instance, G. Crossick, *An Artisan Elite in Victorian Society: Kentish London, 1840–1880* (Croom Helm, London: 1978); J. Foster, *Class Struggle and the Industrial Revolution: Early Industrial Capitalism in Three English Towns* (Weidenfeld and Nicolson, London: 1974); R. Q. Gray, *The Labour Aristocracy in Victorian Edinburgh* (Clarendon Press, Oxford: 1976); P. Joyce, *Work, Society and Politics: The Culture of the Factory in Later Victorian England* (Harvester, London: 1980); N. Kirk, *The Growth of Working Class Reformism in Mid-Victorian England* (Croom Helm, London: 1985).

7. See, for instance, G. Stedman Jones, *Languages of Class: Studies in English Working-Class History, 1832–1982* (Cambridge University Press, Cambridge: 1983); P. Joyce, *Visions of the People: Industrial England and the Question of Class, 1848–1914* (Cambridge University Press, Cambridge: 1991); J. Vernon, *Politics and the People: A Study in English Political Culture, c. 1815–1867* (Cambridge University Press, Cambridge: 1993); and, most provocatively, P. Joyce, 'The end of social history?', *Social History* 20 no. 1 (1995); for critical responses see, for instance, B. D. Palmer, 'Critical theory, historical materialism, and the ostensible end of Marxism: the poverty of theory revisited', *International Review of Social History* 38, pt. 2 (1993); N. Kirk, 'History, language, ideas and post-modernism: a materialist view', *Social History* 19, pt. 2 (1994).

8. Zolberg, 'How many exceptionalisms?', p. 433; See also I. Katznelson, 'Working-class formation: constructing cases and comparisons', in the same collection, for further consideration of the varieties of working-class formation in international perspective.

9. Zolberg, 'How many exceptionalisms?', p. 431.

10. T. L. Drinkwater, 'A History of the Trade Unions and Labour Party in Liverpool, 1911 to the General Strike' (unpublished BA thesis, University of Liverpool, 1940); W. Hamling, *A Short History of the Liverpool Trades Council, 1848–1948* (LTCLP, Liverpool: 1948); S. Maddock, 'The Liverpool Trades Council and Politics, 1878–1918' (unpublished MA thesis, University of Liverpool, 1959); J. D. Walsh, 'Aspects of Labour and Industrial Relations in Liverpool, 1891–1932' (unpublished MA thesis, University of Liverpool, 1976).

11. D. A. Roberts, 'Religion and Politics in Liverpool since 1900' (unpublished M. Sc. thesis, University of London, 1965), p. 1.

12. Roberts, 'Religion and Politics in Liverpool', p. 154.

13. R. Baxter, 'The Liverpool Labour Party, 1918–1963' (unpublished D.Phil. thesis, University of Oxford, 1969); R. Baxter, 'The working-class and labour politics', *Political Studies* XX (1972).

14. Baxter, 'The Liverpool Labour Party', especially Chs. 7–10.

15. Baxter, 'The Liverpool Labour Party', pp. 1–2, and especially Chs. 4–6.
16. See M. Shefter, 'Trade unions and political machines: The organization and disorganization of the American working class in the late nineteenth century', in Katznelson and Zolberg (eds), *Working Class Formation*, pp. 197–213, 267–71; see also A. Bridges, *A City in the Republic: Antebellum New York and the Origins of Machine Politics* (Cambridge University Press, Cambridge: 1984), pp. 103–24, 146–61.
17. Quoted in P. J. Waller, *Democracy and Sectarianism: A Political and Social History of Liverpool, 1868–1939* (Liverpool University Press, Liverpool: 1981), p. 313.
18. Baxter, 'The Liverpool Labour Party', p. 1.
19. *Ibid.*, p. 3.
20. Waller, *Democracy and Sectarianism*, p. xix.
21. *Ibid.*, p. xvi.
22. J. Smith, 'Commonsense Thought and Working Class Consciousness: Some Aspects of the Liverpool and Glasgow Labour Movement in the Early Years of the Twentieth Century' (unpublished Ph.D. thesis, University of Edinburgh, 1981); 'Labour tradition in Glasgow and Liverpool', *History Workshop* 17 (1984); 'Class, skill and sectarianism in Glasgow and Liverpool, 1880–1914', in R. J. Morris (ed.), *Class, Power and Social Structure in British Nineteenth-Century Towns* (Leicester University Press, Leicester: 1986).
23. Smith, 'Labour tradition', p. 33.
24. *Ibid.*, p. 44.
25. *Ibid.*, pp. 48–9.
26. *Ibid.*, p. 49.
27. *Ibid.*, p. 44.
28. *Ibid.*
29. *Ibid.*, pp. 44–6.
30. *Ibid.*, p. 46.
31. *Ibid.*, p. 47.
32. *Ibid.*, pp. 47–8.
33. See especially, Smith, 'Class, skill and sectarianism', pp. 173–80.
34. On the problems of interpreting Gramsci's terminology in his prison writings, see Q. Hoare and G. Nowell Smith (eds), *Selections from the Prison Notebooks of Antonio Gramsci*, (Lawrence and Wishart, London: 1971), pp. x–xiv; for Gramsci's writings on 'commonsense', etc., see pp. 323–31.
35. Smith, 'Labour tradition', p. 50.
36. *Ibid.*
37. *Ibid.*, pp. 40–2.
38. R. J. Holton, 'Syndicalism and labour on Merseyside, 1906–14', in H. R. Hikins (ed.), *Building the Union: Studies on the Growth of the Workers' Movement: Merseyside, 1756–1967* (Toulouse Press, Liverpool: 1973), p. 122.
39. Smith, 'Labour tradition', p. 48; J. Des Forges, '"We make millions of pairs of boots, but not one pair of millionaires": co-operation and the working-class in Liverpool and the Rhondda', *North West Labour History* 19 (1994/5), pp. 48–64; J. Des Forges, 'Co-operation, labour, and consumption in Liverpool, c.1890–1914', in B. Lancaster and P. Maguire (eds), *Towards the Co-operative Commonwealth: Essays in the History of the Co-operative Movement* (Keele University Press, Keele: forthcoming).
40. Des Forges, '"We make millions of pairs of boots', pp. 50–5.

41. Holton, 'Syndicalism and labour on Merseyside', pp. 127, 131–3. Also, see E. L. Taplin, *The Dockers' Union: A Study of the National Union of Dock Labourers, 1889–1922* (Leicester University Press, Leicester: 1986), pp. 67–79.

42. J. Belchem, 'Introduction: The peculiarities of Liverpool', in J. Belchem (ed.), *Popular Politics, Riot and Labour: Essays in Liverpool History, 1790–1940* (Liverpool University Press, Liverpool: 1992), p. 9. See also Belchem, 'Liverpool in the year of revolution: the political and associational culture of the Irish immigrant community in 1848', in *Popular Politics, Riot and Labour,* pp. 75–95.

43. A. Shallice, 'Liverpool Labourism and Irish Nationalism in the 1920s and 1930s', *Bulletin of the North West Labour History Society* 8 (1982–3), pp. 19–21.

44. Smith, 'Labour tradition', p. 39.

45. Waller, *Democracy and Sectarianism*, pp. 165, 197; Smith, 'Class, skill and sectarianism', pp. 181–2.

46. *Liverpool Official Red Book* (1920), p. 63.

47. Baxter, 'The Liverpool Labour Party', pp. 108–10.

48. Waller, *Democracy and Sectarianism*, pp. xvii–xix, 119, 153, 160.

49. F. Bealey, J. Blondel and W. P. McCann, *Constituency Politics: A Study of Newcastle-under-Lyme* (Faber, London: 1965); G. W. Jones, *Borough Politics: A Study of the Wolverhampton Borough Council, 1888–1964* (Macmillan, London: 1969); W. Hampton, *Democracy and Community: A Study of Politics in Sheffield* (Oxford University Press, London: 1970).

50. Hampton, *Democracy and Community*, pp. 24–48, 153–82.

51. Jones, *Borough Politics*, pp. 58–74.

52. Bealey *et al.*, *Constituency Politics*, pp. 77–97.

53. *Ibid.*, p. 104.

54. See, for instance, J. A. Gillespie, 'Economic and Political Change in the East End of London during the 1920s' (unpublished D. Phil. thesis, University of Cambridge, 1984); S. Goss, *Local Labour and Local Government: A Study of Changing Interests, Politics and Policy in Southwark from 1919 to 1982* (Edinburgh University Press, Edinburgh: 1988); J. Holford, *Reshaping Labour: Organisation, Work and Politics in Edinburgh in the Great War and After* (Croom Helm, London: 1988); B. Lancaster, *Radicalism, Cooperation and Socialism: Leicester Working Class Politics, 1860–1906* (Leicester University Press, Leicester: 1987); B. Lancaster and T. Mason (eds), *Life and Labour in a Twentieth Century City: The Experience of Coventry* (P. Cryfield, Coventry: 1986); J. Mark-Lawson, *et al.*, 'Gender and local politics: struggles over welfare policies, 1918–1939', in L. Murgatroyd *et al.* (eds), *Localities, Class and Gender* (Pion, London: 1985); J. Marriott, *The Culture of Labourism: The East End Between the Wars* (Edinburgh University Press, Edinburgh: 1991); M. Savage, *The Dynamics of Working-Class Politics: The Labour Movement in Preston, 1880–1940* (Cambridge University Press, Cambridge: 1987); A. Warde, 'Conditions of dependence: working-class quiescence in Lancaster in the twentieth century', *International Review of Social History* 35 (1990).

55. Lancaster, *Radicalism, Cooperation and Socialism*, p. xix.

56. *Ibid.*, p. xviii.

57. Savage, *The Dynamics of Working-Class Politics*, Ch.1.

58. *Ibid.*, pp. 20–8.

59. *Ibid.*, pp. 41–63.

60. *Ibid.*, ch. 4.
61. *Ibid.*, pp. 140–1.
62. *Ibid.*, p. 152.
63. *Ibid.*, pp. 162–79.
64. *Ibid.*, pp. 180–7.
65. *Ibid.*, p. 187.
66. *Ibid.*, pp. 192–4.
67. *Ibid.*, p. 3.
68. For a useful discussion of this, see N. Kirk, 'Traditional working-class culture and the "rise of labour": some preliminary questions and observations', *Social History* 16 (1991). Also see E. P. Thompson, 'The poverty of theory: or an orrery of errors', in *The Poverty of Theory and Other Essays* (Merlin Press, London: 1978), and the succeeding debate in the pages of *History Workshop Journal* 6 (Autumn 1978); 7 (Spring 1979); and 8 (Autumn 1979).
69. See, for instance, R. Aminzade, *Class, Politics and Early Industrial Capitalism: A Study of Mid-Nineteenth Century Toulouse, France* (State University of New York Press, Albany: 1981); D. C. Wright, 'Socialist Municipal Politics in Twentieth Century Limoges, France' (unpublished Ph.D. thesis, University of Wisconsin-Madison, 1991); W. J. Chase, *Workers, Society and the Soviet State: Labor and Life in Moscow, 1918–29* (University of Illinois Press, Urbana: 1990); S. A. Smith, *Red Petrograd: Revolution in the Factories 1917–1918* (Cambridge University Press, Cambridge: 1983); R. A. Comfort, *Revolutionary Hamburg: Labor Politics in the Early Weimar Republic* (Stanford University Press, Stanford: 1966); C. Lis, *Social Change and the Laboring Poor: Antwerp, 1770–1860* (Yale University Press, New Haven: 1986).
70. L. R. Berlanstein, *The Working People of Paris, 1871–1914* (Johns Hopkins University Press, Baltimore: 1984).
71. *Ibid.*, pp. 3–38, 74–121, 151–97.
72. For the earliest period of working-class formation, see, for example, A. Dawley, *Class and Community: The Industrial Revolution in Lynn* (Harvard University Press, Cambridge, Mass.: 1976); S. E. Hirsch, *Roots of the American Working Class: The Industrialization of Crafts in Newark, 1800–1860* (The Temple University Press, Philadelphia: 1978); B. Laurie, *Working People of Philadelphia, 1800–1850* (University of Pennsylvania Press, Philadelphia: 1980); C. G. Steffen, *The Mechanics of Baltimore: Workers and Politics in the Age of Revolution, 1763–1812* (University of Chicago Press, Chicago: 1984); S. Wilentz, *Chants Democratic: New York City and the Rise of the American Working Class, 1788–1850* (Oxford University Press, Oxford: 1984). For a later period, see, for instance, S. J. Ross, *Workers on the Edge: Work, Leisure and Politics in Industrializing Cincinnati, 1788–1890* (Columbia University Press, New York: 1985); Bridges, *A City in the Republic*; B. Greenberg, *Worker and Community: Response to Industrialization in a Nineteenth Century American City, Albany, New York 1850–1884* (State University of New York Press, Albany: 1985); S. J. Kleinberg, *The Shadow of the Mills: Working-Class Families in Pittsburgh, 1870–1907* (University of Pittsburgh Press, Pittsburgh: 1989). For the twentieth century, the history of the Chicago working class is extensive, due in part to the accident of the University of Chicago becoming the centre of social scientific research in the USA in the inter-war period. Notable recent work includes: R. A. Slayton, *Back of the Yards: The Making of a Local Democracy* (University of

Chicago Press, Chicago: 1986); J. R. Barrett, *Work and Community in the Jungle: Chicago's Packinghouse Workers, 1894–1922* (University of Illinois Press, Urbana: 1987); L. Cohen, *Making a New Deal: Industrial Workers in Chicago, 1919–1939* (Cambridge University Press, Cambridge: 1990). See also, J. E. Argersinger, *Toward a New Deal in Baltimore: People and Government in the Great Depression* (University of North Carolina Press, Chapel Hill: 1988); E. Faue, *Community of Suffering and Struggle: Women, Men and the Labor Movement in Minneapolis, 1915–1945* (University of North Carolina Press, Chapel Hill: 1991); D. Frank, *Purchasing Power: Consumer Organizing, Gender, and the Seattle Labor Movement, 1919–1929* (Cambridge University Press, Cambridge: 1994); G. Gerstle, *Working-Class Americanism: The Politics of Labor in a Textile City, 1914–1960* (Cambridge University Press, Cambridge: 1989).

73. Bridges, *A City in the Republic*, pp. 39–57.
74. *Ibid.*, pp. 43, 73–7.
75. *Ibid.*, p. 124.
76. *Ibid.*, p. 158.
77. *Ibid.*, pp. 57–8, 154–7.
78. Cohen, *Making a New Deal*, pp. 17–38.
79. *Ibid.*, pp. 24–6, 53–97.
80. *Ibid.*, pp. 38, 252–4.
81. *Ibid.*, pp. 252–360.
82. *Ibid.*, p. 7.
83. B. Nelson, 'The uneven development of class and consciousness', *Labor History* 32 (1991), p. 589.
84. Bridges, *A City in the Republic*, p. 14.

2 The extent of Labour's failure: organization, structure and links with the working class

Even for a party as strongly committed to electoralism as the British Labour Party has always been, its strength and success cannot be measured purely in electoral terms. Its mode of organization and structure, and the relationship between it and its intended supporters was also indicative of its performance. For the period of this study it is assumed that Labour's relationship to the working class was the key indicator of performance. This is not to say that Labour was unable to appeal to other sectors of society, but the whole historical trajectory of the party from its inception was shaped by the notion of the independent representation of labour. The founding conference, after all, declared its aim as the representation of working-class opinion 'by men sympathetic with the aims and demands of the Labour movement'.[1] The strong link with the trade unions from the beginning ensured that the centrality of the working class to Labour's progress was to persist.

That the organized labour movement and the working class were by no means synonymous is undeniable. Different levels of trade-union and political organization according to occupation and skill levels, but also according to gender, inherently placed constraints on Labour's appeal. But it does not alter the fact that it was primarily working-class support that remained the bedrock of Labour's strength nationally. In that sense this book rejects recent suggestions that the Labour Party's growth in this period 'had little to do with declining class fragmentation, or growing class consciousness', and that its development was hindered by its failure to develop 'a means of mobilising support from more affluent voters'.[2] Class politics, whatever its limitations, remained central to Labour, and it is the relationship with the working class that is relevant here.

There was much in the structure and organization of the Liverpool party up to 1918 that was indistinguishable from others across the country. The confederal nature of the national organization, linking trade unions and political groups, was faithfully reflected locally. Membership of the party was not direct, but only through affiliated bodies, and political activity was dependent upon the strength of those bodies. Two institutions provided the central structure of the party: the Liverpool Trades Council (LTC) and the local Independent Labour Party (ILP). It was the members of the individual affiliated unions and ILP branches who comprised the rank-and-file activists of the party. None of this was exceptional.[3]

However, variations on this basic theme were widespread, and Liverpool varied in a number of ways. One significant difference from other city Labour parties was that there was virtually no organization at a ward or divisional level.[4] Divisional councils were formed to fight elections, and lapsed afterwards. No permanent ward parties were established before 1918. This meant that the party was strongly dependent on the central structures of the organization, the LTC and the ILP, and it was the relationship of those two bodies with the wider working class that determined Labour's connection with that class. Inevitably, then, the limitations of the LTC and the ILP were crucial.

The Liverpool Trades Council and the origins of the Labour Party in Liverpool

The LTC claimed to be the oldest Trades Council in the country, having its origins in 1848. However, it was certainly not the case that it could claim to be highly representative of the working class of Liverpool as a whole, nor could it have been expected to be before 1889, given the chronology of trade-union development in Britain. Union organization nationally was mainly confined to skilled or semi-skilled, and almost exclusively male, workers before the new unionism of the late 1880s. Liverpool's economy was heavily dependent on port-related activity and the unskilled and often casual labour that went with it. Inevitably, only a small proportion of Liverpool's working class had been permanently organized by 1889. The LTC therefore was initially based upon the craft unions established in the city, which were relatively unrepresentative of the local working class as a whole. In 1887, trade unions of engineers, printers, tailors, saddlers, bookbinders, railwaymen, gilders, cabinet-makers, sawyers, brushmakers, bootmakers, mastblock-makers, and upholsterers were affiliated to the LTC. Between them they represented 3,000 workers.[5] This constituted a fraction of the 230,000 men and women classified as being in paid employment in Liverpool in the 1891 census.[6]

The new unionist strike wave of 1889–90 broadened the base of support for the LTC to some extent. Organization among dockers, seafarers, gasworkers, post-office workers, and tramway employees was developed in Liverpool in 1889 and 1890, and women workers in the workshop trades of cigar-making, book-folding, coat-making, upholstering, sack- and bag-making and laundering were also organized around this period.[7] By March 1891 the LTC had 47 affiliated unions, representing 46,000 workers.[8] However, much of this growth only lasted for a short period before the steep decline of the new unions from 1891. Most of the women's organization in Liverpool, for instance, collapsed, with only the uphol-stresses surviving by joining with the men's Upholsterers' Union, and all the other unions saw a sharp decline in membership.[9] The National Union of Dock Labourers (NUDL) barely survived through the 1890s, and the National Amalgamated Sailors' and Firemen's Union (NASFU) collapsed in 1894, not to be fully revived until 1910.[10] Other significant groups that were organized in this period in Liverpool stayed permanently distanced from the LTC, most notably the carters, organized in 1889 in the Mersey Quay and Railway Carters' Union,[11] and the clerical workers, who belonged to the strictly non-political Liverpool Clerks' Association.[12]

Moreover, the relationship between the LTC and the NUDL, the union that represented the largest single group of male workers in the city, was tenuous from the beginning. This was to be a portent of later develop-ments up to the 1920s. When the NUDL had begun to grow in Liverpool in 1889–90, it had not initially affiliated to the LTC, despite being invited to do so. When the dockers went on strike in March 1890 the LTC gave only tepid support, and the dockers only joined eventually in July 1890. Subsequent relations were strained, not least because of a series of disputes between the leader of the NUDL, James Sexton, and the LTC. This cul-minated in Sexton implying that the LTC was giving tacit support to the recruitment of scab labour in Liverpool to break the crucial Hull dock strike of 1893. In 1894 the NUDL disaffiliated, only allowing its branches to affiliate again in 1906. There seemed no great rush by the dockers to join even then, no NUDL branch being recorded in a list of affiliated organizations in 1907.[13]

Sexton's powerful position in the NUDL, and his idiosyncratic person-ality, had something to do with this tangled story, but it was also caused by the differences in outlook between the 'would-be aristocratic artisans', as Sexton described them, of the LTC and the newly organized dockers.[14] The differences were complex. Many dockers, along with seafarers and other dockside workers, had been only recently dissuaded by the NUDL from supporting the US-based Knights of Labor in a scheme to unite all unskilled workers, a scheme that was anathema to the mainly skilled members of the LTC.[15] The LTC argued strongly that it was a non-political body, and rejected Sexton's proposal in 1893 for it to affiliate to the ILP.[16] Sexton's description, quoted above, of the LTC hinted at the social and cultural gulf that lay between the regularly-employed, relatively well-paid, time-served workers that dominated it, and the low-paid, casually-employed workers whom he represented. From the other side, the attitude towards maritime workers was expressed succinctly in the pages of a local socialist newspaper as follows: 'The ways of those amphibious trade unionists who work "along the line of the docks" are not easily understood by those who find employment on terra firma.'[17]

By 1896, then, the LTC still represented only 35,000 workers,[18] drawn from a numerically small sector of Liverpool's organized labour force, let alone the working class as a whole. A much fuller understanding of the basis of its support can be gained from a detailed analysis of the delegates to the LTC. Up until 1907, a list of delegates from all affiliated unions was published, including their home addresses. From this can be calculated which unions were best represented on the LTC, and also where in the city members of these unions were concentrated. The last complete list with all addresses was in 1905, and it is for this year that the analysis has been undertaken, tracing the wards in which all delegates lived. The full list can be found in Appendix I, and a summary of the data is shown in Table 2.1. Two important points flow from this evidence. First of all, the predominance of skilled, craft unions and the lack of representation of casual, unskilled dock-related workers, or of general unskilled unions, is marked. The lone delegate representing the sailors and the seven delegates from the National Amalgamated Union of Labour (NAUL) were very much the exceptions amongst the painters, shipwrights, carpenters, engineers and other craftsmen who predominated. The unrepresentative nature of the list can be best conveyed by expressing it in terms of the occupational breakdown that has been used for the analysis of wards in Chapter Eight, and then comparing it with the figures for Liverpool as a whole. This comparison is also included in Table 2.1.

Table 2.1 Male occupations in Liverpool, 1911, and of LTC delegates, 1905 (in %)

Occupational group	Liverpool 1911	LTC 1905
Building trades	8	32
Furnishing trades	3	5
Railwaymen	4	5
Engineering and metal trades	10	22
Workshop trades	1	9
Printing trades	2	6
Clothing trades	3	4
Retail and services	10	1
Transport and associated	32	4
White-collar and supervisory	18	5
Miscellaneous	8	9

Source: Calculated from 1911 census for Liverpool, and from data in Appendix I for Liverpool Trades Council, 1905.

Second, the residences of the LTC delegates were limited to certain parts of the city. The full significance of this can only be appreciated when it is put into context with an analysis of the electoral strength of Labour by ward, and an analysis of the occupational and other economic and social characteristics of wards. This will be found in Chapter Eight but, for the moment, what can be seen clearly is that the LTC's delegates resided only in certain of the working-class wards of the city, and were notably absent in others. This is summarized in Table 2.2, and expressed in map form in Figure 2.1.

Table 2.2   Wards where LTC delegates were resident, 1905*

Ward	Number of LTC delegates resident
Kensington	13
Everton	9
Dingle	8
Low Hill	8
Edge Hill	6
Kirkdale	6
Wavertree West	5
St Anne's	4
Prince's Park	4
Abercromby	4
Breckfield	4
Netherfield	4
Garston	3
Fairfield	3
Old Swan	3
St Domingo	3
Granby	3
Sandhills	3
Anfield	2
Brunswick	1
Gt George	1
Sefton Park East	1
Total	98

* 13 delegates living outside Liverpool excluded.

Most of the LTC delegates were concentrated in a number of adjacent wards near the city centre but some distance uphill from the river – Edge Hill, Low Hill, Kensington, Everton, and St Anne's – mainly Protestant areas with a relatively large proportion of permanently employed and skilled workers, as will be demonstrated in Chapter Eight. In the mainly Protestant, and less skilled wards to the north of the city and some distance inland – Kirkdale, Netherfield, Breckfield and St Domingo – there was less representation. In the dockside areas there was some LTC presence in the mainly Protestant south, in Dingle and Garston, but in the strongly Catholic and unskilled north end there was virtually no representation.

Figure 2.1 Trades Council delegates per ward, 1905

2   1911 Transport Strike Committee. Personnel with affiliation where known.
Back row (l. to r.): J. Bromley (unknown); T. Williamson (NAUL); W. Edwards (Bakers); W. Quilliam (Carters); A. W. Short (Ships' stewards); J. Connolly or Connor (Sailors); A. Williams (Railway servants); R. Allen (Dock board coopers).   *Second row:* H. McDonagh (unknown); W. Jones (Carters); E. Lamb (Engineers); J. Cotter (Ships' stewards); J. Hanratty (Coalheavers); G. Milligan (Dockers); W. Murray (Dockers); M. McGrath (Dockers); J. Wood (Dockers); J. Phipps (unknown).   *Third row:* F. Kilkelly (Dockers); T. Chambers (Sailors); J. Stephenson (Ships' steward, member of the LTC); Tom Mann (Chairman); J. Sexton (Dockers); T. Ditchfield (Carters); P. Kean (Coalheavers); P. Casey (Coalheavers).   *Front row:* J. Hessom (Sailors); R. Bell (Sailors); J. Clark (Warehousemen); J. Dickson (Sailors); J. Gardner (Navvies and general labourers).

Running along the river between Sandhills in the north to Brunswick in the south, nine adjacent wards with a total population in 1911 of over 125,000 people had only five LTC delegates resident.

This spatial pattern will become more familiar later in this book. What can be stated now is that the trade-union side of the Labour Party, represented by the LTC, had a foothold in only some of the working-class neighbourhoods of Liverpool, and that not only differences of occupation and skill-levels but also religion played a part in determining this pattern.

It was the narrow labour movement represented by the early LTC that helped to found the Labour Party in Liverpool. Earlier forays into political representation in 1887 and 1893 had been attempted by the LTC,[19] but its refusal to accede to Sexton's demand to amalgamate with the ILP in 1893 showed the reluctance of the skilled unions to commit themselves to independent labour representation initially. It was in 1900, though, that the LTC joined with the ILP, the Fabians, the Social Democratic Federation (SDF), and the Edge Hill and Garston Labour Clubs to form what became

3 Liverpool Trades Council, Executive Committee, c.1906. Personnel with affiliations where known.
Back row (l. to r.): G. Donkersley (Litho. printers); F. Norris (Bootmakers); G. Parkin (Engineers); H. Gough (Carpenters); J. Stephenson (Cabinetmakers [c.f. Illustration 2]); E. Peters (Glassworkers). *Front row:* G. Nelson (Typo. printers), J. Shannon (Carpenters); A. Short (Carpenters); J. Moore (Painters); J. Naylor (Coachmakers).
Note the predominance of skilled trades represented here, and contrast with the unskilled groups represented in Illustration 2.

by 1903 the Liverpool Labour Representation Committee (LLRC), which in turn affiliated to the national Labour Party in 1907.[20] Up to 1918, the LTC remained vital to the central organization of the party.

The nature of the LTC did change somewhat following the upsurge of unskilled and general associations in 1911. Unions representing dockers, seafarers, and other dockside workers, shop, distributive and clerical workers, and municipal employees were all recruited. However, the dominance of the LTC by the older skilled unions persisted. Moreover, the relationship between the new and the old was never a harmonious one, and turned to open conflict during the First World War.

Disputes over conscription and the Russian Revolution of February 1917 increasingly divided the leadership of the NUDL from the more left-wing and ILP-influenced mainstream of the LTC. The NUDL eventually seceded before it could be expelled in July 1917, and set up a rival organization, the Liverpool Trade Union Labour Representation Council, which attracted 47 delegates to its first meeting, representing dockers, seafarers, carters, ships' stewards, enginemen and cranemen, farriers, and the NAUL.[21] It was claimed that 55,000 workers were represented by this body, but it was not only its size that was significant, but also the predominantly unskilled and casualized sectors of the Liverpool working class that distinguished it from the LTC. The leading historian of the Dockers' Union asserts with some understatement that the split 'seriously weakened the Liverpool labour movement' in 1917,[22] but it also revealed a much deeper fault-line running beneath the surface of the organized labour movement that had its origins much earlier and which was to persist long afterwards. At the end of the war, the formal split was healed, with many of the defectors rejoining the LTC, although some not for very long, as will be seen later.

The ILP and the development of the Labour Party in Liverpool

The political wing of the early Labour Party in Liverpool was dominated by the ILP. Although the Fabians and SDF and other socialists were also involved in its foundation in 1900, only the ILP had a local base of support and an organizational structure sufficient to play a major role in the party. This is not to say that the ILP was particularly strong in Liverpool as compared with other areas. David Howell, the leading historian of the early years of the ILP, adjudges Merseyside to be an extremely weak area for the party. This he attributes to the combination of religious sectarianism with the predominance of casual, unskilled labour in the area.[23]

Nevertheless, the ILP did establish an early presence on Merseyside, as shown by the the fact that in conjunction with the Fabian Society it was producing a local newspaper, the *Liverpool Labour Chronicle*, in 1895. Other evidence of the number of Liverpool supporters buying shares in the *Labour Leader* in 1904 suggests that there was some ILP strength locally.[24] A number of notable figures in the local labour movement also had early connections with the ILP, including union leaders of contrasting style like James Sexton and Jim Larkin of the Dockers' Union, and Bob Tissyman of the Policemen's Union. Other leading lights of the Labour Party, like John Wolfe Tone Morrisey, one of its earliest councillors, and Fred Richardson, the first Labour mayor of Liverpool, had early ILP connections.

All of this still amounted to only a limited growth, both in terms of size of membership and the spread of the ILP through the local working class. By 1920 the Liverpool Federation claimed 900 members, but that included branches in Bootle, Prescot, Southport and across the river in Birkenhead, Wallasey and Ellesmere Port.[25] In Liverpool itself, branches were established permanently in only a small number of wards. In 1895 there were seven branches, in Breckfield, Edge Hill, Kensington, Old Swan, Kirkdale, West Toxteth and Wavertree.[26] Twenty-five years later, in 1920, all but Breckfield had survived, but no new branches had been added to the list. Once again it is notable that the ILP presence was confined to areas predominated mainly by Protestants and by skilled workers. The dockside wards, the Catholic areas, and the areas of predominantly unskilled, casual labour were notable by their absence.

Where the ILP was established was where Labour had its main strength up to 1918, for these were the only areas with any continuous Labour presence between elections, as well as being the sorts of areas where the party was most likely to find support among the local electorate. Of the ten municipal election contests in which Labour won seats before 1914 (discounting the 1914 electoral truce when all Labour councillors were unopposed), eight were in the city centre wards concentrated around the Edge Hill / Kensington area where the ILP was dominant – Edge Hill, Kensington, Low Hill, St Anne's and Everton. One other was in Brunswick, which was organized by the West Toxteth ILP. The only other victory was a freak result in St Domingo in 1911 where Labour won with only 38 per cent of the votes cast due to an Independent Conservative splitting the Tory vote. ILP members also provided a significant proportion of the successful candidates before 1914, including Sexton in St Anne's, Morrisey in Kensington, and Richardson in Edge Hill.[27]

Organizational development from 1918

The new constitution of the national party of 1918, allowing for individual membership for the first time, was obviously influential in changing the nature of the local party, but reorganization was slow to take effect. The Liverpool party had attempted to set up ward organization in 1916 and 1917, but with little success outside the ILP strongholds, and further attempts in 1918 and 1919 were again ineffectual.[28] The LLRC now became known as the Liverpool Labour Party, and remained the central structure of the organization. The lack of ward activity was shown by the selection procedures for the 1918 general election. There were no operative divisional parties to select candidates, and a special meeting of the whole LLP had to be called to select five candidates.[29] By April 1919 the position was still highly unsatisfactory, and the Executive Committee was reported to have 'reviewed the whole position of lack of proper ward organization, apathy of candidates, etc'.[30]

At the same time, the upsurge in trade-union activity during and immediately after the war, together with the return of most of the unions that had defected in 1917, meant that the base of the LTC was broadened. When the LLP and the LTC were amalgamated in March 1921 to form the Liverpool Trades Council and Labour Party (LTCLP), the new body inherited an organization in transition, as can be shown by looking at the affiliated societies in the first year of its existence. Among the political affiliations, six ILP branches were recorded – Kirkdale, Wavertree, Kensington, West Toxteth, Edge Hill and the Liverpool Federation – representing much the same areas in which the ILP had had its strength before the war. The Fabian Society was also affiliated, as well as four divisional Labour parties (there were eleven divisions in all) – West Toxteth, Edge Hill, Everton and West Derby. On the industrial side, fifty-two unions were affiliated, including the older craft unions like the engineers, woodworkers, bootmakers and printers, but also unskilled and general unions, such as those of the dockers, seafarers, distributive workers, shop assistants and the NAUL.[31]

By 1924, when a full-time paid secretary was first appointed by the LTCLP, ward organization had been improved, but was still unsatisfactory. There were eight divisional parties operative by March 1924; only the strongly Protestant Kirkdale, the strongly Catholic Exchange and the markedly middle-class East Toxteth were unorganized.[32] Officially, there were twenty-two ward secretaries listed by July of that year also, although the secretary doubted if more than six wards actually had functioning parties.[33] In November it was agreed to reorganize the whole party to conform with national model rules, and an Elections and Organization Subcommittee was established. The minutes of this committee, to which all divisional parties were supposed to submit monthly reports on membership and organization, provides a valuable insight into the real state of the party organization. The committee met regularly between February and August 1925, and a summary of the divisional party reports can be found in Table 2.3.

What do these reports tell us about the state of the party in 1925? First, it is quite clear that it was going through a period of growth and change. Second, there was a very serious attempt by the membership at the time to develop the ward and divisional organization of the party, and recruit new members. It is also notable that the women's sections seemed to be playing a particularly active role at this time. This conforms with the picture of a growing influence by women on the party in the mid- to late 1920s, which is dealt with more thoroughly in Chapter Seven. On the surface, moreover, there did appear to be some activity in all the divisions.

However, organizational weakness can also be discerned in these reports. The 'difficulties' in wards like Netherfield and Kirkdale were a euphemism for the sectarianism of the strongly Protestant parts of the city, and Labour's failure to win widespread support in these areas. On the other hand, in the strongly Catholic areas of the Scotland and Exchange divisions, the reassurances that the membership figures quoted represented a 'paying membership' obviously reflected some scepticism from the rest of the party as to the accuracy of their reports. The picture of Scotland division seems particularly dubious. Labour had made no attempt to set up ward parties in this division until Davie Logan had defected from the Nationalists in early 1923, yet the delegate from Scotland division, Logan himself, was claiming the largest divisional and ward (for Scotland North) membership in the city, and a phenomenal increase from around 750 to 1,000 members between May and June of that year alone.

The financial accounts of the party for this period provide a rather different, and perhaps more realistic, estimation of its organizational strength. Up to 1928 detailed accounts recording the affiliation fees paid by divisional parties were published, although there are some gaps in the surviving records. Complete accounts survive for the successive twelve month periods to March 1925 and March 1926. Affiliation fees were paid at the rate of 6d. per member, with a minimum of £1.10s. (representing up to 60 members), then rising to £3 (for 60–120 members), £4.10s.

Table 2.3 Divisional Labour Party reports, February–August 1925

Division	Reports on organization
East Toxteth	'About 120 members' (May).
Edge Hill	Ward parties in Kensington, with 57 members; Low Hill, with 90 members; and Edge Hill, with 153 members. Edge Hill party had been recently reformed, as previously it had been run by the ILP (Apr.)
Everton	Netherfield ward defunct, Everton ward had 110 members, 45 recently recruited, and women's section also growing (Apr). 'Many difficulties in Netherfield' (May). 135 members (Jun).
Exchange	Ward parties in St Anne's and Abercromby, but none in Exchange, Vauxhall or Gt George (Feb). Gt George and Vauxhall parties established, total membership in Division 110 (Apr). 'A paying membership existed' (May).
Fairfield	Fairfield ward had 'fine women's section with a membership around 100', Old Swan ward recently reconstituted (May).
Kirkdale	100 members in St Domingo ward, but 'difficulties' in Kirkdale ward (Feb). 100 members in St Domingo, 127 in Kirkdale, women's sections in both (Apr).
Scotland	Scotland N. ward 600 members, Scotland S. 56, Sandhills 103, a 'paying membership' (May). Davie Logan 'believed they had 1,000 members' (Jun).
Walton	450 members in all, 116 recruited in previous four weeks (Feb). Over 500 members (Apr).
Wavertree	Total membership 860, Wavertree and Wavertree W. wards 'very healthy', Garston 'settling down' (Apr). Over 900 members (May). Reconstituting party in Woolton (Jun). Separate Garston TC and ward party, need to reconcile both bodies (Aug).
West Derby	Total membership 150, women 'most active' (Apr). 160 members (May).
West Toxteth	120 members in Brunswick ward, and women's section 'particularly active', Dingle ward gaining 'new members every day', total membership c.500 (Apr). 550 members (May).

Source: LTCLP, Elections and Organization Subcommittee, *Minutes* (24 February, 28 April, 26 May, 24 June, 28 July, 25 August, 1925).

(120–180 members), and so on.[34] For the year to March 1925, only Exchange and Kirkdale divisions were not affiliated at all, East Toxteth paid the minimum fee, and the other eight divisions paid at the 60–120 member level. In the following year, East Toxteth disappeared from the list, but Exchange and Kirkdale were added at the 120–180 member level, and all the others, with the exception of Edge Hill, also paid at the higher 120–180 level.[35]

These figures confirm that there was indeed an increase in membership at this time, but at much lower levels than some of the reports above would indicate. Assuming that the affiliation fees paid represented the maximum possible numbers of members at the appropriate level, the figures for 1924–5 give a total individual membership for the whole city of 960, rising to 1,740 in 1925–6. This was an impressive increase, no doubt, reflecting much hard work by the active membership of the time, but far less impressive than some of the reports above would indicate. Certainly, the reports of nearly 1,000 members in the Wavertree and Scotland divisions must have been wildly overstated.

It is also clear that some of the gains made around this time were only temporary. Looking at the lists of ward parties and their secretaries which were published each year, a number of wards appear to have been only sporadically organized up to 1939. In the East Toxteth division, Sefton Park East ward was not established until 1927, and disappeared between 1932 and 1938, and Aigburth ward was not organized until 1931, only to disappear again between 1933 and 1937. In Exchange division, Exchange and St Peter's ward were not organized until 1937 and 1931 respectively, and Great George ward was only intermittently active until 1932. In Scotland division, neither Sandhills nor Vauxhall wards had a permanent existence through the 1920s and 1930s. In West Toxteth, Brunswick ward disappeared in 1928 and again between 1934 and 1937. Finally, in Kirkdale the ward party disappeared in 1934.[36] Even making the dubious assumption that the public listing of a ward secretary always guaranteed that an actual ward party was active, it is clear that the party never established a city-wide organization in the inter-war period. This was probably not a situation unique to Liverpool. Significantly, though, in Liverpool many of the wards where organization seemed weakest were in strongly working-class, and mainly Catholic, dockside neighbourhoods. Vauxhall ward was typical: in 1932 the LTCLP was still discussing attempts to set up a ward party there, seven years after the supposedly comprehensive reorganization of 1925.[37]

This conclusion was confirmed in 1939 when the NEC of the Labour Party investigated the local party. Its findings were highly critical of local organization, stating that:

> the Committees of many Wards in Liverpool did not desire a large individual membership, it being suggested that this made control much easier ... Ward organisation in the city is out of touch with the centre ... most Constituency Parties were in a state of financial embarrassment.[38]

The recommendations of this enquiry were unequivocal:

> The City Labour Party can only succeed on the basis of good constituency organisation ... while suggestions are made below for the

improvement of organisation in each constituency, it is suggested that the Liverpool Trades' Council and Labour Party should act more vigorously in pushing forward co-ordinated efforts in propaganda, publicity and the working out of constructive policy for the whole city. Unless this can be secured the imagination of Liverpool people is not likely to be awakened ... The Liverpool Trades' Council and Labour Party should undertake more frequent and more active participation in the organisation of the Party in Constituencies and Wards.[39]

It is hard to avoid the conclusion that the Labour Party never succeeded in building a genuinely effective party organization covering the whole of the city and with deep roots in the local community. However, there is still the trade-union side of the party structure to consider. Perhaps there at least the party could claim a close connection with the organized part of the working class.

Trade-unionism and the Labour Party between the wars

What of the trade-union side of the party? There had been a broadening of support from local unions after 1918, as already stated. Again, the financial accounts of the Liverpool Trades Council and Labour Party provide a useful insight into the affiliated unions. Unions affiliated at the rate of 6*d.* for each member who paid the political levy, and it is quite easy to calculate the number affiliated from each union in the detailed accounts provided up to 1928. The accounts for the year ending in March 1925 give a good indication of the situation just before the traumas of the General Strike and the Trade Disputes Act which had a significant impact on affiliations, as will be demonstrated later. The full list of affiliations for 1924–5 can be found in Appendix II. A simplified version classifying the unions according to the types of occupation they mainly represented can be found in Table 2.4. The same system of occupational classification that has been adopted throughout this book has been used.

These figures show that there had been a significant change in the trade-union base of the LTCLP. The skilled trades had become less dominant than before, and the transport, service and retail, and railway sectors had all correspondingly increased their representation. The transport sector was still under-represented proportionally, even though the dockers, through the Transport and General Workers' Union (TGWU), and the seafarers, through the NSFU and Amalgamated Marine Workers' Union (AMWU), had over 5,000 members affiliated. By comparison, railway workers were relatively over-represented, with over 4,000 affiliated, and the skilled trades, even though much reduced, were still the biggest single group, with over 10,000 affiliated. Nevertheless, as a cross-section of the organized Liverpool working class as a whole, the 1924–5 LTCLP was more representative, even if still not perfectly so, than the 1905 Trades Council had been.

Table 2.4 LTCLP occupations represented by affiliated unions, year ending 31 March, 1925

Occupational group	Numbers affiliated	%
Building trades	3,136	10.8
Furnishing trades	1,045	3.6
Railwaymen	4,152	14.3
Engineering and metal trades	2,801	9.7
Workshop trades	1,197	4.1
Printing trades	2,926	10.1
Clothing trades	390	1.3
Retail and services	3,875	13.4
Transport and associated	5,040	17.4
White-collar and supervisory	1,585	5.5
Miscellaneous	2,875	9.9
Total	29,022	

However, the situation was still in a state of flux. In 1926, the NSFU, or National Union of Seamen (NUS) as it became known from that year, was thrown out of the LTCLP after sacking its local officials who had supported the General Strike. It was also thrown out of the TUC in 1928 over its opposition to the General Strike and its subsequent support for the breakaway Spencer union in the East Midlands coalfield.[40] However, even when the NUS was reconciled with the TUC and readmitted after the death of its long-time leader, Havelock Wilson, in 1929, relations locally between the LTCLP and the NUS remained poor. This was demonstrated when, in September 1929, the TUC wrote asking the LTCLP's advice on readmitting the NUS. The TUC received a rather dusty answer, which opposed readmittance unless the NUS reinstated all its local officials who had been sacked for carrying out TUC instructions during the general strike.[41] For the whole of the 1930s relations remained embittered, and a union representing a key group of Liverpool workers was estranged from Labour.

Other unions left the LTCLP after the Trade Disputes and Trade Union Act of 1927 came into effect. The imposition of the contracting-in to the political levy system, and the necessity to keep the political and industrial funds of the LTCLP strictly apart, forced branches of many unions to withdraw. Between late 1927 and the end of the decade branches of the National Union of General and Municipal Workers (NUGMW) and others representing post-office engineers, railwaymen, woodworkers, coopers, and lithographic artists, all disaffiliated for varying lengths of time.[42]

Moreover, the real involvement in the activities of, and influence upon, the LTCLP by key local unions may not have been as great as their superficial affiliation figures might have suggested. This can be shown through an analysis of the union delegates elected to the Executive Committee (EC) of the LTCLP. Obviously these elections were not simply decided on the basis of which unions were the most important or influential in the LTCLP as a whole. The personal abilities and political ambitions of individual delegates were influential to some extent, as was the nature of some of the posts on the EC. Thus, powerful figures like Luke Hogan or W. A. Robinson from the Distributive Workers' Union were elected regardless of their union's importance to the LTCLP, and clerical and white-collar unions tended to be over-represented through elections for secretarial and financial posts. Nevertheless, the EC elections must have reflected, to some extent, the relative importance of the various affiliated bodies. A summary of all EC elections between 1921 and 1939 can be found in Appendix III. A simplified version, placing all trade-union delegates elected to the EC in the occupational groups used throughout this book can be found in Table 2.5.

Table 2.5 Trade-union delegates elected to the Executive Committee of the LTCLP, classified by occupational group represented, 1921–1939

Occupational group	1921–1930		1931–1939	
	Delegates	%	Delegates	%
Building trades	11	8.5	34	29.1
Furnishing trades	2	1.6	0	
Railwaymen	12	9.3	14	12.0
Engineering and metal trades	19	14.7	9	7.7
Workshop trades	1	0.8	7	6.0
Printing trades	7	5.4	1	0.9
Clothing trades	6	4.7	3	2.6
Retail and services	20	15.5	12	10.3
Transport and associated	2	1.6	10	8.5
White-collar and supervisory	36	27.9	18	15.4
Miscellaneous	15	11.6	9	7.7
Total	129		117	

These figures show that key groups like the transport workers, which had grown by 1925 in terms of their affiliation to the LTCLP, were not as well represented on the EC, particularly up to 1930. The figure for transport workers after 1930 is also probably slightly exaggerated, due to the fact that the TGWU has been put in this category. When the TGWU was formed in 1922 there is no doubt that in Liverpool it mainly represented dockers, but later mergers with general unions and recruitment of general workers meant that, by the 1930s, it was less predominantly a transport union.[43] Conversely, the skilled trades were still highly influential, occupying almost half of all trade-union positions on the EC in the 1930s. There had been some change in the nature of the LTCLP, but it was still a long way from accurately reflecting the structure of the local working class.

Another writer's analysis can serve as the final words on the fragile relationship between the Liverpool working class and the Trades Council. As Eric Taplin has remarked:

> ... the major groups of the city had never looked on the Trades Council as a premier organisation deserving allegiance. These major workers' groups were to be found along the waterfront; seamen, ships' stewards, dockers, coalheavers, warehousemen, bargemen, tugboatmen and the like ... In most cities with a more diversified occupational structure, the Trades Council might be looked upon as the hub of united trade union activity. This was very much less the case in Liverpool.[44]

The Labour group and the Catholic caucus

There were two other significant elements of the party structure that have not yet been considered in any detail. First, there was the Labour group in the council-chamber, which became a significant force from the mid-1920s as the Labour presence increased. Second, there was the Catholic caucus within that group, which grew in importance from the late1920s, as Labour gained control of the Catholic wards of the city.

Although the LTCLP was formally the overall ruling body of the party, as elsewhere the Labour group in Liverpool developed an autonomy of its own. This became a major issue in 1930. The saga began in February when the city council decided to sell off the site of the old workhouse on Brownlow Hill, as a consequence of the demise of the Poor Law system. The suggested buyer of the valuable city-centre site was the Catholic church, which proposed to build a cathedral there. It says something about the subtleties of the implicitly sectarian Toryism of the city that it was the ruling Conservative group that pushed forward this proposal. The effect on Labour was disastrous.

Party policy, reaffirmed at the time by the LTCLP, was that publicly owned land should not be sold into private hands. On the crucial motion approving the sale, 21 Labour councillors voted against. A further 37 Labour members voted for selling to the Catholic church. Significantly, of the Catholic members of the Labour group, only 1 supported party policy, while 27 others supported the cathedral proposal.[45]

In March, the LTCLP disbanded the Labour group, and reformed it on the basis that members would have to agree to a new set of conditions. These included a commitment to uphold the constitution of the Labour

69

Party, and also: 'To acknowledge that in local affairs the Trades Council and Labour Party is the Executive governing body on Party programme, policy and discipline.'[46] Only 27 councillors were willing to accept the conditions, and the whip was withdrawn from the rest, formally splitting the party in the council-chamber. An enquiry into the whole affair was then instigated by the National Executive Committee of the Labour Party. In April, the results of the national enquiry came through, recommending the reinstatement of the old standing orders for the Labour group. Despite strong opposition from some sections of the LTCLP, the recommendation was accepted, and the original Labour group was reformed in May.[47]

Repercussions of the cathedral dispute rumbled on through 1930. Councillor Duffy, the only Catholic councillor originally to have opposed the sale of the Brownlow Hill site, was deselected by his ward party in Scotland North.[48] On the other hand, Councillor Mrs Hughes, who had supported the sale, was deselected in St Anne's ward, and replaced by Bessie Braddock. Mrs Hughes subsequently stood as an Independent Labour candidate in the November election, gaining 40 per cent of the vote against Mrs Braddock.[49] Another councillor, Bob Tissyman, resigned his seat in Edge Hill ward in protest at the failure to make the group follow party policy, precipitating a by-election in August. Also standing as an Independent Labour candidate, Tissyman defeated the official Labour nominee, only to lose the seat in the subsequent November election by splitting the Labour vote and letting in the Conservatives.[50]

In September, the LTCLP made further representations to the National Executive Committee, deploring the 'loss of prestige and authority, consequent upon the publication of the findings of the recent Sub-Committee of Inquiry appointed by the National Executive Committee'.[51] This was a last forlorn attempt to curb the independence of the Labour group. Essentially though, the group was now free to implement policy as it saw fit. For the rest of the decade it reigned supreme within the party.

At the same time, the cathedral dispute also confirmed the powerful position of the Catholic caucus within the Labour group. The Labour Party had displaced the Irish Nationalist Party (INP) as the dominant political force in the Catholic wards of the city during the 1920s. After the formation of the Irish Free State in 1922, there was little support for the continuation of the INP in Liverpool. The party changed its name to the Irish Party, then the Catholic Party, and finally the Centre Party. Even as it changed, some prominent members began to throw in their lot with the Labour Party. The first Nationalist councillor to defect to Labour was Davie Logan in 1923.[52] A fierce electoral battle ensued in the predominantly Catholic wards in the north of the city in the mid-1920s, which Labour was clearly winning by 1928. In that year as well, a new Catholic archbishop signalled a greater emphasis on assimilation, rather than defence of the faith, for the local Catholic population. A separate Catholic Party seemed increasingly inappropriate, and an electoral truce was declared in the 1928 municipal elections. Finally, the Labour Party's

4 Luke Hogan, nicknamed 'the iron duke'. Educated at St Sylvester's Roman Catholic School (Scotland North ward); trade-union official (NUDAW) – first elected to Brunswick ward 1921; leader of the Liverpool Labour Group and the Catholic caucus during the 1930s: Lord Mayor 1945–6; and freeman of the city 1946.

sweeping gains in the general election of 1929 precipitated wholesale defections to Labour.[53] Those councillors who subsequently represented the safe Catholic seats formed a numerical majority of the Labour group for most of the 1930s. Their victory over the cathedral issue welded them into a powerful caucus.

It would not be true to say that these Catholic councillors had no sympathy with socialism. Their leader, Luke Hogan, for instance, had his political origins in the Distributive Workers' Union and the Trades Council, and probably owed his eventual leadership of the party to the fact that he was the one figure who could claim to be a member of both camps. Others, such as P. J. Kelly, proclaimed their support for 'the claims of labour' even before they defected to the party.[54] Those ex-Nationalists who were genuinely anti-Labour, such as Austin Harford, remained in a Centre Party that became increasingly dependent on Tory patronage for survival in the 1930s. Nevertheless, the Catholic caucus' main political function was not the advancing of socialism but remained the representation of the Catholic community. They had done this surprisingly well for several decades in a strongly anti-Catholic city by working through the established political system. From an openly anti-Catholic Tory council, they won for the Catholic population of the city a considerable share of the housing improvements and other social amenities that the municipality provided. They continued to do this within the Labour Party in the 1930s. It is relevant to ask whether the Labour group and the Catholic caucus perhaps provided an alternative to the ward and divisional parties and the affiliated unions as a link with the local working class. To what extent were Labour councillors a real part of the neighbourhoods that they claimed to represent? Baxter analysed the residence and social origins of the Labour group as a whole in his 1969 thesis. His evidence suggests that Labour councillors in Liverpool were highly unrepresentative of the communities that they represented. Fewer than 10 per cent of councillors actually lived within the wards for which they stood in the 1930s, and in terms of social class almost 60 per cent of them were defined as middle class in the 1920s, and over 40 per cent in the 1930s.[55] These figures hardly suggest that Labour councillors sprang from within the neighbourhoods in which they were elected.

However, as far as the Catholic caucus was concerned, the relationship between elector and elected may have been more complex, and less distant. For those councillors in predominantly Catholic wards, religion provided a common link with their electors, and it was perhaps inevitable, given the cohesiveness of the Catholic community, that these councillors were much more likely to come from within this community itself. The evidence quoted above seems to bear this out, as far more councillors elected in these wards were also resident in them than in the rest of the city.[56]

On the other hand, it would be wrong to overstate the case, as evidence of the social composition of this group does not appear to distinguish them markedly from other Labour councillors. An investigation of the occupations of the Labour councillors and aldermen in 1930 who had been elected in the six most clearly Catholic wards gives the results shown in Table 2.6.

As can be seen very distinctly, the members of the caucus came overwhelmingly from business, white-collar and supervisory backgrounds. A number had connections with the trade-union movement as officials, but only one out of the nineteen whose occupations can be traced had an unequivocally working-class job, and that was as a skilled plasterer. This was certainly not a mirror image of the unskilled, casual workforce that predominated in the Catholic areas of the city at this time. These councillors were undoubtedly of the Catholic community, but they were also from a particular higher-status segment of it. Whether they truly expressed the beliefs and aspirations of their working-class Catholic electors, or whether they acted more as authority figures within their own community, are difficult questions to resolve conclusively.

Table 2.6 Occupations of Labour councillors and aldermen in 1930 who had been elected in predominantly Catholic wards

Name	Ward	Occupation
T. Hanley	Brunswick	Insurance agent
L. King	Brunswick	Paper stock merchant
P. Moorhead	Brunswick	Authority on economics
Ald. L. Hogan	Ex-Brunswick	Trade-union official
H. L. Gaffeney	Gt George	Unknown
M. Grogan	Gt George	Unknown
J. Loughlin	Gt George	Schools' agent
P. H. Hayes	Vauxhall	Surgeon
A. B. Hoer	Vauxhall	Window-cleaning contractor
J. Belger	Vauxhall	Accountant
Ald. P. J. Kelly	Ex-Vauxhall	Insurance agent
J. Sheehan	Scotland S	Plasterer
M. J. Reppion	Scotland S	Cartage contractor
J. Harrington	Scotland S	Team owner
P. Duffy	Scotland N	Unknown
P. Fay	Scotland N	Trade-union official
Mrs M. McFarlane	Scotland N	Unknown
Ald. W. A. Robinson	Ex-Scotland N	Trade-union official
Ald. D. G. Logan	Ex-Scotland N	Pawnbroker
J. W. Baker	Sandhills	Dentist
T. H. Dunford	Sandhills	Trade-union official
J. W. T. Morrisey	Sandhills	Insurance agent
Ald. T. W. Byrne	Ex-Sandhills	Dentist

Source: *Liverpool Official Red Books*, Who's Who section (various dates, 1920–39).

Political divisions within the party

By the 1930s political divisions within the Liverpool Labour Party were extremely complex. The Catholic caucus formed a solid bloc generally on the right wing of the party. Its dominant position in the Labour group assured the caucus a powerful position in the party. A second influential group was the predominantly moderate wing based in the Trades Council. There were close connections between this group and the local trade unions long associated with the Trades Council's activities. Leading councillors, such as W. A. Robinson of the Distributive Workers' Union, Fred Richardson of the Post Office Workers, Herbert Rose of the Life Assurance Agents and Bertie Kirby of the Clerks, typified this group. In the main these were party loyalists and evolutionary socialists. After the discord over the cathedral issue, the caucus and the Trades Council bloc formed an unofficial right-wing alliance which dominated the party overall. If, as has been argued, machine politics of the Tammany Hall type eventually came to dominate Labour in Liverpool, then it had its origins in this alliance.

Ranged against the moderate majority, was a disparate left-wing minority. Mainly having its strength in the divisional and ward parties, it could be sub-divided into two main parts in this period. The first was centred around the ILP, which still had its main base of support in the Edge Hill division, and was the leading force of the left through the 1920s. Its most prominent councillors, Bob Tissyman and Bob Edwards, were a continual thorn in the flesh of their party leaders, as will be shown later in Chapter Six. Their political ardour was matched by the only ILP MP for Liverpool, Elijah Sandham, who held Kirkdale between 1929 and 1931. Sandham scandalized his colleagues in Parliament by launching 'an extra-ordinary attack on the sobriety and morality of MPs' at an ILP conference in July 1930, for which he was referred to the Committee of Privileges and eventually censured for committing a 'gross libel'.[57] Tissyman and the ILP's opposition to the party leadership over the Catholic cathedral dispute eventually led to the disaffiliation of the entire Edge Hill divisional party in 1930.[58] Although the Edge Hill party was reinstated the following year, this was only a prelude to national disaffiliation of the ILP in 1932, which marked the end of its influence on the local party.[59]

Overlapping briefly with the ILP in the late 1920s and early 1930s was a second group, centred around activists based mainly in ward and divisional parties. Jack and Bessie Braddock, and Sidney Silverman, were leading figures in this group. Many of them were ex-Communists, including the Braddocks themselves. Ardent socialists, their focus of political activity was as much on the streets as in the council-chamber. Their involvement with the National Unemployed Workers' Movement, a proscribed organization with strong Communist Party links, first brought them into conflict with the party leadership.[60] Their support for anti-fascist campaigns, and for republican Spain, also led to clashes within the party. Equally, Bessie Braddock's advocacy of birth-control for working-class women attracted the furious attention of members of the Catholic caucus, as will be shown later in Chapter Seven.

Political alignments within the party, then, were complex. Given the equally complex structure and organization of the party, conflict was endemic. There were conflicts between the divisional delegates and the union delegates on the Trades Council, between the Trades Council and the Labour group, and between the Catholic caucus and the remainder of the group. All these conflicts had political overtones, but very often they also had religious undertones associated with them. Over questions such as birth-control, gender differences were also significant.

Some of these conflicts will be explored in more detail in later chapters. What can be asserted now, though, is that the inherently unstable structure of the party and the degree of conflict within it was not conducive to united or effective political campaigning. There were, of course, conflicts within parties in all other areas as well, but religious sectarianism provided a complicating dimension in Liverpool not commonly found elsewhere. A systematic comparison with other areas is not possible, however, simply because there are not enough local studies available as yet.

Organizational and structural failure and electoral politics

In summary, then, this chapter has shown that the Liverpool Labour Party was riddled with organizational and structural weaknesses. Its relationship with the local working class via trade-unionism was limited, and its ward and divisional parties were active and influential in only a few districts of the city. In the light of these problems, great electoral success for the party seemed unlikely. Yet it is also the case that poor organization elsewhere did not necessarily mean that Labour was unable to win electoral support, as the example of Newcastle-under-Lyme, referred to in Chapter One above, shows.[61] In Liverpool, though, Labour's lack of electoral success appeared undeniable. It is, therefore, necessary now to turn to that electoral record, and to the electoral system itself, to see how much they confirm Labour's failure. These are the subjects of Part Two of this book.

References

1. Quoted in R. Miliband, *Parliamentary Socialism: A Study in the Politics of Labour* (2nd edn., Merlin Press, London: 1972), p.17.
2. D. Tanner, *Political Change and the Labour Party, 1900–1918* (Cambridge University Press, Cambridge: 1990), pp.434, 441.
3. See R. McKibbin, *The Evolution of the Labour Party, 1910–1924* (Oxford University Press, London: 1974), pp.3–11.
4. *Ibid.*, p.5.
5. W. Hamling, *A Short History of the Liverpool Trades Council, 1848–1948* (LTCLP, Liverpool: 1948), p.18; P. J. Waller, *Democracy and Sectarianism: A Political and Social History of Liverpool, 1868–1939* (Liverpool University Press, Liverpool: 1981), p.100.
6. 1891 census, Vol. III, pp.352–9.
7. Hamling, *A Short History of the Liverpool Trades Council*, pp.19–26.
8. *Ibid.*, p.26.
9. *Ibid.*, p.25.
10. E. L. Taplin, *The Dockers' Union: A Study of the National Union of Dock Labourers, 1889–1922* (Leicester University Press, Leicester: 1986), pp.27, 81.
11. *Ibid.*, pp.32, 86–7.
12. *Liverpool Official Red Book* (1905), p.260.
13. Taplin, *The Dockers' Union*, p.54; *Liverpool Official Red Book* (1907), pp.244–5.
14. Quoted in Waller, *Democracy and Sectarianism*, p.105.
15. Taplin, *The Dockers' Union*, pp.31–2; see also R. Bean, 'A note on the Knights of Labour in Liverpool, 1889–90, *Labor History* 13, no. 1 (1972), pp. 68–78.

16. Waller, *Democracy and Sectarianism*, p.143.
17. *Liverpool Labour Chronicle* (1 July 1995).
18. Waller, *Democracy and Sectarianism*, p.152.
19. *Ibid.*, pp.101, 143–4.
20. R. Baxter, 'The Liverpool Labour Party, 1918–1963' (unpublished D. Phil. thesis, University of Oxford, 1969), pp.11–12.
21. Taplin, *The Dockers' Union*, pp.134–6.
22. *Ibid.*, p.136.
23. D. Howell, *British Workers and the Independent Labour Party, 1888–1906* (Manchester University Press, Manchester: 1983), p.205.
24. D. Hopkin, 'The membership of the Independent Labour Party, 1904–10: a spatial and occupational analysis', *International Review of Social History* 20, pt.2 (1975), pp.181–2.
25. *Liverpool Official Red Book* (1920), p.293.
26. Waller, *Democracy and Sectarianism*, p.159.
27. For details, see election results by ward in Appendix IV.
28. Baxter, 'The Liverpool Labour Party', pp.29–30.
29. Liverpool Labour Party, *Minutes* (24 November 1918).
30. *Ibid.* (28 March and 2 April 1919).
31. LTCLP, *Minutes*, balance sheets for 6 months ending 30 September 1921, 31 March 1922 (incorrectly printed as 1921 on original).
32. *Ibid.*, balance sheet for 12 months ending 31 March 1924.
33. *Ibid.* (1 July 1924).
34. *Ibid.* (7 March 1921).
35. *Ibid.*, financial statements, 6 months ending 30 September 1924; 31 March 1925, 30 September 1925, 21 March 1926.
36. *Liverpool Official Red Books* (1926–39).
37. LTCLP, *Minutes* (8 June 1932).
38. *Ibid.*, findings of NEC Inquiry, dated 22 February 1939.
39. *Ibid.*, 26 April 1939.
40. J. Eaton and C. Gill, *The Trade Union Directory: A Guide to all TUC Unions* (Pluto Press, London: 1981), p.54; A. Marsh and V. Ryan, *Historical Directory of Trade Unions*, Vol.3 (Gower, Aldershot: 1987), p.188.
41. LTCLP, *Minutes*, 13 September 1929.
42. *Ibid.*, 2 November and December 1927, 4 April, 14 June and 12 August 1929.
43. Eaton and Gill, *The Trade Union Directory*, pp.59–62.
44. E. L. Taplin, 'The Liverpool Trades Council, 1880–1914', *Bulletin of the North West Group for the Study of Labour History* 3 (1976), p. 15.
45. Liverpool City Council, *Council Proceedings* (5 February 1930), pp. 188–90.
46. LTCLP, *Minutes of Special Executive Committee Meeting* (16 March 1930).
47. *Ibid.*, *Minutes* (3 April 1930); *Executive Committee Minutes* (25 April 1930).
48. *Ibid.*, *Executive Committee Minutes* (4 September 1930).
49. See Appendix IV, p. 311.
50. LTCLP, *Minutes* (17 July, 15 August, 4 September and 6 October 1930); for election results, see Appendix IV, p. 272.
51. *Ibid.*, *Executive Committee Minutes* (4, 12 and 30 September 1930).
52. *Ibid.*, *Minutes* (3 January 1923).
53. *Ibid.*, *Labour Group Minutes* (16 August, 26 and 30 September, 8 November, 1929).
54. *Liverpool Official Red Book* (1926), p. 554.

55. Baxter, 'The Liverpool Labour Party', pp. 193, 198–9.

56. *Ibid.*, p.193.

57. *Liverpool Daily Post*, 27 July 1930; *Liverpool Official Red Book* (1931), p.594.

58. LTCLP, *Minutes*, special EC meeting (6 October 1930).

59. *Ibid.*, *Executive Committee Minutes* (10 April 1931).

60. See S. Davies *et al.*, *Genuinely Seeking Work: Mass Unemployment on Merseyside in the 1930s* (Liverpress, Liverpool: 1992), pp. 159–62.

61. See Chapter One, above p. 27, and F. Bealey, J. Blondel and W. P. McCann, *Constituency Politics: A Study of Newcastle-under-Lyme* (Faber, London: 1965), pp. 77–104.

PART TWO

The Labour Party and the electoral system

3 The scale of Labour's failure: municipal elections

Labour's electoral record in Liverpool

First of all, it is necessary to establish the precise degree of electoral failure by the Labour Party in Liverpool up to 1939. While performance at elections is not the only indicator of the success of any political party, it is certainly the case that the British Labour Party has always placed a great emphasis on electoral politics. It has been argued that this has, in turn, shaped its policies, organization and activities. Ralph Miliband has pursued this argument most forcefully, suggesting that 'the Labour party has always been one of the most dogmatic – not about socialism, but about the parliamentary system,' and that it 'has not only been a parliamentary party; it has been a party deeply imbued by parliamentarism.' Moreover, Miliband has suggested that this concentration on the electoral path to socialism has been stronger in the British case than in comparable reformist socialist parties elsewhere.[1] If Labour could claim to be the main party of the British working class for much of the twentieth century, that claim would have to be based primarily on its electoral record, not the size of its active membership.

Much of the literature on Labour in Liverpool has started, justifiably, with the electoral record, and in this regard the party has been found wanting. Ramsay MacDonald's assessment in 1910, that from Labour's perspective 'Liverpool is rotten and we had better recognise it',[2] seemed to be borne out for the next half century or more. In both parliamentary and municipal elections, the Labour Party in Liverpool was slow in making progress, perhaps slower than in any other major British town or city.

The first Labour MP for a Liverpool seat was elected at a by-election in March 1923, well after the first successes in most other industrial centres. By 1918 Labour had already won for the first time in 50 parliamentary divisions and, in the general elections of 1918 and 1922, another 132 divisions were newly won. The regional spread of their success was extensive. Starting with Derby and Merthyr in 1900, they had subsequently won contests in such places as Woolwich (1903), Glasgow, Dundee, Newcastle, Sunderland, Leeds, Manchester, Bolton, Leicester, Wolverhampton and Deptford (1906), Sheffield (1909), Nuneaton, the Rhondda and the Gower (1910) and Nottingham (1918). Only the far south and south-west

5 J. H. Hayes.
Born in Wolverhampton;
Metropolitan police officer
1909–1919 and secretary
of the Police and Prison
Officers' Union; first
Labour MP in Liverpool,
elected for Edge Hill
division in by-election
March 1923, holding his
seat until 1931; junior
whip in Parliament
1925–31.

remained untouched. In the rest of England, Scotland and Wales, the only major city to compare with Liverpool was Birmingham, which elected its first Labour MP even later, in 1924.[3] Nor did Labour make up for lost time in Liverpool subsequently. In 1939, only 3 of Liverpool's 11 divisions had Labour MPs, and 5 divisions had still never elected a Labour candidate to Parliament.

In municipal elections the record seemed even worse. Labour won its first seats on the council in 1905, but by 1914 they had only 7 councillors out of a total of 140. Between the wars they never remotely looked like becoming the ruling party on the council, their best position being in 1929 and 1934, when they held 59 and 57 seats respectively, out of a total of 157 seats. Even after 1945 Labour's progress was slow in Liverpool, control of the council only being won as late as 1955. The contrast with other parts of the country was stark. It was estimated that, by 1914, at least 196 Labour councillors were sitting on borough councils, and 420 on councils of all kinds nationally.[4] When Labour won control of the London county council for the first time in 1934 it had already gained many town halls throughout the country. The earliest victories were in 1919, when the first major borough council, Bradford, fell to Labour, and when county councils in Durham, Glamorgan and Monmouthshire and 12 London boroughs were also won.[5] Sheffield, Leeds, Hull, Swansea, Barnsley, Blackburn, Norwich, Derby, Stoke and Oldham were all examples of councils that subsequently fell to Labour in the inter-war period.[6] The peak was reached in 1937, when Labour controlled the London county council, 17 London boroughs, 3 county councils, 42 provincial boroughs, and 15 Scottish burghs.[7] The contrast between Liverpool and Sheffield is one of the most illustrative examples that is available: by the time Labour had gained overall control in Liverpool in 1955, it had ruled Sheffield continuously for almost 30 years from 1926, apart from one year in 1932–3.[8]

All this comparative evidence is rather spasmodic, and it is unfortunate for the purposes of this study that local election results were not officially collated in the inter-war period. Subsequent historical study has also tended to concentrate on the parliamentary rather than the municipal level.[9] However, one comparative measure of Labour's weakness in Liverpool can be calculated from election results given in *The Times*. Annually from 1927, this newspaper listed the position in terms of seats held on all large councils immediately after the results were announced at the beginning of November. It must be stressed that these figures were given before any changes of aldermen and subsequent by-elections had taken place, and therefore may not exactly reflect the final position on the councils for the following year. Nevertheless, the proportion of seats held by Labour on each council can be calculated. The figures for 1927, 1929, 1932, 1935 and 1938 in all county boroughs with a population of over 100,000 are shown in Table 3.1, from which it can be seen that Liverpool appears to be one of the weaker boroughs in the country as far as Labour was concerned. At best, in 1929, Liverpool ranked 26th out of 40. At worst, in 1927, it ranked 35th. Generally it appears that the worse Labour did nationally, the lower down the ranking Liverpool was placed. Of the 12 largest boroughs with populations of over a quarter of a million, only Birmingham had a worse record, being ranked below Liverpool in every year except 1927. The others in this group all ranked above Liverpool in every year, in most cases by wide margins. They included all the other major northern industrial centres of Manchester, Bradford, Leeds, Newcastle, Hull and Sheffield. Also in this group were the Midlands towns of Nottingham and Stoke, and Bristol and West Ham in the south.

The proportion of seats held by Labour in Liverpool was also consistently and substantially below the average for all the boroughs combined. In good years for Labour the gap was narrower, so in 1929 the differential was 33 per cent in Liverpool compared to 39 per cent nationally, and in 1935 it was 35 per cent compared to 40 per cent. In poorer years the gap widened – in 1927 the proportion was 16 per cent in Liverpool compared to 31 per cent nationally, in 1932, 23 per cent compared to 32 per cent, and in 1938, 25 per cent compared to 38 per cent. The evidence of these figures seems to point overwhelmingly to the conclusion that, in terms of electoral politics at the municipal level, Labour failed badly in Liverpool between the wars. Combined with the parliamentary record outlined earlier, Labour's weakness in Liverpool seems clear.

Table 3.1 Labour representation in county boroughs with population over 100,000, 1927–1939 (in descending order of Labour strength; percentage of all seats held by Labour given in brackets)

	1927	1929	1932	1935	1938
1	West Ham (80)	West Ham (86)	West Ham (86)	West Ham (84)	West Ham (84)
2	St Helens (69)	St Helens (75)	East Ham (73)	East Ham (83)	East Ham (78)
3	Sheffield (57)	Sheffield (65)	St Helens (69)	St Helens (69)	St Helens (67)
4	Birkenhead (52)	Derby (59)	Sheffield (49)	Swansea (59)	Swansea (63)
5	Leeds (49)	Birkenhead (55)	Swansea (48)	Norwich (58)	Norwich (56)
6	Swansea (47)	Bradford (53)	Norwich (47)	Sheffield (55)	Coventry (56)
7	Bradford (45)	Leeds (53)	Hull (44)	Hull (54)	Derby (55)
8	Leicester (43)	Stoke (53)	South Shields (42)	Burnley (54)	Sheffield (54)
9	Gateshead (40)	East Ham (53)	Birkenhead (42)	Derby (53)	Gateshead (53)
10	Norwich (39)	Swansea (51)	Leeds (40)	Stoke (53)	South Shields (52)
11	East Ham (38)	Leicester (48)	Walsall (40)	Birkenhead (51)	Hull (50)
12	Preston (38)	Gateshead (48)	Stoke (39)	Oldham (49)	Bristol (50)
13	South Shields (37)	Salford (47)	Coventry (38)	Sunderland (49)	Burnley (48)
14	Hull (36)	Norwich (45)	Derby (38)	Leeds (47)	Stoke (47)
15	Nottingham (36)	Hull (45)	Leicester (36)	Leicester (47)	Sunderland (47)
16	Derby (36)	Preston (44)	Bradford (35)	Coventry (46)	Leeds (46)
17	Stoke (35)	Nottingham (41)	Gateshead (35)	Nottingham (45)	Birkenhead (44)
18	Salford (33)	Blackburn (39)	Nottingham (34)	Gateshead (45)	Nottingham (44)
19	Manchester (32)	Plymouth (38)	Newcastle (34)	Newcastle (45)	Salford (44)
20	Bolton (32)	Bristol (37)	Bristol (34)	Blackburn (45)	Leicester (41)
21	Newcastle (32)	South Shields (37)	Burnley (32)	Bradford (43)	Walsall (39)
22	Plymouth (29)	Cardiff (37)	Oldham (31)	Salford (42)	Middlesbrough (39)

	1927	1929	1932	1935	1938
23	Halifax (28)	Manchester (36)	Preston (31)	Preston (42)	Southampton (37)
24	Bristol (28)	Bolton (35)	Sunderland (31)	South Shields (40)	Manchester (35)
25	Birmingham (28)	Burnley (33)	Bolton (31)	Walsall (40)	Bradford (35)
26	Middlesbrough (26)	Liverpool (33)	Halifax (30)	Bolton (39)	Blackburn (34)
27	Cardiff (25)	Oldham (31)	Blackburn (29)	Bristol (38)	Plymouth (33)
28	Wolverhampton (25)	Birmingham (30)	Middlesbrough (27)	Southampton (37)	Oldham (32)
29	Walsall (22)	Middlesbrough (30)	Manchester (27)	Manchester (36)	Newcastle (32)
30	Stockport (21)	Halifax (29)	Southampton (25)	Liverpool (36)	Preston (31)
31	Blackburn (20)	Southampton (28)	Wolverhampton (23)	Middlesbrough (32)	Wolverhampton (31)
32	Oldham (19)	Walsall (28)	Cardiff (23)	Cardiff (31)	Halifax (28)
33	Southampton (18)	Coventry (27)	Liverpool (23)	Halifax (30)	Cardiff (27)
34	Burnley (17)	Sunderland (26)	Salford (20)	Plymouth (29)	Liverpool (25)
35	Liverpool (16)	Wolverhampton (25)	Plymouth (20)	Birmingham (24)	Croydon (25)
36	Sunderland (14)	Stockport (21)	Stockport (19)	Wolverhampton (24)	Bolton (22)
37	Croydon (9)	Croydon (18)	Birmingham (19)	Stockport (19)	Huddersfield (20)
38	Southend (8)	Portsmouth (11)	Southend (10)	Bournemouth (13)	Birmingham (16)
39	Huddersfield (7)	Huddersfield (8)	Croydon (10)	Southend (13)	Stockport (14)
40	Portsmouth (5)	Southend (8)	Portsmouth (8)	Croydon (12)	Southend (14)
41*			Huddersfield (2)	Portsmouth (11)	Bournemouth (13)
42*				Huddersfield (8)	Portsmouth (11)

* No figures given for Bournemouth in 1927, 1929 or 1932, Coventry in 1927, 1929 or 1932, Coventry in 1927 or Newcastle in 1929.

Source: Calculated from reports in *The Times*, 2 November 1927, 2 and 4 November 1929, 2 November 1932, 2 November 1935, 2 November 1938.

However, a more detailed analysis of election results is needed to establish the real extent of the party's poor performance. Such analysis may begin to suggest that a partial revision of the traditional view of Labour's failings in Liverpool is necessary. The first part of that analysis will be concerned with the municipal political system.

Votes and seats in municipal politics

The full record of all municipal election results in every ward in Liverpool between 1905 and 1938 can be found in Appendix IV. A summary of Labour's performance in the inter-war years can be found in Table 3.2, which shows that, at first sight, evidence of Labour's failure seems overwhelming. When the Tory performance is calculated for the same period, also shown in Table 3.2, the contrast is sharply defined. Combining the

Table 3.2 Seats held by Labour (L) and Tories (C) on Liverpool city council, 1919–1938*

Year	Seats held		Total seats on council		% of total seats	
	L	C	L	C	L	C
1919	22	78	147	147	15	53
1920	20	79	148	148	14	53
1921	14	83	148	148	9	56
1922	5	92	148	148	3	62
1923	4	91	149	149	3	61
1924	9	96	151	151	6	64
1925	11	96	151	151	7	64
1926	18	96	151	151	12	64
1927	25	91	152	152	16	60
1928	37	88	153	153	24	58
1929	59	77	157	157	38	49
1930	47	84	157	157	30	54
1931	37	92	157	157	24	59
1932	37	91	157	157	24	58
1933	44	86	157	157	28	55
1934	57	72	157	157	36	46
1935	56	76	157	157	36	48
1936	53	78	157	157	34	50
1937	45	87	157	157	29	55
1938	38	97	157	157	24	62

* Figures calculated at the end of the calendar year following annual elections in November of each year. Where seats were vacant at that date, the subsequent filling of vacancies have been added to the totals.

Source: Election results in *Liverpool Official Red Books* (1920–39).

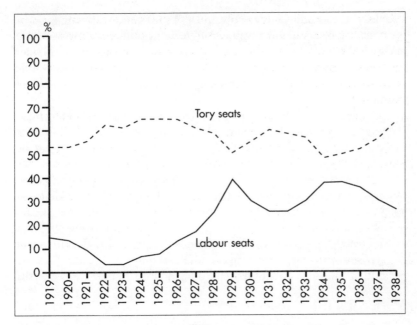

%

Figure 3.1 Labour and Tory seats held on council, 1919–1938

performances of the two parties, as shown in Figure 3.1, makes the comparison even clearer. Labour's dismal record in Liverpool and, conversely, the Conservative domination of the council-chamber, seem to be perfectly reflected here.

Most previous analyses have jumped straight from here to attempting to explain Labour weakness and Tory strength. In most of those explanations the centrality of religious differentiation within the working class has been emphasized. Implicitly or explicitly, religious sectarianism is portrayed as sapping working-class solidarity and therefore Labour support, while strengthening working-class Toryism.

However, before considering these traditional lines of thought, it is necessary to look at the municipal election results in greater depth. In particular, the electoral institutions within which the Labour Party was forced to fight need to be analysed in some detail. Labour was a late arrival in the early twentieth century on a playing field where the rules of the game had already been well established by their political opponents. The party's only consistent challenge to those rules was over the franchise, and the extensions of 1918 and 1928 are often assumed to have removed any major in-built advantage to their rivals, both at parliamentary and municipal levels. That assumption has already been challenged by some historians,[10] and further doubts may creep in when a detailed study of local elections is undertaken. Nationally, Labour also toyed with the idea of electoral reform, to the extent of including it in their legislative programme in 1929, but nothing came of this.[11] Electoral reform was

87

also discussed locally. For example, in 1919 a resolution pressing for proportional representation in municipal elections was passed by the local party.[12] This was never followed up, however, and the electoral rules remained essentially untouched during the inter-war period. The possible significance of this factor in disadvantaging Labour needs to be considered carefully.

The idea that the electoral institutions may have partially determined Labour's performance at the municipal level is supported by the evidence of the actual numbers of votes cast for each party in elections between the wars. Such evidence has to be treated with some caution, given the number of uncontested ward elections common in Liverpool in this period. For the moment, however, and keeping that proviso in mind, the raw evidence of votes cast set out in Table 3.3 and Figure 3.2 gives a rather different picture of Labour's performance.

The voting figures suggest that Labour actually performed quite well in comparison with the Conservatives, and certainly a lot better than the position of seats held on the council would indicate. In the early 1920s the

Table 3.3 Share of vote won by Labour and Tory Parties in municipal elections in Liverpool, 1919–1938

| Year | Labour share of votes (%) | Tory share of votes (%) | Uncontested wins | | | | |
			Lab.	Con.	Lib.	Nat.	Other
1919	36	46	0	2	3	5	0
1920	25	50	0	6	1	1	1
1921	27	45	0	3	3	1	0
1922	29	43	0	8	1	4	0
1923	25	39	0	9	2	0	1
1924	39	43	0	6	3	1	1
1925	36	46	0	4	1	3	0
1926	45	41	0	4	1	1	0
1927	44	39	0	1	1	0	0
1928	47	45	6	5	1	1	0
1929	52	42	0	1	0	0	1
1930	35	48	1	1	1	2	0
1931	35	55	2	6	1	0	0
1932	46	39	1	4	0	0	1
1933	47	41	4	5	4	0	0
1934	43	46	5	3	0	0	1
1935	48	44	3	3	1	0	0
1936	39	50	5	0	2	0	0
1937	37	57	5	2	1	0	0
1938	36	58	8	4	0	0	0

Source: *Liverpool Official Red Books* (1919–39).

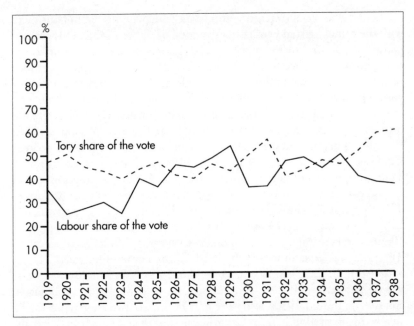

Figure 3.2 Labour and Tory share of vote in local elections, 1919–1938

Tory advantage over Labour was still strong, but as early as 1926 Labour received a higher total of votes. In the ten years between 1926 and 1935, despite a massive setback in 1930 and 1931, Labour actually gained more votes than the Conservatives on seven occasions. The Labour vote did collapse badly in the late 1930s, but overall the picture is hardly one of total domination by the Conservatives. The discrepancy between seats held and votes won certainly suggests that there were elements of the electoral system which disadvantaged the Labour Party.

However, the problem of uncontested seats was a major one in Liverpool politics at this time, and has to be taken into account in order to get a more accurate picture of voting patterns. As Table 3.3 shows, as many as thirteen seats might be uncontested in any one year, which constituted almost a third of all the seats due for election in the city. Given that these seats were usually very safe seats, where the uncontested winners could expect to win an extremely large proportion of the vote, their omission from the figures could obviously result in a serious under-representation of voting strength for the party or parties concerned.

An impressionistic view of the possible impact of this factor on voting strength would suggest that the Conservative vote was probably seriously depressed by the large number of uncontested elections in many of their strongholds in the early and mid-1920s. However, in the late 1920s and early 1930s the effect would seem to be more evenly spread between Labour and the Conservatives, with both parties usually having uncontested victories in a roughly similar number of wards. By the late 1930s the effect seems to have been more important in depressing the Labour vote, with their uncontested wins rising to a total of eight in 1938. This general picture is still inadequate, however, as it ignores the question of differential turn-out in different types of ward, and also the fact that the number of voters in each ward might vary considerably. The detailed analysis of voting patterns by ward will be found in Chapter Eight, but, for the moment, some of the more obvious features of these patterns will illustrate the problem. There were two main types of ward where the Conservative Party won uncontested seats: suburban, predominantly middle-class wards like West Derby, Aigburth or Little Woolton; and city-centre wards with a high proportion of voters actually resident elsewhere, but entitled to a second vote at their business addresses, such as Castle Street and St Peter's. The electorate in these Tory wards varied from as low as 433 voters in Little Woolton or 2,514 voters in Castle Street in 1922, to as high as 10,993 voters in Aigburth or even 20,742 voters in West Derby in 1938. Turn-out was equally varied. In West Derby it varied between 31 and 35 per cent in the early 1930s, whereas in Little Woolton, the turn-out was 65 per cent in 1937. Uncontested Labour strongholds, particularly common in the late 1930s, also varied. They were of two main types: dockside wards in predominantly Catholic parts of the city, such as Vauxhall, Sandhills and Scotland North and South; and new wards on the outskirts of the city where council-house estates were developing rapidly, most obviously Croxteth ward in this period. Vauxhall had only 3,123 voters in 1938, whereas Sandhills had 8,490, and Croxteth 20,489 in the same year. Turn-out was also varied, rising to 63 per cent in Scotland North in 1927, for instance, but dropping as low as 29 per cent in Croxteth in 1937. A final complication needs to be added. In general terms, the dominant party in these wards would always receive a high proportion of votes cast, but nevertheless that proportion could vary considerably. The Conservative Party won 88 per cent of the votes in Little Woolton and only 59 per cent in Aigburth in 1937. In the same year, Labour picked up as much as 97 per cent in Scotland South and only 62 per cent in Croxteth.

It is clear then that the impact of uncontested seats on voting patterns is too important to be ignored, but also too complex to be dealt with in merely impressionistic terms. A formula needs to be constructed to compensate the parties for uncontested wins which takes into account ward size, expected turn-out and anticipated share of votes won. In applying such a formula it is assumed here that it is only the winning parties which could have expected a significant vote in these wards and therefore need to be compensated. Losing parties, by definition, would only expect a low vote in opposition strongholds where they often did not put up candidates, and this vote would be insignificant in comparison to total votes won. Estimates for losing parties have been ignored, then, although it must be recognized that this results in a slight underestimation of total expected vote for the losers. A second assumption made is that uncontested winners for parties other than Labour and Tory were for the most part in wards where neither of the two main parties could have been expected to win many votes. These fell into three main categories.

First, there were Irish Nationalist candidates in predominantly Catholic wards up to the mid-1920s. In these wards neither Labour nor the Conservatives could expect to win many votes, even though, later in the 1930s, the same wards were to become Labour strongholds, as shown in Chapter Eight. Consequently these non-contests can be safely ignored as they could have had little effect on either the Tory or Labour vote even if elections had actually been contested.

Second, there were Independent candidates dependent mainly on a personal vote. The best example is that of Peter Kavanagh, well-known publican and local celebrity in the Catholic community. Originally standing as a Nationalist, by the 1930s he was being regularly returned unopposed in Exchange ward as an Independent. Again, neither of the main parties could expect to win many votes against this kind of candidate, and thus these non-contests can be ignored.

Third, there were uncontested Liberals in a small number of wards in the 1930s. These were the result of electoral understandings between the Tory and Liberal parties in certain wards where the Liberals refrained from standing against the Tories in some years in return for which the Tories did likewise in other years. A good example was Anfield, one of the few areas where, by the 1930s, the Liberals had any significant strength. To avoid the possibility of Labour winning in a three-way contest, the Conservatives put up candidates in 1931, 1934 and 1937 with no Liberal opposition, while the Liberals were unopposed by the Conservatives in the intervening years. When Labour also refrained from putting up a candidate, as in 1933 and 1936, the result was uncontested Liberal wins. However, for those particular years some Tory votes were not cast. These sorts of cases were sporadic and confined to three or four wards in total, so their impact overall was limited. They have also been ignored, therefore, although this means that the Conservative vote in the mid-1930s may be marginally underestimated.

The focus is on Labour and Tory uncontested wins, and a formula has been applied to compensate these two parties with extra hypothetical votes whenever their candidates were unopposed. This formula takes into account the expected turn-out and the percentage of the vote that the winner might have been expected to win, based on earlier and later performance in the ward concerned. The full calculations can be found in Appendix V. It must be emphasized that this gives rough estimates only. No formula could be guaranteed to be absolutely accurate, and counterfactual constructions of this kind should always be treated with caution. Nevertheless, some idea of Labour and Tory performance compensating for uncontested elections can be gained, as shown in summary form in Table 3.4 and Figure 3.3.

The revised estimates for the share of votes give a slightly different picture from the earlier one drawn from the actual votes cast. The

Table 3.4 Hypothetical share of vote won by Labour and Tory Parties in municipal elections in Liverpool, 1919–1938, including estimates for uncontested seats (in %)

Year	Labour share of votes	Tory share of votes
1919	35	47
1920	23	51
1921	25	47
1922	24	47
1923	19	46
1924	34	47
1925	33	48
1926	41	43
1927	43	40
1928	45	40
1929	52	42
1930	35	47
1931	33	54
1932	44	41
1933	43	40
1934	46	42
1935	48	42
1936	44	45
1937	39	53
1938	39	49

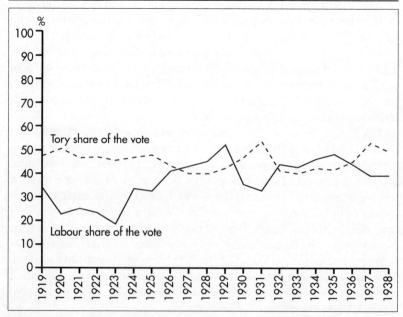

Figure 3.3 Labour and Tory share of vote adjusted for uncontested seats, 1919–1938

dominance of the Conservatives over Labour in the first half of the 1920s is even more marked, and extends slightly longer, up to 1926. However, the subsequent improvement in Labour's performance is again evident, despite the temporary slump in 1930 and 1931. Indeed, between 1927 and 1935, Labour led the Conservative Party in seven out of nine years, with 1934 being transformed into a winning year for Labour. The decline in Labour's fortunes in the late 1930s is also still apparent, but the gap between the two parties is narrowed significantly. If anything, from the mid-1920s these estimates make Labour's performance appear even better, relative to the actual seats held on the council.

One final point needs to be made in relation to the analysis so far. The first-past-the-post electoral system that has prevailed in municipal politics can always throw up anomalies in the relationship between votes and seats, as numerous modern studies have shown.[13] However, the disparity between Labour's share of the vote, and the percentage of the seats they held on the council, seems too great to be passed over without further comment. This disparity is shown very clearly in Figures 3.4 and 3.5. When the Tory and Labour performance in terms of votes and seats are directly compared in this way, what is striking is the consistency of the pattern. Labour's position on the council was always considerably worse than its support at elections warranted. The Tory Party, in comparison, by a substantial margin was always better represented than its support at the polls justified. In both cases the gap between support and representation narrowed slightly in the early and mid-1930s, yet by 1938 the disparity

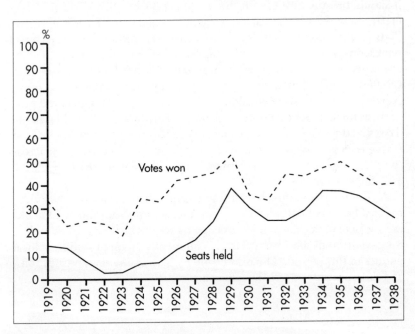

Figure 3.4 Labour seats and votes (adjusted), 1919–1938

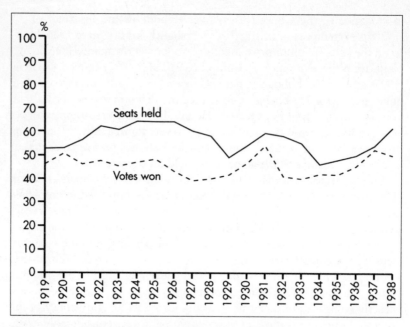

Figure 3.5 Tory seats and votes (adjusted), 1919–1938

between the two was almost as great as it had ever been between the wars. It should be said at this point that there is evidence that other parties – in particular the Liberal Party and the successors to the Irish Nationalist Party (under a number of titles) – also increasingly seem to have been over-represented in the 1930s. As minority parties with small numbers of votes and seats, the inflation of their representation on the council was less substantial in absolute terms, representing only a handful of seats at most. Nevertheless, they were an additional barrier to Labour's electoral progress, as for all practical purposes these two parties were close allies of the Tories by the 1930s. It is not possible to quantify their over-representation with any degree of precision, as they did not put up candidates across the city. However, some specific instances of the way in which they were artificially boosted will be dealt with later.

All the analysis in this chapter suggests that there must have been institutional factors of considerable importance which disadvantaged Labour in Liverpool municipal politics, whether by accident or design. These electoral institutions have been scarcely commented upon in studies of local politics in this period. The next chapter will examine these institutions, and their possible effects, in some detail.

References

1. R. Miliband, *Parliamentary Socialism: A Study in the Politics of Labour* (2nd edn., Merlin Press, London: 1972), pp. 13–14. See also T. Forester, *The Labour Party and the Working Class* (Heinemann, London: 1976), pp. 52–67.
2. Quoted in R. McKibbin, *The Evolution of the Labour Party, 1910–24* (Oxford University Press, London: 1974), p. 14.
3. All figures calculated from tables in F. W. S. Craig, *British Electoral Facts, 1885–1975* (3rd. edn., Macmillan, London: 1976), pp. 108–36.
4. G. D. H. Cole, *A History of the Labour Party from 1914* (Routledge and Kegan Paul, London: 1948), pp. 445–7.
5. *Ibid.*, p. 448.
6. These examples are quoted in J. Stevenson and C. Cook, *The Slump: Society and Politics During the Depression* (Jonathan Cape, London: 1977), pp. 96–119.
7. Cole, *A History of the Labour Party*, pp. 458–9.
8. Calculated from table given in W. Hampton, *Democracy and Community: A Study of Politics in Sheffield* (Oxford University Press, London: 1970), pp. 313–14.
9. The best attempt to consider the municipal pattern in the 1920s is in C. Cook, *The Age of Alignment: Electoral Politics in Britain, 1922–1929* (Macmillan, London: 1975), Ch. 3; see also C. Cook, 'Liberals, Labour and local elections', in G. Peele and C. Cook (eds), *The Politics of Re-appraisal, 1918–1939* (Macmillan, London: 1975); and also Stevenson and Cook, *The Slump*, Ch. 13, for some consideration of the 1930s' trends.
10. On the parliamentary franchise, see N. Blewett, 'The franchise in the United Kingdom, 1885–1918', *Past and Present* 32 (1965); on the municipal franchise see B. Keith-Lucas, *The English Local Government Franchise: A Short History* (Blackwell, Oxford: 1952).
11. On the 1929 Labour government's attitude to electoral reform, see Cole, *A History of the Labour Party*, pp. 229, 244; J. D. Fair, 'The second Labour Government and the politics of electoral reform, 1929–31', *Albion* 13, No.3 (1981).
12. See Liverpool Labour Party, *Minutes* (5 February 1919).
13. See, for instance, V. Bogdanor, *The People and the Party System: The Referendum and Electoral Reform in British Politics*, (Cambridge University Press, Cambridge: 1981); S. E. Finer (ed.), *Adversary Politics and Electoral Reform* (Anthony Wigram, London: 1975); J. Hart, *Proportional Representation: Critics of the British Electoral System, 1820–1945*, (Oxford University Press, Oxford: 1992); D. Butler, 'Electoral systems' in D. Butler, H. R. Penniman and A. Ranney (eds), *Democracy at the Polls: A Comparative Study of Competitive National Elections* (American Enterprise Institute for Public Policy Research, Washington: 1981).

4 The structure of municipal politics in Liverpool

Borough and ward boundaries

In a first-past-the-post, or plurality, electoral system, the boundaries of electoral units and their relationship to population numbers can have a crucial effect on electoral outcomes. The British system, at both parliamentary and local levels, had developed with a strong emphasis on the idea that the representation of communities should be a primary consideration.[1] As a result, ward and divisional boundaries had to fulfil a dual purpose. They had to correspond with some idea of a locality with coherent economic, social and cultural features, often related to long-changed historical realities. Yet they also had to represent roughly equal numbers of voters in the population. To achieve a perfect balance between these two functions was difficult enough in any circumstances, but it was even more difficult over time as economic, social, cultural and demographic shifts altered the picture. The case of Liverpool in this period illustrated these problems very clearly.

External boundaries

Liverpool's internal and external boundaries between 1894 and 1953 can be seen in Figure 4.1. As far as the external boundaries of the borough were concerned, the degree to which they represented Liverpool accurately is open to question. As an entity, Merseyside, including both sides of the River Mersey, probably had a stronger economic rationale by the inter-war years, even if historical and cultural factors dictated otherwise. Even on one side of the river, however, the boundaries were debatable. In particular, the fact that Bootle, for historical reasons, remained a separate borough was anomalous. If anything gave Liverpool an economic identity, it was the docks, even more so before 1939 than later, when industrial expansion on the outer-city estates became significant. The Brocklebank, Langton, Alexandra, Hornby, and Gladstone docks were the northern outposts of the Liverpool docks, yet the people who lived in the surrounding streets voted in the county borough of Bootle – and this was not merely an economic anomaly. Bootle was an extension of the

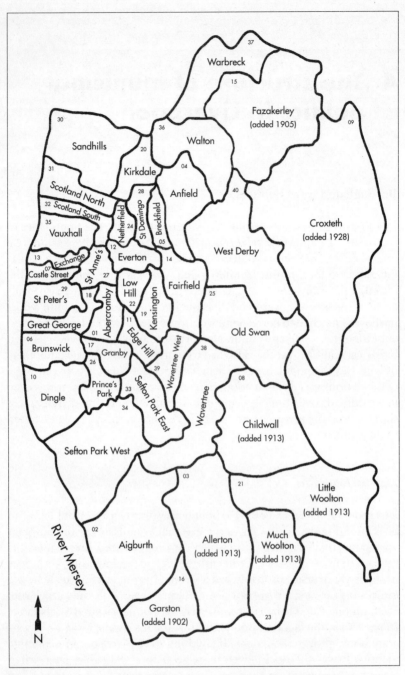

Figure 4.1 County borough of Liverpool, ward boundaries, 1895–1953

strongly Catholic north dockside area of the city, an area with a distinct political, social and cultural identity, as shown later in this book. In political terms, the significance of Bootle's separate status is made very clear by the fact that, from 1933, Labour gained overall control of its council.

The system of revising boundaries after 1888 ensured that anomalies such as this were difficult to rectify. The Acts of 1888 and 1894 established the basic structure of local government which was to last until the reorganization of the early 1970s.[2] While revisions were possible through application to the Home Office, fundamental change was barred. Moreover, changes could only involve the extension of county boroughs into surrounding counties; the boroughs themselves were sacrosanct. As two authorities on local government have stated:

> The institutions of local government [as established in 1888] ... were not the outcome of any planned concept, such as Bentham had expounded, or such as Napoleon had introduced in France. They had grown, haphazard, out of the institutions of the previous centuries, adapted, adjusted, and democratised. The boundaries of the counties owed more to the Anglo-Saxons and the Conquerer than they did to contemporary political scientists; the boroughs had their roots deep in the municipal institutions of the Middle Ages, in the guilds and the courts leet.[3]

Where boroughs adjoined each other, as in the case of Bootle and Liverpool, the traditional boundaries between them remained unalterable until the wholesale restructuring of the 1970s.

By contrast with Bootle, to the south the Garston dock and surrounding area was incorporated into Liverpool in 1902. Separated from the city and the main dock complex by the prosperous suburbs of Sefton Park, Aigburth and Grassendale, Garston was generally viewed as an exotic southern colony, popularly called the 'banana-boat republic'. The name referred as much to its geographical and social distance from Liverpool as its distinctive economic features.[4] Until the post-1945 expansion of the Speke housing and industrial estate, its links with Liverpool were tenuous. Even in terms of Labour Party politics it was distinctive, with the Liverpool party as late as 1925 complaining that Garston was acting independently of its control.[5] The point here is not to argue the respective merits of Bootle and Garston as integral parts of Liverpool, but to point out that Garston, with a population of 14,000 in 1911, was absorbed by Liverpool, while Bootle, with five times as many people, remained outside.[6]

Other extensions of the city boundaries in the inter-war years had variable effects on the electoral geography of Liverpool. Fazakerley was added in 1905 and Allerton, Childwall and Much and Little Woolton in 1913. All these wards were the result of new private housing estates for the middle class on the outskirts of the city, and represented new Tory strongholds. By contrast, Croxteth ward, added in 1928, and Speke, included into Garston ward in 1932, were the result of council-house building. In the case of Croxteth, a new Labour stronghold was created, while the population of Speke was still so small in 1939 as to have had little impact.

The net effect of all these extensions clearly favoured the Tory Party in the political arithmetic of the city. In 1938, the Labour strongholds of Garston and Croxteth had six seats between them on the council, and a combined electorate of 28,956. Fazakerley, Allerton, Childwall and the two Woolton wards, all strongly Tory, had thirteen seats, and a combined electorate of 31,650. The new Tory voters of the suburbs had been allocated almost exactly twice as many seats per head as the new Labour voters.

There is one further anomaly in the external boundaries of the city that arose specifically in the 1930s. As council housing developed on the outskirts of the built-up area, so more and more of the city's tenants were situated outside the city boundaries. Most still continued to work in the city, yet they were disenfranchised as far as city politics were concerned. In 1939, four estates – Longview, Finch House, Woolfall Heath and Huyton Farm – lay outside the city,[7] on which 4,082 council houses were built, making up approximately 12 per cent of all council houses built between the wars.[8] They constituted about 8,000 predominantly working-class voters who had no vote in Liverpool, roughly equivalent to one ward with three councillors and an alderman on the council.

In their evidence to the 1921 Royal Commission, the county boroughs had argued that 'their boundaries should be extended as far as would enable them to catch all persons who slept outside the borough but came into it to work'.[9] While this principle was not strictly applied, due to conflicting arguments from the counties and the problem of adjoining boroughs alluded to above, it was used extensively after 1929. Between 1929 and 1937, forty-nine boroughs received extensions of their boundaries, thereby gaining, on average, roughly 2,000 acres and 3,000 people. Many gained substantially more than this, including Coventry (11,000 people), Leicester (10,000), Newport, Southend and York (9,000), Huddersfield and Nottingham (7,000), and Sheffield (6,500).[10] While Liverpool had extended to take in Croxteth in 1928, as mentioned above, in the comparable period, 1929–37, only the 2,500 acres and the then negligible population of Speke was added.[11] While the political affiliation of the 8,000 council-house voters left outside the city cannot be established precisely, it seems likely that they would have included many potential Labour voters, given the evidence of Labour strength in Croxteth from 1928. Whether by intention or design, Labour again seems to have been the loser.

The final irony in all this was that there was one occasion between the wars when the idea of amalgamating Liverpool with surrounding boroughs was raised. This proposal had nothing to do with the equity of the electoral system, however, but was intended to keep the rates low. Moreover, it was the Tories who proposed it. With the abolition of the Poor Law in

1929, and the transfer of its functions to local authorities, there was concern raised on Merseyside that the overlapping of provision by the various local boroughs would push up the cost of administration – and therefore the rates – unnecessarily. At the council meeting in September 1929, which considered the creation of a Public Assistance Committee for Liverpool, the Tory leader, Thomas White, moved an amendment calling for the setting up of a 'City of Merseyside'. This entity, it was proposed, was to incorporate the boroughs of Liverpool, Bootle, Wallasey and Birkenhead and adjoining parts of Lancashire County. W. A. Robinson opposed the amendment on behalf of the Labour Party, arguing that it was merely a ploy by the Tories to resolve differences between Tory-controlled boroughs over how to divide up the old Poor Law Unions. Eventually the amendment was dropped, the general feeling being that it could only be a long-term prospect that would need a lot of discussion and much consultation with the other boroughs concerned.[12] Subsequently, the idea was quietly shelved. On the only occasion when radical change to the external boundaries of the city was possible in this period, Labour stood for the *status quo*.

Internal boundaries

When ward boundaries within the city are considered as well, the disadvantageous position of Labour is just as clear. Ward boundaries had last been redistributed in 1894–5, ironically as a result of several years of Tory pressure on the then ruling Liberals. The previous boundaries had increasingly favoured the Liberals, whose support was mainly concentrated in the prosperous areas just to the south of the city centre, and the Irish Nationalists, whose support was concentrated in the northern dockside wards. Tory support was located mostly in the rapidly growing suburban wards, which had become severely under-represented by the 1890s. The Liberals were still able to prevent a completely fair redistribution by arguing that rateable value, as well as population, should be taken into account. This meant that the highly rated city centre wards received a proportionately larger representation per head of population. Nevertheless, at the first elections held with the new boundaries in 1895, the Tories were swept to power, almost tripling their representation on the council.[13] In the same year the Tories also enjoyed a general election victory, and perhaps they would have won control in Liverpool irrespective of the boundary changes, but probably not as convincingly. Moreover, this victory marked the beginning of sixty years of unbroken Tory rule in the city – unbroken until ward boundaries were again redistributed in 1953. It took several years of pressure, this time from Labour, to force the ruling party into accepting redistribution.[14] Within a year, the Tories had lost their overall majority, and a year later Labour took power for the first time, even though the general election of that year saw a Conservative victory.

What was glaringly obvious by the 1950s – that unreformed ward boundaries handicapped Labour – had already become a problem by the inter-war years. A quarter of a century of population shift had already taken place since the last redistribution, and massive rehousing schemes in the next two decades caused further change. Some of the inter-war trends actually worked in Labour's favour. The predominantly Catholic wards in the north of the city, inherited from the Nationalists by the mid-1920s, were relatively small, and became smaller as slum clearance took place. However, the over-representation of Labour in these wards still did not compensate for under-representation in the rest of the city. The effect of huge variations in the size of wards generally worked to the advantage of Labour's opponents. This can be quantified by analysing the size of the electorate in Labour's strongest and weakest wards during the inter-war period, as calculated in Appendix VI; the results are summarized in Table 4.1. They demonstrate that Labour strongholds were under-represented on the council when compared with non-Labour strongholds throughout the inter-war period, by a factor of roughly a third in the early 1920s, rising to a half by 1928, then back to a third by the early 1930s, and finally falling nearer to parity by 1938.

The nature of the local economy and consequent social structure, and in turn the spatial distribution of economic activity and population, could increase the potential for inequitable ward boundaries. The dominance of trade and shipping in the Liverpool economy, for instance, meant that a large and distinct area in the city centre, comprised primarily of offices connected with trade, finance, insurance and shipping, developed from the nineteenth century. Wards such as Castle Street, packed with business voters and few others, had their origins in these developments. It needs to be stressed that this development was particularly marked in Liverpool. Retail and manufacturing functions may have played a similar role in some other cities, but not to the same degree. Equally, the concentration of large numbers of mainly casually employed workers in the dockside areas of the city led to other wards with very large numbers of voters by the late nineteenth century. Further structural change in the twentieth century affected ward boundaries. The beginning of the decline of the docks, and the first stages in the development of new industries on the outskirts of the city by the 1930s, resulted in a decline of population in the old dockside wards, and a corresponding growth in some of the suburban wards.

In the end, however, these patterns of population growth and decline only provided the potential for distortion of the electoral system, and comparable situations no doubt existed elsewhere. Ward boundaries were not immutable, pre-ordained features of the landscape. They were to some extent the result of long-established social and cultural traditions, but they were even more so the result of political decision. The fact that boundaries were not redrawn for sixty years, or that tiny new middle-class wards like Little Woolton and enormous working-class wards like Croxteth were created, was ultimately a political outcome. Moreover, economic and social change could be sustained, or enhanced, by local government policies. Thus, expenditure by the council on the new housing estates of the inter-war period encouraged the movement of population and accelerated the shift in economic activity from the city centre to the periphery.

This particular combination of social change and political action may have been echoed elsewhere, but it could not have been repeated exactly in every other borough. One example shows how much the local circumstances could vary, and with it the potential for inequity in ward boundaries. W. A. Hampton's study of Sheffield shows how the economic development of the town led to a sharp and rigid distinction between an area of working-class housing to the east, and another of middle-class housing to the west. As a result, a clear line could be drawn through the city, east of which were a group of safe Labour wards, and west of which were a group of safe Tory wards, leaving a tiny handful of politically marginal wards straddling the line.[15] This contrasts with Liverpool, where there was much more of a patchwork effect of distinct working-class areas interspersed with middle-class areas. Thus, north-east from the city centre, working-class St Domingo and Breckfield adjoined middle-class Anfield and West Derby, which in turn bordered working-class Croxteth further out from the city. Equally, to the south, working-class Dingle adjoined middle-class Sefton Park and Aigburth, which themselves bordered working-class Garston and Speke. Thus there were literally more boundaries which were politically sensitive in Liverpool than in Sheffield. It is also clear that the relatively small scale of concentration of business voters in city-centre wards could not have posed the political problem in Sheffield that it proved to be in Liverpool. Sheffield's narrow industrial base, its failure to develop commercial activities, and its overshadowing by the older-established regional centre of Leeds, ensured that the business vote was both numerically smaller and geographically less concentrated than it was in Liverpool.[16]

As long as the plurality system prevailed, of course, no boundaries could have guaranteed an absolutely accurate reflection of voters and representation. The longer they were unchanged, however, the more likely they were to be unsatisfactory. Boundaries in Sheffield were redrawn in 1928. Councils adjacent to Liverpool also saw the need for redistribution. Wallasey was redistributed in 1920, Bootle in 1928, and Birkenhead in 1934.[17] Nationally, the redistribution process was modified in line with the findings of the Royal Commission on Local Government appointed in 1922–3. After the Local Government Acts of 1926 and 1929, widespread revisions took place. Between 1929 and 1937, 50 county boroughs out of a total of 83 across the country had boundary revisions successfully approved.[18] But there was no change in Liverpool. That this worked against the interest of Labour locally seems indisputable.

Some idea of how the variation in ward size in Liverpool compared to other boroughs can be gained by analysing the population in wards for various boroughs as listed in the 1931 census. The standard deviation as a

Table 4.1 Size of electorate in Labour's ten strongest and ten weakest wards, 1919–1938

Ten strongest Labour wards

1919–1923		1924–1928		1929–1933		1934–1938	
Ward	Electorate (1923)	Ward	Electorate (1928)	Ward	Electorate (1933)	Ward	Electorate (1938)
Everton	12,350	Brunswick	8,447	Scotland N	8,703	Brunswick	7,815
Scotland N	8,075	Croxteth	5,886	Sandhills	9,308	Sandhills	8,490
Scotland S	8,289	Everton	12,194	Brunswick	8,746	Scotland S	7,477
Edge Hill	12,228	Sandhills	8,656	St Anne's	8,983	Scotland N	7,547
Garston	5,897	Edge Hill	12,188	Scotland S	8,602	St Anne's	6,812
Dingle	13,968	Low Hill	10,095	Everton	13,243	Vauxhall	3,123
St Anne's	8,412	St Anne's	8,473	Croxteth	15,544	Everton	11,583
Kensington	10,677	Scotland N	8,025	Gt George	4,912	Croxteth	20,489
St Domingo	10,762	Netherfield	11,178	Garston	7,741	Gt George	4,144
St Peters	2,729	Dingle	14,084	Low Hill	11,253	Garston	8,467
Total	93,387		99,226		97,035		85,947
Seats allocated	30		28		30		30
Voters per seat	3,113		3,544		3,235		2,865

Ten weakest Labour wards

	1919–1923		1924–1928		1929–1933		1934–1938	
	Ward	*Electorate (1923)*	*Ward*	*Electorate (1928)*	*Ward*	*Electorate (1933)*	*Ward*	*Electorate (1938)*
	Sandhills	8,711	Much Woolton	1,861	Sefton Park W	6,453	Wavertree	8,620
	Granby	9,075	Vauxhall	3,565	St Domingo	11,669	Warbreck	13,363
	Abercomby	7,504	Sefton Park W	5,948	Aigburth	9,165	Allerton	6,459
	Fairfield	9,159	Allerton	3,359	Anfield	10,703	Sefton Park W	6,839
	Allerton	1,355	Anfield	10,088	Allerton	4,802	Sefton Park E	8,809
	Exchange	2,747	Exchange	2,582	Much Woolton	2,558	Much Woolton	2,975
	Little Woolton	424	Little Woolton	444	Exchange	2,404	Childwall	8,252
	Sefton Park E	8,667	Sefton Park E	8,629	Childwall	3,357	Little Woolton	925
	Aigburth	5,085	Aigburth	6,899	Little Woolton	698	Castle St	2,010
	Castle St.	2,643	Castle St.	2,576	Castle St.	2,246	Aigburth	10,993
Total		55,370		45,951		54,055		69,245
Seats allocated		28		27		28		28
Voters per seat		1,978		1,702		1,931		2,473

proportion of the mean ward population size has been calculated for the eight largest county boroughs in England, as shown in Table 4.2. As a counter-check, figures for the municipal electorate in wards for eight boroughs have also been collated where they have been listed in local newspapers or other available sources in the late 1930s. Due to variations in press coverage, these boroughs do not coincide exactly with the set for 1931, and the figures for them have had to be drawn from a three-year range of 1936 to 1938. The standard deviations as a proportion of the mean ward electorate size for these boroughs are also included in Table 4.2. As can be seen in both sets of data, Liverpool had almost the highest degree of variation from the mean among these boroughs. Only Bristol

Table 4.2 Ward population size, 1931, and ward electorate size, 1936-1938, for various county boroughs

Borough	No. of wards	Largest ward	Smallest ward	Mean ward size	Standard deviation (SD)	SD as proportion of mean (%)
1931 population						
Birmingham	31	58,516	15,712	32,342	8,567	26.5
Bradford	22	24,261	2,717	13,547	5,616	41.5
Bristol	23	35,013	999	17,261	8,664	50.2
Hull	21	20,723	7,071	14,931	3,404	22.8
Leeds	26	24,260	14,324	18,570	2,621	14.1
Liverpool	40	41,855	366	21,392	10,460	48.9
Manchester	36	44,600	235	21,288	9,615	45.2
Sheffield	24	26,636	16,538	21,323	2,603	12.2
1936–1938 electorate						
Barrow ('37)	8	5,414	3,501	4,202	692	16.5
Birkenhead ('36)	16	5,842	2,357	4,281	903	21.1
Bristol ('37)	28	9,663	4,517	7,730	1,345	17.4
Leeds ('38)	26	15,158	5,175	10,033	2,700	26.9
Liverpool ('37)	40	20,686	874	9,726	4,755	48.9
Manchester ('37)	36	24,520	1,227	9,813	4,944	50.4
Salford ('37)	16	7,247	4,964	6,113	685	11.2
Southampton ('37)	17	10,404	3,081	5,328	2,013	37.8

Sources: 1931 census, county tables; *Liverpool Official Red Book* (1937 and 1938); *Manchester Official Red Book* (1938); *North-Western Daily Mail* (2 November 1937); *Southern Daily Echo* (2 November 1937); *Western Daily Press and Bristol Mirror* (2 November 1937); *Yorkshire Post* (2 November 1938).

exceeded it in the 1931 population figures, and Manchester in the 1936–8 electorate figures. Liverpool was by no means unique, then, but it was, nevertheless, one of the most extreme among these boroughs. It is notable that by contrast two boroughs that had been recently re-distributed before 1931, Sheffield and Hull, had wards very much more equal in size, and the same applied to Birkenhead for 1936–8.

It is also interesting that ward size generally seems to have been more equal where Labour was stronger, and vice versa. If the eight boroughs for 1931 are ordered according to their degree of equality of ward size, and compared with their order in terms of Labour strength in 1932 as shown earlier in Table 3.1, there appears to be a strong correlation between the two factors. Equally, if the boroughs quoted for 1936–38 are similarly compared with their order of Labour strength for 1938, again there seems to be some correlation. This is shown in Table 4.3. To calculate the degree of statistical correlation between Labour strength and more equal ward size, a Spearman's rank order correlation test was carried out for the two sets of data. In both cases, the tests gave a correlation coefficient of +0.7 between the two factors, which indicates a high level of statistical correlation. It is tempting to draw from this the conclusion that Labour strength is directly caused, or at least aided, by the degree of equality of wards. However, statistical analysis of this sort has to be viewed with great caution. Statistical correlation can be quite accidental, and there is no necessary causation implied between the two factors. Equally, it could just as well be that Labour strength caused more equal ward size, which is quite plausible in the sense that, where Labour was stronger, it could more successfully force through boundary revision in its favour. Only further detailed study of the actual circumstances prevailing in the various boroughs could resolve this question. What can be said now is that there appears to be some connection between the state of ward boundaries and Labour success in municipal elections.

While no systematic analysis of the electoral impact of redistributions elsewhere in this period has been carried out, some examples can be inferred from the evidence given earlier in Table 3.1. Of the roughly forty county boroughs with populations of over 100,000 listed there, at least a dozen must have had either substantial extensions to their borough boundaries or significant redrawing of internal boundaries between 1927 and 1938, judging by the changes in the total number of representatives on these councils. Others may also have had a redistribution without changing the overall total of representation, so they are not identifiable from the list. Birkenhead's boundaries, for instance, were totally redrawn in 1933–4, but total representation stayed fixed at 64.[19] Of the dozen redistributions identifiable in the list, several appear to have been neutral in their impact, such as those in Sheffield, Leeds and Wolverhampton. In two of those examples, Sheffield and Wolverhampton, there are also local studies which tend to support this view. G. W. Jones' study of Wolverhampton notes the redrawing of boundaries in 1927 but argues that this

Table 4.3 Equality of ward size in 1931 and 1936–8, and Labour strength in 1932 and 1938, for various county boroughs

1931	1932	1936–8	1938
Standard deviation as a proportion of mean ward population size (%)	Labour strength (% of seats held)	Standard deviation as a proportion of mean ward electorate size (%)	Labour strength (% of seats held)
1. Sheffield 12.2	1. Sheffield 49	1. Salford 11.2	1. Barrow 63*
2. Leeds 14.1	2. Hull 44	2. Barrow 16.5	2. Bristol 50
3. Hull 22.8	3. Leeds 40	3. Bristol 17.4	3. Leeds 46
4. Birmingham 26.5	4. Bradford 35	4. Birkenhead 21.1	4. Birkenhead 44
5. Bradford 41.5	5. Bristol 34	5. Leeds 26.9	5. Salford 44
6. Manchester 45.2	6. Manchester 27	6. Southampton 37.8	6. Southampton 37
7. Liverpool 48.9	7. Liverpool 23	7. Liverpool 48.9	7. Manchester 35
8. Bristol 50.2	8. Birmingham 19	8. Manchester 50.4	8. Liverpool 25

* Barrow is not listed in Table 3.1, as it was a borough with less than 100,000 population. The figure for Labour strength given here has been calculated separately from *North-Western Daily Mail* (2 November 1938).

had only a marginal impact on the wards themselves. His detailed tabulation of seats held in this period also shows no discernible impact on the standing of the main parties.[20] Hampton's study of Sheffield was more concerned with the post-war period, and was much concerned with contemporary debates on local government reform centred on the Maud Committee proposals. The earlier redistribution of seats in 1928–9 was not commented on directly in this work, but again it seems to have had no obvious effect on the election results listed.[21]

In some of the cases of redistribution identified, however, it is tempting to infer that there may have been an impact on electoral trends. Hull, redrawn between 1929 and 1932, subsequently became one of Labour's strongest boroughs having previously been only a modest stronghold. Sunderland's surprisingly low ranking in 1927 seems to have improved steadily after the redistribution between 1927 and 1929. Walsall also seems to have seen a marked improvement for Labour after boundary changes between 1929 and 1932. Most notably, Bristol, which is consistently in the lower half of the table up to 1935, sees an abrupt improvement after the redistribution between 1935 and 1938. Of course, these improvements in Labour's fortunes may have been caused by any number of other political factors, and merely coincided with boundary revisions.

However, one local study does show how redistribution could help Labour. Coventry was redistributed in 1928, and when all the seats were subsequently contested, Labour made eleven gains, never before having made more than two in any one year in the previous decade. From being a minor party on the council, it became a contender for power, eventually gaining control in 1937.[22] Until other cases like this are revealed, it is impossible to be definite, but for the moment the distinct possibility that electoral trends may have been influenced by changes in ward boundaries can be registered.

There are examples from Northern Ireland after partition, which vividly illustrate how blatant gerrymandering of ward boundaries can alter voting patterns. For instance, the three wards of Omagh were redistributed in 1934, resulting in the council, on which two-thirds of the seats were held by Nationalists at the time, passing into Unionist control. Again, in 1936, as a study of the electoral system in Northern Ireland showed, Derry was redistributed so that control was '... confirmed ... in the hands of a religious and political minority when the trend was for that minority to become smaller in relation to the expanding Roman Catholic population'.[23]

To conclude: whether or not redistribution of ward boundaries was desirable, whether such redistribution was carried out, and with what impact on electoral performance, were all questions which depended on a number of interrelated factors. The problem could not have applied on a uniform basis across the country, therefore, and the disadvantaging of Labour in Liverpool is unlikely to have been repeated in every other borough.

The aldermanic system

A second key feature of the municipal electoral system that might have distorted the relative strength of parties was the aldermanic system. In county boroughs, including Liverpool, each ward usually had three councillors and one alderman, so aldermen made up a quarter of the council. Before 1910, they were elected for a term of six years by all the members of the council, and after that date by the sitting councillors only. The criteria for election were at the discretion of the councillors themselves, and different councils applied completely different rules. In some cases, seniority was the sole criterion; in others, aldermen were elected strictly to reflect the balance of parties in the council; others again used the system to maintain or increase the dominance of one party; and in many councils a combination of any or all of these methods was used.[24]

As with much of the rest of the structure of local government, the origins of the system of aldermen lay in distant medieval custom, and its relevance to twentieth-century political life was open to question. They were only included under the 1835 legislation on municipal corporations by accident. The Whig government intended that town councils should be directly elected by the ratepayers, but the Tories wanted to water down the democratic element. The House of Lords, dominated by the Tories, introduced amendments to ensure that aldermen would make up a quarter of the councils. Deadlock between the Lords and the Commons over the issue near the end of the parliamentary session meant that the whole legislation was in danger of falling. Melbourne's government was anxious to clear the old municipal corporations out of the way as soon as possible, and therefore conceded to the Lords' demands to ensure the passing of the bill.[25] The aldermanic system was an unintended compromise, and despite the fact that it was 'so contrary to the general democratic tendencies of the time',[26] it survived attempts to abolish it in 1889 and 1933, only to be abolished finally in 1974.[27] It was also included in the new county councils in 1888 and the metropolitan boroughs in 1899, although in the latter case aldermen were only to make up one-seventh of the councils.[28] An attempt to amend the 1888 Local Government Bill so that aldermen would have been elected on the basis of proportional representation was also rejected, by only eleven votes,[29] so the system survived unchanged apart from the 1910 exclusion of sitting aldermen from aldermanic elections.

In 1933 J. J. Tinker, the Labour MP for Leigh, commented in the debate on the abolition of aldermen: 'Whatever may have been the reason for Aldermen when they were first appointed, for the life of me I cannot see any need for them now.' The Tory MP Michael Beaumont provided a reason in reply, claiming that: 'the Aldermen's bench saves our local government system from the twin evils of democracy and equality'.[30] This opinion may not have been shared by all Tories, but even if such blatantly undemocratic sentiments were kept in check, the system could throw up anomalies. This was especially the case when party allegiances were in flux.

If seniority counted, then old and declining parties, with plenty of long-serving members, would tend to gain, at the expense of growing new parties whose members would only recently have been elected. The system was inherently conservative in its effects. However, if dominant parties were also deliberately to use the aldermanic system to bolster their position, then it could produce even greater distortions.

In Liverpool, the controlling Tories appeared on the face of it to have no consistent policy on aldermanic elections, seeming instead to respond in a pragmatic fashion to changing circumstances. Seniority, proportionality and party advantage were all factors of varying importance to them. However, the net effect of their decisions always seemed to disadvantage Labour the most, even if they did not necessarily directly benefit themselves at the same time. The full list of aldermen elected in Liverpool between 1919 and 1938 can be found in Appendix VII; their impact on party strength can be seen in Figures 4.2 and 4.3.

The general trend is quite clear. Until Labour made their great gains in 1929, they were denied all but the most derisory representation on the aldermen's bench. Their nadir was reached in 1926, when they had no aldermen, despite having eighteen councillors. After 1929 the principle of proportionality was too strong for the Tories to ignore completely any longer, and Labour's representation was allowed to leap from one to nine aldermen, a position more or less maintained until 1938. However, it should be pointed out that, even in 1929, Labour was substantially under-represented proportionally – a figure of seventeen aldermen would have

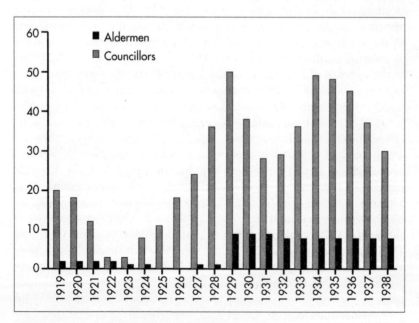

Figure 4.2 Labour councillors and aldermen, Liverpool, 1919–1938

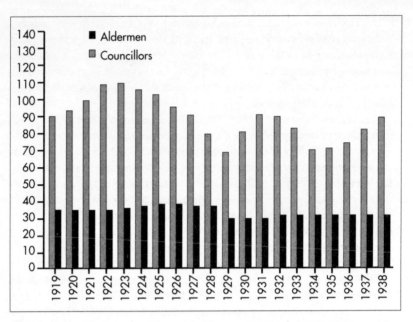

Figure 4.3 All other councillors and aldermen, Liverpool, 1919–1938

been fairer – and throughout the 1930s they remained under-represented to varying degrees.

By contrast, the Tories maintained a position of slightly above their proportional share for almost the entire two decades. They did not, however, appear to be blatantly using the system to their own advantage by hogging all the aldermanic places. Instead they allowed the over-representation of other small parties to develop in the 1920s, and more clearly in the 1930s, at the expense of Labour. Thus the Centre Party, the right-wing rump of former Nationalist councillors who refused to throw in their lot with Labour, were boosted by aldermen to a grotesque extent after 1927, so that by 1936 they had four aldermen despite having no elected councillors left in the city. The Liberals were equally over-represented in the mid-1920s and late 1930s when their total of elected councillors declined.

It might be argued that the inherent bias of the system in favour of old parties at the expense of the new, partially explains Labour's disadvantage. However, analysis of aldermanic elections shows that conscious manipulation by the Tories and others kept Labour out. The clearest example of this in the 1920s took place after the municipal elections in November 1925. Labour at this point had eleven councillors and one alderman, their leader at that time in the council, W. A. Robinson. His term of office of six years was due to expire, and the filling of aldermanic vacancies took place at the first council meeting after the election. It was customary for retiring aldermen to be re-elected unopposed, but in this case custom came a poor second to party interest. Tories and Liberals abstained in the vote, allowing the Catholic Party nominee, P. J. Kelly, representation up to four aldermen and seventeen councillors. Proportionality clearly had nothing to do with this result, but neither did the principle of seniority. Robinson had served on the council since 1911, Kelly since 1914. More to the point, Kelly was not even a councillor, having been defeated in the polls twelve months previously.

The nomination of someone from outside the council was quite legal, if rare. In the ancient origins of the system there had been a principle that 'men or women of outstanding ability or experience' could be brought into the council as aldermen, and nationally at least one other case was recorded between the wars.[32] It is doubtful that Kelly's ability or experience was the point here, however, but rather the complex relationship between the various parties in Liverpool at this juncture. This relationship needs careful analysis to reveal the full significance of Kelly's election.

P. J. Kelly had been the leader of the Irish Party (as it was then called) in 1924 and had led moves to come to an electoral understanding with Labour. He was described as 'a supporter of the claims of Labour and generally of the programme of the Labour Party'.[33] This did not prevent him from threatening to attack them if they failed to agree to a pact. As he put it: '… if the fight continues, we shall not cease reprisals … we have an extraordinary capacity for destruction, and we are not at all particular when we set out in that capacity'.[34] Nevertheless, Labour refused an agreement[35] and, in the subsequent elections in November 1924, defeated Irish Party opponents in four out of the five wards where they were challenged.[36] Kelly himself was comfortably beaten in Scotland South ward, Labour's majority being almost 600 votes out of a poll of just over 4,000. This was a humiliating defeat after his aggressive words only months earlier. Labour made significant gains overall in the 1924 elections, and their opponents rallied their forces in response. Archbishop Keating was instrumental in transforming the Irish Party into the Catholic Representation Association, soon to be known as the Catholic Party.[37] The Coalition Liberals began their move to join the Tory Party, declaring themselves as Independents in March 1925.[38] The subsequent 1925 elections saw an unprecedented attack on Labour, with the Tory leader, Salvidge, mounting a fierce campaign appealing for unity between all 'responsible' parties against the 'socialist and communist threat'.[39] W. A. Robinson responded for Labour, in particular aiming his fire at the new Catholic Party. On the eve of the poll he stated:

I am condemning that formation in this city of the so-called Catholic Party as I will also condemn the formation of any other religious Party … the Labour Party has never failed to do the right thing by any body of citizens, irrespective of the religion to which they belonged. The Labour Party was broad enough to receive into its ranks people of all religions … I sincerely hope that any attempt to divide the working class people in this way would fail.[40]

Overall, Labour increased their representation by three in the 1925 elections, although they lost in four of the five wards where they were opposed by the Catholic Party.[41] Labour's advance had been checked, and it was in the aftermath of this bruising election campaign that P. J. Kelly was then catapulted back into the council as an alderman, while W. A. Robinson suffered the humiliation of having to leave the chamber. He departed with the words, '*Au revoir*, gentlemen, I shall return',[42] leaving it to his successor as leader, Luke Hogan, to make a public statement on the whole affair. Hogan said this:

> The Catholics have established a new precedent. To fill an Aldermanic vacancy they have brought in a man who was beaten at the polls a year ago, and driven out the leader of a party which, at the present moment, commands at least 48,000 votes … it is unfortunate that the Liberals and Conservatives took no part in the election; if they had done the result would have been different, we are sure … the Catholics will have to face the situation they have created in their own constituencies, and that on every possible occasion we shall test the feeling of those wards on what can only be described as an outrage on the decency of public life. On the proportional principle, Labour, with eleven coun- cillors, is entitled to three Aldermen. Now we have none.[43]

The 1925 incident was a blatant example of how the aldermanic system was used against Labour, but there was an ironic postscript to it a few years later. In September 1929, four months after the advent of the minority Labour government, a total of five Centre (formerly Catholic) Party aldermen and councillors defected to Labour.[44] In the local elections two months later the Centre Party lost four out of the five contests where it was challenged by Labour.[45] With the Tories having lost their overall majority for the first time since the 1890s, the tide seemed to be very much with Labour. Mindful, no doubt, of the fact that he would come up for re- election as an alderman in 1931, P. J. Kelly joined the Labour group within a week,[46] to be joined on the aldermanic benches a few days later by W. A. Robinson. Kelly remained on the council until his death in December 1936. Having first been returned unopposed to the council in the electoral truce of 1914, and again having been unchallenged in 1921, P. J. Kelly had the dubious distinction of serving on the council for twenty-two years, with only a twelve-month break between 1924 and 1925, having never actually won a municipal election.

The case of P. J. Kelly revealed the quirks that the aldermanic system could produce in a supposedly democratic electoral system. After 1929 his unelected presence in the council worked in Labour's favour, but an equally clear series of events in the 1930s showed how the system was still being used to Labour's overall detriment. This is illustrated by the case of Lawrence King, one of the former Nationalist councillors who had joined

114

Labour in September 1929. Between June 1932 and June 1936 he was proposed by Labour in aldermanic elections eight times, and defeated every time.[47] On every occasion he had seniority over his opponent. On the first occasion he was defeated by a Centre Party nominee, bringing that party's total to five aldermen and seven councillors. The election had been caused by the death of a Labour alderman, so Labour's already disproportionately low representation actually worsened. In three elections in a row, between July 1934 and February 1935, he was defeated by Liberal nominees replacing deceased Liberal aldermen, thus maintaining their proportional parity, while at the same time keeping Labour under-represented by roughly a half. Again, in June 1936, he was defeated by two Liberal nominees, which resulted in the Liberal Party moving from parity to over-representation. King was eventually elected in January 1937, replacing a deceased Labour alderman merely to maintain Labour's still grossly under-represented position.[48] The Labour group registered its discontent at the obvious collusion between the Tory, Liberal and Centre Parties in this period only once: in February 1933 it abstained on an aldermanic vote as a protest.[49]

The political significance of the manipulation of the system was considerable in that it magnified Labour weakness and Tory strength. When Labour was at its lowest ebb in the mid-1920s and early and late 1930s this magnification was only marginal in relation to the huge majority that the Tories had in the council. But when Labour was at a high point in the late 1920s and mid-1930s, the distortion produced by the aldermanic system was crucial. The Tories only lost their overall majority on the council on four occasions between the wars: in 1929, and in three consecutive years between 1934 and 1937. They were still by far the largest party in those years, however, and needed only a handful of Protestant or Centre Party votes to maintain their control. However, if aldermen had been kept proportionate to the number of elected councillors for each party, the Tories would also have lost their overall majority in 1919 and 1920. In 1929 and 1934 not only would their overall majority have gone, but they would have been only narrowly ahead of Labour. In 1934 Labour in fact had forty-nine elected councillors compared to the Tory Party's fifty, and the possibility of unseating the Tories through an alliance with Liberals and/or the Centre Party might have been feasible. As it was, with aldermen included, the Tories had seventy-two seats to the Labour Party's fifty-seven, and their control was unchallengeable.

Anomalies produced by the aldermanic system were very much the product of political will. Whichever party dominated at a local level, its attitude to other parties, and its degree of commitment to fair and democratic procedure in the council-chamber determined the way in which the system was applied. In Liverpool, it was used quite blatantly against the interest of Labour in the council. The Tory leader in the 1930s, Sir Thomas White, admitted as much in private correspondence in 1935: he acknowledged collusion in the recent elevation to the aldermanic bench of the Revd Harry Longbottom, leader of the Protestant Party; he listed five previous occasions when the Tory Party had assisted Centre Party councillors to aldermanships; and he revealed that three Centre Party aldermen would be re-elected when their term of office expired three years later, thus preventing the party from disappearing from the municipal scene.[50]

There is only scattered evidence to show how the aldermanic system was used elsewhere. In the parliamentary debate in 1923, on a proposal to allow proportional representation in local government elections, various MPs cited evidence of how affairs were carried out in their own areas. In Burnley, it was revealed, Labour was allocated no aldermen despite having won considerable support in recent elections. On the other hand, it was claimed that in Plymouth aldermen were elected strictly on the principle of proportionality.[51]

One local example which is documented is the Lancashire county council, where the principle of seniority was adhered to. Even this could cause distortions, though, as was proved by the case in 1946, when large gains by Labour were negated by the survival of long-lived aldermen from before the war. The consequent controversy led eventually to the concession of the principle of proportionality.[52] Keith-Lucas' 1952 study of the local government franchise, in arguing strongly against the continued existence of aldermen, gave a number of other examples of how the system was operated, although none was from the inter-war period. Norwich, Liverpool, Exeter and Leeds were all quoted as examples of where ruling parties gave no aldermanic places to opposition parties in the late nineteenth century.[53] On the London county council, after the first elections in 1889, a Liberal/Socialist alliance, having won a majority of the seats, filled eighteen out of the nineteen aldermanic places with its own supporters, so securing its control of the council. By contrast, in 1910 the Municipal Reform Party bolstered a two-seat majority by only appointing aldermen from its own ranks. Again, in 1949 on the London county council, when Labour and the Tories had an equal number of elected councillors, Labour secured a majority through the choice of Labour aldermen.[54] Michael Savage, in his study of Preston, also provides an example in passing, stating that Labour was only prevented from taking power in 1929 by the presence of Tory aldermen.[55]

These are only a few examples, and do not show how the system might have been applied over a long period of time, but at the very least they show that practice did vary between boroughs. The only local study that allows a more detailed and long-term picture is again that of G. W. Jones in Wolverhampton. In referring to the operation of the aldermanic system, Jones claimed that:

> ... it was difficult to balance the many criteria for an Aldermanic seat in the 1920s and 1930s without upsetting somebody's feelings. Yet up to 1945 a balance was roughly kept between the Mayoral qualification, [i.e. appointing all ex-mayors automatically as aldermen] promoting

the senior Councillor and sharing the seats in some relation to party strength on the council.[56]

This supposedly reasonable behaviour by a council dominated by an alliance of Tories, Liberals and Independent Ratepayers is contrasted with the later tactics of the Labour Party in 1961–2, when packing the aldermanic benches with Labour supporters in order to retain control of the council led to applications to the High Court and a general crisis of municipal politics in Wolverhampton. Jones argued that these events made Wolverhampton 'notorious for displaying the evil effects of party politics in local government'.[57]

However, this contrast between inter-war propriety and post-war Labour gerrymandering of the system hardly seems to be borne out by other evidence that Jones himself provides. He records that the Labour Party itself complained in the 1920s that they were not given adequate representation in proportion to the seats they held, and that the long service of some of their councillors was ignored. He also reports that the only example of an ex-mayor not being automatically put on the aldermanic bench between the wars was that of a Labour ex-mayor in 1930, preference being given instead to a Liberal councillor.[58] Jones also gives detailed figures of the party composition of the council, including both councillors and aldermen, throughout the inter-war period, and analysis of these figures shows quite clearly that the aldermanic system was operated in a way that disadvantaged Labour. A comparison of the situation in Liverpool, as shown earlier, and in Wolverhampton, derived from Jones' data,[59] can be seen by comparing Figures 4.2 and 4.3 (Liverpool) with Figures 4.4 and 4.5 (Wolverhampton). The pattern in the two cities seems similar. Minimal representation on the aldermanic bench for Labour in the 1920s, a slight improvement in the 1930s, but still proportionally far less than the other main parties on the council. The similarities go further than that if the details of each party's representation are examined. Just as in Liverpool, the Tories in Wolverhampton did not hog all the aldermanic places themselves. Instead they allowed their allies, in this case the Liberals and the Independent Ratepayers, to increase their representation well above their entitlement at the expense of the Labour Party. Thus, by 1938, the Liberals had five aldermen to three councillors, the Independents had five aldermen to ten councillors, while Labour still had only three aldermen to sixteen councillors. The 'rough balance' seemed particularly 'rough' for Labour.

It is also worth noting that this form of the aldermanic system was specific to the county boroughs and councils of England and Wales. When the district and parish councils were created in 1894 aldermen were not introduced[60] and, as already noted, they made up only one-seventh of the council body in the metropolitan boroughs.[61] In Scotland, the role of aldermen was taken by bailies, who were also chosen from among the sitting councillors but, crucially, only held office for as long as their term

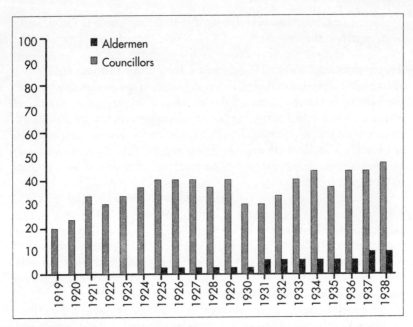

Figure 4.4   Labour councillors and aldermen, Wolverhampton, 1919–1938

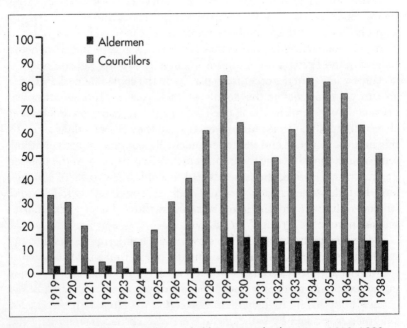

Figure 4.5   All other councillors and aldermen, Wolverhampton, 1919–1938

118

as councillors.[62] In the Irish municipal corporations, established from 1840, and persisting in the North after partition, aldermen were directly elected by the public.[63] In all these cases, the potential for misuse of the aldermanic system was either reduced or eliminated altogether.

From these few examples, it can be concluded that if there was a potential for abuse of the aldermanic system in all boroughs, it seems that it depended on local political conditions, whether or not it was manifested. In some cases, the system was worked in Labour's favour. In others it may have been neutral. In others again, Labour was as disadvantaged as in Liverpool. It is certainly not the case that what happened in Liverpool can be assumed to apply to all other boroughs.

Exclusions from the municipal franchise

The third key element of the electoral system for local government that may have affected Labour's performance was the limited nature of the municipal franchise. A significant proportion of the population was enfranchised for parliamentary elections but disenfranchised at a local level during the inter-war years, to an extent that has been little investigated. Among recent historical works, J. S. Rowett, in his study of the Labour Party and local government, notes the problem, but does not attempt to estimate its effect on Labour. Duncan Tanner, in his study of Labour in the Edwardian period, also touches on the problem in the inter-war years.[64] Tanner concludes, however, that municipal disenfranchisement was of little significance to Labour.[65] For most other historians, the assumption that, with the extension of the vote to women by the Acts of 1918 and 1928, complete adult suffrage had been achieved is a deep-rooted one. It is also erroneous as far as municipal elections were concerned.

Once again, the origins of the municipal franchise are to be found in the distant past. Hasluck's history of English local government states that: 'The right of the ratepayer as such to participate in Local Government was recognised in thousands of parishes "from time immemorial".'[66] By the time of the Poor Law Amendment Act in 1834: 'The argument that local administration should be kept in the hands of those who provided the money was particularly cogent ... it justified the exclusion from the franchise of every person who did not directly contribute to the funds of the local authorities.'[66] What this meant in practice was that the vote was restricted to ratepayers. The 1888 Local Government Act more specifically embodied the principle that all owners or occupiers of land or property were entitled to the vote. This meant that, until 1918, the municipal franchise was in advance of the parliamentary franchise as far as women were concerned, as female owners or occupiers were qualified to vote. The 1918 Representation of the People Act extended the principle to the wives (aged 30 or over) or husbands of owners or occupiers, and the 1928 Act brought the age limit down to 21 for all women.[68]

Even after all these extensions to the franchise, there were still large numbers who were not qualified to vote in local elections. Hasluck, writing in 1936, expressed the essential difference between the parliamentary and the municipal franchise, which was to be maintained until 1945:

During the long conflicts of the nineteenth century when Democracy was struggling for national recognition, disputes concerning the franchise usually revolved round the opposition of two principles, the rights of citizenship and the rights of property. One school of thought held that every individual had an inherent right to participate in the government of his country owing to the mere fact of citizenship; another held that responsible government could be carried out only by those who had 'a stake in the country' in the form of financial interest. After many struggles, the principle of citizenship triumphed in the constitutional system of Central Government; but the other principle still holds the field in Local Government.[69]

Those who were disenfranchised municipally included the following significant groups: sons and daughters, and other family members such as aged parents, who lived with the owner or occupier; servants who lived in the home of the owner or occupier; and tenants of furnished premises.[70] Furthermore, others could be temporarily disenfranchised. Until 1926 the voter had to prove that he or she had been resident in the ward for six months prior to registration on 1 June. In 1926 this qualifying period was reduced to three months.[71]

The net effect of all these exclusions is hard to establish precisely, due to the lack of official statistics for municipal elections in this period.[72] The figures for all Liverpool parliamentary divisions have been calculated here, comparing municipal and parliamentary voters for the inter-war period. These figures are shown in Appendix VIII; a summary of the data for the city as a whole is shown in Table 4.4. It reveals that the extent of municipal disenfranchisement in Liverpool was substantial.

As Table 4.4 shows, over 20 per cent of municipal voters in Liverpool were disenfranchised in 1919, with the percentage then falling gradually to 16.5 per cent by 1928. After the extension of the vote to women under 30, the proportion excluded rose again to almost 30 per cent. This was due to the fact that many women below the age of 30, who could not vote previously in either municipal or parliamentary elections, had now won the right to vote at the parliamentary level, but were still barred from the municipal franchise. The rate of exclusion then remained high for the rest of the 1930s, still amounting to 27.2 per cent in 1938. This was plainly a factor of considerable significance in Liverpool, therefore.

Some idea of how typical Liverpool was in this regard can be ascertained from data given in the *Registrar General's Statistical Review*. The figures for 1938 for the whole of England and Wales, for the London metropolitan

Table 4.4 Parliamentary and municipal voters in Liverpool, 1919–1938*

Year	Parliamentary voters	Municipal voters	Difference (%)
1919	352,407	275,320	21.9
1920	355,755	283,762	20.2
1921	357,034	289,817	18.8
1922	362,208	297,164	18.0
1923	373,283	307,514	17.6
1924	381,527	315,859	17.2
1925	389,569	321,660	17.4
1926	392,640	324,913	17.2
1927	396,960	330,345	16.8
1928	396,271	331,015	16.5
1929	510,410	365,208	28.4
1930	513,099	364,781	28.9
1931	518,468	367,436	29.1
1932	520,102	368,768	29.1
1933	520,316	369,320	29.0
1934	519,718	368,545	29.1
1935	519,634	370,568	28.7
1936	517,695	370,933	28.3
1937	509,466	368,942	27.6
1938	504,041	366,980	27.2

* The municipal electorate for Croxteth ward, incorporated from 1928, has not been included in this table, as, for parliamentary elections, this ward remained in the Ormskirk division, rather than being brought in to one of the Liverpool divisions. The total figure for municipal electors given here, then, is slightly lower than the full municipal electorate from 1928.

boroughs, and a number of municipal boroughs, have been collated in Table 4.5. This shows that the overall extent of exclusions was considerable, with 24.2 per cent of voters excluded from the municipal franchise at all levels of local government for England and Wales as a whole. They also show a wide variation nationally, with boroughs such as Derby, Cardiff and Stoke having less than 10 per cent excluded, while others, like Preston and East and West Ham, had 25 per cent or more excluded. The combined metropolitan boroughs of London also had a high level of exclusion, at 28.4 per cent. Liverpool, at 23.1 per cent, appears to have a fairly high exclusion rate according to these figures, although by no means the highest. However, attentive readers will have noted that this figure for Liverpool differs from the calculations shown above in Table 4.4, where a figure of 27.2 per cent was recorded for 1938. This is due to the exclusion of Croxteth ward from the figures, as explained in the note to Table 4.4.

Table 4.5 Parliamentary and municipal voters in London and various county boroughs, 1938–1939

	Parliamentary voters	Municipal voters	Difference (%)
Birmingham	667,333	519,447	22.2
Blackburn	82,638	63,522	23.1
Bradford	205,536	158,152	23.1
Bristol	272,035	219,118	19.5
Cardiff	122,862	112,720	8.3
Derby	79,392	72,526	8.7
East Ham	91,659	68,555	25.2
Hull	175,978	154,932	12.0
Leeds	327,389	261,012	20.3
Leicester	165,841	139,121	16.1
Liverpool	504,041	387,481	23.1
Manchester	467,135	354,312	24.2
Newcastle	187,957	144,972	22.9
Nottingham	171,406	139,742	18.5
Preston	84,225	60,223	28.5
Sheffield	316,498	275,664	22.9
Stoke	141,681	128,618	9.2
West Ham	162,476	121,836	25.0
Wolverhampton	93,675	72,039	23.1
All London boroughs	2,804,051	2,008,120	28.4
England and Wales*	28,183,422	21,354,421	24.2

Source: *Registrar General's Statistical Review of England and Wales* (1938), tables, pt. II – Civil, pp. 61–93.   * All levels of local government

The true exclusion rate for Liverpool, then, is 27.2 per cent, one of the highest in the country. A general note of caution needs to be sounded, however, about the Registrar General's figures. It may well have been the case in other boroughs that the external boundaries at the parliamentary and municipal level were not precisely the same, especially if there had been recent extensions of the borough boundaries.[73] Only a detailed examination of each borough could eliminate this problem completely. The raw figures as they stand can only be taken as a rough guide to the relative position nationally. On that basis, it can be asserted that Liverpool plainly had a relatively high exclusion rate, and that the rate varied considerably across the country.

The political significance of these figures is hard to quantify for an age when there were no such things as opinion polls. Nevertheless, it seems likely that the exclusions from the municipal franchise would have disadvantaged Labour more than the Tories, on the assumption that working-class electors were more likely to be prospective Labour than Tory voters. Furnished rooms and lodgings were likely to be tenanted by the most transient members of the population, not all of whom would have necessarily been working class, although it is probable that a majority would have been, in a city like Liverpool with its strong tradition of casual employment. Live-in servants, by definition, would have been working class, and in Liverpool they would also have constituted a significant proportion of the working population, and especially of women workers.

Adult sons and daughters living at home may have been as prevalent, or even more common, in middle-class as in working-class homes. The wealthy may have been more able to support children and other relations at home, and also would have had more room to do so. On the other hand, the low wages of young workers may have made it difficult for many of them to set up their own home. Hasluck records that some parents entered into formal agreements with their children, legally transferring the ownership of the furniture in their bedrooms to them and providing them with a rent-book so that they could qualify as tenants of 'unfurnished lodgings'.[74] Such legalistic responses were presumably economically beyond the reach of most working-class families. Overall, the impact of this particular group on electoral fortunes is particularly difficult to identify.

Again, the residential qualification would have affected all classes, but in Liverpool between the wars, when slum clearance and council-house building was extensive, it may have particularly affected working-class voters. Evidence for parliamentary electors before the First World War, when a twelve-month qualification period still applied, certainly shows the extent of the problem. Between the drawing up of the electoral register in July 1909 and the election of December 1910, the proportion of electors who had moved ranged between 26 and 39 per cent in a variety of urban constituencies. In Liverpool, the proportion was 31 per cent.[75] A Liberal MP had earlier commented: 'It is when you come to the working-classes, who have to follow the tide of industry from one place to another, that the hardship of twelve months occupation most harshly operates.'[76]

Some indication of the variation in exclusions from the municipal franchise within the city can be gained by comparing the exclusion rate for each parliamentary division in Liverpool. This data is to be found in Appendix VIII; a summary for 1938 is shown in Table 4.6. As can be seen, there was considerable variation between divisions, exclusion rates ranging from 22.9 to 31.2 per cent. What precisely caused this variation, however, is hard to ascertain. It might seem significant that West Toxteth, which contained some of the wealthiest streets in the city, had a low exclusion rate of 22.9 per cent, whereas Scotland/Exchange, with some of the worst slums, had a high rate at 28.5 per cent. But other divisions contradict this pattern. East Toxteth, which also contained some very prosperous districts, had the highest exclusion rate of all, at 31.2 per cent, while Everton, with some very poor streets, had one of the lowest, at 23.1 per cent. Clearly, there was more than one factor at work here. The large size of

Table 4.6 Parliamentary and municipal voters for all Liverpool parliamentary divisions, 1938*

Division(s)	Parliamentary voters	Municipal voters	Difference (%)
East Toxteth	52,432	36,063	31.2
Edge Hill/Fairfield	83,629	60,529	27.6
Everton	28,454	21,882	23.1
Kirkdale	36,321	26,964	25.8
Scotland/Exchange	74,954	53,615	28.5
Walton	58,807	42,903	27.0
Wavertree	68,803	51,189	25.6
West Derby	59,061	41,960	29.0
West Toxteth	41,580	32,044	22.9

* Scotland and Exchange divisions, and Edge Hill and Fairfield, have had to be combined, as they had wards divided between them. See Appendix VIII for details.

parliamentary divisions, often encompassing widely differing areas in terms of social class, housing stock and population density, also makes it difficult to reach any firm conclusion from this data.

Only a ward, or even street-level investigation, of the electoral registers for this period could give a clearer picture of variations in the exclusion rate from the municipal franchise. An examination of the registers of a number of wards in Liverpool for 1939 gives the results shown in Table 4.7. The figures show that the more prosperous wards of Sefton Park West and Little Woolton clearly had higher rates of exclusion than poorer wards such as Netherfield and Scotland North. However, the reasons for exclusion might vary considerably between different areas, as analysis of

Table 4.7 Parliamentary and municipal voters in five Liverpool wards, 1938–1939

Ward	Parliamentary voters	Municipal voters	% Excluded
Little Woolton	1,354	946	31.3
Netherfield	12,918	10,300	20.3
St Anne's	9,051	6,614	26.9
Sefton Park W	10,343	6,820	34.1
Scotland N	9,486	7,334	22.7

Source: Liverpool Electoral Registers, 1938–9.

the surnames of excluded voters shows. In one polling district in Scotland North, 73 per cent of excluded voters had the same surname as the head of household, while the corresponding figure for Netherfield was 63 per cent, and for Little Woolton only 47 per cent.[77] This would suggest that family members made up a high proportion of excluded voters in poorer areas, whereas, in more prosperous areas, servants, and possibly furnished tenants, were more significant.

Street level investigation of the electoral register reveals further variation, as shown for a part of St Anne's ward in Table 4.8. As can be seen, there was a great deal of variation even within this small area. It is also notable that some notoriously poor streets grouped close together near the city centre, such as Richmond Row and Springfield, had extremely high rates of exclusion from the municipal franchise. Extraordinarily, in Trinity Place, adjacent to Springfield, all but one of the parliamentary voters were excluded. These figures suggest strongly that poor areas of cheap lodging houses had the highest exclusion rates of all.

Table 4.8 Parliamentary and municipal voters in selected streets, St Anne's ward (polling district BE), 1938–1939

Street	Parliamentary voters	Municipal voters	% Excluded
Bidder St.	260	226	13
Canterbury St.	264	198	25
Gt Richmond St.	130	99	24
Islington	187	112	40
Mansfield St.	49	40	18
Page St.	151	131	13
Queen Anne St.	35	31	11
Richmond Row	215	73	66
Soho St.	272	212	22
Springfield	138	64	54
Trinity Place	21	1	95
Whole polling district	3,289	2,461	25

Source: Electoral Register, polling district BE, St Anne's ward, 1938–9.

A fuller investigation of electoral registers is needed to establish definitively the impact of exclusions from the municipal franchise between the wars.[78] What can be stated now is that these exclusions, which were to last until 1945,[79] were significant, not least in Liverpool. The suggestion that working-class voters were more likely to be excluded from the municipal franchise seems plausible, but it cannot be proved as yet. Moreover, it needs to be remembered that because a ward was more working class did not automatically mean that it should be a Labour ward, or vice versa. In Liverpool, especially, that was a dangerous assumption. Nevertheless, any exclusion from the franchise that particularly affected the working class was more likely to disadvantage Labour than any other party.

Plural voting and the municipal franchise

There was also the problem of the inclusion of business voters distorting the franchise. This again stemmed from the traditional association of the right to vote in local elections with property-ownership and the payment of rates. Non-resident shopkeepers and other owners of business premises were entitled to a vote in the ward in which their businesses were situated, in addition to their vote in the ward in which they resided. In some cases, plural voters may not have lived within the borough at all, yet they were still entitled to vote in it. The contrast between their inclusion in the franchise and the exclusion of council tenants living outside the city boundaries shows the bias inherent in the system. Plural voting also survived in the parliamentary franchise until 1948, but it was not until 1969 that it was excluded from the local franchise.[80] In parliamentary constituencies, the plural vote was probably only marginally significant in relation to the large numbers of voters on the register. In the smaller municipal wards, particularly in city centres, and especially where boundary revision was long delayed, the business vote could be influential; that it was likely to benefit the opponents of Labour, and in particular the Tories, is hardly open to question.

The national significance of plural voting can be gauged from figures derived from the *Registrar General's Statistical Review*, which are shown in Table 4.9. The figures show that the business vote was most significant in the largest cities, and was usually concentrated in city-centre constituencies. London, Manchester and Liverpool stand out as the three cities where plural voting must have had a real political effect, especially in the retail and business districts. With a quarter of the voters in Liverpool Exchange qualifying by their property ownership alone, parliamentary elections clearly would have been influenced strongly by the business vote. At municipal elections, where plural voters might be even more concentrated in city-centre wards, the effect was likely to be even more significant.

Some idea of the impact of plural voting on the municipal franchise in Liverpool can be derived from Table 4.10, which shows the municipal electorate for each ward in the city in 1931 compared to the estimated population, aged 21 or over, living in the wards. (For the method of calculation of these estimates, see Appendix IX.) These figures provide clear evidence of the impact of plural voting. The business vote was particularly evident, as one would expect, in the wards near the city centre. This was

Table 4.9 Business voters on parliamentary electoral register in selected parliamentary boroughs, 1938–1939

Borough	No. of constituencies	All voters	Business voters	Difference (%)	Constituency with highest % of business voters
Birmingham	12	667,333	16,547	2.5	West (8.6)
Bolton	1	121,791	1,023	0.8	Bolton (0.8)
Bradford	4	205,536	5,407	2.6	Central (10.2)
Bristol	5	272,035	5,353	2.0	Central (10.2)
Hull	4	175,978	4,780	2.7	Central (9.5)
Leeds	6	327,389	8,923	2.7	Central (14.2)
Liverpool	11	504,041	17,170	3.4	Exchange (25.9)
London	61	2,804,051	126,059	4.5	City of (83.9)
Manchester	10	467,135	19,840	4.3	Exchange (33.5)
Newcastle	4	187,957	5,680	3.0	Central (10.8)
Nottingham	4	171,406	4,716	2.8	Central (6.7)
Preston	1	84,225	733	0.9	Preston (0.9)
St Helens	1	64,655	689	1.1	St Helens (1.1)
Sheffield	7	316,498	8,492	2.7	Central (17.6)
Southampton	1	113,678	608	0.5	Southampton (0.5)
All constituencies, England and Wales		28,183,422	360,644	1.3	City of London (83.9)

Source: *Registrar General's Statistical Review of England and Wales* (1938), tables, pt. II – Civil, pp. 61–93.

Table 4.10 Municipal electorate as a proportion of estimated population, aged 21 or over, living in wards, 1931 (in descending order)

Ward	Municipal electorate (1)	Estimated population 21+ (2)	(1) as a % of (2)
Castle St.	2,360	254	930
Exchange	2,492	1,879	133
St Peter's	2,979	3,429	87
Croxteth	10,851	13,050	83
Aigburth	8,493	10,771	79
Vauxhall	3,783	4,843	78
Fazakerley	10,866	13,923	78
Allerton	4,379	5,682	77
Netherfield	12,090	15,779	77
West Derby	18,498	24,437	76
Walton	16,395	21,692	76
St Domingo	11,734	15,600	75
Dingle	15,469	20,580	75
Garston	7,131	9,501	75
Wavertree	14,575	19,491	75
Breckfield	10,3691	13,892	75
Childwall	3,105	4,163	75
Old Swan	15,881	21,302	75
Scotland N	8,758	11,762	74
Wavertree W	8,906	12,037	74
Sefton Park W	6,438	8,776	73
Edge Hill	13,274	18,183	73
Kensington	11,351	15,605	73
Sandhills	9,499	13,101	73
Scotland S	8,712	12,025	72
Much Woolton	2,299	3,182	72
Kirkdale	17,017	23,738	72
Prince's Park	9,913	13,878	71
Anfield	10,869	15,360	71
Fairfield	10,220	14,472	71
Brunswick	9,088	12,897	70
St Anne's	9,253	13,360	69
Low Hill	11,271	16,293	69
Warbreck	12,376	17,966	69
Sefton Park E	8,969	13,155	68
Granby	9,918	14,854	67
Everton	13,501	20,346	66
Little Woolton	592	935	63
Gt George	5,043	8,139	62
Abercromby	9,493	16,270	58
Total	378,287	516,619	73

Source: 1931 census; *Liverpool Official Red Book* (1933), p. 100.

most obvious in Castle Street ward, where there were over nine times as many voters as residents of voting age. This ward already stood out as an anomaly resulting from inequitable internal boundaries, but it was clearly even more anomalous given that its electorate must have been made up almost entirely of non-resident plural voters. There were three seats here that were solidly anti-Labour, as the results for this ward listed in Appendix IV show. Exchange and St Peter's were also city-centre wards, and although not as grossly out of line with the rest of the city, they were nevertheless significantly above average for the ratio of electors to residents. There were another six seats here that were unshakeably anti-Labour. In 1931, these three wards together accounted for roughly 8 per cent of the elected seats on the council, whereas their combined electorate amounted to only 2 per cent of the total in the city. Even more striking, their resident population old enough to vote amounted to just 1 per cent of the total for the city. What this clearly shows is that the system of plural voting, combined with eccentric ward boundaries, produced a substantial anti-Labour bias.

Table 4.10 might also provide another way of measuring the differential effect of the exclusions from the franchise dealt with earlier. The proportion of the population enfranchised tends to be higher in some of the middle-class wards, such as Aigburth, Allerton, West Derby and Walton, and lower in some of the poorer wards such as Great George, Everton, St Anne's, Brunswick and Scotland South, but the relationship is by no means uniform. Prosperous wards, like Sefton Park East and Little Woolton, and working-class wards, like Vauxhall and Netherfield, show quite the opposite relationship. In the case of Vauxhall, it may be that the business vote was marginally significant. It was a ward on the edge of the central business district of the city, and its electorate was probably increased to some degree by non-resident plural voters. On the other hand, a large number of resident domestic servants may have increased the numbers excluded from the municipal franchise in Sefton Park East. Again, as with the earlier evidence, there are too many unquantifiable variables to make definite conclusions.

Liverpool as the exception?

There are reasons for believing that the effects of the franchise factor would not have applied in a uniform fashion across the country. For instance, business voters would have existed everywhere else, of course, but their electoral significance would have depended on both their numbers and the distribution of their business premises. As Table 4.9 above showed clearly, their impact varied considerably. That variation was mainly a product of the structure of the local economy. Large cities of regional importance, with major retail and distributive functions, were more likely to have a concentration of business voters in the city centre, and Liverpool undoubtedly came into that category. On the other hand, their influence was clearly much exaggerated in Liverpool by political decision. The 1893 boundary revision by the Liberals, by deciding ward size not only relative to population but also according to rateable value, meant that the city-centre wards were inevitably over-represented. The failure of the Tory council to redraw the boundaries for the next sixty years both perpetuated and exacerbated that initial imbalance.

Exclusions from the franchise were also not likely to be on an identical scale throughout the country. There were a number of factors that were relevant. The local economy and housing market could affect the situation in some cases. Family size and the availability of both jobs and housing for young workers would determine how many children of voting age lived with their parents, and therefore were deprived of the vote. The availability of casual and part-time work, combined with the housing stock, would have determined the numbers living in furnished lodgings, who again would have been disenfranchised. The number of live-in servants not entitled to the municipal vote would also have varied according to local economic and social circumstances. The larger and richer the middle class, the greater the number of servants would have been employed, and the greater the degree of disenfranchisement. There was also a gender factor which would have affected this last point up to the equalization of the franchise for men and women in 1928. Domestic service was a major source of employment for young women, so, where it was concentrated, there would have been large numbers of women below the age of 30, whether living-in or not, who were not enfranchised until 1928. All these factors seem to have been significant in Liverpool. The casual nature of much employment in the city, the poor housing stock, the existence of a large and rich middle class, the huge domestic-service sector, with particularly large numbers of young women employed, all meant that if the exclusions from the franchise disadvantaged Labour, then they may have been more marked in Liverpool than in some other parts of the country.

Other problems in the municipal electoral system

Finally, there may have been other factors that could have had some effect on Labour's performance in local elections. One issue that has to be considered is registration. It is possible that middle-class residents were more likely to register for voting. Evidence for different countries in other periods, most notably the United States in the post-war period, suggest that this may be so. However, analysis of the 1931 census figures for Liverpool proves decisively that non-registration of voters was not a problem. The total population of Liverpool in 1931 was 855,688, whereas the total population below the age of 21 was 338,043, leaving a total of 517,645 people of voting age.[81] The total parliamentary electorate in 1931 was 518,468.[82] The slight difference in timing of the census and the registration process, the recording of visitors in the census and other factors, meant that the figures for the electorate and the population of voting age could not have been identical. However, they were so similar in 1931 that it seems that non-registration of voters for parliamentary elections could not have been a significant problem. As registration for both parliamentary and municipal levels was carried out at the same time, and only one joint electoral roll was actually published, with parliamentary voters who were excluded from the municipal franchise being clearly distinguished from the rest, then it can be assumed that non-registration was also not a problem at the municipal level. Nearly everyone who was entitled to register did so, and any variations in registration between classes could not therefore have been significant.

Other factors included the timing of elections – in early November – and the hours of polling – from 8 a.m. to 8 p.m.[83] – which probably affected Labour detrimentally. This again requires the assumption that the conventional wisdom amongst post-1945 pollsters about the effects of bad weather, the duration of daylight, and class differences in the length of the working day, can be retrospectively applied to the inter-war period.

Again, the sequence of one-third of the seats coming up for election each year may also have benefited older, established parties, as it would require a steady rise in electoral support over several years for new parties to displace them. If all seats had been up for re-election every three years, for instance, as they were in London metropolitan boroughs, then one good year for the challenger might have been enough to unseat the controlling party. At the very least, the pattern of elections probably reduced the volatility of political shifts at a local level, and was therefore inherently conservative in its impact. The effects of these distortions in the electoral system are difficult to establish, and were probably only marginal. The major factors of boundaries, the aldermanic system, and the franchise appear to have been much more significant.

The combined effect of anomalies in the municipal electoral system

Various reasons have been advanced above for believing that the factors that determined the extent of distortion of the electoral process varied from one borough to another, and that Liverpool was a borough where the distortion was likely to be more significant, and which particularly damaged the Labour Party. The problem, though, is that there is very little evidence for the rest of the country to compare with the Liverpool experience. There have been no systematic studies of municipal politics on a national scale in this period, nor have there have been any local studies which have looked at the details of election results and their relationship to the electoral system in a locality. Until such studies are carried out, firm conclusions are not possible. Some suggestions can, however, be made on the basis of the limited evidence that is available.

There are two general points that need to be made first. One is that the Labour Party could not have been equally as disadvantaged by the electoral system in every other borough as it was in Liverpool, for if it had been, then it would have been receiving an extraordinarily high proportion of the votes in some boroughs where it held large numbers of seats. The figures quoted in Table 3.1 earlier make this point very clearly. With the Labour Party consistently holding 80 per cent or more of the seats in West Ham from 1927 to 1938, it was scarcely possible for it to have gained an even higher proportion of the votes cast. West Ham, of course, was exceptional in the degree to which it was dominated by Labour, but in other boroughs, like St Helens, Sheffield, Swansea and East Ham, where the proportion of seats held was frequently in the 60–70 per cent range, it is equally unlikely that their share of the vote could have been substantially higher than this.

Second, the extent to which the electoral system either benefitted or damaged a party was primarily a product of the overall balance of political power in the locality. The operation of the aldermanic system and the state of the ward boundaries in a borough might have been decided on an all-party basis, but it was more likely that the dominant party prevailed in these sorts of decisions. Certainly this was the case in Liverpool. What this meant in general for the Labour Party in this period is clear: once Labour had gained power in those areas where it was strongest, it could proceed to operate the system in its own favour, and thus its political strength would be subsequently exaggerated; once Labour aldermen were drafted in in numbers, they were in place for six years; and once boundaries were redrawn fairly, or even unfairly, in Labour's favour, then the party's political position was improved for the foreseeable future. In general, where Labour was strong, its strength would have been amplified. Where it was weak, its weakness would have been magnified. The latter would have applied to Liverpool. The relative weakness of the Labour Party in Liverpool compared to other parts of the country was almost certainly exaggerated by the electoral system.

The only local study over a long period of time which can be directly compared with Liverpool is that provided for Sheffield by W. A. Hampton. Although providing no analysis himself, Hampton did collate data relating to seats and votes won in local elections,[84] and from this it is possible to calculate Labour's record in Sheffield between the wars and compare it with the figures calculated for Liverpool in Chapter Three.

The results of this comparison are shown in Figures 4.6 (a–d). There is no account taken of non-contests in Hampton's figures, and therefore the figures used for Liverpool are also the raw votes cast with no compensation for non-contests. This reduces the reliability of the vote-share figures, but, nevertheless, the picture conveyed by the comparison is so clear as to be incontrovertible. Figures 4.6 (a) and (b) show that the share of seats held by Labour in Liverpool was consistently lower than its share of votes won. In Sheffield, Labour's share of the seats was also lower than its share

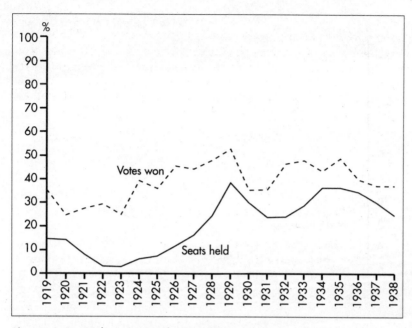

Figure 4.6a   Labour seats and votes, Liverpool, 1919–1938

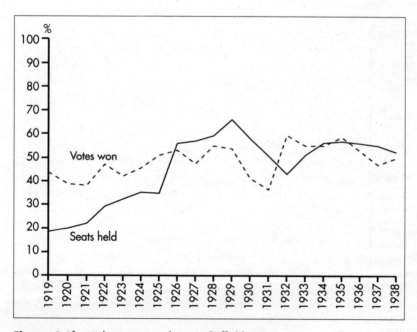

Figure 4.6b   Labour seats and votes, Sheffield, 1919–1938

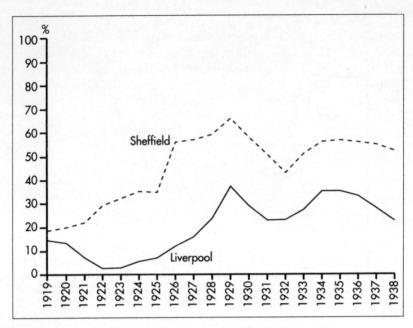

Figure 4.6c   Labour seats in Liverpool and Sheffield, 1919–1938

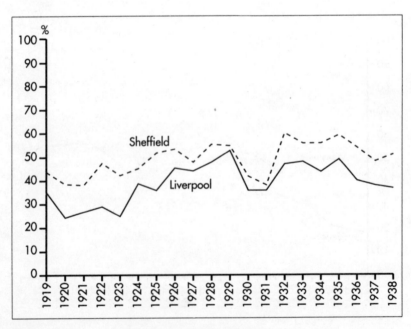

Figure 4.6d   Labour votes in Liverpool and Sheffield, 1919–1938

of votes for as long as it was the minority party, but once it gained a majority, in 1925, it then moved into a position where it usually had more seats
than votes. The electoral system, which so consistently seemed to disadvantage Labour in Liverpool, conversely began to benefit it in Sheffield.
The overall effect is to magnify the difference between Labour's performance in the two cities. Figures 4.6 (c) and (d) reinforce this conclusion.
In terms of seats held, Labour was clearly far more successful in Sheffield
than in Liverpool, but in terms of votes, while Labour was more popular
in Sheffield, the difference was far narrower.

There were also a handful of examples of disparity between votes and
seats in local government which were quoted in the parliamentary debate
on proportional representation in 1923, mentioned before. Various MPs
pointed to the situation in their own locality to show the anomalies that
were possible. In Burnley, at the 1922 elections, for instance, 10,000
Labour votes won one seat, whereas 13,000 Tory and Liberal votes won
nine seats. In the same year in Plymouth, 11,000 Labour votes won one
seat, and 20,000 Tory votes won thirteen seats. In Bradford, in 1920,
Labour gained the most votes, 32,000, yet won no seats at all, while the
Tories gained the fewest votes, 29,000, but won twelve seats, and the Liberals, with 30,000 votes, won eleven seats. In the metropolitan borough of
Islington, in 1922, 131,000 votes for the Municipal Reformers and 90,000
votes for Labour resulted in forty-nine seats for the former, while Labour
won only five. One case also showed that the anomalies of the system could
work in Labour's favour. In Hackney, in 1919, the vote was split three ways:
Labour gained 50,000 votes, the Progressives and Municipal Reformers
49,000 each. This resulted in Labour winning thirty-two seats, the Municipal Reformers fifteen, and the Progressives thirteen.[85] A Scottish example
from a contemporary source was Glasgow in 1933, where Labour won
less than one-third of the votes and yet secured 60 per cent of the seats
contested.[86] Whether this case has any relevance to the comparison by
Joan Smith between the Liverpool and Glasgow labour movements
remains unclear without further detailed study, but it certainly suggests
that Labour's better showing in Glasgow may have had something to do
with differences in the electoral system. All these examples help to confirm
that the municipal electoral system could produce major distortions,
and that those distortions varied widely from one borough to another
according to local circumstances.

The municipal election system and Liverpool Labour

The main point of this chapter has been to identify elements of the electoral system at the municipal level which seemed to work against Labour's
interest locally. It appears that Labour's poor performance in gaining seats
on the local council, which has been cited as evidence of its weakness in
Liverpool in this period, was in part caused by the anomalies of the

135

electoral system itself. If the aldermanic system had not operated, or at least if it had been operated on a proportional basis, if ward boundaries had been revised more thoroughly to take account of population movement, and if the municipal franchise had not been distorted by the persistence of the principle of ratepayers having the right to decide local affairs, then the Labour Party would have had a stronger position on the local council.

However, it is not the intention of this analysis simply to make a counter-factual argument that Labour was actually strong in Liverpool in this period. As the rest of this book shows, there are other ways to demonstrate Labour's failure to become a successful party representing all sections of the working class in Liverpool. Nevertheless, the traditional story of abject failure by Labour has to be modified. No doubt the party was weaker in Liverpool than in many other comparable cities. That weakness, however, at the level of municipal politics, was much exaggerated by the vagaries of the electoral system. That, in turn, raises further questions: how was Labour's weakness in Liverpool reflected in parliamentary elections? To what extent was the Labour Party compliant, or even complicit, in the inequities of the system, and could it have done otherwise? Ultimately, might it not be the case that Labour's weakness in Liverpool was really confirmed by the party's failure to respond to the situation as adequately as in other parts of the country? These are the questions that are addressed in the following two chapters.

References

1. V. Bogdanor, *The People and the Party System: The Referendum and Electoral Reform in British Politics* (Cambridge University Press, Cambridge: 1981), pp. 177–8.
2. V. D. Lipman, *Local Government Areas, 1834–1945* (Blackwell, Oxford: 1949), pp. 167–8; B. Keith-Lucas and P. G. Richards, *A History of Local Government in the Twentieth Century* (George Allen and Unwin, London: 1978), p. 11.
3. Keith-Lucas and Richards, *A History of Local Government*, p. 12.
4. Approximately one-third of all bananas imported into Britain came through Liverpool between the wars, and most of them were landed at Garston Dock. See D. Caradog Jones, *The Social Survey of Merseyside, Vol. II* (Liverpool University Press, Liverpool: 1934), p. 69; G. C. Allen, F. E. Hyde, D. J. Morgan and W. J. Corlett, *The Import Trade of the Port of Liverpool: Future Prospects* (Liverpool University Press, Liverpool: 1946), p. 92.
5. LTCLP, *Elections and Organisation Sub-Committee Minutes* (25 August 1925).
6. 1911 census figures for Bootle and Garston.
7. M. McKenna, 'The suburbanization of the working-class population of

Liverpool between the wars', *Social History* 16 (1991), p. 186.

8.   M. McKenna, 'The Development of Suburban Council Housing Estates in Liverpool between the Wars' (unpublished Ph.D. thesis, University of Liverpool, 1986), pp. 362–3.

9.   Lipman, *Local Government Areas*, p. 181.

10. *Ibid.*, pp. 185–6.

11. *Liverpool Official Red Book* (1933), p. 97.

12. *Ibid.* (1930), p. 605.

13. P. J. Waller, *Democracy and Sectarianism: A Political and Social History of Liverpool, 1868–1939* (Liverpool University Press, Liverpool: 1981), pp. 135–6, 150, 160.

14. R. Baxter, 'The Liverpool Labour Party, 1918–1963' (unpublished D. Phil. thesis, University of Oxford, 1969), pp. 109–10.

15. W. Hampton, *Democracy and Community: A Study of Politics in Sheffield* (Oxford University Press, London: 1970), pp. 164–6.

16. Hampton, *Democracy and Community*, pp. 24–8.

17. *Liverpool Official Red Book* (1923), pp. 124–5; (1929), p. 594; (1935), p. 137.

18. Lipman, *Local Government Areas*, pp. 171–86.

19. *Liverpool Official Red Book* (1935), p. 137.

20. G. W. Jones, *Borough Politics: A Study of the Wolverhampton Borough Council, 1888–1964* (Macmillan, London: 1969), pp. 74, 359–62.

21. Hampton, *Democracy and Community*, pp. 313–14.

22. F. Carr, 'Municipal socialism: Labour's rise to power', in B. Lancaster and T. Mason (eds), *Life and Labour in a Twentieth Century City: The Experience of Coventry* (P. Cryfield, Coventry: 1986), p. 197.

23. S. Elliott, 'The Electoral System in Northern Ireland since 1920' (unpublished Ph.D. thesis, Queen's University, Belfast, 1971), pp. 75–383, 404–33.

24. Keith-Lucas and Richards, *A History of Local Government*, p. 23.

25. E. L. Hasluck, *Local Government in England* (Cambridge University Press, Cambridge: 1936), pp. 175–6; B. Keith-Lucas, *The English Local Government Franchise: A Short History* (Blackwell, Oxford: 1952), pp. 187–8.

26. Hasluck, *Local Government in England*, p. 176.

27. Keith-Lucas, *The English Local Government Franchise*, p. 189; Keith-Lucas and Richards, *A History of Local Government*, pp. 23, 24.

28. Hasluck, *Local Government in England*, p. 177.

29. Bogdanor, *The People and the Party System*, p. 43.

30. *Parliamentary Debates*, Vol. 281, cols. 766, 770 (14 November 1933).

31. *Liverpool Daily Post* (10 November 1925), p. 5.

32. Keith-Lucas and Richards, *A History of Local Government*, p. 23.

33. *Liverpool Official Red Book* (1926), p. 554.

34. LTCLP, *Executive Committee Minutes* (24 August 1924).

35. *Ibid.*

36. Labour defeated the Irish Party in St Anne's, Sandhills, Scotland North, and Scotland South wards, and only lost to them in Vauxhall. See Appendix IV.

37. *Liverpool Daily Post* (17 October 1925).

38. *Ibid.* (16 March 1925).

39. *Ibid.* (2 November 1925), p. 4; (3 November 1925), p. 5.

40. *Ibid.* (2 November 1925), p. 4.

41. Labour beat the Catholic Party in Sandhills, but lost to them in Great George, St Anne's, Scotland North and Scotland South. See Appendix IV.

42. *Liverpool Daily Post* (10 November 1925), p. 5.
43. *Ibid.*
44. LTCLP, *Labour Group Minutes* (16 August, 26 and 30 September 1929).
45. Centre Party candidates lost to Labour in Great George, St Anne's, Scotland South and Vauxhall wards, and only beat Labour in Exchange ward. See Appendix IV.
46. LTCLP, *Labour Group Minutes* (8 November 1929).
47. *Liverpool Official Red Book* (1933), pp. 580, 581; (1935), pp. 577, 579, 580; (1936), pp. 585, 586; (1937), p. 560.
48. *Ibid.* (1938), p. 517.
49. *Ibid.* (1934), p. 575.
50. Quoted in Waller, *Democracy and Sectarianism*, p. 340.
51. *Parliamentary Debates*, Vol.160, cols. 1462, 1472, (23 February 1923).
52. J. D. Marshall (ed.), *The History of Lancashire County Council, 1889 to 1974* (Martin Robertson, London: 1977), pp. 71, 201–4.
53. Keith-Lucas, *The English Local Government Franchise*, p. 189.
54. *Ibid.*, p. 190.
55. M. Savage, *The Dynamics of Working-Class Politics: The Labour Movement in Preston 1880–1940* (Cambridge University Press, Cambridge: 1987), pp. 162–3.
56. Jones, *Borough Politics*, p. 261.
57. *Ibid.*, p. 325.
58. *Ibid.*, p. 261.
59. *Ibid.*, pp. 360–1.
60. Keith-Lucas and Richards, *A History of Local Government*, p. 23; Hasluck, *Local Government in England*, p. 177.
61. Hasluck, *Local Government in England*, p. 177.
62. Keith-Lucas, *The English Local Government Franchise*, pp. 9–10.
63. *Ibid.*, pp. 190–1.
64. J. S. Rowett, 'The Labour Party and Local Government: Theory and Practice in the Inter-War Years' (unpublished D. Phil. thesis, University of Oxford, 1979), pp. 4–10; D. Tanner, *Political Change and the Labour Party, 1900–1918* (Cambridge University Press, Cambridge: 1990), pp. 99–129, 384–417.
65. Tanner, *Political Change and the Labour Party*, pp. 127, 413.
66. Hasluck, *Local Government in England*, p. 23.
67. Keith-Lucas, *The English Local Government Franchise*, pp. 9–10.
68. *Ibid.*, pp. 74–6.
69. Hasluck, *Local Government in England*, p. 22.
70. *Ibid.*, pp. 25–6; H. Finer, *English Local Government* (Methuen, London: 1933), p. 17.
71. Keith-Lucas, *The English Local Government Franchise*, p. 75; Finer, *English Local Government*, p. 17; Hasluck, *Local Government in England*, pp. 26–7.
72. H. Finer, *English Local Government*, p. 18.
73. A point noted in D. Tanner, 'Elections, statistics, and the rise of the Labour Party, 1906–1931', *Historical Journal* 34, no. 4 (1991), p. 899.
74. Hasluck, *Local Government in England*, p. 25.
75. N. Blewett, 'The franchise in the United Kingdom, 1885–1918', *Past and Present* 32 (1965), pp. 36–7.
76. Quoted in Blewett, 'The franchise in the United Kingdom', p. 36.

77. The full figures are:

	All excluded voters	Excluded voters with same surname as head of household
Polling district AE, Scotland North	435	206
Polling district FG, Netherfield	385	241
Polling districts MP and MQ, Little Woolton	766	560

78. The author is engaged in this fuller investigation at present.
79. Keith-Lucas, *The English Local Government Franchise*, p. 75; Finer, *English Local Government*, p. 17; Hasluck, *Local Government in England*, pp. 26–7.
80. See Keith-Lucas and Richards, *A History of Local Government*, p. 20; Hasluck, *Local Government in England*, p. 25–6; G. Alderman, *British Elections: Myth and Reality* (Batsford, London: 1978), pp. 21–2.
81. The slight difference between this figure and that given in Table 4.2 is due to the statistical complexity of the calculations used to construct Table 4.2. For details see Appendix IX.
82. 1931 census, Lancashire report, pp. 6, 114; *Liverpool Official Red Book* (1932), p. 98.
83. R. Simon, *Local Councils and the Citizen* (Stevens, London: 1948), pp. 17–18.
84. Hampton, *Democracy and Community*, pp. 313–14.
85. *Parliamentary Debates*, Vol.160, cols. 1472, 1462, 1430 (23 February 1923).
86. S. R. Daniels, *The Case for Electoral Reform* (Allen and Unwin, London: 1938), p. 107.

5 The scale of Labour's failure: parliamentary elections

Elections at the parliamentary level provide another way to assess the scale of Labour's failure in Liverpool. The brief summary provided earlier suggested once again that Labour's performance in Liverpool was not impressive in this period. It is easier to show how accurate this picture is, simply because there were far fewer parliamentary elections than at the municipal level. At the same time, this limits the usefulness of these results in providing indications of political allegiances locally. The longer gaps between elections and the much larger size of constituencies gives a less detailed analysis. The parliamentary results are also useful, however, in providing a comparison with the municipal level, which may help to sustain the arguments of the previous chapter. There were significant differences between the process of boundary revision, the franchise, and other institutional factors in the two electoral systems. Generally, these differences meant that Labour was probably less disadvantaged at the parliamentary level. Comparing the two may confirm this expectation.

A full record of all parliamentary election results in every division in Liverpool between 1918 and 1939 can be found in Appendix X. A summary of Labour and Tory performances in terms of seats won can be found in Table 5.1 which, at first sight, again seems to show that Labour's performance in Liverpool was poor. Apart from 1929 – the high point for Labour nationally in this period – the overwhelming majority of Liverpool seats were won by the Tories in inter-war general elections. Both 1918 and 1922 saw almost total Tory dominance, with Labour failing to win a single seat. Only the unopposed Nationalist, T. P. O'Connor, in Scotland division, prevented a clean sweep for the Tories. In 1923 Labour hung on to its first seat won at a by-election nine months previously in Edge Hill, but the Tory stranglehold was more noticeably affected by two rather unexpected Liberal gains in Wavertree and West Derby. Labour doubled its representation in 1924, but the Tories still increased their seats by winning back Wavertree and West Derby from the Liberals. Even at their lowest point in 1929 the Tories still won six of the eleven seats in the city, compared to Labour's best performance of four. Two years later the débâcle of the Labour cabinet split led to the party being almost entirely wiped out in Liverpool at the subsequent election, only Scotland Division being retained. Finally, in 1935, Labour raised its representation to three seats

Table 5.1 Seats won by Labour and Tories in Liverpool at general elections, 1918–1935*

Election	Seats contested	Seats won	Total seats
Labour			
Dec. 1918	7 (1)	0	11
Nov. 1922	6 (1)	0 (1)	11
Dec. 1923	4 (1)	1 (1)	11
Oct. 1924	9	2	11
May 1929	10 (3)	4 (1)	11
Oct. 1931	10 (3)	1 (2)	11
Nov. 1935	10	3	11
Tory			
Dec. 1918	10 (1)	10 (0)	11
Nov. 1922	10 (1)	10 (−1)	11
Dec. 1923	10 (1)	7 (−1)	11
Oct. 1924	10	8	11
May 1929	10 (2)	6 (0)	11
Oct. 1931	11 (4)	10 (−2)	11
Nov. 1935	11	8	11

* Figures in brackets show net gains or losses in by-elections between general elections.

Source: *Liverpool Official Red Books* (1919–39).

compared to the Tory Party's eight. Labour had clearly established itself as the main opposition party in Liverpool, but the Tories were still dominant.

This initial picture of Labour failure has to be revised to some extent when the parliamentary electoral results are analysed in greater detail. First of all, it is important to stress, that if by-election results are taken into account, then Labour's record appears rather more impressive. Overall, Labour won five out of the nine by-elections that it contested between the wars. The Labour victories in Edge Hill in March 1923, West Toxteth in May 1924, Scotland division in December 1929, Wavertree in February 1935, and West Toxteth again in July 1935, all boosted Labour's representation significantly. Davie Logan's unopposed inheritance of T. P. O'Connor's old seat at the very end of the 1920s represented Labour's real high point, for, at this time, Labour held five Liverpool seats compared to the Tory Party's six, a position it maintained until the disaster of October 1931. Before the next general election in 1935 two seats had been won back again, and it was surprising that further gains were not made in 1935, given the apparent trend shown in the by-elections of the early part of the year.

THE TORY LAMENT.

Sir Archie lifted up his voice and cried with might and main,
Why can't the safe and happy days come back to me again,
Oh! we have served you years and years, yea we have served you long,
So pray have patience with us yet and listen to our song.

We were a merry Party in the good old days of yore,
And never did we ever think those days we would deplore,
And never did we ever think that grief would lay us low,
When we entered on the battle, where the Edge Hill Breezes Blow.

Oh, once we were a merry band with all our seats complete,
The ten of us felt very safe until we got cold feet,
And never did we ever think that TEN could fall to NINE
Till Jack Hayes came and slaughtered us, but we did not repine.

But Hayes came here and stayed awhile, and wasn't satisfied,
He brought a little brother, so his number multiplied,
For Gibbins was the brother's name, and it was very sad
When Gibbins said " I'm lonely, and we'll have another lad."

Now " Mercer " was this brother's name, turns out to be a girl,
And consequently dangerous, it made our sleek hair curl,
With Mercer there came three or four, or five or six or seven,
And naught was left for us to do but ready get for heaven.

So now we stand as soldiers stand, our backs against the wall,
And being thus without a fuss, we know we cannot fall,
No longer fear we Labour, that Party Red and New,
Unless they come with Ramsay's gun, and then they'll push us through.

VOTE FOR JACK HAYES
THE LABOUR CANDIDATE.

Printed and Published by The Sutherland Printing Service Liverpool.

6 Labour Party leaflet, October 1924 general election, Edge Hill division. The optimism of the verse was not borne out by the results; Mrs Mercer lost in Fairfield, and six other Labour candidates were defeated, although Jack Hayes and (Joseph) Gibbins retained their seats – Sir Archie (Salvidge) did not need to lament so much after all.

The disappointment of 1935, though, illustrates two significant points about the parliamentary record. First, by-elections in this period, just as much as in the post-war years, were often poor indicators of longer-term trends in electoral support. The opportunity for voters to register a protest vote against the government of the day which may not be repeated at a general election was one factor which made by-elections rather unpredictable. Another was the appearance of party rebels at by-elections who might split the vote. Randolph Churchill's candidature in Wavertree in February 1935 was a classic case. Standing as an Independent Conservative as a protest both against the national government's policy on India and the machinations of the local party caucus, he split the vote so successfully that the Labour candidate, J. J. Cleary, was elected with only 35 per cent of the vote. The following November, by which time Churchill had been reconciled with the Tory Party to the extent that he was the official candidate in West Toxteth, Cleary increased his share of the vote to 41 per cent, but still lost comfortably in a straight fight.[1]

Second, the failure of the 1935 general election results to live up to the expectations raised by the preceding local elections and by-elections in

Liverpool was a reflection of the national experience.[2] This was generally the case throughout this period, in the sense that Labour's record in Liverpool did not significantly depart from the national trends. Perhaps the failure to win a seat in 1918 and 1922 showed a slight lag behind the national gains, especially those of 1922, but the pattern thereafter is unexceptional. Moderate gains in 1923, substantial improvement in 1929, collapse in 1931, and moderate, if in the end disappointing, recovery by 1935 describe the national picture for Labour as well as the local scene in these years. This is not to suggest that Labour was particularly strong in Liverpool in parliamentary elections. Nevertheless, it is the case that the supposed exceptionalism of Liverpool that was so often remarked upon in municipal politics was not so evident at the parliamentary level.

This impression of a slight divergence between the municipal and the parliamentary experience in Liverpool was much more clearly expressed in the post-1945 period. This lies beyond the ambit of this particular study, but it is worth noting that the 1945 general election saw Labour take eight of the eleven Liverpool seats, and yet in the subsequent municipal elections the party only increased its representation on the council from the 24 per cent of 1938 to 33 per cent. However, even confining the analysis to the inter-war period, there are other indications of this divergence. This is particularly the case in the mid-1920s, when Labour's first parliamentary seats were won at a time when its fortunes were never lower on the council. In 1922, Labour won only one seat in the November municipal elections, and in 1923 it failed to win any. Yet the party took Edge Hill division in March 1923 in a straight fight with the Tories and held it again in December. It also lost West Toxteth in the December general election by only 139 votes and then took the seat at the by-election the following May. A comparison with the results in the wards that made up these two constituencies makes these victories seem even more surprising.

Edge Hill division comprised Edge Hill ward, part of Kensington and Low Hill, so the comparison is not perfect, but nevertheless the general picture is clear. In November 1922, four months before the parliamentary by-election, Labour lost sitting councillors in all three of these wards, picking up 38 per cent, 31 per cent and 27 per cent of the vote respectively. Having won the parliamentary seat with 53 per cent of the vote, it again lost all three wards in November 1923, with 46 per cent, 41 per cent and 36 per cent of the vote. The parliamentary seat was then retained a month later with 57 per cent of the vote, and again in October 1924 with 53 per cent, but in the November 1924 local elections only Edge Hill ward was won back by the narrowest of margins.

West Toxteth was made up of Brunswick, Dingle and Prince's Park wards. In November 1923 Labour got a derisory 4 per cent of the vote in Brunswick against an Irish Party candidate, 42 per cent in Dingle, and put up no candidate in Prince's Park. A by-election took place only three weeks later in Prince's Park, but Labour could win only 30 per cent of the vote. In the December general election Joseph Gibbins just failed to win the division, and then took it in the May 1924 by-election with 54 per cent, and held it again in October with 51 per cent. In a by-election in Dingle in July, Labour again failed to win the ward and, finally, in November, won Brunswick comfortably, but received only 38 per cent of the vote in Dingle and put up no candidate in Prince's Park.

Parliamentary and municipal politics in these two constituencies at this point seemed to be operating almost independently of each other. Moreover, at the parliamentary level, Labour seemed to be performing much more impressively. There are two possible explanations. On the one hand, it is possible that local and national politics were fought out over very different issues, so that many voters who might have supported Labour as a national party might not have voted for it as an expression of local politics. To some extent this is bound to have applied to some voters, but in Liverpool there were special reasons why this might have been the case.

The familiar explanation of the importance of religious sectarianism in the local working class was the key point. Sectarianism may have been a very real political force in local, municipal elections, but when it came to national politics it may have been far less significant. A Protestant voter in the predominantly Protestant Dingle ward might have cast what he or she perceived as an anti-Catholic vote for the Tories in November 1923, yet in December voted for Labour in a general election that had no significant sectarian overtones. A Catholic in Brunswick might equally have voted for the Irish candidate as a display of communal solidarity in November, but for Labour against the Tories in the subsequent general election. The Brunswick municipal elections are particularly suggestive of this explanation. When Labour stood against the Irish Party in 1923 they won only 4 per cent of the votes. One year later, after a *rapprochement* with some sections of the Irish Party, and with a candidate, Luke Hogan, who was a well-known figure in the Catholic community, Labour gained 69 per cent of the vote against the Tories. Clearly, religion was an important factor at this local level. Whether this alone explains the differences between local and parliamentary voting patterns is difficult to assess, but it will be considered again later in this study.

At this stage, though, one other possibility needs to be explored, namely that differences in the electoral systems at the municipal and parliamentary level might have been a factor. Of the three major features of the municipal system that were identified in the last chapter as possible sources of bias against Labour, two at least can be largely discounted as a factor at the parliamentary level. The aldermanic system was confined to the municipal arena. It might be argued that the House of Lords played a similar role in a symbolic sense at the national level. The debate in Parliament over the inclusion of aldermen in the municipal boroughs in 1835 certainly showed that as far as the Lords themselves were concerned the two institutions were intimately connected. The mover of the amendment to retain aldermen, Lord Lyndhurst, saw the original bill for directly elected councils as threatening not only the boroughs themselves, but also the established

145

church and the hereditary peerage. Another Tory, Lord Wharncliffe, spelt out this threat more clearly:

> He confessed that he felt the more anxious with respect to the amend-ment when he remembered the degree in which adoption or rejection might affect the principle of aristocracy throughout the kingdom, for if it were determined that a body of aldermen or life members were un-necessary to a corporation, hereditary members of the House of Lords would be deemed equally unnecessary. The Clause, as it stood, went to the root of aristocracy, and went to the destruction of all that hitherto formed a check upon the democratic principle.[3]

Whatever the symbolic similarities, however, the House of Lords was at least formally distinct from the electoral process itself, and anyway quite divorced from any local influence or control.

The problem of exclusions from the franchise was also irrelevant at the parliamentary level once women were put on the same footing as men in 1928, as the franchise had by then been extended to all citizens. If the ex-clusion of young women between 1918 and 1928 worked against Labour's interest – a factor that will be considered later – then it was something that equally affected the municipal and parliamentary franchise, and can also be discounted at this point as a source of difference at the two levels. Only the inclusion of plural voters was a definite source of bias against Labour in the parliamentary franchise, and even then it was almost cer-tainly much dissipated given the much greater size of divisions.

It was only the third factor, the question of boundaries, that was still potentially a source of disadvantage to Labour at the parliamentary level, but even this problem becomes subsumed by the much wider question of the plurality system itself over the whole country. The control of divisional boundaries was not, of course, a purely local issue, nor was Liverpool, as an entity, in any way represented in Parliament. Therefore, the boundaries question, inasmuch as it affected a specific locality like Liverpool, was almost a random factor that could cut both ways. In fact it may be the case that, overall, this factor could have worked in Labour's favour in Liverpool for at least some of the inter-war period. By the end of the 1930s rapid pop-ulation movement within the city meant that many of Labour's strongest parliamentary divisions, which tended to be those nearest the city centre, had significantly smaller electorates than the Tory-dominated divisions in the suburbs. The Labour Party's strongest five divisions, all of which it held in 1930, had become the smallest by 1938. Edge Hill (35,000), Everton (28,000), Kirkdale (36,000), Scotland (33,000) and West Toxteth (41,000) had a combined electorate in 1938 of 175,000, an average of 35,000 per division. By contrast, the other six divisions of Exchange (41,000), East Toxteth (52,000), Fairfield (47,000), Walton (58,000), Wavertree (68,000) and West Derby (59,000), all of which were Tory strongholds, had a combined electorate of 328,000, an average of almost 55,000 per division.[4]

The Labour Party was quite aware of the advantage the divisional boundaries in Liverpool gave them. When an inquiry into the local party was carried out by the National Executive Committee in 1939, the first problem that local leaders alerted them to was the following: 'There has been a large movement of population from the Central Parliamentary Divisions to the outlying constituencies ... It is claimed that Liverpool will lose at least one seat at the next re-distribution.'[5] The implication was that Labour would be the main loser from redistribution, as one of its stronger city-centre seats would go. The fact that there were no general elections in the late 1930s meant that this in-built boundary advantage to Labour was not tested. However, it was certainly part of the explanation of the sweeping gains in 1945, by which time the population movement between divisions had been further intensified, but redistribution had still not taken place. By then, Scotland division was down to 21,000 voters and Everton to 22,000, while West Derby had 59,000, Walton 60,000 and Wavertree 72,000.[6]

It needs to be stressed again, however, that this problem could only be fully analysed at the national level. Any advantage to Labour in Liverpool may well have been counter-balanced by Tory advantage elsewhere. It is certainly the case, though, that, at the national level, Labour began to be increasingly a beneficiary of the electoral system once it replaced the Liberals as the second major party. The tendency of the plurality system to squeeze out third parties ensured that. Moreover, it is precisely in the inter-war period that population movements away from the traditional urban industrial centres meant that, for the first time since 1832, unreformed parliamentary boundaries might actually benefit urban rather than rural areas. This in turn was most likely to benefit the Labour Party at a national level.

It is the case, then, that Labour was less disadvantaged by the electoral system at the parliamentary level than at the municipal, first, because the aldermanic system did not apply; second, because any boundary distortion increasingly moved in its favour by the 1930s, although the scarcity of general elections after 1931 meant there was little chance for this to be manifested; and third, perhaps, because of the wider parliamentary franchise, although there is little hard evidence to support this supposition. Whether this all helps to explain the apparent divergence in Labour's performance at these two levels in Liverpool is again hard to quantify, but some further analysis of the two systems is still possible. A comparison of votes and seats similar to that done for municipal results earlier can also be constructed for the parliamentary results. This is shown in Figures 5.1 and 5.2 and appears to show a disparity between votes and seats for the two main parties, rather similar to that shown for municipal elections earlier. Labour seems to be generally under-represented, and the Tories generally over-represented, although perhaps not so dramatically as in the municipal sphere. The disparity also seems to decline by the late 1920s. If the analysis were to be taken into the post-war period then the trend in favour of

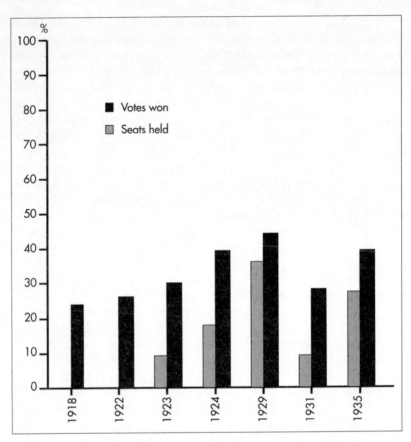

%

Figure 5.1 Labour seats and votes won at general elections in Liverpool, 1918–1935

Labour would become much clearer. In 1945 Labour won eight out of eleven seats in Liverpool with 47 per cent of the votes cast, while the Tories won only three seats with 44 per cent of the votes cast.[7]

However, it would be unwise to read too much into these figures for the inter-war period, as there are sound reasons for suggesting that the parliamentary figures for the share of the vote won are far less reliable as a real indicator of party support than their municipal counterparts. This is due to the fact that there were proportionally far fewer straight fights between the two main parties at general elections. Uncontested seats, and contests where three or more parties stood, were far more common, a state of affairs which is shown in Table 5.2.

The various different types of contests that took place at general elections, in varying proportions each time, meant that the share of the vote won by the two main parties was subject to all sorts of influences. For example, the four uncontested Tory wins in 1923 meant that their share

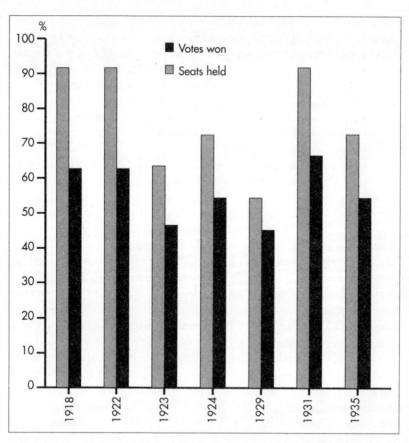

Figure 5.2 Tory seats and votes won at general elections in Liverpool, 1918–1935

Table 5.2 Types of electoral contests at general elections in Liverpool, 1918–1935

Election	Straight fights Tory/Labour	Other straight fights	Uncontested seats	Three or more candidates	Total seats
1918	5	2	2	2	11
1922	6	2	3	—	11
1923	3	2	5	1	11
1924	5	—	2	4	11
1929	5	—	1	5	11
1931	7	1	—	3	11
1935	8	1	—	2	11

of the vote overall was seriously depressed. On the other hand, Labour's decision to contest only four seats in 1923 meant that their vote would also have been depressed to some degree. Equally, the decision by the Liberals to contest no seats in 1922, compared with five in 1929, would have had incalculable effects on the vote-share of the two main parties. Unlike municipal elections, where three-way contests were relatively rare, and the regularity of elections meant that reasonable estimates can be made of the vote-share in uncontested seats, the comparable figures for parliamentary contests are highly unreliable.

However, it is also possible to investigate the relationship between the two types of electoral system in a way which isolates many of the imponderable elements. This can be done by comparing the voting figures in local elections for the combined wards which made up constituencies, with the figures in parliamentary elections for the same constituencies around the same time. The example above of the parliamentary and municipal votes in the West Toxteth and Edge Hill divisions in the 1923–4 period was used in an illustrative way, but such an approach can be applied in a more systematic fashion. Differences in parliamentary and municipal boundaries, and uncontested wards, mean that these comparisons cannot be made in all cases, but where they are possible they have been calculated in Appendix XI; a summary of the Labour vote is shown in Table 5.3. It would be difficult to claim too much for these comparisons, as the difference in dates between local and national elections, however small in many cases in this period, may still have been significant. This is most obvious in the largest difference, between the December 1918 general election and the November 1919 local elections. The much larger Labour vote at a local level eleven months after the national poll was almost certainly a reflection of rapidly growing Labour support in that tumultuous year.[8] But even where the time-lag was much smaller, it may still have been significant. The factor of third parties entering in to some of the elections also makes it difficult to read off straightforward conclusions from these comparisons.

However, there are several important points that can be made about these figures. First, there was no consistent pattern in the relationship between local and national voting trends. At times, such as 1923, the parliamentary vote for Labour was consistently higher than the local vote. At others, such as 1935, the opposite was true. At others again, such as 1931, the parliamentary vote was higher in some divisions, and lower in others. This may seem rather an indeterminate conclusion, but in fact it is of some importance.

Given that, in terms of the electoral system, the only difference that could be reflected in these comparisons is that between the municipal and parliamentary franchise, it suggests that the franchise factor was not so important as to skew decisively and consistently the voting patterns one way or the other. This in turn means that the other main factors disadvantaging Labour in the municipal electoral system, the aldermanic

Table 5.3 Labour vote in parliamentary and municipal elections compared, 1918–1935 (share of vote in %)

Elections	Division	Parliamentary vote (1)	Municipal vote (2)	(1) as % of (2)
Dec. 1918 (P)/	Kirkdale	33	47	70
Nov. 1919 (M)	Walton	29	42	69
	West Derby	33	44	75
Nov. 1922 (P)/	Everton	39	41	95
Nov. 1922 (M)	West Derby	30	26	115
Dec. 1923 (P)/	Everton	46	22	209
Nov. 1923 (M)	West Toxteth	50	30	167
Oct. 1924 (P)/	Everton	48	58	83
Nov. 1924 (M)	Kirkdale	39	35	111
	West Derby	30	23	130
May 1929 (P)/	Everton	53	58	91
Nov. 1929 (M)	Kirkdale	51	49	104
	Walton	42	49	86
	Wavertree	32	43	74
	West Derby	36	41	88
	West Toxteth	55	58	95
Oct. 1931 (P)/	Everton	31	46	67
Nov. 1931 (M)	Kirkdale	30	29	103
	Walton	26	25	104
	West Toxteth	42	44	95
Nov. 1935 (P)/	Everton	50	57	88
Nov. 1935 (M)	Kirkdale	37	51	73
	Walton	38	39	97

system and the boundaries question, must be viewed as relatively more important in explaining the inherent bias against Labour at that level.

Another implication is that it also does not appear to be the case that specific local political factors, such as the importance of religious sectarianism in Liverpool, were so strong or so permanent as to skew the figures in a consistent fashion. If sectarianism did affect voting behaviour at a local level, then its effects were mediated by a number of other factors. One other point is much more clear-cut. The turn-out at municipal elections was consistently and substantially lower than at general elections, a pattern which is consistent with later post-war trends. For the inter-war period, given the smaller franchise that then pertained for local elections, it meant that a far smaller number of voters decided elections at a municipal than at a parliamentary level. For example, in all three divisions where a direct comparison was possible in 1935, at least twice as many people voted in the general election of that year as in the local elections. In the most extreme case – Walton – over 36,000 votes were cast at the general election, but only 16,000 in the local elections two weeks earlier. What this again implies is that the municipal electoral system in Liverpool in this period was an imperfect way of reflecting political allegiances, as only a small proportion of those of voting age actually voted. Any sweeping conclusions drawn from its results have to be questioned. If the conventional wisdom for post-1945 politics, i.e. that low turn-out generally hurts Labour more than the Tories, applied to this period as well, then again the implication would be that municipal election results would tend to underestimate Labour's real level of support.

In conclusion, then, the analysis of parliamentary election results confirms Labour's weakness in Liverpool between the wars, but at the same time suggests that institutional factors were less important in disadvantaging Labour than at the municipal level. This still leaves the question of how adequate Labour's response was to the whole problem of the inequities of the electoral system. Chapter Six will take up this question in detail.

References

1. P. J. Waller, *Democracy and Sectarianism: A Political and Social History of Liverpool, 1868–1939* (Liverpool University Press, Liverpool: 1981), pp. 335–9.
2. J. Stevenson and C. Cook, *The Slump: Society and Politics During the Depression* (Jonathan Cape, London: 1977), pp. 245–60.
3. Quoted in B. Keith-Lucas, *The English Local Government Franchise: A Short History* (Blackwell, Oxford: 1952), p. 187.
4. *Liverpool Official Red Book* (1939), p. 97.
5. LTCLP, *Minutes*, notes of NEC Inquiry, dated 22 February 1939.
6. *Liverpool Official Red Book* (1949), pp. 115–16.
7. *Ibid.*
8. C. Cook, *The Age of Alignment: Electoral Politics in Britain, 1922–1929* (Macmillan, London: 1975), p. 51.

6 The Labour Party and the electoral system

> ... the modern state in most civilized communities is democratic, and in spite of remaining anomalies and imperfections, if the mass of the ordinary people are agreed upon any policy neither electors, privileged peers nor reigning houses could stand in their way.
>
> (Ramsay MacDonald, 1905)[1]

> The clamour for a socialist party is a remnant of the revolutionary period, or a copying of methods proper to countries where parliamentary government is but a name. What is needed here is a party which accepts the socialist point of view and approaches the industrial problems of society with socialist assumptions in mind ... socialism is to come through a socialistic party, and not through a socialist one ... socialism will be retarded by a socialist party which thinks it can do better than a socialistic party, because its methods would be contrary to those by which society evolves.
>
> (Ramsay MacDonald, 1909)[2]

The words of Labour's first Prime Minister, quoted above, who by the 1920s 'exercised an awesome domination over his party',[3] have been used before by other writers to demonstrate the reformist, evolutionary philosophy of social change that guided the party from its inception. They are quoted here, though, to show how that philosophy also encouraged a tolerant attitude towards the whole system of governmental and political structures that the Labour Party found itself engaged in once it had committed itself to the 'representation of labour' through parliamentary means.

MacDonald was arguing for a distinctively British form of evolutionary socialism to work within a distinctively British, and superior, political system. Britain was evidently a 'civilized community', to be contrasted with other countries 'where parliamentary government was but a name'. Moreover, its superior political system guaranteed the eventual triumph of socialism, for, 'in spite of remaining anomalies and imperfections', the system in some mystical fashion would inevitably reflect the people's will. MacDonald, it should be noted, was writing at a time when the parliamentary franchise, through the exclusion of all women and a significant

153

proportion of mainly working-class men, included less than 30 per cent of the adult population, when parliamentary constituencies were so unequal that some were eight times larger than others,[4] and when an unelected assembly of hereditary peers could still effectively block legislation by the House of Commons, to name but some of the most obvious 'anomalies and imperfections'. Nevertheless, this 'democracy', constructed in piecemeal fashion in the nineteenth century by an entirely aristocratic and bourgeois parliament, was expected to allow the evolution of society towards socialism.

MacDonald's views had their antecedents even earlier in the origins of the Labour Party. A Fabian tract of 1896 stated:

> ... since England now possesses an elaborate democratic State machinery, graduated from the parish Council or Vestry up to the central Parliament, and elected under a franchise which enables the working-class vote to overwhelm all others, the opposition which exists in the Continental monarchies between the State and the people does not hamper English Socialists.[5]

The British Labour Party was influenced strongly by this reverential attitude to the political system, and for this reason constitutional and electoral reform has never been a major preoccupation of the party. This contrasts markedly with earlier working-class movements such as Chartism, whose main focus was on the reform of a corrupt and unjust political system as a precursor for economic and social change. For Labour, political reform was complete, and economic and social change would follow inevitably. This uncritical attitude toward the political system explains why Labour in office has never carried through any significant measure of political reform, while its main rivals have both instituted major reforms, most notably in 1911, 1918 and 1928.

It is also the case, though, that this generalized acceptance of the political system meant that municipal, as well as parliamentary, structures were uncritically treated by Labour. Labour groups in council-chambers throughout the country between the wars have been described as adhering to an ethos of 'Morrisonian aldermanic socialism'.[6] Herbert Morrison, the archetypal municipal socialist, defined his own attitude, and that of 'the great bulk of organised Labour', towards the local government system as one of 'democratic constitutionalism'. This was to be contrasted with 'Popularism', which he strongly opposed.[7] Thus, in the inter-war period, when some of the most obvious imperfections at the parliamentary level had been removed, but when the system of local government remained deeply flawed, Labour failed to mount any real challenge to this state of affairs. This chapter will show how Labour failed in this regard both at a national level and locally in Liverpool as well. More than that, it will demonstrate that the party became increasingly complicit in the very practices that disadvantaged it in Liverpool.

The Labour Party and the parliamentary electoral system

The quotations from MacDonald at the start of this chapter illustrated some of the dominant attitudes to electoral reform held by the leaders of the party. There were variations on this approach, however. Before 1914 there was some consideration of reform of the electoral system, particularly in the ranks of the ILP. At the founding conference of the ILP in Bradford in 1893, a general statement supporting 'every proposal for extending electoral rights and democratising the system of Government' was passed, and restated in the policy document drawn up in 1896–7. The vagueness of this commitment and the brevity of the discussion of it at the Bradford conference was indicative, though, of the low priority that the ILP placed on this issue. In 1904 'the immediate extension of the franchise to women on the same terms as granted to men' and the longer-term aim of full adult suffrage was added to the programme, along with other political reforms such as the second ballot electoral system and triennial parliaments.[8] At its 1911 conference the ILP voted in favour of proportional representation,[9] but of course the ILP was only one part of the Labour Party, and by no means the dominant one.

Within both the ILP and the Labour Party as a whole the leading figure in support of proportional representation in the years before the First World War was Philip Snowden. He suggested that PR would help the party to develop a more independent identity by encouraging it to put up candidates in as many constituencies as possible to maximize its vote.[10] This contrasted with the tactic under the plurality system of relying on electoral pacts with the Liberals. Nearly all the seats that Labour won before 1914 had been uncontested by the Liberals, in return for which Labour had stood down in favour of the Liberals in other constituencies.[11] Ultimately, though, Snowden lost the debate to MacDonald. As Bogdanor states:

> ... at its conference in 1914, the Labour Party decisively rejected proportional representation at the behest of the Party's chairman, Ramsay MacDonald, and in large part as a tribute to his personal authority over the movement. MacDonald's hostility to proportional representation derived from his conception of the future development of socialism which differed in important respects from that held by Snowden.[12]

MacDonald argued that, in the short term, Labour's interests were best served by working closely with other sympathetic parties in a Progressive Alliance, in much the same way that it had co-operated with the Liberals from 1903. PR would force the party to stand against the Liberals whenever possible, thus differentiating them more clearly and lessening the chances of co-operation. In the longer term, the inevitability of the growth of socialism would make Labour a major party, and thus the plurality system would work in its favour. Pragmatism, not principle, was the order of the day.[13]

When the peculiar circumstances of war-time coalition led to the first Speaker's Conference on electoral reform in 1916–7, and subsequent recommendations for proportional representation in borough constituencies, the alternative vote system in rural constituencies, and female suffrage, Labour was split. PR was supported at the 1918 party conference, but in the series of votes in Parliament, a small majority of Labour MPs in favour of PR in the first three votes between June and November 1917 was replaced by a majority against in the votes of January and May 1918.[14]

As the plurality system began to be seen to benefit Labour at the expense of the Liberals in the course of the 1920s, so Labour's attitude towards PR began to harden. When a private member's bill in favour of PR was put forward in May 1924, Labour MPs voted by a margin of 90 to 28 against it.[15] The distortions of the three-party system at the parliamentary level up to 1929 produced an exaggeration of Labour's real strength, especially in relation to the Liberals.[16] The 1929 election saw Labour gain 37 per cent of the vote, but 47 per cent of the seats – and power – while the Liberals, with 23 per cent of the vote, gained only 10 per cent of the seats. A pragmatic complicity in the inequity of the system was adopted, although the danger of this pragmatism was revealed in 1931, when a 30 per cent poll for Labour gave it only 8 per cent of seats, and to a lesser extent in 1935. But by then the die was cast. MacDonald, in a spirit of seeking to reduce party conflict that was a precursor of his later coalitionism, set up a committee to look at electoral reform in 1929. Any form of proportional representation was ruled out by Labour, though, and a bill to introduce the far less radical alternative vote system eventually foundered on the rocks of opposition from the House of Lords. Before it could be refloated, the 1931 crisis intervened, and Labour was condemned to political impotence for the rest of the decade.[17]

The Labour Party and the municipal electoral system

As far as local government was concerned, the Labour Party's attitude nationally to the manifest defects of the system was a mixture of complacency and cynicism. In the early 1920s resolutions in favour of equalizing the parliamentary and municipal franchises were put to the Annual Conference, and the parliamentary party raised the issue in the Commons in 1921 and 1924. From the mid-1920s onwards, however, the issue faded as a serious concern for Labour, and disappeared from view entirely after 1931.[18] When the exclusions from the municipal franchise were eventually abolished in the 1945 Representation of the People Act, it was due to a fortuitous accident of wartime conditions. Local government elections were suspended in 1939, and the annual registration of voters was also abandoned. At the same time a National Register was compiled for conscription purposes. In 1943 it was decided that parliamentary by-elections, which still took place, should be based on this National Register, as the old electoral rolls had become outdated, a process hastened by the effects of bombing, conscription and evacuation. It was decided in 1944 that, when local elections were to be resumed, initially they would also be based on this National Register until a new register could be prepared in the customary way. Once the principle of a common electoral roll had been established in this accidental way, it was a short step to formalizing it in the 1945 Act, and eight million new voters were added to the municipal lists.[19] Significantly, though, the Act of 1945 did not apply to Northern Ireland, and the situation was to remain unchanged there until as late as 1968.[20]

This still left plural voting intact at both levels, though. Despite having an overall majority of well over a hundred seats in the Commons, when the Labour government eventually acted to abolish the business vote in 1948 it bowed to opposition pressure and retained it for local elections. As Keith-Lucas observed:

> The simple principle of 'one man [sic], one vote' was thus applied only to Parliament, and the Labour Government, in retaining the property qualification for local government purposes, roused strong opposition from its own followers, but gained the support of many members of the Conservative Party.[21]

It was not until 1969 that a later Labour administration finally abolished plural voting for local government elections.[22]

Labour's attitude to the aldermanic system was, if anything, even more cynical. When a proposal to abolish it was raised in Parliament in 1933, it was supported by individual MPs, but only thirty-four votes were cast in its favour and the motion was overwhelmingly lost.[23] Benign indifference turned to blatant abuse when Labour began to gain control of councils, and by the post-war years it was the Labour Party which increasingly stood accused of manipulating the system to its advantage. At their 1961 Conference it was the Tories who moved to abolish the system, followed by the Maud Commission in 1966, and it finally went in the 1972 Local Government Bill.[24]

Much the same pattern can be seen in Labour's attitude to other aspects of the municipal system. When PR was proposed for local government in 1923, Labour was divided over the issue, with notable figures such as George Lansbury voting against.[25] As far as boundary revisions were concerned, Labour was content to go along with the elaborate system evolved by 1929 which was so dependent on local initiative and ministerial response. Labour did nothing to alter the system in 1945, and it was not until 1972 that an independent Local Government Boundary Commission was set up to ensure that boundaries were fairly redrawn.[26]

Labour's record, then, on reform of the electoral system was uninspiring in the inter-war years and later. This is perhaps not surprising, given the political philosophy that informed Labour, and also the fact that at both parliamentary and local levels the party was increasingly advantaged by the system by the 1920s. However, in Liverpool, where at the municipal level at least Labour was clearly disadvantaged, opposition to the system was clearly in the party's interest. Such opposition, however, was limited.

The Liverpool Labour Party and the electoral system

What is striking about municipal politics in Liverpool between the wars is that the Labour Party seems hardly to have appreciated the contribution that the distortions of the electoral system may have made to its poor performance. Religious sectarianism was always the first excuse that Labour leaders turned to when faced with electoral disappointment, to the extent that they seemed blinded to any other possible reason.

The question of the equity of ward boundaries and the new wards added to the borough between the wars seems never to have been discussed formally within the party, nor was it ever raised in the council-chamber by Labour or considered for inclusion in the municipal election programme. As already noted, when the possibility of reconsidering ward boundaries and amalgamating with surrounding boroughs was raised in the council in 1929, Labour opposed the proposal.[27] Labour's acquiescence in the existing and unequal boundaries contrasts strongly with the earlier Tory campaign to force the Liberals into redistributing boundaries in 1893–4. Only in the early 1950s did Labour finally take up the issue. Proportional representation for municipal elections, which of course would have obviated any necessity to equalize ward size to achieve equity, was raised within the party in 1919. A resolution was passed that 'The National Labour Party be asked to support the principle of proportional representation for Municipal Elections, and to try to secure a clause to that effect being inserted in any legislation dealing with local Government elections.'[28] This was the first and last time that the issue was raised in the local party between the wars, however.

Nor was it the case that the issue of distortions of election results locally was ignored in public debate. After the 1925 elections the local press provided a detailed analysis of votes cast and seats won, and it was noted that the Tories had maintained their position in terms of seats, and yet were the only party that appeared to have shown a fall in their share of the vote.[29] This analysis was based on the average of votes won in seats actually contested by each party, which is rather different from the proportion of the total votes cast in all seats, as shown in Table 4.3 earlier. On that calculation, the Tory share of the vote actually increased from 43 to 46 per cent in 1925. Nevertheless, whether or not the *Daily Post*'s analysis was correct, the paper still remarked very pointedly that an apparent fall in Tory support did not translate into a loss of seats. However, nobody, including the Labour Party, appeared interested enough in this anomaly of the electoral system to follow it up subsequently.

The question of the municipal franchise was also totally ignored by

Labour in this period, and only the obvious manipulation of the aldermanic system by their opponents roused Labour to some protest. Luke Hogan's complaint at the election of P. J. Kelly to the aldermanic bench at the expense of W. A. Robinson in 1925 has already been noted, and there were further, less public attempts to press Labour's claims to fairer treatment. After Labour's successes in November 1929, for instance, there were negotiations with the Tory and Liberal leaders which resulted in seven Labour aldermen being elected.[30] In 1933 Luke Hogan was instructed by the Labour group to see the Tory leader about an aldermanic vacancy and to claim it for Labour, but to no avail in this case.[31] Again, in October 1936, after the repeated rejection of Labour's nominee, Lawrence King, Hogan proposed at a meeting of the Labour group to put forward a motion in the council complaining about the selection of aldermen.[32] In the end, no motion was put, but presumably Hogan successfully made his point in private to the other party leaders, as King was elected in January 1937, the first new Labour alderman for six years. However, it needs to be stressed that Labour never challenged the validity of the aldermanic system itself, and despite their back-stage attempts to get a fairer deal from their opponents, they remained consistently under-represented.

In fact, the Labour group on the council seemed far more concerned about selection procedures for the purely honorary position of Lord Mayor. Complaints that no Labour mayor had ever been selected were made consistently through the 1920s and early 1930s. Finally, in 1934, a deal was struck between the party leaders whereby Labour agreed to support the freedom of the city being given to the Tory leader, Sir Thomas White, and the Liberal shipping magnate, Sir Frederick Bowring, in return for which Labour's Sir James Sexton would also be granted the freedom and Fred Richardson would become the next mayor. Bessie Braddock and Sidney Silverman were outraged by this honouring of Labour's chief political enemy and the extravagantly wealthy Bowring, and broke ranks with the rest of the Labour group by voting against them.[33] For their pains they were both expelled from the group for a while, and Richardson was duly elected as mayor in November 1934. Luke Hogan spoke ringingly of his pride at this recognition of Labour's claim, as if this purely symbolic gesture was a great political triumph.[34]

Moreover, the whole question of aldermanic selection became far more an issue that revealed political division within the Labour Party than one used by Labour to condemn its political opponents. Dissension within the party started in October 1927, when Luke Hogan was elected to an aldermanic vacancy. He was the first new Labour aldermen since the débâcle over P. J. Kelly's election and W. A. Robinson's deselection in 1925 referred to in Chapter Four. However, Hogan was selected ahead of Robinson, by then back on the council and with ten years longer service. There was a great deal of criticism of the Labour group's action by the LTCLP, and eventually a resolution emanating from the ILP demanded that the principle of seniority be applied in future. This was accepted, but a further demand that aldermanic nominations should be approved by the full LTCLP was rejected by the group.[35] The issue rumbled on until March 1928 when the ILP councillor, Bob Tissyman, moved that Hogan's elevation be fully reconsidered and all correspondence relating to it made public. This was only averted by the calling of a special meeting on the general issue, which eventually restated the principle of seniority.[36]

But this was not the end of the affair. When a number of long-standing Centre Party councillors defected to Labour in 1929,[37] they immediately became the senior members of the Labour group and would have prior claim to aldermanic nomination over loyal councillors, who in many cases had been party members for years. This came to a head when Lawrence King was first nominated, on the basis of seniority, to a vacancy in May 1932.[38] An attempt to suspend the standing orders of the group, in order to block his nomination, failed, and the issue rumbled on again until 1935. At that year's AGM, the standing orders were amended so that only 'seniority of actual service in the Labour Party on the city council' should count, although a special clause was inserted to exempt King from this ruling.[39] Eight years of disputes between left and right, between the group and the LTCLP, and between Catholic and non-Catholic in the party had taken place over the issue. Eventually the principle of seniority for aldermanic nominations had been established within the party, but in the council-chamber Labour's opponents flouted the principle at will. Meanwhile Labour's under-representation on the aldermanic benches remained unchanged.

Labour's failure to take up the issue of the anomalies of the municipal electoral system in Liverpool was quite clear, then, but there is one final point to consider. For the various groups that made up the Liverpool party by the 1930s, their failure on this score was not surprising, precisely because in most cases their political priorities lay elsewhere.

As shown earlier in Chapter Two, by the 1930s there were three main groups that were allied within the Liverpool party. There was, first of all, the moderate wing associated with the Trades Council. To a great extent, this group reflected MacDonald's views on the electoral system quoted earlier. Its acceptance of all the trappings of the council-chamber was symbolized by Fred Richardson's elevation to the mayoralty in 1934. For this faction, Labour's time would come, and only the sectarian menace delayed it in Liverpool.

The second main group was the Catholic caucus on the Labour group. Its main political concern was with representing the interests of the Catholic community. As already indicated, it had succeeded in doing this quite well by working through the established political system over several decades, and continued to do so in the Labour Party in the 1930s. There was therefore no reason why this group should need to challenge a system within which it achieved its primary political aims.

The third main wing of the party was the left. That faction of it led by the Braddocks was far too busy campaigning outside the narrow

7 The Braddocks. Jack Braddock (2nd left), born in Hanley, member of the Communist Party until 1924; Labour councillor in Everton ward from 1929 and leading member of the left in the Labour Group throughout the 1930s; leader of the Labour Group from 1948; died 1963. Bessie Braddock (right), born in Liverpool, member of the Communist Party until 1924; Labour councillor in St Anne's ward from 1930 and also leading member of the left; MP for Liverpool Exchange division from 1945; died 1970.

framework of the council-chamber to be very much concerned with the equity of the electoral system. Its battle was to win active support within the working class itself, and at the same time to combat the right wing within the party. The municipal electoral system was probably very low down this group's list of political priorities.

The other main left-wing faction, led by the ILP, had a slightly different perspective however, and in fact was the only group within the party that had much interest at all in the justice of the political system itself. The Liverpool ILP was clearly on the left of the party, but also very clearly committed to fighting for socialism through the ballot box. It maintained a principled, but critical, commitment to the electoral system. Its leading figures, Bob Tissyman and Bob Edwards, were the most prominent councillors to object in principle to sharp practice in the council-chamber. As a result, they both frequently ended up disturbing the peace and decorum of the chamber. This sometimes resulted in their being expelled from the chamber when they refused to give way. Tissyman, the ex-police sergeant sacked for his part in the 1919 police strike, was escorted out by police constables on at least three occasions.[40]

It was the ILP that so assiduously followed up the question of the selection of aldermen within the party, as mentioned above. Both Edwards and Tissyman also consistently exposed the undemocratic elections decided behind closed doors, much to the disapproval of their fellow Labour colleagues. In October 1931, for instance, Tissyman proposed himself for an aldermanic vacancy in opposition to Sir Thomas White, and gained one vote.[41] Edwards proposed Tissyman for the Watch Committee in September 1930, only six months after Tissyman had shocked his own party by proposing a reduction of £10,000 in police expenses for the year. He got four votes.[42] In November 1930 Edwards proposed himself as mayor, but got no seconder from among Labour ranks.[43] Perhaps the protest that was most instructive about the nature of the left in Liverpool took place much earlier. In 1924, John Nield, elected as an Independent Labour councillor in St Anne's ward in 1922 even though he had recently declared himself to be a Communist, proposed Tissyman as Lord Mayor. He said Tissyman had every right to assume the post as 'he represented a section of the general public'. Someone shouted out 'what about yourself?', to which Nield replied 'I don't represent the public: I represent the working classes'. In the event there was no seconder for Tissyman.[44]

Tissyman and Edwards fought a lonely battle, then, but they were entirely unrepresentative of the rest of the party, and once outside the party they were soon ousted from the council. Any broader attack on the electoral system was not forthcoming from Labour. While not forgetting that it was their opponents, and most notably the controlling Tories, who operated the system in their favour with ruthless pragmatism, Labour's failure to respond adequately meant they were also partly guilty by default.

Concluding remarks on the significance of the electoral system

The analysis of the electoral system and its impact on Labour contained in the second part of this book can be summarized simply. While the Labour Party, both locally and nationally, was remiss in failing to tackle the imperfections of the electoral system, it is plainly the case that the system did disadvantage Labour to some degree in Liverpool. This fact, and the earlier demonstration of the weakness of the structure and organization of the local party, both go some way to explain the Labour Party's failure in Liverpool.

Nevertheless, other local parties were organizationally weak, and no doubt others also suffered to some degree from the vagaries of the electoral system, and yet many were still able to perform better than the Liverpool party. Whatever qualifications need to be made in the light of the new evidence presented in this book, it is still undeniable that Labour's record in Liverpool was unimpressive.

There is still a third major problem that needs to be explored if Labour's weakness in Liverpool is to be understood fully. That problem is the relationship between the Liverpool working class and the Labour Party. It is therefore necessary in the final part of this book to turn to the social characteristics of the working-class voters of Liverpool, and their political allegiances.

References

1. Quoted in R. Miliband, *Parliamentary Socialism: A Study in the Politics of Labour* (2nd edn, Merlin Press, London: 1972) pp. 18–19.
2. Miliband, *Parliamentary Socialism*, p. 31.
3. D. Howell, *British Social Democracy: A Study in Development and Decay* (Croom Helm, London: 1976), p. 18.
4. N. Blewett, 'The franchise in the United Kingdom, 1885–1918', *Past and Present* 32 (1965), p. 27.
5. Quoted in R. Miliband, *Capitalist Democracy in Britain* (Oxford University Press, Oxford: 1982), p. 23.
6. *Ibid.*, p. 143.
7. *Ibid.*, p. 144.
8. D. Howell, *British Workers and the Independent Labour Party, 1888–1906* (Manchester University Press, Manchester: 1983), pp. 297, 344.
9. V. Bogdanor, *The People and the Party System: The Referendum and Electoral Reform in British Politics* (Cambridge University Press, Cambridge: 1981), p. 122.
10. *Ibid.*, pp. 122–3.
11. Miliband, *Parliamentary Socialism*, pp. 21–3.
12. Bogdanor, *The People and the Party System*, pp. 123–4.
13. *Ibid.*, pp. 124–5.
14. *Ibid.*, pp. 126–31.
15. *Ibid.*, p. 134.
16. Howell, *British Social Democracy*, p. 25.
17. Bogdanor, *The People and the Party System*, pp. 138–9.
18. J. S. Rowett, 'The Labour Party and Local Government: Theory and Practice in the Inter-War Years' (unpublished D. Phil. thesis, University of Oxford: 1979), pp. 7–8.
19. B. Keith-Lucas, *The English Local Government Franchise: A Short History* (Oxford University Press, Oxford: 1952), pp. 76–7; B. Keith-Lucas and P. G. Richards, *A History of Local Government in the Twentieth Century* (George Allen and Unwin, London: 1978), pp. 19–20.
20. S. Elliott, 'The Electoral System in Northern Ireland Since 1920' (unpublished Ph.D. thesis, Queen's University, Belfast: 1971), p. 791.
21. Keith-Lucas, *The English Local Government Franchise*, p. 77.
22. Keith-Lucas and Richards, *A History of Local Government*, p. 20.
23. *Parliamentary Debates*, Vol. 281, cols. 765–774 (14 November 1933).
24. Keith-Lucas and Richards, *A History of Local Government*, p. 24.
25. *Parliamentary Debates*, Vol. 160, cols. 1429–1510 (23 February 1923).
26. Keith-Lucas and Richards, *A History of Local Government*, p. 2.
27. *Liverpool Official Red Book* (1930), p. 605.
28. Liverpool Labour Party, *Minutes* (5 February 1919).

29.   *Liverpool Daily Post* (4 November 1925), p. 5.
30.   LTCLP, *City Council Group Minutes* (8 November 1929); *Liverpool Official Red Book* (1930), p. 609.
31.   LTCLP, *Group Minutes* (5 November 1933).
32.   *Ibid.* (1 October 1936).
33.   *Liverpool Official Red Book* (1935), p. 581.
34.   *Ibid.* (1935), p. 584.
35.   LTCLP, *Group Minutes* (7 November 1927; 29 December 1927; 26 January 1928).
36.   *Ibid.* (2 March 1928, 26 April 1928).
37.   See Chapter four, p. 97.
38.   LTCLP, *Group Minutes* (28 May 1932).
39.   *Ibid., Group Minutes* (7 January 1935).
40.   *Liverpool Official Red Book* (1928), p. 602; (1929), p. 619; (1931), p. 581.
41.   *Ibid.* (1932), p. 580.
42.   *Ibid.* (1931), p. 585, 579.
43.   *Ibid.*, p. 587.
44.   *Ibid.* (1925), p. 587.

Part Three

The Labour Party and the Liverpool working class

Part Two

The Labour Party and the
Liverpool working class

7 The Labour Party and women[1]

The idea that gender is a social category which labour historians should be keenly aware of is hardly a new one. Almost two decades ago, for example, the argument was put as follows:

> We have made of sex a category as fundamental to our analysis of the social order as other classifications, such as class and race. And we consider the relation of the sexes, as those of class and race, to be socially rather than naturally constituted, to have its own development varying with changes in social organization. Embedded in and shaped by the social order, the relation of the sexes must be integral to any study of it.[2]

The extent to which gender has been generally accepted by historians as an integral part of explaining historical change is debatable. However, there is no doubt that it has become increasingly influential in labour history. Much excellent work has been done to show how gender relations have been of profound importance in shaping the process of class formation. It is significant, as well, that much of this writing has been in the form of local studies.[3] In a recent survey of trends in British labour history, Neville Kirk stressed 'the importance of issues of gender and neighbourhood to a full understanding of popular politics', and pointed to local studies to illustrate the point.[4]

This chapter is placed firmly in this historiographical context, in that it assumes that gender relations are integral to the understanding of working-class politics in Liverpool. The relationship between class and religion has already been much emphasized in studies of Liverpool, as indicated earlier in Chapter One.[5] The significance of gender has been much less studied, however.[6] To help to redress the balance, the relationship between the Liverpool Labour Party and women will be addressed here. As will become clear, gender was an important influence on the development of the local party.

Women in the Liverpool Labour Party

One possible way of examining the impact of issues of gender on the local party is to look at how women fared within the party itself and, conversely, at how much they were able to influence the party from within, either in terms of political practices or policies. The problems of examining these relationships are, however, extremely difficult, given the state of the existing records for the inter-war years. There are no surviving records of any women's section or any other constituent part of the Liverpool Labour Party specifically involving women. All that are available are the records of the central institutions of the local party which have been referred to throughout this book. Nevertheless, from these it is possible to piece together some picture of women's involvement.

From 1906 to 1918 women, nationally, had been organized separately in support of the party through the Women's Labour League.[7] Under the new Constitution of February 1918 they were absorbed into the party, and the formation of women's sections at a local level became a priority. In Liverpool, however, the development of a women's organization seems to have been a rather long-drawn-out affair. By September 1918 there was a Women's Association organizing public meetings over the issue of war pensions and allowances for soldiers' wives and dependents.[8] This body was organized well enough to have its secretary elected to the Executive Committee of the Party at its AGM in April 1919. Its candidate was nominated under the 'other affiliated organisations' section alongside the ILP, Fabians, and the Trades Council, so clearly it was perceived as a separate body at this time. It also seems to have withered away fairly quickly after this, and does not appear to be have been represented at the 1920 AGM.[9]

In April 1921 local reorganization came with the merger of the Trades Council and the Labour Party, and at its first Executive Committee meeting a Women's Subcommittee was established. However, the title of this subcommittee seems to have been rather a misnomer, as it consisted of three men and only one woman, and it was unable to find a delegate to represent the local divisional parties, suggesting that organization of women in the city was not well-advanced at this stage. In fact, the subcommittee seems to have collapsed fairly quickly, and did not re-appear at the next AGM in April 1922.[10] Eventually, in May 1922, a proposal came forward to form a Liverpool Women's Central Council, and it is from this date that women's organization within the party began to take shape. The inaugural meeting of the Women's Council consisted of thirty delegates from ward and divisional parties, and the formation of separate women's sections in the local wards was much encouraged.[11] By August 1923 six wards and one parliamentary division were recorded as having a women's section, and their subsequent development in Liverpool can be seen in the full list of ward women's sections between 1923 and 1939 in the tables contained in Appendix XII; the situation is summarized in Figures 7.1 and 7.2. As the tables show, separate women's sections were certainly not established throughout the whole of the city at any time in the inter-war period. In fact, at the height of their achievement in 1933, only twenty out of a total of forty wards were organized, and close analysis shows that only about a dozen wards had women's sections operating for most of the period.

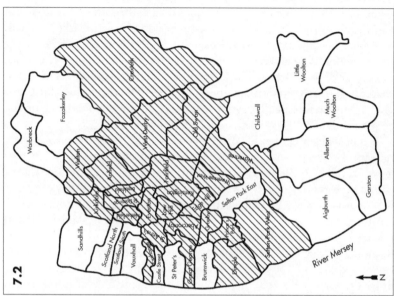

Figure 7.1 Labour Party wards with women's sections, August 1923–June 1930

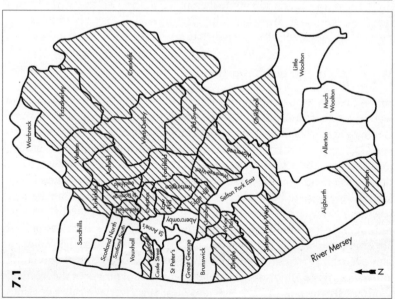

Figure 7.2 Labour Party wards with women's sections, January 1931–June 1939

Of the unorganized wards, many were in the suburbs like Aigburth, Allerton, Much and Little Woolton, and Warbreck, and others were in the city-centre areas such as Castle Street and St Peter's, which were packed with business voters. Most of these wards were so solidly anti-Labour that it is no surprise that the party had little organization there. What is more striking, however, is that in a number of working-class areas where Labour was extremely strong for at least the latter part of this period, women's organization was non-existent. These consisted of a swathe of dockside wards extending from the northern boundary of the city down as far as the Brunswick Dock – Sandhills, Scotland North and South, Vauxhall, Great George and Brunswick. These were the predominantly Catholic wards, which had become safe Labour seats in the 1920s when the Irish National-ist councillors who had represented them either switched their allegiance to Labour or were deposed by Labour opponents, as described in earlier chapters. It was the councillors from these areas who also formed the Cath-olic caucus led by Luke Hogan that dominated the Labour group on the council in the 1930s.

It is probable that the lack of women's organization in these areas was a reflection of the general organizational vacuum shown earlier in Chapter Two. By the early 1930s, Labour usually won unopposed in these wards, and there was no necessity for any organized electioneering by the party there. In fact, ward Labour Parties, let alone women's sections, were a rarity, and an informal political organization based on close-knit ethnic and neighbourhood ties dominated. Nevertheless, what is particularly signi-ficant here is that Catholic women were clearly not organized to any great extent within the Labour Party during this period. Women's organization in Liverpool was limited, then, mainly to one side only of the sectarian divide, and for that reason alone its impact on the local party would have been lessened. But there are other factors which may be important in explaining the effect of women's sections on the party.

Work, family and neighbourhood

Among feminists involved in socialist and labour politics, there were some who feared that absorption into separate sections within a male-dominated Labour Party would result in women being confined to a powerless ghetto, and at the same time isolated from a wider feminist movement. At national level, at least, these fears were borne out to some extent. The fact that in the 1918 constitution the four female members of the National Executive Committee were to be elected by the party, and not by the women's con-ference, was an early indication that women members were to be kept on a tight rein. It was significant also that the women's conference was only an advisory body, with no direct access to shaping party policy. The failure to win over the party conference on the issues of birth-control and family allowances were important examples of the lack of power of the women's sections. By the late 1920s it was also clear that over a number of issues, such as equal pay and protective legislation for women workers, Labour women had diverged sharply from feminists in non-party organizations such as the National Union of Societies for Equal Citizenship (NUSEC).[12]

However, this analysis pitched at a national level may be too simplistic to explain the complex reality of women's involvement in the Labour Party. A number of writers associated with the Lancaster Regionalism Group have shown that, at a local level, the relationship of women to the Labour Party varied greatly. Thus, Jane Mark-Lawson *et al*. have shown how differences in women's participation in the local labour market – and also the gender relations involved in their work – explain marked differences in women's impact on local Labour parties in Lancaster, Preston and Nelson. In Lancaster, the relatively low participation of women in paid employment was linked to a lack of female political activity, and a consequent lack of impact on Labour Party organization and policies. In Preston, on the other hand, a much higher level of paid female employment nevertheless resulted again in a restricted women's impact on the local party. The patriarchal structure of work relations in the local cotton-weaving industry meant that skilled male trade-unionists saw female labour as a threat, and carried over these attitudes into Labour Party practices and policies. In Nelson, however, a similarly high level of female employment resulted in a quite different relationship to Labour. Here, men and women were employed in the weaving industry on a more or less equal basis, and also participated in trade-union and political life much more equally. Thus, women had a significant impact on the Nelson Labour Party, being highly organized and influencing policy considerably, particularly pushing the party towards local state intervention in various welfare services.[13]

Michael Savage has shown that changing economic circumstances can also affect the relationship between Labour and women. Thus, in the mid-1920s, when employment in Preston was relatively high and therefore the perceived threat of female labour to skilled male workers was reduced, women were able to influence the party considerably. This resulted in a development of neighbourhood-based politics which benefited the local party electorally. When high unemployment returned in 1929, however, male attitudes to female labour reverted to their earlier hostility, partly explaining a decline in women's involvement in the party and a shift in policy away from local state welfare initiatives.[14]

Members of the Manchester Women's History Group have developed a rather different perspective in looking at the impact of women on council-house provision in Manchester between the wars. They have shown that women in the Labour Party, and also in the closely linked Women's Co-operative Guild, were very active in attempting to influence the provision of public housing in the city. However, the effect of this campaigning is difficult to assess. The view that housing quality and design was a non-party issue, and therefore to be decided upon in the council on a free vote, allowed male councillors to ignore recommendations emanating from the Women's Advisory Council which meant, for instance, that

Labour Party women's opposition to flats in principle seems to have been ineffectual. So despite the evidence of women being well organized and politically active within the Manchester party, over the issue of housing at least their impact on policy was limited.[15] The same was apparently true of their impact on education and maternity services.

More recently, Pat Thane has argued that women in the party should not be viewed merely as 'puppets of male leaders or as traitors to a feminist movement', as such a view 'does less than justice to their organizational importance and independence of mind, to the coherence of their analysis of the role of women in society and of their strategies for change'. While she concedes that their overall achievement was 'minimal' compared with their ambitions, she also argues that in London at a municipal level women had an important influence on the Labour Party in the 1930s. They were elected in large numbers and had a considerable effect on policy, especially with regard to improved levels of health care.[16]

Turning to the local experience in Liverpool, there are a number of interconnected factors which need to be taken into account in examining women's impact on the Labour Party. As far as the local labour market was concerned, women were in a particularly disadvantageous position. In the 1931 census, 36 per cent of women over the age of 14 in Liverpool were in paid employment or registered as unemployed.[17] Of course, there were many unemployed married women excluded from this total, due to the vagaries of the Unemployment Insurance system, and women's work has always tended to be underestimated in the census,[18] but as a comparative measure the figure is instructive. By comparison, the national proportion was 35 per cent, and in Lancaster it was 33 per cent, in Preston 53 per cent and in Nelson 57 per cent.[19] Female participation in the paid labour force was low, then, but in the most detailed examination of women's work locally, Linda Grant has also shown that 'women workers remained concentrated in an extremely limited range of industries'.[20] Domestic service, the 'sweated trades' in the clothing industry, food, tobacco and paper production, sack making and mending, retail trades and clerical work were the only significant areas of paid women's work.

Linda Grant has also argued that the particularly strong dependence on work in dock-related jobs for men in Liverpool, coupled with the restricted areas of female employment, created a highly distinctive sexual division of labour. The distinction between 'men's work' and 'women's work' was sharply defined, 'producing and reproducing a model of masculinity which implicitly constructed a model of femininity'. In turn, this sexual division of labour 'meshed perfectly with the assumptions of a society which drew sharp lines of distinction between the male and female worlds'.[21] She quotes the example of Liverpool dockers in 1916 resolutely refusing to work with women on the docks as indicative of the strength of this sexual division of labour.[22] On the face of it, then, the structural context of women's work seemed unfavourable for the prospects of women being able to influence the local Labour Party significantly.

However, there were also distinctive features of the local Labour Party and its connections with the working class which have to be taken into account. As shown in Chapter Two, at least up to the 1920s the Liverpool Labour Party was dominated by trades and trade unions which hardly reflected the pattern of employment of male workers in the city. The party that emerged in Liverpool was based mainly on the support of relatively small sections of skilled and semi-skilled workers generally unrepresentative of the working class as a whole. By contrast, the largest unions representing dockers and seafarers had only a spasmodic and often stormy relationship with Labour.[23] The dominant sectors in the party can be seen in the list of union delegates elected to the Executive Committee of the LTCLP, shown in Appendix III. In 1927, for instance, delegates of distributive workers, clerks, postal workers, electricians, engineering workers, railwaymen, sheet-metal workers, painters, insurance workers and the League of the Blind were elected. One would hardly guess that this group represented the working class of the largest port in Britain.

The unrepresentative nature of the Labour Party up to the mid-1920s paradoxically meant that women had a better chance of influencing the party overall. Skilled craft unions representing predominantly male workers might also have seen female labour as a threat, especially as the very concept of 'skilled' work often had clear gender implications in its exclusivity.[24] On the other hand, unions representing significant sectors of female employment were well represented in the party. Most notable of these were the National Union of Distributive and Allied Workers (NUDAW) and the National Union of General and Municipal Workers (NUGMW), but dressmakers, shop assistants, clerical workers, tailors and garment workers were also well represented.

Women's progress in the party in the 1920s

There are clear signs that the party looked quite favourably on women's involvement, and women were able to win significant support and influence policy up to the mid-1920s. Even before the war, the Trades Council voted to support votes for women in July 1910, December 1911, and again in October 1912.[25] The then separate Labour Representation Committee (LRC) also supported the following motion in July 1913:

> This LRC strongly protest against the treatment of Mrs. Pankhurst and other members of the Women's Social and Political Union by the Liberal Government. Considering the method of dragging them in and out of prison to be an inhuman form of torture and that no body of men suffering under the same indignities and oppression as women are suffering under would be treated in such a manner for rebelling.[26]

Again, in January 1914, the LRC supported the National Union of Suffrage Societies in its campaign for votes for women, and agreed to send a delegate to its conference and demonstration in London.[27]

After the war women were also able to influence policy to some extent. Labour's programme for the 1919 municipal elections, for instance, called for the development of municipal nursery schools, for more provision of playgrounds for children, more public wash-houses, and the establishment of municipal laundries.[28] Again, in 1925, the manifesto called for the municipalization of child welfare services.[29] After the elections that year the Secretary of the LTCLP was minuted as saying that 'he desired to thank all the workers in the various wards for the fine work done by the various women's sections'.[30] Later that year the LTCLP even lifted its head from parochial concerns when it received a motion from one of the women's sections calling for the banning of submarines, which was passed unanimously.[31] Even on the issue of birth-control the women's sections made progress within the party. In 1927, the LTCLP was persuaded to invite a speaker to present the case for a mother's welfare clinic – the same clinic that was to split the party nine years later over the issue of birth control, as shown later in this chapter. The speaker was listened to with interest and received the thanks of the meeting, and no dissent was recorded in the minutes.[32] One other sign of women's impact on policy can be seen in the influence of the Women's Co-operative Guild. It had mounted a major national campaign in the 1920s over the issue of food purity, improved hygiene in the preparation, packing and distribution of food, and especially the importance of a pure, healthy milk supply.[33] This campaign was taken up locally, and was eventually reflected in the 1928 Municipal election programme. Two new demands were inserted in the programme, that 'a pure milk supply' be guaranteed for Liverpool, and 'that attention to be called for the need for hygienic conditions in all shops dealing with food supplies'.[34]

The clearest sign of women's impact within the Labour Party up to the mid-1920s, however, was the party's willingness to campaign over women's working conditions and trade-unionism. On these issues, both before and after the First World War, the key position of Mary Bamber (the mother of Bessie Braddock) in the Liverpool Labour movement was significant. As a NUDAW delegate, Mary Bamber was one of the leading figures in the LTCLP for many years. She was re-elected onto the Executive Committee year after year, and continually worked for improvements in the working conditions and the unionization of women. Most of this activity was concerned with women in low-paid and poorly organized sectors of the local economy, but there is also evidence that the relatively small number of women in skilled trades was defended by the LTCLP in this period. Thus, in 1923, a resolution from the Printing and Paper Workers' Union was passed unanimously, condemning the fact that women workers who had served apprenticeships in a trade were being disallowed unemployment benefit if they refused to take work as domestic servants.[35]

The Labour Party took up the question of women's trade-unionism most enthusiastically in June 1926, when the Industrial Committee of the LTCLP met to launch a major campaign to organize women workers. All affiliated unions were to be contacted, public speakers were to be made available for all meetings, an advert was to be placed in the *Liverpool Echo*, and a major conference was to be organized with other parties in the area. This was perhaps the highpoint of women's activity in the Labour Party between the wars, but it was also a turning point. The campaign ran until the conference in April 1927, but ultimately it petered out due to the poor response of affiliated unions. By December 1926 only 18 unions had taken up the offer of a speaker, and at the conference only 55 organizations were represented, although 486 had been contacted. In the context of the defeat of the General Strike and the subsequent downturn in trade-union fortunes, perhaps no more should have been expected.[36]

A new phase in the relationship between the Liverpool Labour Party and women came by the late 1920s. The women's sections seemed to become more marginal to the party, and their impact on policy seemed to decline. Symbolic of the change, perhaps, was the special appeal made by the LTCLP to the women's sections to provide a decorative lorry or tableau for the May Day demonstration of 1927.[37] This stress on women's domestic skills within the party was a pointer to the future.

The decline in women's influence on the party

The politics of the Labour Party changed in the second half of the 1920s. At a national level, the party, along with the TUC, became more inward-looking. Joint action with any organizations outside the party, particularly those that had any connection with the Communist Party, was frowned upon. The end of joint work with the National Unemployed Workers' Movement (NUWM) was the most notable sign of this trend.[38] At the same time, work with feminists outside the party was also terminated. Disagreement over protective legislation for women workers led to the 1927 decision to prohibit joint action with NUSEC, the leading non-party feminist organization of the time.[39] Labour women's isolation was only increased by the performance of their leaders in Parliament. Margaret Bondfield's assent to the 1927 Unemployment Insurance Act, which imposed a cut in benefit from 15*s*. to 8*s*. (75p to 40p) for women under 21, was a severe defeat for the women's sections. Even more damaging was the Anomalies Act introduced by Margaret Bondfield as Minister of Labour in 1931. This Act disallowed benefit to large numbers of married women, discounting their National Insurance contributions prior to marriage and also for any periods of temporary or seasonal work. By April 1933, half a million married women had had their benefit stopped under the terms of the Act.[40]

These national trends were reflected locally. Joint action with the NUWM was wound down from April 1926, and by March 1928 the LTCLP was setting up its own rival Unemployed Association.[41] Work with the Women's Co-operative Guild was also run down gradually. As early as October 1926 the Liverpool Co-operative Society was meeting increasing difficulties in coming to agreements with the Labour Party over mutually acceptable candidates for local elections. Labour began to insist that the co-operative movement should simply be absorbed fully into the party, and joint work was steadily eroded as relations between the two organizations worsened in to the late 1920s.[42] Labour women were at the same time increasingly isolated from local feminists in the Liverpool Women's Citizens Association (WCA), which was affiliated to NUSEC, over the issue of family allowances. The leading proponent of this measure, Eleanor Rathbone, was a Liverpool city councillor with whom Labour women had worked in the early 1920s. By the late 1920s, such co-operation had ceased. The WCA wrote to all local parliamentary candidates prior to the 1929 general election asking them to support family allowances, but only four out of the ten Labour candidates agreed to do so.[43] At the 1930 Labour Women's Conference, Bessie Braddock opposed family allowances, arguing that they would encourage employers to cut men's wages, and defended the trade union concept of the 'family wage'.[44] The impact of the Anomalies Act, which had caused 3,000 women in Liverpool to lose their benefit by November 1931,[45] further disheartened the women's sections in the party.

There was another significant change locally in the late 1920s which adversely affected women's organization in the party. The arrival of the group of Catholic councillors, as described earlier, had a profound impact on the party. They brought with them few new ward organizations or women's sections, and therefore had little effect on the structure of the LTCLP. On the other hand, most of them had little sympathy with socialist ideas, but they soon formed a majority in the Labour group on the council, and began to shape policy there. The 1930 dispute over the Catholic cathedral, described above in Chapter Two, resulted in the Labour group being confirmed as the dominant force in the party.[46]

For women, this meant that, however effective they might have been within the party organization, their efforts could always be negated by the decisions of the Labour group. The fact that, as in the case of Manchester mentioned earlier, many issues of importance to women were seen as non-party issues and were therefore left to a free vote by Labour councillors, only served to magnify this major political problem for women in the party. The only way that women could effectively influence the party thereafter was by election to the council and, with a few notable exceptions, this proved difficult.

The other important effect that this change had as far as women were concerned was to bring religion to the centre of Labour politics. Over a key issue for feminists in the 1930s – birth-control – this was damaging. A major controversy over the issue in Liverpool illustrates this very clearly.

On 1 April 1936 Liverpool city council discussed a motion that the annual grant of £100 to the mothers' welfare clinic in Clarence Street be renewed. The leader of the Labour group and of the Catholic caucus, Luke

Hogan, led the opposition to the grant being extended to one of the few institutions in the city where women could get advice on birth-control. It was reported that:

> He fully acknowledged the difficulties which maternity involved. He paid tribute to the clean-minded women who endured them, but he questioned whether birth control was the right way of approaching those difficulties ... Hogan disagreed with birth control because it was the negation of socialism.

In a bitter debate, the main supporter of the grant was a leading member of the left of the Labour Party at that time, Bessie Braddock. She pointed out that in the previous year eighty-seven women had died in the city because of childbirth, and argued that three-quarters of them would still have been alive if they had been able to avoid pregnancy. She added that the sale of drugs for abortion was growing enormously, and that the alternative was 'decent, clean, scientific advice such as was given at the Mothers' Welfare Clinic'. She was supported 'warmly' in the debate by another Labour woman, Mary Cumella, and also by the virulently anti-Catholic leader of the Protestant Party, the Revd Harry Longbottom.

In the end, the vote was taken. In favour of renewing the grant were 15 Labour members, 4 Protestants, 5 Liberals and 48 Tories, while against were 34 Labour, 4 Independents and 3 Tories. The motion was carried by 72 votes to 41, and a curious alliance of left and right had triumphed over the majority Catholic caucus in the Labour group. In a final twist, the four Labour women in the council were also divided over the issue, with Bessie Braddock and Mary Cumella finding themselves in opposition to Mary Hamilton and Agnes Mitton.[47]

Nationally, as well, the Labour Party was often divided over the question of birth-control in the inter-war period. Male hostility to the provision of contraceptive advice and facilities usually won out in motions on the issue at the annual conference. These motions were usually supported by women's sections.[48] The issue was partially resolved by the Labour government in 1930, which allowed Ministry of Health clinics to give free advice on contraception 'in cases where further pregnancy would be detrimental to health'.[49] In other localities, like West Yorkshire and Manchester, birth-control and Catholicism were an explosive mix, but less so in the 1930s than in the 1920s.[50]

However, what the division in Liverpool in 1936 graphically illustrated was the complex interconnection of class, religion and gender in the politics of the local party. The religious complexion of the Labour group kept the issue of birth-control alive. This is not to suggest, of course, that religion alone accounts for opposition to birth-control within the Labour Party. Opposition on the grounds that population-control would be forced on the working class to reduce or even eliminate the 'lower orders' had a history going back to the ideas of Malthus over a century earlier. The eugenicist idea of population-control for the poor to eliminate social problems was a significant early twentieth-century variant, and many orthodox socialists opposed contraception on these grounds. Oswald Mosley's advocacy of birth-control in the 1930s as part of the fascist plan to 'improve the race' and eliminate the 'unfit' only served to revive the fears of some socialists.[51] But in Liverpool it was religion that was the main factor in stirring up the controversy in the 1930s.

In Parliament, Liverpool's Labour MPs continued to oppose birth-control. Davie Logan, who had been the first Nationalist councillor to defect to Labour in January 1923,[52] became the MP for Scotland division in Liverpool in 1929. In his first speech to Parliament he stated his principles: 'I stand for the great things that go to make the family life and to help to make the manhood of the nation great and strong, because of deep religious convictions.'[53] In 1932 he defended the sanctity of marriage by arguing against divorce, even in cases where a spouse was clinically diagnosed as 'incurably insane'.[54] In 1935 and 1936 he opposed any measures to allow contraceptive advice to be given to married women by the Ministry of Health.[55] A father of ten children, he argued in the 1935 debate:

> If the Ministry of Health wishes to encourage the welfare of the nation, it will not be by the scientific dispensation of the knowledge of Marie Stopes. The welfare of the nation will depend upon a healthy manhood and womanhood, not so much the knowledge of the prostitute as the knowledge that goes to make for human happiness and the welfare of the people. This nation was never made on the scientific dissemination of material. It is only fit for the gutter. It is not for decent homes to have any knowledge of ... I believe it is pernicious. I believe it is the worst kind of propaganda that was ever introduced ... The object of the speech that has been made tonight is that, without denying the pleasure of sexual delectation, there must be no children. I am against this doctrine.

Despite much barracking and several attempted interruptions by other members of the House, Logan continued in this vein for ten minutes. For some sections of the Liverpool Labour Party this was clearly still a contentious issue.

It is far less clear, though, to what extent Labour leaders like Logan and Hogan accurately reflected the views of Catholic voters, and particularly Catholic women, on this and other issues. In the 1936 council debate on birth-control the Protestant leader Longbottom sniped away at his sectarian enemies by questioning their right as an all-male group to speak for Catholic women. He was quoted as saying that: '... he did not believe the opposition [to birth control] was a layman's opposition; it certainly was not a laywoman's opposition. If this was a free issue there was no doubt the women would have something to say about it.' Of course Longbottom's

8 Davie Logan. Educated at St Anthony's and St Sylvester's Roman Catholic Schools (Scotland North ward); Irish Nationalist councillor for Scotland South ward from 1920, but converted to Labour and represented them in Scotland North ward from 1924; succeeded T. P. O'Connor as MP for Scotland division in December 1929, O'Connor having held it for the INP since 1885; Logan retained the seat for Labour until 1964.

intervention was a purely sectarian rather than feminist point, but it raised an important issue about the nature of political representation in the Catholic community of Liverpool. The councillors who ran the Catholic caucus in the Labour Party were potentially as much nominees of a their religion's hierarchy as representatives of its electorate, and they appeared to determine as much as reflect Catholic opinion. The internal political and cultural life of Catholic Manchester in this period has been studied in some detail, but in Liverpool similar studies are still awaited.[56] In the meantime one has to be cautious about generalizing about Catholic attitudes as a whole from the discourse of the Catholic caucus. Nevertheless, this imposed a new context on women's activities in the Labour Party.

Women on the defensive in the 1930s

In this new context, women's influence in the Liverpool Labour Party was limited in the 1930s. The women's sections faded into insignificance. The only important arena was the council-chamber, and only one woman was able to make a major impact there, namely Bessie Braddock. Elected to the council in 1930, she put on almost a one-woman show there for a decade. Significantly, she seems to have avoided working in the women's sections at all, and in fact fell out with them at times. Martin Pugh has described the women who came to predominate in the inter-war Labour Party as 'orthodox party loyalists … who put party and class before sex'.[57] Bessie Braddock certainly put party and class before sex, but she was most emphatically not an orthodox party loyalist. After 1945 she became in Parliament a prominent figure on the right of the party, but in the 1930s she was firmly on the left, and she was constantly involved in disputes with the party leadership.

Not long after she had clashed with Luke Hogan over the mothers' welfare clinic in April 1936, she was disciplined for publicly criticizing a municipal candidate, Mrs Elliot, who was the chairwoman of the Liverpool Labour Women's Central Council from its inception in 1922 right through to 1939. She was reported as stating:

> … that Mrs. Elliott was a bad candidate … That Mrs. Elliott was not class-conscious … That on a P.A.C. Committee in St Anne's ward that Mrs. Elliott remarked to a woman applying for extra nourishment money and receiving 45/– (having a large family) that she was better off than a Railwayman who had only 40/10d. whatever the size of his family.

In the same speech, Mrs Braddock also criticized another Labour councillor, Reginald Bevins, as he 'had voted against the best interests of the working class mothers on the birth control issue … That Mr. Bevins should have got instructions from his ward as to how he was to vote and obeyed those instruction.'[58] She was disciplined again in 1938 for speaking on a public platform with the NUWM.[59]

She would never have described herself as a feminist, but chaired the Maternity and Child-Welfare Subcommittee of the council from its creation in 1934, and in that capacity did much work on behalf of women. In June 1936 her committee was responsible for the opening of a maternity and child-care centre in Everton which was claimed to be the only one of its kind in the country.[60] Only a few days later she organized a major national conference on maternity and child welfare in Liverpool, working with many other non-party women's organizations. The conference called for birth-control clinics to be established by all health authorities, and improved pre- and post-natal care, and received much publicity in the local press.[61]

It is difficult to place Bessie Braddock in the context of the feminist movement of the inter-war years. It has been claimed that a 'new feminism', placing a stress on the special attributes and needs of women, began to predominate over the pre-war 'equality feminism'. The implications of this new feminism are controversial. Some historians see it as failing to challenge, and in fact contributing to, 'a reconstruction of gender that circumscribed the roles, activities and possibilities of women'.[62] Others have argued that the 'new feminism' showed a new confidence by women in their rightful and equal place in society.[63] Others again have written that

9 Bessie Braddock.

stressing distinctions between 'old' and 'new' feminism is too simplistic, and obscures a much more complex range of opinion.[64] However new feminism is judged, Eleanor Rathbone was seen as the leading exponent of it. Her presidential address to NUSEC in 1925 expressed the shift of emphasis clearly: 'We can demand what we want for women, not because it is what men have got, but because it is what women need to fulfil the potentialities of their own natures and to adjust ourselves to the circumstances of their own lives.'[65] Protective legislation for women at work, family allowances, and the availability of birth-control were the key demands of the new feminism. As we have seen, Bessie Braddock campaigned vigorously for birth control, but also strongly opposed family allowances. It is the case, perhaps, that she and Eleanor Rathbone represented two quite different discourses by the 1930s, with issues of class as well as gender contributing to the difference.

But of course Bessie Braddock was only one individual, and there were very few women to assist her in the council. The number of women involved in municipal politics in Liverpool in this period was very small. Even before women had been enfranchised nationally, they had been involved in municipal politics, as Patricia Hollis has recently shown.[66] In Liverpool, the only party to select a woman candidate before the First World War was the Liberal Party, for whom a Miss Johnson stood unsuccessfully in 1907 and again in 1910. The only other woman who stood for election before 1914 was Eleanor Rathbone, who was returned as an Independent in 1910 and again in 1913. Labour's first woman candidate was Mary Bamber, winning in a by-election in 1919. But, as Table 7.1 shows, very few women were selected by any of the major parties before 1938.

181

Table 7.1 Women candidates in municipal elections in Liverpool, 1905–1938

	All candidates	All wins No.	All wins %	Women candidates No.	Women candidates %	Women wins No.	Women wins %
Labour							
1905–9	18	3	(17)	0		0	
1910–14	52	14	(27)	0		0	
1919–23	108	16	(15)	2	(2)	1	(50)
1924–28	166	51	(31)	14	(8)	1	(7)
1929–33	191	75	(39)	18	(9)	10	(56)
1934–38	192	73	(38)	23	(12)	6	(26)
Total	727	232	(32)	57	(8)	18	(32)
Tory							
1905–9	130	102	(79)	0		0	
1910–14	119	99	(83)	0		0	
1919–23	137	116	(85)	2	(1)	2	(100)
1924–28	152	122	(80)	8	(5)	6	(75)
1929–33	165	120	(73)	10	(6)	7	(70)
1934–38	161	122	(76)	7	(4)	3	(43)
Total	864	681	(79)	27	(3)	18	(67)
Liberal							
1905–9	102	61	(60)	1	(1)	0	
1910–14	60	46	(77)	1	(2)	0	
1919–23	59	28	(48)	6	(10)	5	(83)
1924–28	43	16	(37)	0		0	
1929–33	33	16	(49)	2	(6)	2	(100)
1934–38	25	16	(64)	2	(8)	2	(100)
Total	322	183	(57)	12	(4)	9	(75)
Other							
1905–9	52	23	(44)	0		0	
1910–14	41	25	(61)	2	(5)	2	(100)
1919–23	96	45	(47)	7	(7)	3	(43)
1924–28	64	27	(42)	5	(8)	5	(100)
1929–33	80	21	(26)	10	(13)	6	(60)
1934–38	45	15	(33)	11	(24)	3	(27)
Total	378	156	(41)	35	(9)	19	(54)
Total							
1905–9	302	189	(63)	1	(0.3)	0	
1910–14	272	184	(68)	3	(1)	2	(67)
1919–23	400	205	(51)	17	(4)	11	(65)
1924–28	425	216	(51)	27	(6)	12	(44)
1929–33	469	232	(50)	40	(9)	25	(63)
1934–38	423	226	(53)	43	(10)	14	(33)
Total	2,291	1,252	(55)	131	(6)	64	(49)

Source: Municipal Election Results, *Liverpool Official Red Books* (1906–1939).

The Labour Party did at least do better than the others, with 8 per cent of all their candidates between 1905 and 1938 being women, as opposed to 4 and 3 per cent respectively for the Liberals and Tories. But, in total, on only 18 occasions were Labour women ever successfully elected onto the council between the wars, and only 10 Labour women actually became councillors over the whole period (some of them were elected more than once). This compares very unfavourably with the experience in London recorded by Pat Thane. There, 150 out of a total of 729 successful Labour candidates were women in the 1934 elections, a proportion of almost 20 per cent.[67] In Liverpool, by contrast, only 6 out of 73 Labour winners between 1934 and 1938 were women, a proportion of less than 10 per cent.

Even when women were selected as candidates, they were often selected in wards where they had little chance of winning. To take one example, Sarah McArd, a leading local member of the ILP and the Women's Co-operative Guild and a stalwart of the women's sections, whose unswerving loyalty to Labour was demonstrated when she remained in the party when the ILP was disaffiliated in 1932, was rewarded for her tireless work with the following: in 1925 she was selected for St Domingo ward, the stronghold of Harry Longbottom's Protestant Party, and lost. In 1926, 1927 and 1928 she unsuccessfully contested the safe Tory ward of Old Swan. In 1929 she was selected for a by-election in the fairly safe Labour ward of Edge Hill, and won, but in the 1931 elections she was swept away in the aftermath of the Catholic cathedral controversy and the collapse of the Labour government. In 1934 she stood unsuccessfully in Wavertree West, another safe Tory seat; in 1936 she gamely contested St Domingo again and lost; and finally, in 1938, she lost in the safe Tory seat of Fazakerley. Sarah McArd did get elected after the war in Bessie Braddock's ward of St Anne's, but lesser persons must surely have given up early against these sort of odds, and it is no surprise that so few Labour women got on the council.

As far as parliamentary elections were concerned, no woman stood for Labour before the war. Bessie Braddock was selected for the Exchange division, but war intervened before she could mount a challenge. Nationally, the highest proportion of women candidates for Labour in a general election before the war was only 7 per cent in 1931.[68] It has been suggested that many women within the Labour Party positively chose not to stand for Parliament and preferred to stay close to their support in the local community.[69] This was perhaps borne out in Liverpool when candidates were selected for the 1918 election. Mary Bamber was nominated, but withdrew, stating that she did not think the time opportune for women parliamentary candidates.[70]

Whatever the reason, Davie Logan never had a local Labour woman to challenge him in Parliament before the war. Local feminists were represented indirectly from 1929, when Eleanor Rathbone was elected as an Independent for a Combined Universities seat. The political parties in Liverpool, however, retained an all-male approach to Parliament.

Women and municipal services

Another way of attempting to assess women's impact on Labour is by linking it to local spending on those municipal services that might be seen as particularly relevant to women's welfare. This approach was used by Jane Mark-Lawson and her colleagues in their study of Preston, Lancaster and Nelson. The stronger the women's influence was in a local party, the more it might have been reflected in local municipal policies, and therefore in council spending. There are serious methodological problems in using this kind of financial data, as they point out in their work, but nevertheless it might be useful to compare similar figures for Liverpool; the results are shown in Table 7.2. As can be seen, the figures for Lancaster, Preston and

Table 7.2 Approximate per capita net expenditure on some services in financial years 1924–1925 and 1935–1936

Years	Liverpool	Lancaster	Preston	Nelson
Education (per child under 15 years old)				
1924–5	£2 17s. 0d.	£2 13s. 8d.	£2 17s. 7d.	£4 1s. 4d.
1935–6	£4 3s. 5d.	£3 8s. 1d.	£4 13s. 10d.	£5 1s. 8d.
Maternity and child welfare (per woman 15–44 years old)				
1924–5	3s. 2d.	7d.	8d.	5s. 11d.
1935–6	9s. 6d.	4s. 1d.	5s. 6d.	8s. 2d.
Parks, baths, libraries and recreation (per capita)				
1924–5	5s. 0d.	8d.	3s. 4d.	4s. 11d.
1935–6	6s. 4d.	2s. 9d.	4s. 7d.	6s. 8d.

Source: Liverpool City Council, Treasurer's Accounts, 1924–5 and 1935–6; census of population, 1921 and 1931; Jane Mark-Lawson *et al.*, *Gender and Local Politics*, p. 200.

Nelson seemed to bear out Mark-Lawson's estimation of the relative impact of women on the Labour Party in each town. The figures for Liverpool are extremely interesting, if less clear-cut in their implications. On education, Liverpool's expenditure seemed similar to Preston's. On maternity and child welfare, and parks, baths, etc., Liverpool appeared to rank alongside Nelson. Taken overall, Liverpool's provision in these areas was perhaps surprisingly generous. This may have reflected the impact that women had on Labour policy in the 1920s, but also perhaps their impact on the other main parties. The importance of an extremely effective feminist like Eleanor Rathbone sitting as an Independent councillor throughout the 1920s may also be reflected in the figures.

The continued or even increased generosity of provision in the 1930s is again intriguing. All councils were affected to some degree by the phasing out of the Poor Law and the increased municipal responsibility for aspects of social provision from 1929. The increase in Liverpool nevertheless seems relatively high. With the rise of Labour in the late 1920s, the increasing dependence of the Tories in Liverpool on a sectarian Protestant working-class vote to maintain their hold on the council may have been relevant. Working-class Tory voters' demands in terms of council provision had to be met if the sectarian alliance was to be maintained. At the same time, the delicate political balance that kept the Tories in power also required them to make concessions to the Catholic interest, as has been shown earlier. This was not so much a case of 'jobs for the Protestant boys',[71] but rather, separate municipal services for Catholic and Protestant voters alike.

It is also interesting that expenditure on maternity and child welfare was higher in Liverpool in the 1930s than in all the other areas. It seems likely that this reflected the key position of Bessie Braddock in chairing the maternity subcommittee throughout this period and very forcefully and publicly campaigning for provision in this area.

The fact that we are comparing councils of such different size, and that Labour was never politically in power in Liverpool in the inter-war years, makes the link between council expenditure and women's impact on the Labour Party difficult to assess conclusively. The evidence, though, does seem to suggest there was a connection between the two, even if other factors lying outside the party also have to be taken into account.

Women voters and the Labour Party

One last way of assessing the relationship between the Labour Party and women in Liverpool might be by considering female voting trends. There are difficulties in attempting this, of course, as there are no opinion surveys to consult for this period, and women's votes cannot be identified in the election records themselves. The issue has also been clouded by certain assumptions about women voters that have prevailed in much social scientific research. These include the following: that women are more apolitical than men, and that therefore they are less firmly committed to support for political parties, and also less likely to vote; that they are less independent, in that their voting decisions may be influenced by their husbands' (or fathers') opinions; and, most commonly, that women voters are inherently more conservative in politics than men.[72] The problem has been summarized thus: 'Too often, where voting studies have actually looked at women voters, prejudice has posed as analysis and ideology as science.'[73]

Despite the fact that evidence is so scarce, these attitudes have pervaded analysis of the inter-war period as well. One study has concluded: 'Labour did not gain, but rather suffered, from the effects of the 1918 Representation of the people Act. Women ... were more reluctant than established voters to support Labour.' A recent history of women concurred with this view, stating that Labour 'was disadvantaged by the electoral reforms of 1928'. Another study stated that 'Labour's electoral support during the interwar period varied inversely according to the proportion of the electorate that was female'.[74] The problem has been further confused by the questionable statistical methods employed in many of these studies.

The evidence quoted most often comes from Jorgen Rasmussen, who compared the proportion of women voters with the votes gained by Labour in every parliamentary division for the four general elections between 1924 and 1935. He found a negative statistical correlation in all four cases.[75] In simple terms, this means that overall the more women voters there were in a division, the fewer votes Labour tended to win. Testing this approach for Liverpool, the comparable figures are as shown in Figure 7.3 which, on the face of it, suggest that in Liverpool, too, Labour tended to do less well where there was a higher proportion of women voters. Statistical testing confirms this impression, with a high negative correlation showing up for the 1929, 1931 and 1935 elections, and only the 1924 election revealing no significant correlation.[76] However, there are serious problems in using evidence like this to draw firm conclusions about the women's vote.

A careful reading of Table 7.3 leads in quite a different direction. What is striking about it is that the divisions where the proportion of women voters was lower were clearly the most working class, and vice versa. This tendency also appeared to increase after the extension of the women's franchise in 1928. At the one extreme, Scotland division – in the heart of the strongly working-class northern dockside area – had the lowest proportion of women voters. Exchange, Everton, Edge Hill, Kirkdale and West Toxteth – all predominantly working class – showed a slightly higher figure. West Derby, Wavertree and Fairfield, comprised mainly of middle-class suburban areas, had a larger proportion of women again. At the other extreme, East Toxteth, representing the plushest middle-class areas in the south of the city, had the highest figure. (The evidence in Chapter Eight on the social composition of wards will confirm this pattern quite clearly.) It takes no expertise in statistics to see that the Labour Party was unlikely to garner many votes from the mansions of Sefton Park, but was likely to do far better in the courts and cellars of Scotland Road. It seems plausible to suggest that it was the varying class composition that was the decisive factor, rather than the relative proportion of women voters.

Liverpool's eleven divisions were only a very small sample, of course, and may have been unrepresentative of the national picture. Rasmussen's figures, on the other hand, were based on all seats contested by Labour. As a counter-check, the proportion of women voters in all 474 English

Table 7.3 Women voters and Labour votes in Liverpool parliamentary divisions, 1924–1935 (in %)

Year	Division	Women voters	Labour share of vote
1924	East Toxteth	45	25
	Edge Hill	43	53
	Everton	43	48
	Exchange	43	No candidate
	Fairfield	44	37
	Kirkdale	42	39
	Scotland	42	No candidate
	Walton	43	37
	Wavertree	43	35
	West Derby	43	30
	West Toxteth	43	51
	All contested	43	39
1929	East Toxteth	56	27
	Edge Hill	52	55
	Everton	53	53
	Exchange	51	50
	Fairfield	54	47
	Kirkdale	52	51
	Scotland	50	No candidate
	Walton	53	42
	Wavertree	54	32
	West Derby	55	36
	West Toxteth	52	55
	All contested	53	44
1931	East Toxteth	57	No candidate
	Edge Hill	52	37
	Everton	53	31
	Exchange	51	31
	Fairfield	55	24
	Kirkdale	52	30
	Scotland	51	57
	Walton	53	26
	Wavertree	54	22
	West Derby	54	22
	West Toxteth	53	42
	All contested	53	31
1935	East Toxteth	56	No candidate
	Edge Hill	52	49
	Everton	52	50
	Exchange	50	43
	Fairfield	54	37
	Kirkdale	52	37
	Scotland	46	66
	Walton	53	38
	Wavertree	54	41
	West Derby	54	28
	West Toxteth	53	53
	All contested	53	43

divisions in 1929 have been analysed here. As an indication of the general trend, the top and bottom 25 divisions are shown in Table 7.4. The contrast between the predominantly middle-class seats in the left-hand column of the table, and the mainly working-class ones on the right, is clear-cut, and confirms the impression given by the Liverpool figures. The proportion of women voters did not vary at random, but was closely linked to the class-composition of parliamentary divisions. It should come as no surprise, therefore, that Labour did worse where women voters were more prevalent, as Rasmussen found. This says nothing about the supposed conservatism of women voters, though, but rather emphasizes the fatuous nature of some statistical exercises like these.

Table 7.4 English parliamentary divisions with highest and lowest proportions of women voters, 1929 (% in brackets)

Highest *(in descending order)*	*Lowest* *(in ascending order)*
1. Kensington South (68.6)	1. Hemsworth (45.2)
2. Hampstead (62.3)	2. City of London (45.8)
3. Bournemouth (62.0)	3. Clay Cross (46.3)
4. Chelsea (61.4)	4. Don Valley (46.3)
5. Paddington (61.3)	5. Wentworth (46.6)
6. Westminster, St George's (61.1)	6. Normanton (46.9)
7. Hastings (61.0)	7. Seaham (47.1)
8. St Marylebone (60.5)	8. Rother Valley (47.2)
9. Cheltenham (60.0)	9. Derbyshire NE (47.7)
10. Southport (59.5)	10. Consett (47.7)
11. Bath (59.1)	11. St Helens (48.0)
12. Bristol W (58.9)	12. Sedgefield (48.2)
13. Blackpool (58.6)	13. Blaydon (48.2)
14. Brighton (58.6)	14. Morpeth (48.4)
15. Eastbourne (58.5)	15. Spennymoor (48.5)
16. Streatham (58.2)	16. Forest of Dean (48.5)
17. Hornsey (57.9)	17. Middlesborough E (48.8)
18. Ealing (57.7)	18. Jarrow (48.8)
19. Hythe (57.6)	19. Chester Le Street (48.8)
20. Torquay (57.5)	20. Rotherham (48.9)
21. Isle of Thanet (57.5)	21. Doncaster (48.9)
22. Southend (57.3)	22. Cannock (49.0)
23. Richmond (57.1)	23. Nuneaton (49.0)
24. Scarborough (57.1)	24. Sheffield Attercliffe (49.0)
25. Tonbridge (57.0)	25. Workington (49.1)

Source: Calculated from figures given in *Registrar General's Statistical Review* (1929), pp. 83–94.

Of more interest is the question of why there tended to be more women voters in middle-class areas. As Table 7.3 suggests, for some reason this tendency became more pronounced after 1928, when women voters achieved universal suffrage for all those aged 21 or over. Women's parliamentary franchise had been limited previously not only by the exclusion of all women below the age of 30, but also by the fact that women, unlike men, only qualified as householders (or their spouses). In this regard the 1918–1928 women's franchise was similar to the municipal franchise outlined in Chapter Four, excluding domestic servants, tenants of furnished rooms, and family members other than spouses living with householders.

The *Liverpool Daily Post* noted the higher proportion of women in the better-off districts of the city when the electoral register for 1929 was published. Three possible reasons for this were put forward. First, the preponderance of 'female domestic servants in the best residential districts' was cited. Second, it was suggested that there were 'more unmarried daughters in well-to-do than in working-class homes'. Third, it was suggested that 'unmarried professional and business women have their rooms and flats in the most attractive of the suburbs'.[77] Only the first of these three factors seems plausible. Even if the second could be proved, it is unclear why a lower marriage-rate among middle-class daughters should have affected the electoral register at all, once the householder qualification for women had been abolished. The third suggestion appears to be something of a tautology.

A fourth possibility should perhaps be added. Life expectancy for women was generally higher than for men, and had been skewed even more so in this period by the effects of the First World War.[78] Greater longevity was probably accentuated even more for middle-class women. They had the advantages over working-class women of lower birth-rates in earlier decades, better nutrition and health-care, and far better prospects of pensions and other forms of social security in old age.[79] The prevalence of middle-class retirement resorts among the constituencies with the highest proportion of women voters in Table 7.4 would seem to confirm this factor.

For cities like Liverpool, however, the concentration of domestic servants in middle-class areas was probably decisive. There were almost 20,000 female domestic servants recorded in the 1931 census for Liverpool, and the number had actually increased by 3,000 over the 1921 figure. Many still resided in the households of their employers, and many others lived in lodgings near to their place of employment. Most of them would have been excluded from the parliamentary franchise before 1928 as non-householders, regardless of their age. Their impact would have been most noticeable after 1928, therefore, which is confirmed by Table 7.3.

These are the likely causes, then, of the higher proportion of female voters found in middle-class divisions. The statistical relationships they produced tell us nothing about the way women in general voted. Rasmussen tries to use variations in the correlation in different elections to show trends over time in the women's vote, and also in different types of seat, defined statistically as 'middle-class', 'mining' and so on. In all these exercises, however, the problem remains that it is voting patterns related to social class, and not sex, that are being identified. So the higher correlations he finds for the 1931 election, for instance, may simply reflect a stronger trend against Labour by middle-class voters, rather than any collapse in the women's vote. The correlations in mining constituencies (defined as those with 20 per cent or more of male workers in mining) may reflect differences between those that included some middle-class areas in their boundaries, and those that did not.

In short, the statistical approach to this problem is at best unhelpful, and at worst seriously misleading. As Duncan Tanner has remarked drily, these accounts are 'littered with technical problems', and women's voting behaviour in this period 'remains an open question'.[80] It is necessary to turn to more qualitative evidence, therefore.

In this regard, there were signs that Labour benefitted from the extension of the franchise to women as far as Liverpool was concerned. Special attention was given to the concerns of women voters by the party. In August 1922, for instance, Mrs Anderson, the national women's organiser, was invited to address the LTCLP 'on that important portion of the electorate, "the woman voter"'.[82] She was 'warmly received', and argued that women would 'become a force over our [Labour] electoral organisation machinery'. She hoped that 'sympathetic consideration' would be given, especially with regard to financing women's activities in the party. Her arguments appear to have been accepted, in that women's influence in the party did increase through the early and mid-1920s, as shown earlier.

There is little evidence in the early 1920s that this awareness of the importance of women voters was translated into electoral support. However, the extension of the women's franchise in 1928 focused local attention on the question, and discussion of the impact on the succeeding general election of May 1929 throws some light on the issue. Local press coverage emphasized two points: first, that women voted in large numbers and second, that their votes favoured Labour. One newspaper reported: 'The women electors, matrons as well as 'flappers', are believed to have polled heavily. At many of the booths the women predominated, at any rate until tea time, and even from then onward till the close at 9 pm the male majority, if existent, was quite small.'[82] In a number of local seats it was also reported that women supported Labour strongly. Ironically, the only woman candidate in Liverpool, Margaret Beavan, stood for the Tories in Everton. Labour captured the seat for the first time, though, suggesting that her sex was of no benefit to her as far as attracting the new voters was concerned. In Kirkdale, also won for the first time by Labour, it was reported that 'here again the bulk of the newcomers proved to be supporters of the Labour Party'. In West Toxteth, Labour increased its majority, and 'here too the new voters ... favoured Labour'. In Fairfield,

Labour lost narrowly, but nevertheless increased its share of the vote from 37 to 47 per cent. The Labour candidate attributed this to 'the magnificent work of the women'.[83]

There is certainly no sign of apathy, nor of greater conservatism, amongst women voters from this evidence. It remains an open question whether women's electoral support for Labour remained strong through the 1930s. As argued earlier, shifts both locally and nationally in party policy and structure gave good cause for some women at least to turn away from Labour. The reduced role of women within the local party, notwithstanding Bessie Braddock's individual efforts, could not have helped to attract women's votes either. Definitive confirmation of these speculations remains elusive, however.

Women, gender and the Labour Party

To summarize, the relationship between the Labour Party and women in Liverpool was a complex one. It varied over time, with women's influence in the party being stronger in the 1920s than the 1930s. It was influenced by the nature of gender relations in the local labour market, and also by the particular occupational groups that made up the early Labour Party. It was strongly affected by religious considerations from the late 1920s, and was also linked to national changes in the Labour Party in the late 1920s and early 1930s. Comparing the relationship with the few local studies from other parts of the country that we have, women seemed to have had less impact on Labour in Liverpool than they did in either London or Nelson, but more than in Lancaster. The nearest comparison seems to be with Preston, with greater influence in the 1920s declining in the 1930s, but for rather different reasons.

To put these conclusions in the context of the debate raised near the beginning of this chapter on working-class culture and politics, it could be argued that gender, along with religion and occupational differences, influenced working-class life and culture crucially in Liverpool, and in turn affected the relationship between that culture and Labour politics. Neither an economic nor a cultural reductionism can do full justice to these complex historical relationships.

The final concern of this book is to round off the analysis by considering other connections between work, community, and politics in as much as they affected the fortunes of the Labour Party. To do this, the religious, occupational and political disposition of Liverpool's population needs to be established. This is the task of Chapter Eight.

References

1. An earlier version of this chapter appeared as 'Class, religion and gender: Liverpool Labour Party and women, 1918–1939', in J. Belchem (ed.),

Popular Politics, Riot and Labour: Essays in Liverpool History, 1790–1940 (Liverpool University Press, Liverpool: 1992).

2.   Joan Kelly, quoted in M. J. Buhle, 'Gender and labor history', in J. Carroll Moody and A. Kessler-Harris (eds), *Perspectives on American Labor History: The Problem of Synthesis* (N. Illinois University Press, De Kalb: 1989), pp. 61–2.

3.   See, for instance, M. Savage, *The Dynamics of Working-Class Politics: The Labour Movement in Preston, 1880–1940* (Cambridge University Press, Cambridge: 1987); J. Mark-Lawson, *et al.*, 'Gender and Local politics: struggles over welfare policies, 1918–1939', in L. Murgatroyd *et al.* (eds), *Localities, Class and Gender* (Pion, London: 1985); A. Baron (ed.), *Work Engendered: Toward a New History of American Labor* (Cornell University Press, Ithaca: 1991); E. Faue, *Community of Suffering and Struggle: Women, Men and the Labor Movement in Minneapolis, 1915–1945* (University of North Carolina Press, Chapel Hill: 1991); D.Frank, *Purchasing Power: Consumer Organizing, Gender, and the Seattle Labor Movement, 1919–1929* (Cambridge University Press, New York: 1994).

4.   N. Kirk, 'Traditional working-class culture and the "Rise of Labour": some preliminary questions and observations', *Social History* 16, no. 2 (May 1991), p. 213; Kirk points to the local studies by Savage and Mark-Lawson quoted above.

5.   See, for instance, A. Shallice, 'Liverpool Labourism and Irish Nationalism in the 1920s and 1930s', *Bulletin of the North West Labour History Society* 8 (1982); J.Smith, 'Labour tradition in Glasgow and Liverpool', *History Workshop* 17 (Spring 1984); P. J. Waller, *Democracy and Sectarianism: A Political and Social History of Liverpool, 1868–1939* (Liverpool University Press, Liverpool: 1981).

6.   The notable exception is L. Grant, 'Women Workers and the Sexual Division of Labour: Liverpool 1890–1939' (unpublished Ph. D. thesis, University of Liverpool: 1987), p. 102.

7.   For the history of the Women's Labour League, see M. Rendel, 'The contribution of the Women's Labour League to the winning of the franchise', in L. Middleton (ed.), *Women in the Labour Movement* (Croom Helm, London: 1977); C. Collette, *For Labour and for Women: The Women's Labour League, 1906–14* (Manchester University Press, Manchester: 1989).

8.   Liverpool Labour Party, Executive Committee, *Minutes* (27 September 1918).

9.   *Ibid., Minutes* (2 April 1919, 7 April 1920).

10.   LTCLP, Executive Committee, *Minutes* (11 April 1921; 12 April 1922).

11.   *Ibid.*

12.   On these developments, see H. Wainwright, *Labour: A Tale of Two Parties* (Hogarth Press, London: 1987), pp. 177–9; H. Smith, 'Sex vs. class: British feminists and the labour movement, 1919–1929', *The Historian* 47 (1984); M Pugh, 'Domesticity and the decline of feminism, 1930–1950', in H. Smith (ed.), *British Feminism in the Twentieth Century* (Edward Elgar, Aldershot, 1990).

13.   Mark-Lawson *et al.*, 'Gender and local politics', pp. 209–13.

14.   Savage, *The Dynamics of Working-class Politics*, pp. 167–87.

15.   Manchester Women's History Group, 'Ideology in bricks and mortar: women's housing in Manchester between the wars', *North West Labour*

History 12 (1987), especially pp. 32–5. Linda Walker has been further developing this work on women and the Labour Party, and the results of her research are awaited with interest.

16. P. Thane, 'The women of the British Labour Party and feminism, 1906–1945', in Smith (ed.), *British Feminism in the Twentieth Century*.

17. 1931 census, tables of occupation.

18. E. Roberts, *Women's Work, 1840–1940* (Macmillan, London: 1988), pp. 18–20.

19. Mark-Lawson *et al.*, 'Gender and local politics', pp. 210–11.

20. Grant, 'Women Workers and the Sexual Division of Labour', p. 102.

21. *Ibid.*, pp. 85–97.

22. *Ibid.*, p. 86.

23. See, for instance, E. Taplin, *The Dockers' Union: A Study of the National Union of Dock Labourers, 1889–1922* (Leicester University Press, Leicester: 1986), pp. 133–7.

24. See A. Phillips and B. Taylor, 'Sex and skill: notes towards a feminist economics', *Feminist Review* 6 (1980).

25. Liverpool Trades Council, *Minutes* (27 July 1910; 13 December 1911; 23 October 1912).

26. Liverpool Labour Representation Committee, *Minutes* (2 July 1913).

27. *Ibid.* (30 January 1914).

28. Liverpool Labour Party, *Minutes* (3 September 1919).

29. LTCLP, *Minutes* (13 September 1925).

30. *Ibid.* (4 November 1925).

31. *Ibid.* (2 December 1925).

32. *Ibid.* (20 April and 19 May 1927).

33. See, for instance, the Women's Co-operative Guild pamphlets, *The Milk We Want* (1925), *Food Purity* (1926), and *Food Values* (1926), in the Labour Archive at the University of Hull Library.

34. LTCLP, *Minutes* (26 September 1928).

35. *Ibid.* (15 August 1923).

36. *Ibid.* (23 June 1926–7 April 1927).

37. *Ibid.* (15 November 1926).

38. See J. Saville, 'May Day 1937', in A. Briggs and J. Saville (eds), *Essays in Labour History, 1918–39* (Macmillan, London: 1977).

39. Smith, 'Sex vs. class', pp. 32–3.

40. On the full implications of the Anomalies Act, see S. Davies *et al.*, *Genuinely Seeking Work: Mass Unemployment on Merseyside in the 1930s* (Liverpress, Liverpool: 1992), Ch. 5.

41. LTCLP, *Minutes* (12 April 1926; 23 March 1928).

42. Liverpool Co-operative Society Ltd., *Quarterly Report* (25 October 1926), pp. 12–13.

43. *Liverpool Daily Post* (28 May 1929).

44. Pugh, 'Domesticity and the decline of feminism', p. 157.

45. Davies *et al.*, *Genuinely Seeking Work*, Ch. 5.

46. M. Nightingale *et al.*, *Merseyside in Crisis* (Manchester Free Press, Manchester: 1980), pp. 76–9; T. Lane, *Liverpool: Gateway of Empire* (Lawrence and Wishart, London: 1987), pp. 137–8.

47. Liverpool City Council, *Minutes* (1 April 1936); *Liverpool Daily Post* (2 April 1936).

48. See S. Rowbotham, *A New World for Women. Stella Brown: Socialist Feminist* (London: 1977), pp. 43–59; J. Lewis, *The Politics of Motherhood: Child and Maternal Welfare in England, 1900–1939* (Croom Helm, London: 1980), pp. 197–8; B. Campbell, *The Iron Ladies: Why do Women Vote Tory?* (Virago, London: 1987), pp. 63–4; Wainwright, *Labour: A Tale of Two Parties*, pp. 178–9.

49. Thane, 'The women of the British Labour Party', p. 137.

50. J. Reynolds and K. Laybourn, *Labour Heartland: A History of the Labour Party in W. Yorkshire during the Inter-War Years, 1918–39* (Bradford University Press, Bradford: 1987), p. 42; S. Fielding, 'The Irish Catholics of Manchester and Salford: Aspects of their Religious and Political History, 1890–1939' (unpublished Ph. D. thesis, University of Warwick, 1988).

51. S. Rowbotham, *Hidden from History: 300 Years of Women's Oppression and the Fight Against It* (Pluto Press, London, 1973), pp. 151–6.

52. LTCLP, *Minutes* (3 January 1923).

53. *Parliamentary Debates*, 5th series, Vol. 234, cols. 538–42 (24 January 1930).

54. *Ibid.*, Vol. 272, cols. 826–28 (30 November 1932).

55. *Ibid.*, Vol. 304, cols. 1136–40 (17 July 1935); Vol. 317, col. 1048 (12 November 1936).

56. Fielding, *The Irish Catholics of Manchester and Salford*; S. Fielding, 'Irish politics in Manchester, 1890–1914', *International Review of Social History* 33 (1988).

57. Pugh, 'Domesticity and the decline of feminism', pp. 156–7.

58. LTCLP, Labour Group Meeting, *Minutes* (2 June 1936).

59. *Ibid.* (11 March 1938).

60. *Liverpool Daily Post* (27 June 1936).

61. National Conference on Maternity and Child Welfare, Liverpool (1–3 July 1936), *Official Programme and Handbook*.

62. S. Kingsley Kent, 'Gender reconstruction after the First World War' in Smith (ed.), *British Feminism in the Twentieth Century*.

63. B. Harrison, *Prudent Revolutionaries: Portraits of British Feminists Between the Wars* (Clarendon Press, Oxford: 1987), p. 104.

64. J. Alberti, *Beyond Suffrage: Feminists in War and Peace, 1914–28* (Macmillan, London: 1989), p. 165; see also M. Pugh, *Women and the Women's Movement in Britain, 1914–1959* (Macmillan, London: 1992), pp. 235–63.

65. Quoted in S. Kingsley Kent, 'The politics of sexual difference: World War I and the demise of British feminism', *Journal of British Studies* 27, no. 3 (1988), p. 240.

66. P. Hollis, *Ladies Elect: Women in English Local Government, 1865–1914* (Clarendon Press, Oxford: 1987).

67. Thane, 'The women of the British Labour Party', p. 140.

68. B. Harrison, *Separate Spheres: The Opposition to Women's Suffrage in Britain* (Croom Helm, London: 1978), pp. 236–7.

69. M. Stacey and M. Price, *Women, Power and Politics* (Clarendon, Oxford: 1981), p. 91.

70. Liverpool Labour Party, *Minutes* (24 November 1918).

71. Smith, 'Labour tradition in Glasgow and Liverpool', p. 39.

72. See M. Goot and E. Reid, 'Women: if not apolitical, then conservative', in J.Siltanen and M. Stanworth (eds), *Women and the Public Sphere: A Critique of Sociology and Politics* (Hutchinson, London: 1984), pp. 122–36; see also

J.Hills, 'Women and voting in Britain', in Siltanen and Stanworth, *Women and the Public Sphere*, pp. 137–9.

73. Goot and Reid, 'Women: if not apolitical, then conservative', p. 125.

74. J.Turner, 'The Labour vote and the franchise after 1918: an investigation of the English evidence', in P. Denley and D. Hopkin (eds), *History and Computing* (Manchester University Press, Manchester: 1987), p. 142; Pugh, *Women and the Women's Movement*, p. 152; J.Rasmussen, 'Women in Labour: the flapper vote and party system transformation in Britain', *Electoral Studies* 3, no. 1 (1984), p. 60.

75. Rasmussen, 'Women in Labour', pp. 56–60.

76. The Pearson's correlation coefficients for the data are as follows: 1924, –0.04; 1929, –0.85; 1931, –0.68; 1935, –0.76.

77. *Liverpool Daily Post* (29 April 1929).

78. H. Jones, *Health and Society in Twentieth-Century Britain* (Longman, London: 1994), p. 196.

79. *Ibid.*, pp. 59–69.

80. D. Tanner, *Political Change and the Labour Party, 1900–1918* (Cambridge University Press, Cambridge: 1990), p. 308.

81. LTCLP, *Minutes* (2 August 1922).

82. *Liverpool Daily Post* (31 May 1929).

83. *Ibid.*

8 The social and political characteristics of the electoral wards of Liverpool

This chapter will analyse variations in social characteristics within the city and their relationship to political allegiance. This will be done on a ward basis, showing how wards in the city varied in their social composition and in their pattern of voting behaviour in local elections. From this it will be possible to distinguish the spatial contours of differentiation within the working class, especially those related to religion and occupation, and in turn to evaluate their impact on Labour's progress.

The religious character of wards

It is a relatively straightforward task to establish the predominant religious composition of each ward in the city. First, it is made easier by the fact that the residential segregation of different ethnic groups in the city was quite clearly defined. Analysis of nineteenth-century Liverpool has shown how different ethnic groups tended to be concentrated in particular areas of the city.[1] While this pattern of residential segregation had begun to change by the beginning of the twentieth century, and was to be changed much more fundamentally in the 1920s and 1930s by slum clearance and the development of council housing, it was still the case that clearly defined Catholic and Protestant areas of the city were recognized. To this day, most of the older inhabitants of Liverpool would identify the north-end dockside areas as traditionally strongly Catholic, or the Dingle in the south and the heights of Netherfield and St Domingo in the north as strongly Protestant. Second, there are a number of historical sources available which confirm these patterns of religious segregation fairly clearly, as will be shown below in the analysis of the distribution of church places and of children in voluntary and board schools.

However, it would be unwise to see the pattern of religious differentiation of Liverpool's population identified here as being too clear-cut. As already stressed in previous chapters, ward boundaries were selected for a combination of reasons, but mainly as a result of traditional notions of what constituted a locality mixed with the political needs of the day. The religious character of a locality may have been part of its traditional rationale, and political expedience might also dictate that boundaries of religion be reflected in wards. In the end, though, there was no guarantee that ward boundaries would coincide precisely with boundaries of religion, or of any other form of social differentiation. The long interval between the redistribution of ward boundaries in Liverpool only made this more unlikely over time, as economic and social change took place. So, however clearly defined religious segregation may have been, wards reflected it only imperfectly.

Turning to the evidence, then, the lists of churches and chapels and elementary schools published each year in the *Liverpool Official Red Book* and the street directories, together with the religious surveys carried out for the *Liverpool Daily Post*, all provide a valuable source of information. It would have been preferable to have used the lists for one particular year, but this was not possible as the detail provided varied from one year to another. The list of schools in the *Red Book* only gave figures for the number of children accommodated at each school in the early 1920s, and so 1923 has been selected. The detail of the number of seats (or sittings) provided in each church, on the other hand, varied from year to year but was never complete. The figures in the 1930 street directory have been selected as they were reasonably comprehensive in that year. For those churches that gave no detail in this period, the figures for their accommodation in the 1902 religious survey have had to be used. Obviously these figures may not be totally accurate, as some churches may have been extended in the intervening period, but this is unlikely to have been very significant. The results of the analysis of these two sources are shown in Tables 8.1 and 8.2.

Neither of these two tables can be taken to represent exact percentages of Catholics, Anglicans and Nonconformists in the city. In the case of both churches and schools, the community that they served would not have coincided precisely with ward boundaries, and those that were situated on or very near to boundary streets in particular could be misleading. For instance, the Catholic Our Lady of Mount Carmel was situated on the corner of High Park Street and Admiral Street, which was in Dingle ward, and its 800 seats have been allocated to Dingle in Table 8.1. However, this church was on the boundary with Prince's Park ward, and also only a block away from Brunswick, and probably served all three wards.

Equally problematic was All Saints Church of England school, situated on Great Nelson Street. Its 403 pupils have been allocated to Scotland South ward, but it was only yards from the boundary with Netherfield ward, and on the other side of Scotland Road from most of the inhabitants of Scotland South. However, these were the two most questionable examples, and most were situated more centrally in the wards. Combining the data from the two tables also alleviates this difficulty, as 'boundary' issues were unlikely to coincide in both. There is also the problem that both schools and churches may have reflected earlier demand from population that had since declined. Consequently, in inner-city areas, where considerable slum clearance had taken place already by the 1920s, the

Table 8.1 Liverpool churches by ward, 1929 (% in brackets)

Ward	Anglican		Catholic		Nonconformist	
	No.	Sittings	No.	Sittings	No.	Sittings
Abercromby	6	1,050 (10)	0	0	10	9,074 (90)
Aigburth	2	1,732 (58)	1	224 (8)	2	1,020 (34)
Allerton	2	1,250 (86)	1	200 (14)	0	0
Anfield	5	3,375 (34)	2	1,100 (11)	11	5,494 (55)
Breckfield	3	2,250 (65)	0	0	2	1,200 (35)
Brunswick	4	2,900 (45)	2	2,074 (32)	4	1,510 (23)
Castle St.	0	0	0	0	0	0
Childwall	1	500 (63)	1	300 (37)	0	0
Croxteth*	—	—	—	—	—	—
Dingle	3	2,480 (41)	1	800 (13)	6	2,700 (45)
Edge Hill	2	1,656 (32)	2	1,300 (25)	4	2,240 (43)
Everton	4	4,870 (43)	2	2,533 (22)	7	3,926 (35)
Exchange	1	1,332 (60)	1	900 (40)	0	0
Fairfield	4	2,650 (43)	1	200 (3)	5	3,303 (54)
Fazakerley	2	1,200 (80)	0	0	1	300 (20)
Garston	2	1,650 (39)	1	320 (7)	8	2,297 (54)
Granby	3	2,050 (46)	1	350 (8)	3	2,010 (46)
Gt George	2	1,950 (30)	3	2,740 (42)	2	1,850 (28)
Kensington	2	1,645 (28)	0	0	9	4,166 (72)
Kirkdale	6	4,695 (43)	1	900 (8)	9	5,350 (49)
Little Woolton	0	0	0	0	0	0
Low Hill	2	1,600 (39)	1	700 (17)	3	1,800 (44)
M Woolton	2	750 (45)	1	200 (12)	3	730 (43)
Netherfield	6	4,752 (67)	0	0	5	2,350 (33)
Old Swan	3	1,414 (34)	2	900 (22)	4	1,790 (44)
Prince's Park	4	4,070 (35)	0	0	11	7,650 (65)
St Anne's	5	4,034 (77)	1	500 (10)	1	700 (13)
St Domingo	3	2,130 (32)	1	575 (9)	7	3,938 (50)
St Peter's	1	900 (41)	1	1,300 (59)	0	0
Sandhills	0	0	2	1,330 (73)	1	500 (27)
Scotland N	1	800 (18)	3	3,000 (67)	1	700 (15)
Scotland S	5	4,760 (53)	5	4,220 (47)	0	0
Sefton Park E	3	1,260 (24)	1	450 (8)	6	3,610 (68)
Sefton Park W	3	2,030 (60)	1	470 (14)	1	900 (26)
Vauxhall	0	0	1	1,500(100)	0	0
Walton	3	2,700 (39)	3	800 (11)	10	3,505 (50)
Warbreck	1	800 (28)	1	650 (23)	3	1,370 (49)
Wavertree	3	2,100 (28)	2	850 (11)	7	4,605 (61)
Wavertree W	1	850 (37)	0	0	3	1,450 (63)
West Derby	1	1,000 (53)	0	0	2	880 (47)

* Croxteth ward only added to city in 1928, and no churches had yet been constructed.

Source: *Liverpool Official Red Book* (1930), pp. 449–81; *Kelly's Directory of Liverpool* (1930), pp. 2005–16; *Liverpool Daily Post*, 11 November 1902.

Table 8.2 Liverpool public elementary schools: summary of accommodation for the month ending 30 September 1922 (% in brackets)

Ward	Catholic		Council		C. of E.		Wesleyan		Total
Abercromby	0		0		1,091	(69)	497	(31)	1,588
Aigburth	133	(10)	1,009	(77)	176	(13)	0		1,318
Allerton	0		0		0		0		0
Anfield	1,373	(44)	243	(8)	1,532	(48)	0		3,148
Breckfield	0		2,489	(100)	0		0		2,489
Brunswick	2,128	(59)	1,174	(32)	336	(9)	0		3,638
Castle St	0		0		0		0		0
Childwall	0		0		0		0		0
Croxteth*	1,979	(20)	7,923	(80)	0		0		9,902
Dingle	925	(12)	5,347	(68)	1,646	(20)	0		7,918
Edge Hill	1,141	(18)	3,752	(59)	1,486	(23)	0		6,379
Everton	3,101	(38)	2,737	(34)	1,704	(21)	574	(7)	8,116
Exchange	839	(63)	0		487	(37)	0		1,326
Fairfield	424	(10)	3,896	(90)	0		0		4,320
Fazakerley	0		346	(74)	120	(26)	0		466
Garston	521	(15)	1,544	(45)	1,391	(40)	0		3,456
Granby	487	(10)	2,514	(54)	1,692	(36)	0		4,693
Gt George	2,333	(54)	1,597	(37)	360	(9)	0		4,290
Kensington	0		2,840	(86)	483	(14)	0		3,323
Kirkdale	2,580	(23)	5,884	(53)	2,592	(24)	0		11,056
Little Woolton	0		0		309	(100)	0		309
Low Hill	990	(26)	2,178	(56)	695	(18)	0		3,863
Much Woolton	399	(41)	0		579	(59)	0		978
Netherfield	0		4,398	(73)	1,600	(27)	0		5,998
Old Swan	1,128	(21)	2,879	(54)	1,296	(25)	0		5,303
Prince's Park	0		662	(30)	1,519	(70)	0		2,181
St Anne's	310	(32)	0		650	(68)	0		960
St Domingo	1,188	(23)	3,189	(62)	746	(15)	0		5,123
St Peter's	1,600	(81)	0		387	(19)	0		1,987
Sandhills	1,926	(48)	1,248	(31)	837	(21)	0		4,011
Scotland N	4,664	(95)	0		229	(5)	0		4,893
Scotland S	5,145	(74)	1,008	(14)	846	(12)	0		6,999
Sefton Park E	0		1,946	(61)	1,239	(39)	0		3,185
Sefton Park W	141	(9)	926	(61)	447	(30)	0		1,514
Vauxhall	785	(66)	0		408	(34)	0		1,193
Walton	336	(4)	7,151	(85)	952	(11)	0		8,439
Warbreck	501	(14)	2,640	(74)	419	(12)	0		3,560
Wavertree	371	(10)	2,054	(55)	1,318	(35)	0		3,743
Wavertree W	856	(28)	1,734	(56)	515	(16)	0		3,105
West Derby	559	(12)	2,628	(58)	1,325	(30)	0		4,512
Total	36,884	(26)	70,013	(50)	31,412	(23)	1,071	(1)	139,380

* Croxteth ward not in existence in 1923 – figures for Croxteth quoted are from *Population Problems of New Estates*, Liverpool University Social Studies Dept. (1937), p. 44, and are not included in totals for whole city.

Source: *Liverpool Official Red Book* (1923), pp. 278–88.

figures were probably over-estimates. Equally, in suburban areas where new housing estates were being developed, the construction of churches and schools probably lagged behind the growth of population. This was certainly the case for Croxteth ward, which already had 25,000 residents by 1931, but no churches built by 1930.

Nevertheless, taken together, these tables provide an indicator of the religious complexion of wards, and show the crucial sectarian divide in the working class. Combining them to give an index of Catholic influence provides clear-cut results. This has been done by calculating the average of the percentages of Catholic school places, and church seats, for each ward. It should be stressed that these averages do not reflect the exact statistical proportions of Catholics within wards, but are an indicator of Catholic influence. The results are shown in Table 8.3, and summarized in Figure 8.1.

A number of groups of wards were distinguishable by their religious complexion. First, there were eight wards – Sandhills, Scotland North, Scotland South, Vauxhall, Exchange, St Peter's, Great George and Brunswick – where Catholic influence was strong. These wards stretched in a line along the river from Sandhills in the north to Brunswick in the south, with only tiny Castle Street ward in the city centre breaking the continuity. Next were a number of predominantly working-class wards with some moderate Catholic influence, namely St Anne's, Everton, Low Hill and Edge Hill. These were situated just inland and uphill from the city centre. Third, there were two predominantly lower-middle-class suburban wards, Anfield and Old Swan, and one semi-rural ward, Much Woolton, where some Catholic influence was found. There were very few Catholic schools and churches in the suburbs as a whole, serving a small Catholic population scattered widely across the middle-class areas of the city. The Catholic presence registered in these specific wards, therefore, is probably misleading, and really reflects the situation for the whole of the suburbs. Lastly, and standing on its own, was Croxteth ward, added to the city in 1928 to allow for the development of council housing. The moderate Catholic influence here was probably a good reflection of the proportion of Catholics and Protestants being relocated in the 1920s and 1930s. Finally, the rest of the wards can be characterized as non-Catholic, but within them can be identified the predominantly working- class wards of Kirkdale, St Domingo and Netherfield in the north of the city, and Dingle and Garston along the river to the south.

The occupational character of wards

The pattern of differentiation of wards according to different types of occupation and related forms of social division is inherently much harder to establish than the religious divide. The definitional problems of social

Table 8.3 Index of Catholic presence in wards

(A)	(B)	(C)
Proportion school places (%)	*Proportion church sittings (%)*	*Index influence (average of A + B)*
1. Scotland N (95)	1. Vauxhall (100)	1. Vauxhall (83)
2. St Peter's (81)	2. Sandhills (73)	2. Scotland N (81)
3. Scotland S (74)	3. Scotland N (67)	3. St Peter's (70)
4. Vauxhall (66)	4. St Peter's (59)	4. Scotland S (61)
5. Exchange (63)	5. Scotland S (47)	5. Sandhills (61)
6. Brunswick (59)	6. Gt George (42)	6. Exchange (52)
7. Gt George (54)	7. Exchange (40)	7. Gt George (48)
8. Sandhills (48)	8. Childwall (37)	8. Brunswick (46)
9. Anfield (44)	9. Brunswick (32)	9. Everton (30)
10. Much Woolton (41)	10. Edge Hill (25)	10. Anfield (28)
11. Everton (38)	11. Warbreck (23)	11. Much Woolton (27)
12. St Anne's (32)	12. Everton (22)	12. Low Hill (22)
13. Wavertree W (28)	13. Old Swan (22)	13. Old Swan (22)
14. Low Hill (26)	14. Low Hill (17)	14. Edge Hill (22)
15. St Domingo (23)	15. Allerton (14)	15. St Anne's (21)
16. Kirkdale (23)	16. Sefton Park W (14)	16. Croxteth (20)*
17. Old Swan (21)	17. Dingle (13)	17. Warbreck (19)
18. Croxteth (20)*	18. Much Woolton (12)	18. Childwall (19)
19. Edge Hill (18)	19. Anfield (11)	19. St Domingo (16)
20. Garston (15)	20. Wavertree (11)	20. Kirkdale (16)
21. Warbreck (14)	21. Walton (11)	21. Wavertree W (14)
22. Dingle (12)	22. St Anne's (10)	22. Dingle (13)
23. West Derby (12)	23. St Domingo (9)	23. Sefton Park W (12)
24. Wavertree (10)*	24. Aigburth (8)	24. Garston (11)
25. Aigburth (10)	25. Granby (8)	25. Wavertree (11)
26. Granby (10)	26. Kirkdale (8)	26. Aigburth (9)
27. Fairfield (10)	27. Sefton Park E (8)	27. Granby (9)
28. Sefton Park W (9)	28. Garston (7)	28. Walton (8)
29. Walton (4)	29. Fairfield (3)	29. Allerton (7)
30. Abercromby (0)	30. Abercromby (0)	30. Fairfield (7)
31. Allerton (0)	31. Breckfield (0)	31. West Derby (6)
32. Breckfield (0)	32. Castle St. (0)	32. Sefton Park E (4)
33. Castle St. (0)	33. Croxteth (–)*	33. Abercromby (0)
34. Childwall (0)	34. Fazakerley (0)	34. Breckfield (0)
35. Fazakerley (0)	35. Kensington (0)	35. Castle St. (0)
36. Kensington (0)	36. Little Woolton (0)	36. Fazakerley (0)
37. Little Woolton (0)	37. Netherfield (0)	37. Kensington (0)
38. Netherfield (0)	38. Prince's Park (0)	38. Little Woolton (0)
39. Prince's Park (0)	39. Wavertree W (0)	39. Netherfield (0)
40. Sefton Park E (0)	40. West Derby (0)	40. Prince's Park (0)
Average (26)	(17)	(21.5)

* Croxteth figure for schools is for 1938, and the index figure for this ward is the schools figure alone, as no churches had been constructed by 1930.

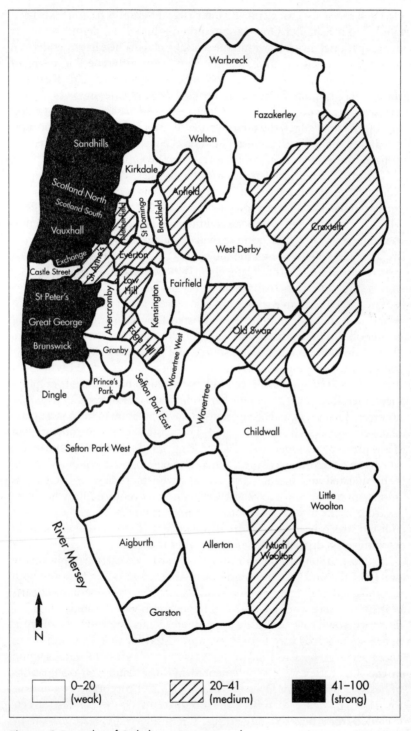

Figure 8.1 Index of Catholic presence in wards

203

class and the analysis of intra- and inter-class differences have already been alluded to in Chapter One. As stated there, there is no definitive model of occupational divisions within the working class. The categories devised here are intended to emphasize the significant differences in terms of occupation within the Liverpool working class. Any such system of categorization has its limitations, and in the most difficult cases involves making almost arbitrary decisions to distinguish between different types of work. Having acknowledged the imperfection of the system, what is important is that it is applied with consistency. The occupational categories that are utilized in this chapter are, therefore, used throughout this book.

The other major problem lies with the sources. While the census provides occupational data for the whole city, it is not broken down into smaller units. Some population data is provided at the ward level, some of which can be analysed to provide additional indicators of social difference, as will be seen later. The occupational characteristics of wards, however, are only accessible through the full census returns, and the one hundred year rule prevents their use later than 1891 at present. For the purposes of this study that is too early to be really useful.

The only alternative sources to the census are the street directories, which were published annually and listed the occupations of heads of households. The fact that other household members were never listed clearly limits the accuracy of this source, and particularly limits any indication of female employment, as men were almost always defined as heads of households. The directories can only be taken to indicate male employment, therefore. There was a further limitation to the directories than this, however. The names and occupations of the population in the poorer parts of the city were less likely to be listed. The reasons for this are obscure, but it was presumably linked to the advertising and distribution purposes for which the directories were used. It may also be supposed that the relatively well-educated and middle-class citizens who must have collected this information may not have been very willing to venture into what were regarded as the most insalubrious streets of the city. It is also the case that unlisted streets became far more common after 1914, so that virtually all working-class districts were excluded after that date.

A survey of some of the working-class wards was carried out using the pre-1914 directories. The wards were selected in order to cover both Catholic and non-Catholic areas, and also the various geographical parts of the city where working-class neighbourhoods were located. The 1911 directory would have been most appropriate, coinciding with a census year, but in some wards very few streets were listed for that year, and it was necessary to go back to 1900 in some cases. In all cases, the figures found in the directories were supplemented by information on occupations of heads of households given in lists of tenants of corporation tenements for 1907, in order to reflect the occupations of the poorest streets excluded from the street directories. The results of these surveys are by no means definitive, but are the best indicator that can be contrived of the occupational characteristics of the selected wards in the period 1900 to 1911. The full explanation of the method used to calculate these figures, and a full list of the results, can be found in Appendix XIII. A summary of the results can be found in Tables 8.4 and 8.5, in which, for comparative purposes, are also included figures for the whole of Liverpool in 1911. These have been calculated from the 1911 census, using exactly the same system of categorization that was used in the surveys. Additionally, figures for Croxteth ward for 1940 have been provided. This is to analyse a very different type of working-class area, a suburban development of council housing in the inter-war years. These are based solely on the 1940 street directory. The new estates were fully listed in the directories in the 1930s, which in itself is an indicator of the social characteristics of these areas, but 1940 was selected to allow for the fullest development of the estates. This survey, unlike the others, does not cover every street, due to the vast scale of this ward, but only a substantial section of the largest and central estate in the ward. This was Norris Green, which it is assumed was representative of the other council estates, most notably Fazakerley and Dovecot, which were partially included at the extremities of Croxteth ward. Additionally, it should be noted that the categorization of employment had to be adjusted slightly to take account of the changing names of some jobs over time, and also the development of new types of occupation. Finally, figures for the whole of Liverpool in 1931, derived from the census, are also included to show any significant changes overall since 1911.

The results of these surveys reveal a great deal about the varying character of the occupational structure of different working-class areas of the city. There is a range of variation between, at one end of the scale, wards with a greater proportion of the male workforce concentrated in occupations defined as unskilled, lower-paid, and casually-employed, and at the other end, in higher-paid, permanent and skilled occupations. The key indicators of this variation are the 'transport and associated' category, and the various 'trades' categories grouped together. Neither of these could be defined as exclusively skilled or unskilled, or casual and non-casual, groups, but most of the occupations grouped in the former were dock-related, casual jobs, while in the latter were concentrated many of the most skilled, permanent jobs in the city. The pattern can best be represented by listing the wards in order according to the proportions in these two categories, as shown in Table 8.6. As can be seen, the predominantly Catholic, dockside wards of Scotland South and Brunswick have the highest proportion in transport and, conversely, almost the lowest proportion in trades. The strongly Protestant ward of St Domingo in the north of the city is also near this end of the scale, while the rather more mixed wards (in religious terms) near the city centre of Everton and St Anne's, and the Protestant Dingle in the south are nearer the middle of the range. Kirkdale and Edge Hill stand out at the other end of the scale. The only ward that is difficult to characterize is Garston, which has a low proportion in transport, yet also

Table 8.4 Male occupations in ten Liverpool wards, 1900, 1911 and 1940 (in %)

	Edge Hill (1900)	Dingle (1900)	Scotland S (1900)	Kirkdale (1900)	Brunswick (1911)	Garston (1911)	Everton (1911)	St Anne's (1911)	St Domingo (1911)	Croxteth (1940)	Liverpool (1911)	Liverpool (1931)
Building trades	14	10	3	9	8	6	10	5	11	9	8	8
Furnishing trades	2	1	1	–	1	–	2	6	1	1	3	1
Railwaymen	5	5	1	5	2	14	2	1	1	3	4	2
Engineering and metal trades	9	15	6	17	8	10	6	5	7	11	10	8
Workshop trades	4	2	4	4	3	1	3	3	3	2	1	1
Printing trades	1	1	–	–	–	1	2	1	1	2	2	1
Clothing trades	3	1	2	1	2	3	3	9	1	–	3	1
Retail and services	6	4	2	5	6	7	9	7	6	7	10	10
Transport and associated	36	46	72	39	58	35	43	50	56	35	32	36
White-collar and supervisory	15	8	1	13	5	12	11	2	12	22	18	19
Miscellaneous	5	7	9	6	8	10	9	11	2	8	8	12

Source: *Gore's Street Directory* (1900, 1911); *Corporation Tenants List* (1907); *Kelly's Street Directory* (1940); census (1911, 1931).

Table 8.5 Ten most common male occupations in ten Liverpool wards, 1900, 1911 and 1940

Edge Hill 1900	%	Dingle 1900	%	Scotland S 1900	%
1. Labourers	12	1. Mariners	10	1. Dock labourers	19
2. Carters	8	2. Dock labourers	10	2. Labourers	18
3. Mariners	6	3. Labourers	8	3. Carters	13
4. Railwaymen	5	4. Carters	8	4. Mariners	13
5. Carpenters and joiners	5	5. Railwaymen	5	5. Porters	5
6. Painters	4	6. Fitters	5	6. Smiths	3
7. Bookkeepers	4	7. Smiths	4	7. Hawkers	3
8. Fitters	3	8. Shipwrights	4	8. Firemen and stokers	2
9. Smiths	3	9. Porters	4	9. Warehousemen	2
10. Porters	3	10. Portworkers	3	10. Coopers	2
% of total	53		61		80

Kirkdale 1900	%	Brunswick 1911	%	Everton 1911	%
1. Mariners	8	1. Labourers	23	1. Labourers	12
2. Carters	8	2. Dock labourers	13	2. Dock labourers	8
3. Fitters	7	3. Mariners	11	3. Carters	8
4. Dock Labourers	5	4. Carters	6	4. Mariners	5
5. Railwaymen	5	5. Firemen and stokers	3	5. Painters	4
6. Carpenters and joiners	5	6. Carpenters and joiners	2	6. Porters	4
7. Smiths	4	7. Painters	2	7. Smiths	3
8. Labourers	4	8. Smiths	2	8. Carpenters and joiners	2
9. Portworkers	4	9. Porters	2	9. Printers	2
10. Boilermakers	3	10. Boilermakers	2	10. Waiters	2
% of total	53		66		50

Garston 1911	%	St Anne's 1911	%	St Domingo 1911	%
1. Railwaymen	14	1. Labourers	15	1. Labourers	17
2. Labourers	10	2. Dock labourers	14	2. Carters	11
3. Dock labourers	9	3. Mariners	7	3. Dock labourers	10
4. Mariners	5	4. Carters	7	4. Mariners	7
5. Smiths	5	5. Tailors	6	5. Painters	5
6. Carters	4	6. Cabinet-makers	4	6. Porters	4
7. Foremen	4	7. Porters	3	7. Carpenters and joiners	3
8. Fitters	3	8. Boot- and shoe-makers	3	8. Police	3
9. Portworkers	3	9. Smiths	3	9. Smiths	3
10. Clerks	2	10. Hawkers	2	10. Clerks	3
% of total	59		64		66

... *Table 8.5 continued*

Croxteth 1940	%	Liverpool 1911	%	Liverpool 1931	%
1. Labourers	15	1. Dock labourers	9	1. Labourers	8
2. Clerks	6	2. Clerks	6	2. Clerks	7
3. Drivers	6	3. Mariners	5	3. Dock labourers	7
4. Fitters	5	4. Porters	5	4. Mariners	5
5. Police	4	5. Carters	5	5. Drivers	5
6. Railwaymen	3	6. Railwaymen	4	6. Porters	5
7. Carpenters and joiners	3	7. Labourers	3	7. Unskilled workers	5
8. Electricians	2	8. Painters	2	8. Fitters	3
9. Commercial travellers	2	9. Carpenters and joiners	2	9. Railwaymen	2
10. Tramwaymen	2	10. Fitters	1	10. Painters	2
% of total	48		42		49

Source: As for Table 8.4.

Table 8.6 Proportion of male workforce in 'transport and associated' and 'trades' categories in nine Liverpool wards, 1900 and 1911 (in %)

	Transport and associated (descending)			Trades (ascending)	
1.	Scotland S	72	1.	Scotland S	16
2.	Brunswick	58	2.	Garston	21
3.	St Domingo	56	3.	Brunswick	22
4.	St Anne's	50	4.	St Domingo	24
5.	Dingle	46	5.	Everton	26
6.	Everton	43	6.	St Anne's	29
7.	Kirkdale	39	7.	Dingle	30
8.	Edge Hill	36	8.	Kirkdale	31
9.	Garston	35	9.	Edge Hill	33

a low proportion in trades, but this is explained mainly by the fact that there was a significantly high proportion of 14 per cent in the railway category in this ward. This is not unexpected, as Garston was the only dock with a major direct rail terminal.

The figures for the top ten occupations listed in each ward confirm this general pattern. In both Scotland South and Brunswick, dock labourers, labourers, carters and mariners occupy the top four places, together making up 63 and 53 per cent respectively of the total in these wards. There were, conversely, no skilled occupations making up more than 3 per cent of the total in these wards. St Domingo, St Anne's, Dingle, and Everton follow next, with the same four most common occupations, but making up lower proportions of the total of 45, 43, 36 and 33 per cent respectively. There were also some concentrations of more skilled occupations in these wards, such as fitters, smiths and shipwrights in Dingle, painters and smiths in Everton, and painters, smiths and carpenters and joiners in St Domingo. St Anne's is exceptional in having a significant number of skilled workshop crafts such as tailors (6 per cent), cabinet-makers (4 per cent) and boot- and shoe-makers (3 per cent). Garston is distinctive in having railwaymen as the most common occupation in the ward. Finally, Kirkdale and Edge Hill had significant concentrations of railwaymen and skilled workers, including carpenters and joiners, fitters and smiths in both, as well as painters in Edge Hill and boilermakers in Kirkdale.

In summary, the key points are these. The two strongly Catholic wards surveyed (Scotland South and Brunswick) were characterized by a preponderance of mainly dockside labour, and a lack of skilled and semi-skilled workers. Of the mainly Protestant wards, St Domingo had a rather similar profile to the Catholic areas, whereas St Anne's, Dingle, Everton and Kirkdale had a more mixed population. At the other end of the scale, Garston and Edge Hill had the smallest proportion of maritime workers, and the highest proportion of skilled workers (in Edge Hill) and railway workers (in Garston).

The figures for Croxteth are not directly comparable due to their being for a much later date, but it is obvious that the population moving into the new suburban estates was drawn disproportionately from the more skilled and better-off sections of the working class, and even the lower echelons of the middle class. Comparison with the 1931 census figures makes this even clearer, as the skilled trades had actually declined since 1911 for the city as a whole. The relatively low proportion in transport in Croxteth is a sure indicator of its difference from the older working-class areas. Skilled craft groups like fitters, carpenters and joiners and electricians were notable here, as well as white-collar and supervisory workers, such as clerks, policemen and commercial travellers.

Other indicators of economic and social differentiation by ward

The picture built up for the limited number of wards surveyed in the street directories can be supplemented by the population data given at a ward level in the census reports. The total number of resident families, structurally separate dwellings, and occupied rooms were all listed for each ward, and from these statistics can be calculated a number of different indices. The two most interesting in this context are those for persons per room and families per dwelling. The number of persons per room was clearly an indicator of overcrowding, and would presumably be a fairly sensitive reflection of levels of income and wealth. Families per dwelling (a structurally separate dwelling being defined as one with its own access to a street or common staircase, so each flat in a block, for instance, was 'structurally separate') would also be an indicator of income and wealth, as presumably most families would not have shared dwellings unless through economic necessity. In both cases, but especially in the latter, differences in housing type could obviously distort the figures to some degree. Areas near the city centre where large Georgian and early Victorian terraces were common, for instance, would be far more likely to have shared dwellings than, say, the suburban council-house estates which had been purpose-built to accommodate working-class families. Despite this proviso, these figures are well worth analysing, and are summarized in Table 8.7, and in Figures 8.2 and 8.3.

These indices tend to confirm the pattern established earlier. The most overcrowded wards were the predominantly Catholic riverside wards. Equally overcrowded was the Protestant ward of Netherfield on the heights above, and also the more mixed city-centre ward of St Anne's. Following them came St Domingo, a little further up the hill in the north end, Protestant Dingle in the south, and Everton. Lower down the scale again came Kirkdale, Edge Hill and Garston, and then Croxteth, which is near the average for the city as a whole. Below that came the increasingly

10 Hopwood Street, Scotland North ward, 1911. The street then ran off Scotland Road, in the heart of the Catholic dockside area of the north end of Liverpool.

Table 8.7 Some indicators of social differentiation, calculated from the 1931 census (by ward, in descending order)

Persons per room		Families per dwelling	
1. Scotland S	1.54	1. Abercromby	1.71
2. St Anne's	1.51	2. St Anne's	1.60
3. Scotland N	1.46	3. Gt George	1.57
4. Netherfield	1.30	4. Brunswick	1.46
5. Exchange	1.26	5. St Peter's	1.46
6. Brunswick	1.26	6. Everton	1.33
7. Vauxhall	1.25	7. Scotland N	1.28
8. St Peter's	1.17	8. Scotland S	1.24
9. Sandhills	1.16	9. Vauxhall	1.24
10. Gt George	1.12	10. Netherfield	1.23
11. Everton	1.10	11. Granby	1.23
12. Dingle	1.07	12. Low Hill	1.21
13. St Domingo	1.06	13. Sandhills	1.20
14. Edge Hill	1.05	14. Prince's Park	1.19
15. Garston	1.03	15. Exchange	1.19
16. Kirkdale	.99	16. Kirkdale	1.18
17. Croxteth	.98	17. Fairfield	1.16
18. Fazakerley	.98	18. Dingle	1.15
19. Low Hill	.97	19. Breckfield	1.15
20. Abercromby	.93	20. Edge Hill	1.14
21. Walton	.89	21. St Domingo	1.14
22. Granby	.88	22. Garston	1.12
23. Prince's Park	.88	23. Sefton Park E	1.11
24. Much Woolton	.85	24. Kensington	1.09
25. Old Swan	.85	25. Warbreck	1.08
26. West Derby	.83	26. Sefton Park W	1.08
27. Breckfield	.83	27. Wavertree W	1.07
28. Kensington	.82	28. Walton	1.07
29. Castle St.	.81	29. West Derby	1.07
30. Wavertree W	.78	30. Old Swan	1.06
31. Warbreck	.77	31. Anfield	1.05
32. Anfield	.76	32. Much Woolton	1.04
33. Allerton	.75	33. Allerton	1.04
34. Fairfield	.74	34. Wavertree	1.04
35. Wavertree	.71	35. Aigburth	1.03
36. Little Woolton	.66	36. Little Woolton	1.02
37. Sefton Park E	.66	37. Fazakerley	1.02
38. Sefton Park W	.65	38. Childwall	1.01
39. Aigburth	.65	39. Castle St.	1.01
40. Childwall	.58	40. Croxteth	1.00
All Liverpool	.93	All Liverpool	1.16

Source: 1931 census.

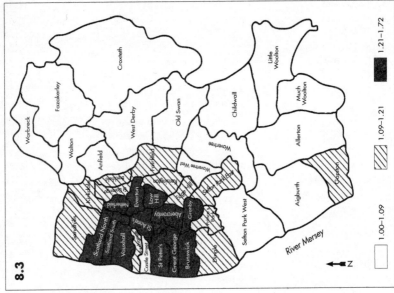

Figure 8.2 Persons per room, 1931

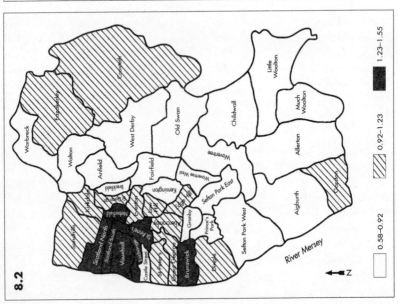

Figure 8.3 Families per dwelling, 1931

212

more prosperous areas of mixed working-class and middle-class occupation, such as Fazakerley, Abercromby, Walton, Granby, Prince's Park, and Old Swan, although the mixture took very different forms here. Abercromby, Prince's Park and Granby were older areas not far from the city centre, with pockets of working-class terraces cheek-by-jowl with the grand terraced mansions of the middle class. Fazakerley and Walton, by contrast, were newer suburban wards with large estates of middle-class terraces and semi-detached housing, increasingly being supplemented in the 1920s and 1930s by council-house estates, notably the major part of the Fazakerley estate in the former case, and a substantial portion of the Norris Green estate in the latter. Finally, at the lower end of the scale came the distinctly middle-class areas, mostly in the south of the city around Sefton Park, Aigburth, Woolton and Childwall.

The figures for families per dwelling show some variations in this pattern, almost certainly due to the greater impact of housing differences. This is very clearly shown by the fact that Abercromby, an area where there was a great concentration of the oldest terraced mansions in the city, had the highest level of multiple occupancy, and adjacent areas such as Granby and Prince's Park were also above the average on this index. Equally clearly, Croxteth had the lowest level of multi-occupancy in the city, which does not indicate that it was the most prosperous, but that it was comprised almost entirely of council houses specifically designed to accommodate working-class families. These figures are thus less reliable as an indicator of income and wealth, but still reflect a broadly similar pattern.

The political allegiances of wards

The final part of this chapter establishes the political allegiance of wards within the city. The analysis of municipal election results already carried out in earlier chapters, and summarized in Appendices IV and VI, provide the basis for this exercise. The primary aim is to establish how support for the Labour Party varied from ward to ward, and also how this pattern changed over time. Linked to this will be the analysis of support for other political parties, particularly those associated with religious sectarianism.

As far as Labour is concerned, an index of support can be constructed using slightly different principles for the pre- and post-1914 periods. Before 1914 Labour only stood candidates in a relatively small number of wards, and won elections in even fewer. They only put up candidates on a regular basis in a handful of wards, so detailed patterns over time within wards are hardly discernible. This means that the only meaningful way of measuring support for Labour is by identifying the wards where the party won at any time before 1914 (including by-elections) as the areas of greatest Labour support, and those where it stood candidates unsuccessfully at any time before 1914 as the areas of moderate, or at least potential, support. It must be assumed that, in those wards where the party put up no candidates, it had the least support. This is by no means a perfect measure of Labour strength, for it assumes that Labour chose to put up its candidates wherever it had its greatest support. At this early stage of the party's development, however, financial considerations, and also the state of organization within wards, limited the choice for Labour. Furthermore, tactical considerations meant that some wards where Labour could probably have won significant support were uncontested so as not to offend potential allies. In other cities at this time this might have applied most to Labour/Liberal relations, but in the Liverpool context it was the Labour/Irish Nationalist relationship that was vital. The strongly Catholic working-class wards along the river may well have given some support to Labour at this time if they had been contested, even if they were likely to remain Nationalist strongholds, but the Labour Party usually chose not to test this support. The pre-1914 index, then, is far from perfect, but the best possible in the circumstances, and the same principles have also been applied in trying to assess support for the Irish Nationalist Party and overtly Protestant candidates in this period. The results of all these calculations can be found below in Table 8.8 and Figures 8.4, 8.5 and 8.6.

After 1918, Labour began to contest elections far more regularly and on a city-wide basis, and calculations of average vote-share become far more meaningful. Calculating averages over five-year periods for each ward also means that uncharacteristic results, due to Independents splitting a party's vote, for instance, are less prone to distort the pattern. Detailed figures for the average Labour vote in each ward for each five-year period between 1919 and 1938 are shown in Appendix VI. A summary of the figures can be found in Table 8.9 and Figures 8.7 to 8.10.

Nationalist/Catholic and Protestant Party candidates were still spasmodic after 1918, and therefore estimations of their support have been calculated on the same basis as the pre-1914 figures. These can be found in Table 8.10 and Figures 8.11 to 8.14. However, Protestantism as a political force was at least as much, if not more, expressed through the Working Men's Conservative Association (WMCA) as through the Protestant Party, as will be shown later. A full list of ward branches of the WMCA between 1920 and 1939 is listed in Appendix XIV. Permanent existence of branches throughout the period has been taken as evidence of their strength. These branches are shown in Table 8.11, and have also been incorporated into Figures 8.13 and 8.14.

Occupation, religion and politics

What pattern of political allegiances can be derived from this data? Taking the pre-1914 situation first, Labour's strength was concentrated mainly in the cluster of wards inland from the city centre focused on the Edge Hill Division, namely Edge Hill, Low Hill, Kensington, St Anne's and Everton. These were predominantly Protestant wards, although there was some

214

Table 8.8 Index of support for Labour, Irish Nationalist and Protestant Parties in municipal elections, 1905–1913

Ward	Candidates stood	Winning candidates
Labour		
St Anne's	3	3
Edge Hill	5	2
Kensington	9	1
Low Hill	7	1
Garston	4	1
Everton	2	1
St Domingo	2	1
Brunswick	1	1
Kirkdale	8	
Old Swan	4	
Walton	4	
Wavertree W	3	
Breckfield	2	
Dingle	2	
Granby	2	
Gt George	1	
Netherfield	1	
Sefton Park E	1	
Warbreck	1	
West Derby	1	
Irish Nationalist		
Scotland N	11	11
Scotland S	10	10
Sandhills	7	7
Vauxhall	7	7
Brunswick	3	3
Gt George	1	1
Fairfield	1	
Fazakerley	1	
St Anne's	1	
Protestant		
Netherfield	8	2
Kirkdale	2	1
St Domingo	4	
Breckfield	1	
Sandhills	1	

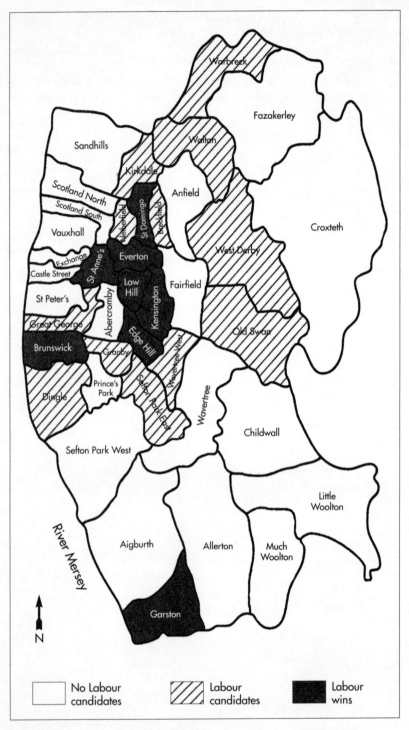

Figure 8.4 Labour strength, 1905–1913

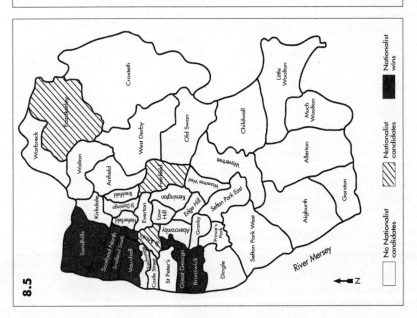

Figure 8.5 Nationalist strength, 1905–1913

Figure 8.6 Protestant strength, 1905–1913

Table 8.9 Index of support for Labour Party in municipal elections, 1919–1938 (average % vote)

1919–1923	1924–1928	1929–1933	1934–1938
Everton (49)	Brunswick (76)	Scotland N (89)	Brunswick (UC)
Scotland N (47)	Croxteth (63)	Sandhills (87)	Sandhills (UC)
Scotland S (46)	Everton (61)	Brunswick (81)	Scotland S (95)
Edge Hill (43)	Sandhills (58)	St Anne's (78)	Scotland N (86)
Garston (42)	Edge Hill (56)	Scotland S (68)	St Anne's (79)
Dingle (40)	Low Hill (55)	Everton (59)	Vauxhall (74)
St Anne's (40)	St Anne's (54)	Croxteth (56)	Everton (69)
Kensington (39)	Scotland N (53)	Gt George (55)	Croxteth (62)
St Domingo (38)	Netherfield (46)	Garston (54)	Gt George (61)
St Peter's (38)	Dingle (46)	Low Hill (51)	Garston (53)
M Woolton (37)	Gt George (45)	Vauxhall (48)	Edge Hill (51)
Low Hill (37)	Kensington (45)	Edge Hill (48)	Abercromby (51)
Fazakerley (37)	Scotland S (45)	Dingle (46)	Granby (50)
Walton (36)	Garston (44)	Old Swan (43)	Dingle (49)
Old Swan (36)	Kirkdale (44)	Fazakerley (41)	Low Hill (49)
Wavertree W (33)	Breckfield (44)	Breckfield (41)	Kirkdale (47)
Breckfield (33)	Walton (44)	Netherfield (41)	St Peter's (43)
Kirkdale (33)	St Domingo (44)	Wavertree W (40)	Prince's Park (42)
Childwall (32)	Granby (42)	Kensington (40)	Old Swan (42)
Brunswick (32)	Old Swan (40)	Prince's Park (39)	Fazakerley (41)
Prince's Park (30)	Prince's Park (40)	Kirkdale (39)	Netherfield (37)
Wavertree (29)	Abercromby (39)	Walton (39)	Wavertree W (37)
West Derby (28)	Fazakerley (39)	Granby (38)	Fairfield (36)
Vauxhall (23)	St Peter's (38)	West Derby (37)	Kensington (36)
Anfield (23)	Wavertree W (37)	Abercromby (36)	Breckfield (34)
Warbreck (22)	Childwall (35)	Wavertree (33)	Walton (33)
Netherfield (19)	Warbreck (34)	Fairfield (32)	St Domingo (33)
Gt George (17)	Fairfield (33)	Warbreck (30)	Exchange (32)
Sefton Park W (14)	Wavertree (32)	St Peter's (29)	West Derby (31)
Sandhills (11)	West Derby (32)	Sefton Park E (29)	Anfield (30)
Abercromby (NC)	Much Woolton (30)	Sefton Park W (29)	Wavertree (30)
Aigburth (NC)	Vauxhall (26)	St Domingo (28)	Warbreck (28)
Allerton (NC)	Sefton Park W (25)	Aigburth (25)	Allerton (24)
Castle St. (NC)	Allerton (23)	Anfield (24)	Sefton Pk W (24)
Exchange (NC)	Anfield (22)	Allerton (23)	Sefton Pk E (23)
Fairfield (NC)	Exchange (17)	Much Woolton (21)	Much Woolton (21)
Granby (NC)	Little Woolton (6)	Exchange (20)	Childwall (12)
Little Woolton (NC)	Aigburth (NC)	Childwall (13)	Little Woolton (12)
Sefton Park E (NC)	Castle St. (NC)	Castle St. (NC)	Aigburth (NC)
	Sefton Park E (NC)	Little Woolton (NC)	Castle St. (NC)
All Liverpool (35)	All Liverpool (44)	All Liverpool (44)	All Liverpool (42)

N.B. NC = No Labour candidates; UC = Uncontested Labour wins; where averages indicated for wards are equal, wards are ranked according to decimal points, which are not shown due to shortage of space.

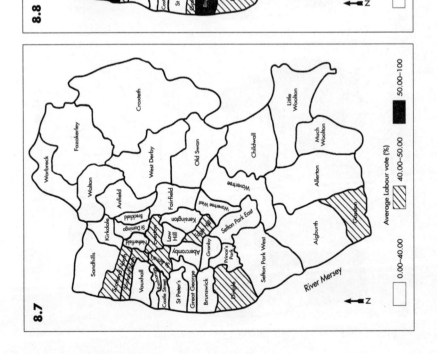

Figure 8.7 Labour strength, 1919–1923

Figure 8.8 Labour strength, 1924–1928

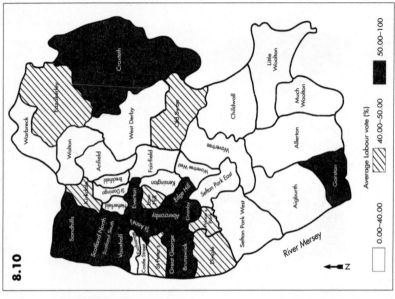

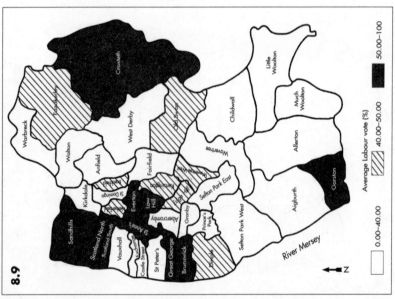

220

Table 8.10 Index of support for Nationalist/Catholic/Centre/Democratic Labour and Protestant Parties, 1919–1938

Ward	Candidates stood	% of vote gained	Winning candidates
1919–1928			
Nat/Cath/Centre			
Exchange	10		10
Vauxhall	9		9
Scotland	9		8
Sandhills	10		7
Gt George	8		7
Scotland N	9		6
Brunswick	6		5
St Anne's	6		3
Low Hill	2	17	
St Peter's	2	10	
Old Swan	2	7	
Edge Hill	2	6	
Breckfield	1	3	
Wavertree	1	3	
Kensington	1	2	
Netherfield	1	1	
West Derby	1	1	
Everton	1	0	
Protestant			
Netherfield	6		2
St Domingo	3		2
Breckfield	1	49	
Fazakerley	1	20	
1929–1938			
Centre/Dem. Labour			
Exchange	10		10
Vauxhall	9		5
Gt George	7		2
Scotland S	4		
St Anne's	3		
Everton	1	18	
Croxteth	1	4	
Much Woolton	1	0	
Protestant			
St Domingo	9		8
Netherfield	6		1
Kirkdale	5		
Dingle	4		
Breckfield	2		
Garston	1	12	
Everton	1	10	
Kensington	1	8	
Croxteth	1	7	
Fazakerley	1	7	
Walton	1	7	

N.B. Where the numbers of candidates put forward in wards were equal, those wards have been ranked according to the percentage of the vote gained by the candidates.

Figure 8.11
Nationalist/Catholic/
Centre strength,
1919–1928

Figure 8.12
Centre/Democratic Labour
strength, 1929–1938

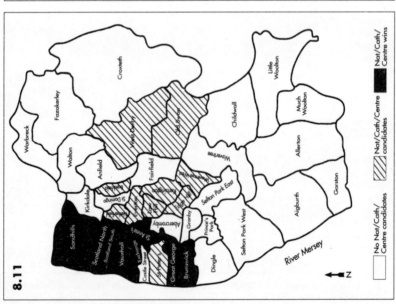

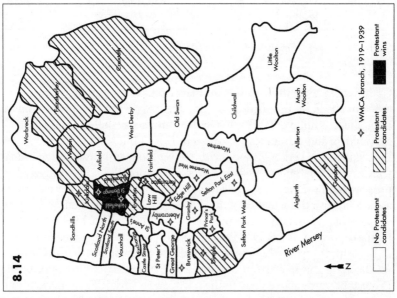

Figure 8.13 Protestant strength, 1919–1928

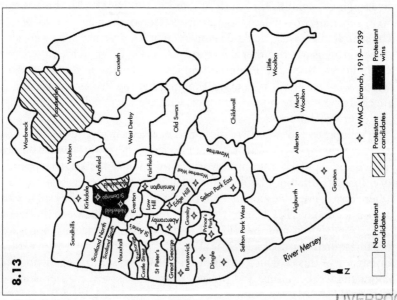

Figure 8.14 Protestant strength, 1929–1938

223

Table 8.11 Liverpool wards with Working Men's Conservative Association branches in continuous existence, 1920–1939

Abercromby	Kensington
Breckfield	Kirkdale
Brunswick	Netherfield
Dingle (2 branches)	Prince's Park
Edge Hill	St Domingo
Garston	Sefton Park East
Granby	Wavertree West

Source: *Liverpool Official Red Books* (1920–39).

Catholic presence in St Anne's and Everton. They were also areas with a relatively high proportion of the male workforce concentrated in permanent-employed and often skilled and semi-skilled occupations – railwaymen and various skilled trades in Edge Hill, Kensington, and Low Hill, skilled workers associated with the building and engineering industries in Everton, and workshop crafts in St Anne's – and a relatively low proportion, by Liverpool standards, in the predominantly casual trades associated with the activities of the docks. Additionally, Labour was strong in Garston, again a mainly Protestant ward, but unusual because of the high proportion of workers associated with the railway terminal here.

By contrast, where Labour was notably weak was, first, in the Catholic wards along the river from Sandhills to Brunswick and, second, in the Protestant wards above them in the north end – Kirkdale, Netherfield and St Domingo – and to the south of them in the Dingle. All these wards were generally areas where a higher proportion of the male workforce was concentrated in casual, dockside employment. Conversely, these were also the main areas where either the Irish Nationalist Party, in the case of the Catholic wards, or the Protestant and Tory Parties, in the Protestant wards, were strong. It is notable, though, that the Protestant Party was much stronger in the north end wards, while, in the Dingle, working-class Toryism was dominant.

It is important to stress here the apparent divergence of the political response of the dockside wards of the city from those wards where more skilled and regularly employed workers were concentrated. Irrespective of religious affiliation, Labour was weak in electoral terms before 1914 where casual, dockside employment predominated. This is consistent with the earlier findings in Chapter Two of the tenuous links between the major waterfront unions and the LTCLP, and also the evidence of poor ward organization in the dockside areas. As has been argued elsewhere in earlier discussion of this evidence, the idea that there was something distinctive about the work, culture and politics of maritime workers seems to be indicated.[2]

One recent comparative study has cast doubts on this suggestion, however. Tony Adams has rejected attempts 'to establish a relationship between the place of workers in the division of labour and their politics'.[3] He focuses on dockside workers, among others, as one of the most common examples of this apparently misguided approach. Looking at the years immediately before and after the First World War, and concentrating on four port cities, he concludes that there was no consistent relationship between Labour support and concentrations of waterfront workers. Labour, he argues, was electorally strong in Hull and dockside London, but weak in Liverpool and Cardiff. Moreover, within these cities, he claims, dockside wards were sometimes the strongest centres of Labour support, especially in London, or at least equally as strong as other areas, in the cases of Hull and Liverpool.[4]

Objections to these claims arise over the nature of the evidence supporting them. It is arguable that the limited time-span covered by Adams' study is inadequate to sustain such conclusions about the strength of Labour support in these four cities. Certainly, the Liverpool evidence that he uses, concentrating on the two very turbulent and untypical years of 1911 and 1919, is unconvincing. The longer time-scale used in this book reveals significantly different patterns of Labour support. The dockside wards, at least up to the mid-1920s, showed far less enthusiasm for Labour than Adams implies. It is also salient to point out that the anomalies of the municipal electoral system outlined earlier in Part Two, make superficial comparisons, based on seat-counts in different boroughs, dubious.

However, even if these objections were unfounded, there are still grounds for arguing that Adams' study misses the point. To state that there is a connection between the work and politics of certain groups of workers does not imply that a simple and unchanging relationship should be expected in the historical evidence. As has been shown in this book, other factors cut across and mediated the basic relationship to varying degrees, according to different historical circumstances. Religion, ethnicity, and gender intersected with the structural features of a predominantly maritime economy to produce a particular pattern of working-class politics. Thus, after the First World War, the political allegiance of the Catholic dockside wards changed significantly. This does not mean that these areas were any less distinctive in their political responses, however, but rather that their singularity was expressed in a different form.

The post-1918 pattern saw Labour retaining its original areas of strength, but extending its support in the 1920s to those Catholic wards along the river that had previously been Nationalist strongholds. This was by no means a uniform shift, with some wards like Vauxhall and Great George being slower to come over to supporting Labour. By the 1930s the process was complete, though, and these wards became Labour's safest seats, often uncontested in the 1930s. The pattern shown here for these wards confirms the analysis of the transition from Nationalism to Labour outlined earlier in Chapter Two. Labour also found strong support from

1928 onwards in the new ward of Croxteth, created by the rapid expansion of the Norris Green and Dovecot council-house estates. This development was again reflected in the neighbouring ward of Fazakerley in the late 1930s, although less strongly due to the greater variety of housing developments in this ward. The only other significant shift to Labour can be identified in the late 1930s, when the previously barren ground of Granby and Abercromby wards became Labour strongholds. This was almost certainly due mainly to the social decline of the area of large Georgian and Victorian mansions in the south end of the city that accelerated in this period. As the middle class increasingly decamped to the outer suburbs, so the mansions began to be converted into flats and rented out to working-class tenants.

Conversely, after 1918 the strength of the Irish Nationalist Party, while held together to some extent by the succeeding Catholic and Centre Parties, declined in inverse proportion to Labour's rise in the strongly Catholic wards along the dockside. In the strongly Protestant areas, on the other hand, the pattern of support for the Protestant and Tory Parties changed little, except that the Protestant Party became increasingly stronger in its north-end redoubts of Netherfield and St Domingo. In the south end, Conservatism appeared to be the primary expression of working-class Protestantism, particularly in Dingle ward.

This general pattern is not absolutely clear-cut, nor could it be expected to be so, given the nature of the data on which it is based. Nevertheless, it is unmistakable and, moreover, where exceptions appear, they can usually be explained by specific factors. For instance, the fact that St Domingo fell to Labour on one occasion would appear to contradict the general picture. However, on closer examination, this was clearly a fluke result in 1911. An Independent Conservative candidate split the Tory vote almost exactly down the middle, allowing the Labour candidate through to win with 38 per cent of the votes cast. This result was an anomaly, confirmed by the fact that the following year, when the Tories put forward a single candidate, Labour was heavily defeated. In the following three decades, despite Labour's general improvement, only once, in 1926, did Labour narrowly win this ward again.

It would appear no less contradictory that the strongly Catholic wards of St Peter's and Exchange were not Nationalist strongholds earlier, nor Labour strongholds later. However, this can be explained by the unusually large number of business voters in these wards, even more significant before 1914 given the restricted franchise as far as the working class was concerned. As a result, elections in these wards were decided mainly by businessmen, and Conservatives and Liberals held sway before 1914, to be joined by Independents, such as the Catholic businessman and publican Peter Kavanagh, in the inter-war years.

There are also variations in the general pattern that can only be explained by more complex combinations of factors. In particular, there are subtle distinctions within the group of Protestant wards that were

226

generally weak areas for Labour. Both Kirkdale and Dingle stand out here. Kirkdale was rather different from the adjacent Protestant wards on the heights above the river, as it had a relatively high proportion of skilled workers – 17 per cent in engineering and metal trades and 9 per cent in building trades, for instance – and a relatively low proportion in the casual sectors – only 39 per cent in transport and associated trades. Its occupational structure was not dissimilar to that of Edge Hill, yet its political allegiance was very different. Labour never won in Kirkdale before 1914, while it was the only ward apart from neighbouring Netherfield where the Protestant Party was successful. By contrast, Dingle, much more influenced by dockside, casual trades, was predictably weak Labour territory, yet had no Protestant Party presence at all.

How can these variations be explained? It is clear that Protestantism was by no means an homogeneous political force. The Protestant Party has been used as one indicator of militant Protestantism, but Toryism, and in particular the WMCA, was another avenue for the political expression of Protestantism. The WMCA, which was organizationally separate from the Tory Party itself, was specifically based in the working class, and even more precisely within the Protestant working-class. Catholics were excluded from membership, and the WMCA's strength was quite explicitly grounded in sectarianism.[5]

Table 8.11 above, showing where ward branches of the WMCA were strongest, indicates that Protestantism as a political force in the south end of the city was extensively catered for within the WMCA. Not only were there, uniquely, two branches in Dingle ward, but also a whole cluster of branches in the surrounding wards of Prince's Park, Sefton Park East, Wavertree West, Edge Hill, Abercromby, Granby and Brunswick. These included wards which were by no means exclusively Protestant (Edge Hill, Wavertree West and most obviously, Brunswick), and also wards that were by no means predominantly working-class (Abercromby, Granby, Prince's Park and Sefton Park East). Working-class Conservatism, deeply intertwined with religious sectarianism, was a force which was strongly entrenched in this part of the city over a long period of time.

In the north-end, by contrast, the WMCA was strictly confined to the strongly Protestant areas of Kirkdale, St Domingo, Netherfield and Breckfield. Moreover, it was much more seriously challenged by rival Protestant organizations as the legitimate expression of sectarian politics in these areas. It was only in the north end that an overtly Protestant political organization, separate from Toryism, took shape.

Why should this be so? Differences of religious affiliation may be partly responsible, with a greater preponderance of Nonconformism, and especially Methodism, in the south end, and a greater influence of low-church Anglicanism and newer forms of evangelical dissent in the north end, producing subtly different forms of Protestantism as a political force. There is no doubt that the significance of the Catholic/Protestant conflict in Liverpool had an effect on the nature of Protestantism in the city.

Whereas Nonconformism in the nineteenth century had a very real political potential in opposition to Anglicanism in many urban centres (Birmingham and Leicester are two obvious examples), in Liverpool it was overshadowed by low-church Anglicanism. As one authority on local Nonconformism has put it:

> Here the great issue which inflamed public opinion in the nineteenth century was not Anglicanism versus Dissent ... but Protestantism versus Rome; not present Reform but past Reformation. It was Evangelical Anglicanism ... which had emerged in Liverpool as a major political force: and with the coming of the Salvidge era and the rise to power of the Layman's [sic] League, the Evangelical-Tory axis was so immeasurably strengthened that Dissent, unless it adopted the whole programme of militant Orangism (which only the Irish Presbyterians were at all prone to do) was regarded as irrelevant to the great issue of the age. In this grand religious controversy there was no room for a third force ...[6]

Differences of religious affiliation between north-end and south-end Protestantism in Liverpool are not immediately apparent from the figures based on church capacity and school attendance produced above. However, a closer analysis of this data is revealing. Anglican, Protestant Reform, and Presbyterian churches were most representative of the evangelical and anti-ritualist wing of Protestantism in Liverpool, whereas Baptist, Welsh Presbyterian and the various branches of Methodist churches were more representative of Nonconformism. This excludes Unitarianism, which was the main expression of middle-class dissent and, as many have argued, was distant from local religious and political conflict.[7] Using this classification for all church sittings in the adjacent north-end wards of Kirkdale, Breckfield, St Domingo and Netherfield, gives a total of 17,915 sittings for the evangelicals, and 9,150 for dissenters. Applying the same classification to the adjacent south-end wards of Dingle, Brunswick and Prince's Park, gives 9,850 for the evangelicals, and 11,160 for dissenters.

In the north-end, then, the evangelical presence outweighed Dissent by a margin of almost two to one. The influence here of the militantly low-church, anti-ritualist Protestant Reformers, and the closely associated Protestant Party led by the Revd H. D. Longbottom in the inter-war period, becomes much more explicable. On the other hand, in the south-end dissenters were marginally in the majority, and reduced the influence of the more extreme elements of Protestantism. The Protestant Party's failure to make serious inroads here is also more understandable in the light of this evidence.

Voting trends in these two main centres of working-class Protestantism also seem to confirm the same pattern. There were two main periods between the wars when an increase in the local Protestant sectarian vote was likely: in 1930 and 1931 after the sale of the old workhouse site for the building of the Catholic cathedral, which highlighted the recently increased Catholic influence in the Labour Party; and between 1936 and 1938, when a dispute over grants for Catholic secondary schools again brought sectarian feeling to the boil. On the other hand, national trends for Labour for these two periods varied; 1930 and 1931 were poor years as the Labour government lost popularity and then collapsed; 1936 to 1938, although the evidence is thin, were not particularly bad years for Labour. In both these periods Labour's support fell drastically in the city as a whole, including all the main Protestant areas. If the turn-out figures are analysed, however, some interesting divergences can be identified. The turnout figures for the city as a whole (extracted from Appendix XV) and for four of the main Protestant wards (extracted from Appendix IV) are given in Table 8.12.

Table 8.12   Turnout in four Protestant wards, 1926–1938 (in %)

Year	Dingle	Kirkdale	Netherfield	St Domingo	All Liverpool
1926	51	36	48	38	41
1927	55	37	54	38	45
1928	66	53	54	53	52
1929	54	47	51	44	46
1930	51	51	60	52	40
1931	56	51	55	48	45
1932	58	44	54	44	43
1933	54	41	59	51	40
1934	43	45	53	39	37
1935	54	46	53	40	44
1936	59	44	56	40	43
1937	64	60	61	54	52
1938	53	51	48	37	42

These figures show a marked difference in the response to sectarian issues in the north-end and south-end wards. In 1930 and 1931, when Labour abstentions might have been expected to be high, as they were nationally, voting turnout for the city as a whole fell compared to the previous three years. Similarly, in Dingle ward in the south-end, there was a fall in 1930, although some recovery in 1931. In the north-end Protestant wards, however, there is a distinct rise in turnout in 1930, presumably reflecting increased sectarian feeling in those areas. Between 1936 and 1938, when there is no reason to suppose nationally that turnout might have been increasing dramatically or that Labour might have been losing support, there was a distinct rise in turnout in Liverpool as a whole for 1937.

This time, though, both in the north-end and the south-end Protestant wards there is a rise in turnout, if anything most sharply and earliest in Dingle, and presumably related to the increasingly sectarian tone of the debate over school grants.

These findings may seem contradictory, but in fact they tend to confirm the pattern revealed earlier. The 1930 cathedral dispute was likely to raise the ire of anti-ritualists, suggesting to them 'Rome on the rates' and increased Catholic influence in the Labour Party.[8] The response was clearest in the north-end wards, where the evangelical presence was strongest, whereas in Dingle, where dissent was much stronger, the sectarian response was muted.

The 1936 school grants dispute, however, was more complex. The origins of the controversy lay in the 1936 Education Act, which allowed for grants to the voluntary sector to build or improve secondary schools.[9] This roused anti-ritualist protest again, but it also offended Methodists and other Dissenters, who resented state assistance to the voluntary sector. Thus it was Dingle, with the greater dissenting presence, which registered the earliest response in 1936. The 1937 local Labour proposals to increase grants specifically to Catholic schools then brought anti-ritualist protest to a peak, accounting for the 1937 surge in turnout in the north-end wards.

Working-class life, culture and politics

The broad patterns of political allegiance and their relationship to occupational and religious differentiation that have been identified in this chapter were by no means straightforward or unchanging. The importance of gender as a factor influencing working-class politics, as shown in the previous chapter, added to the complexity of the process analysed here. This is not unexpected, given the results of other local studies referred to in Chapter One. As Michael Savage has argued most of all, the dynamics of working-class politics were necessarily intricate.[10] The material determinants of working-class life were crucial, but they were expressed in, and intermeshed with, a culture shaped by a number of influences. To echo another local study, 'working-class communities possess both a structure and a nature',[11] and, as some of the earlier studies of Liverpool have argued, political traditions have been formed out of this complicated relationship.[12] Nevertheless, among the complexity there were recognizable patterns which have been highlighted in this chapter.

References

1. See C. G. Pooley, 'The residential segregation of migrant communities in mid-Victorian Liverpool', *Transactions of the Institute of British Geographers*, New Series, vol.2, no.3 (1977).

2. See S. Davies, 'The Liverpool Labour Party and the Liverpool working class, 1900-1939', *Bulletin of the North West Labour History Society* 6 (1979-80); M. Nightingale (ed.), *Merseyside in Crisis* (Manchester Free Press, Manchester: 1980), pp. 77-9; S. Davies *et al.*, *Genuinely Seeking Work: Mass Unemployment on Merseyside in the 1930s* (Liverpress, Liverpool: 1992), pp. 148-50.

3. T. Adams, 'Labour and the First World War: economy, politics and the erosion of local peculiarity', *Journal of Regional and Local Studies* (1990), p. 33.

4. Adams, 'Labour and the First World War', pp. 33-40.

5. P. J. Waller, *Democracy and Sectarianism: A Political and Social History of Liverpool, 1868–1939* (Liverpool University Press, Liverpool: 1981), p. 117.

6. I. Sellers, 'Nonconformist attitudes in later nineteenth-century Liverpool, *Transactions of the Historic Society of Lancashire and Cheshire*, Vol. 114 (1962), pp. 215–16.

7. Waller, *Democracy and Sectarianism*, pp. 13–15, 275–6.

8. Waller, *Democracy and Sectarianism*, pp. 324–6; R. Baxter, 'The Liverpool Labour Party, 1918–1963' (unpublished D.Phil. thesis, University of Oxford, 1969), pp. 49–58.

9. Waller, *Democracy and Sectarianism*, pp. 340–3; Baxter, 'The Liverpool Labour Party', pp. 77–86; D. A. Roberts, 'Religion and Politics in Liverpool since 1900' (unpublished M.Sc. thesis, University of London, 1965), pp. 131–7.

10. M. Savage, *The Dynamics of Working-Class Politics: The Labour Movement in Preston, 1880-1940* (Cambridge University Press, Cambridge: 1987).

11. B. Lancaster, *Radicalism, Cooperation and Socialism: Leicester Working-Class Politics, 1860-1906* (Leicester University Press, Leicester: 1987), p. xix.

12. J. Smith, 'Labour tradition in Glasgow and Liverpool', *History Workshop* 17 (1984); Davies, 'The Liverpool Labour Party and the Liverpool working class'.

Conclusion

At an early stage in the research for this book, I interviewed Hugh Carr, a Labour councillor first elected in 1937. When asked what his explanation was for the weakness of the Liverpool Labour Party before the 1950s, his reply was brief: 'booze and bigotry'. The first part of his answer referred to the prominent role that he claimed the local brewing industry played in financing Liverpool Toryism. The second part was a reference to religious sectarianism. What this book has tried to show is that Labour's historical weakness in Liverpool cannot be explained as simply as this. A number of factors have to be considered to arrive at a satisfactory conclusion.

First, religious sectarianism was almost certainly not as important as twentieth-century convention has made it out to be, but it was still relevant. The analysis in Chapter Eight shows that its effect on voting patterns, especially after 1918, was far from straightforward. In the Catholic wards, Labour support was strong after the mid-1920s, having been non-existent previously. In the Protestant wards, the harnessing of anti-Catholic sentiment to working-class Conservatism was by no means pervasive. In a number of wards, such as Edge Hill, Everton, Garston, St Anne's and Croxteth, the appeal of sectarianism was limited. Only in the north-end wards of St Domingo and Netherfield, overwhelmingly, and Kirkdale, marginally, and in the south-end ward of Dingle, could the sectarian vote be seen to be a major factor adversely affecting Labour. Even then, there were differences in the sectarian response, with the north-end wards adopting overtly Protestant politics, rather than Conservatism, in the 1930s. It was also the case that the sectarian appeal was not a major factor consistently throughout the inter-war years. Only in the mid-1920s and late 1930s was it unequivocally of significance in these wards. Labour's worst years electorally, in 1930 and 1931, were far more linked to the party's national crisis than to any local, sectarian upsurge.

Second, gender was a significant factor in the development of Labour. As Chapter Seven shows, women were drawn into the party's campaigns in the early and mid-1920s. They were important in developing party organization at the ward and constituency levels, and had an impact in shaping policies. However, the neighbourhood-based involvement by women that has been shown to be crucial in other areas was limited in Liverpool. In the Catholic areas of the city, women's formal organization in the party was non-existent. Where women's sections were active, their impact was constrained by the lack of opportunity for women to advance into the leadership of the party. The tiny proportion of female Labour councillors is a clear indication of this. By the 1930s, national and local trends had reduced the role of women in the party considerably. The rise of the Catholic caucus posed special problems for women in the Liverpool party, and only exceptional individuals like Bessie Braddock had any significant impact.

Third, gerrymandering of the municipal electoral system, which has been all but ignored previously, was plainly of considerable significance. As Chapters Three to Six show, the long-unreformed ward boundaries gave a crucial advantage to Labour's opponents in local elections. The manipulation of the aldermanic system provided a further buffer against Labour's advance. Additionally, the restrictions of the municipal franchise and the surviving anomaly of the business vote also disadvantaged Labour. All these effects were potentially significant elsewhere, but the balance of probability is plainly that they were more influential in Liverpool than in many other cities. It is incontestable that Labour's electoral shortcomings in Liverpool relative to other areas were, at the very least, magnified by this factor.

But analytical readjustment of this nature still leaves Liverpool Labour looking weak relative to other cities. This can also be explained by a fourth factor, the labour market structure typical of a port city. The evidence for this lies in Chapters Two and Eight of this book. As shown there, notwithstanding the winning of the Catholic dockside wards from the mid-1920s, overall the Labour Party fared less successfully in those areas where casual, port-related employment was predominant. The party's genuine strength was in those wards where significant numbers of non-waterfront workers were based, and in the support of predominantly craft unions. Labourism, the dominant political strand in the national labour movement, was not the intuitive home of waterfront workers in Liverpool.

In the light of all the evidence put forward in this book, an overall judgement on the development of the Labour Party in Liverpool up to 1939 must be finely balanced. Labour was faced with a range of socio-economic, cultural and political obstacles, the scale and complexity of which might appear insurmountable in retrospect. In terms of Liverpool labour history, any simplistic and easy connections between class and party are simply not tenable. The party's failure in Liverpool may thus seem less abject than some earlier analyses have suggested.

On the other hand, this book has shown that the Labour Party itself contributed to its own problems. The party was poorly organized, structurally weak, and frequently divided internally by religion, occupation, gender, and political ideology. It failed to confront the problems of the local electoral system, and at times was compliant with them. The party was unimaginative in its attempts to meet the political needs and demands of important sections of the local working class, as the evidence relating to women has demonstrated. However unfavourable the historical circumstances were for the Liverpool Labour Party, plainly it failed to cope with them adequately in this period. Structure and agency, then, were both intertwined in explaining the development of Liverpool Labour.

Appendices

APPENDIX I   Delegates to Liverpool Trades Council, 1905

Union	No. of delegates	Wards where delegates lived
Blind basket- and brushmakers	1	Edge Hill
Bootmakers	1	St Anne's
Bookbinders	1	(Birkenhead)
Brassfounders	3	Everton, St Anne's, Prince's Park
Bricklayers (2)	3	Wavertree W, Prince's Park, (Bootle)
Brushmakers	1	Everton
Cabinet-makers	1	Abercromby
Carpenters (2)	17	Wavertree W (2), Kensington (5), Dingle (2), Everton, Edge Hill, Low Hill, Old Swan, Netherfield (Bootle 3)
Carvers	1	St Anne's
Clothiers operatives	1	Low Hill
Coachmakers	3	Everton, Edge Hill, Wavertree W.
Coppersmiths	1	Kirkdale
Engineers	8	Breckfield, Sandhills, Prince's Park, Granby, St Anne's (Bootle 3)
Enginemen and cranemen	4	Dingle, Kirkdale, St Domingo, Prince's Park
Farriers	1	Kensington
Furniture trades	1	Kensington
Gasfitters	1	Dingle
Glassworkers	1	Abercromby
Hammermen	2	Dingle, Abercromby
Iron and steel dressers	1	Netherfield
Life assurance agents	1	Gt George
Litho artists	1	(Birkenhead)
Litho printers	2	Low Hill, Kensington

Loco engineers and firemen	2	Kirkdale, Dingle
Machine workers	1	Granby
Mill sawyers	1	Everton
Musicians	1	Kensington
Masons	3	Low Hill, Everton, Kensington
NAUL	7	Brunswick, Anfield (2), Sandhills, Garston, Kirkdale, Granby
Organ builders	1	Kensington
Packing-case makers	1	Low Hill
Painters (3)	9	Fairfield (2), Dingle, Old Swan, Garston, St Domingo, Kensington, Edge Hill, Low Hill
Plasterers	1	Edge Hill
French polishers	1	Netherfield
Postmen	4	Kensington, Low Hill, Sefton Park E, Everton
Printers cutters	1	Everton
Railway servants	4	Dingle, Garston, Old Swan, Kirkdale
Saddlers	1	Breckfield
Sailors and firemen	1	Sandhills
Scientific instrument makers	1	Netherfield
Shipwrights	3	Kirkdale, Wavertree W, Abercromby
Slaters	1	Low Hill
Stereotypers	1	St Domingo
Tailors	2	Fairfield (Wallasey)
Typographic printers	1	Everton
Upholsterers	2	Breckfield, Edge Hill
Whitesmiths	1	Breckfield
Watermen and porters	3	(Ellesmere Port, Chester, Birkenhead)

Total no. of unions affiliated: 52

Total no. of delegates: 111

Summary of occupational groups represented

	No.	%
Building trades	35	31.5
Furnishing trades	5	4.5
Railwaymen	6	5.4
Engineering and metal trades	24	21.6
Workshop trades	10	9.0
Printing trades	7	6.3
Clothing trades	4	3.6
Retail and services	1	0.9
Transport and associated	4	3.6
White-collar and supervisory	5	4.5
Miscellaneous	10	9.0
Total	111	100.0

Source: Liverpool Official Red Book, 1905.

APPENDIX II   Affiliated trade unions to the Liverpool Trades Council and Labour Party, year ending 31 March 1925

Union	No.	Union	No.
Altogether builders	360	NAFTA	845
Amal. marine workers	300	NUDAW	2,750
Bakers and confectioners	200	Painters	654
Boilermakers	674	Plasterers	400
Boot and shoe operatives	50	Plumbers	300
Brushmakers	22	Police and prison officers	40
Clerks	240	Postal workers	1,000
Coopers	500	PO engineers	200
Dressmakers	200	Printing and paper workers	900
Electricians	400	Railwaymen	2,648
Electro and stereotypers	80	Railway clerks	1,224
Engineers	537	Sailors and firemen	540
Engine and firemen	525	Shop assistants	375
Farriers	200	Saddlers and leather workers	35
Foundry workers	170	Sheet metal workers	440
NATSOPA	200	Street masons	80
NUGMW	1,270	Tailors and garment workers	140
Heating and		Theatrical employees	50
domestic engineers	400	Tobacco workers	60
I&S metal dressers	180	TGWU	4,200
League of blind	320	Typographical society	1,360
Life assurance agents	105	Upholsterers	200
Litho artists	60	Vehicle builders	400
Litho printers	326	Woodcutting machinists	620
Loco engineers – Edge Hill	280	Woodworkers	1,422
Musical instrument makers	40		
Musicians' Union	500	Total	27,422

Source: LTCLP, *Minutes, financial accounts for 6 months ending 30 September 1924; 31 March 1925.*

APPENDIX III Elections to the Executive Committee of the Liverpool Trades Council and Labour Party, 1921–1939

(a) 1921–1930

Name	Division/trade union	1921	1922	1923	1924	1925	1926	1927	1928	1929	1930
R. Armitage	League of Blind	TU		TU		TU	TU	TU	TU	TU	TU
Mrs M. Bamber	NUDAW						TU	TU	TU	TU	TU
W. H. Barton	Secretary, LTCLP				S	S	S	S			
B. G. Bennett	Plasterers										TU
Mrs A. Billinge	Dressmakers	TU	TU								
J. Bond	PO workers			TU							
H. Booth	Unknown	D									
J. H. Borlase	NSFU	TU									
J. Braddock	Fairfield									D	D
A. Broom	NAFTA				TU						
E. Campbell	Scotland		D	D							
T. Cann	Shop assistants		TU								
W. Carlisle	RCA							TU			
G. Chadwick	ETU					TU	TU	TU	TU	TU	TU
Mrs Churchill	Upholsterers		TU								
J. J. Cleary	W. Derby/ILP						O	D	O		
H. A. Cooke	Teachers				TU		O				
A. C. Crosby	Actors			TU							
W. J. Daniel	MEA		TU	TU		P					
A. Davison	Walton		D	V	P	P	D				

Name	Division/trade union	1921	1922	1923	1924	1925	1926	1927	1928	1929	1930
A. Demain	Toxteth/Coopers			D	D					TU	
P. Duffy	RCA										TU
R. Edwards	ILP							O		O	O
Mrs A. Elliott	Wavertree				D	D	D	D	D	D	D
J. G. Elliot	RCA								D	TU	
Dr A. Fitch	Exchange	T	T				D				
F. Fitzpatrick	RCA			D	D	D					
A. Griffin	Edge Hill										
J. Hamilton	AUBTW								T	T	T
A. Hargreaves	West Derby	TU	TU	TU	TU	TU	V		D	D	D
L. Hogan	NUDAW							P	P	P	TU
J. W. Horan	AEU							TU	TU	TU	TU
D. Hornby	NUR							TU	TU	TU	
C. Hoyle	AEU						TU				
J. G. Houston	NUGMW		TU	TU	TU	TU	TU				
B. V. Kirby	NUC		TU	TU			P	V	V	V	P
V. Lloyd	Wood machinists	TU									
D. G. Logan	Scotland					D		D			
Mrs S. McArd	Kirkdale						D				
H. S. Martin	Tailors			TU	TU	TU	TU				
J. Mee	Unknown	D									
T. Millard	ILP						O				
G. Milligan	NUDL	TU									

Name	*Division/ trade union*	1921	1922	1923	1924	1925	1926	1927	1928	1929	1930
J. Mooney	EC, ILP		O								
J. O'Dwyer	MEA	TU				O					
F. Pasco	Low Hill Labour Club							O			
S. Reeves	Fabian Society					O	O	O	O		
J. Revel	Plumbers	TU									
?. Rice	Unknown		D								
F. T. Richardson	UPW	P		D	D	TU	TU	TU			
F. Robinson	Sheet metal workers		TU	TU	TU	TU	TU	TU	TU		
W. A. Robinson	NUDAW		P	P						TU	
H. E. Rose	Life assurance agents	V	V	TU	V	V	TU	TU	TU	TU	TU
T. J. Rowan	NUDAW	AS	AS	AS							TU
J. Scambler	Unknown		D								
S. Silverman	Exchange										D
W. H. Smith	Police	AS			TU	TU					
?. Smithwick	Police	TU									
G. Tatham	Printing and paper workers		TU	TU	TU	TU			TU	TU	TU
C. H. Taunton	UPW	S	S	S	T	T	T	T			
R. Tissyman	ILP										V
J. Troy	Kirkdale								D	D	
H. Walker	Everton					D		D	D	D	
R. Watson	NUR	TU	TU		TU	TU	TU	TU	TU	TU	
C. Wilson	Painters				TU		TU				

(b) 1931–1939

Name	Division/trade union	1931	1932	1933	1934	1935	1936	1937	1938	1939
W. Addison	NUGMW				TU	TU	TU	TU	TU	TU
L. Baines	Unknown								TU	TU
Mrs M. Bamber	NUDAW	TU	TU	TU	TU		TU	TU	TU	TU
C. H. Beeks	Unknown			TU	TU					
B. G. Bennett	Plasterers	TU			TU	TU	TU	TU	TU	TU
J. Braddock	Fairfield	D	D	D	D	D	D	D	D	D
F. H. Cain	Unknown						D	V	V	P
J. D. Carter	League of Blind						TU			
G. Chadwick	ETU	TU								
W. Christian	Printing and paper workers		TU							
Mrs Cund	Kirkdale		D							
E. Darwick	Croxteth		O	O	O					
A. Demain	East Toxteth	D	D	D	D	D				
A. G. Demain	NUDAW						TU	TU	TU	
Mrs C. Doyle	West Derby							D		
P. Duffy	RCA	TU	TU							
H. W. Eden	Heating and domestic engineers			TU	TU					
Mrs A. Elliott	Wavertree	D	D	D	D	D	D	D	D	D
J. G. Elliott	RCA			TU	TU	TU	TU	TU	TU	TU
J. Gibbins	West Toxteth					V				D

244

Name	Division/ trade union	1931	1932	1933	1934	1935	1936	1937	1938	1939
J. Hamilton	AUBTW	T	T	T	T	T	T	T	T	T
L. Hogan	NUDAW	TU	TU	TU	TU	TU	P	P	P	TU
D. Hornby	NUR	TU	TU	TU	TU	TU				
H. Inglis	Unknown	TU								
J. Johnstone	Low Hill Labour Club		O							
?. Kay	Unknown	O								
?. Keeling	Unknown	O								
T. Keeling	Carters							TU	TU	TU
J. T. Kenny	Walton	P	P	P	D	D				
B. V. Kirby	NUC			D	P	P				
?. Lambert	Walton									
Mrs S. McArd	Kirkdale						D	D	D	D
J. McDonald	Kirkdale			D						
T. E. Martin	AUBTW						TU	TU	TU	TU
Miss M. Mee	Unknown						TU	TU	TU	TU
P. O'Brien	Scotland									V
J. Orford	NUVB	TU	TU	TU	TU	TU	V	TU	TU	V
G. Porter	ASW	TU					TU	TU	TU	TU
?. Pugh	ILP		O							
W. J. Riddick	Assurance workers	TU				TU	TU	TU	TU	TU
F. Robinson	Sheet metal workers		TU	TU	TU					
H. E. Rose	Assurance workers	V	TU	TU	TU	V	V	V	TU	TU

Name	Division/ trade union	1931	1932	1933	1934	1935	1936	1937	1938	1939
P. Sherwin	NUVB		TU	TU						
G. Shipton	Painters	TU	TU							
S. Silverman	Exchange	D	V	V	V					
R. Tissyman	Police					TU				
C. R. Torpey	Boilermakers			TU	TU		TU	TU	TU	
J. Whitehead	Low Hill Labour Club					O	O	O	O	O
D. Williams	Everton				D	D	D	D	D	
G. Williams	TGWU	TU	TU	TU	TU	TU	TU	TU		
R. E. Williamson	Painters			TU	TU	TU	TU	TU	TU	

Key: TU, Trade-union section; D, Divisional section; P, President; V, President; O, Other bodies section; S, Secretary; T, Treasurer; AS, Assistant secretary

Source: LTCLP, *Minutes*, AGMs, various dates, 1921–1939.

APPENDIX IV   Ward profiles and municipal election results in Liverpool, by ward, 1905–1938

Abbreviations used for party names are as follows:

Anti-waste	=	Anti-waste
C	=	Conservative
Cath	=	Catholic Party
Centre	=	Centre Party
Comm	=	Communist Party
Co. L	=	Coalition Liberal
C-Lab	=	Conservative-Labour
Co-op.	=	Co-operative
Co-op Lab	=	Co-operative Labour
Dem. C	=	Democratic Conservative
Dem. Lab	=	Democratic Labour
Fasc	=	Fascist
ILP	=	Independent Labour Party
Ind	=	Independent
Ind. C	=	Independent Conservative
Ind. L	=	Independent Liberal
Ind. Lab	=	Independent Labour
Ind. N	=	Independent Nationalist
Ind. P	=	Independent Protestant
Ind. Ratep'rs	=	Independent Ratepayers
IP	=	Irish Party
L	=	Liberal
Lab	=	Labour
MCU	=	Middle Classes Union
N	=	Irish Nationalist
Nat. L	=	National Liberal
P	=	Protestant
Pat. Lab	=	Patriotic Labour
Pat. Prot	=	Patriotic Protestant
People's	=	People's
Prot. Const	=	Protestant Constitutionalist
Ratep'rs	=	Ratepayers
SDF	=	Social Democratic Federation
Soc	=	Socialist
Soldiers	=	Soldiers
Unemp	=	Unemployed
Youth	=	Youth
NC	=	No Contest

NB: In the Summary Tables for each ward, average vote for parties is calculated only for years when they contested seats. Average turnout is also calculated only for the years when seats were contested. 1914 has been excluded from totals as an electoral truce was in force. By-elections are excluded from summaries. Catholic and Centre Party candidates are defined as Nationalists in the summaries. Figures in the Nationalist and Protestant columns represent the number of candidates; any wins are given in brackets.

Sources: Liverpool Official Red Books, 1906–1939; Census Reports, 1911, 1921 and 1931.

ABERCROMBY (1)

	Population	Electorate	Acreage	Persons/Acre
1911	23,326	2,510	268	87.0
1921	24,933	6,916		93.0
1931	23,427	9,493		87.4

1931	Av. family size	Rooms per dwelling	Families per dwelling	Persons per room
	3.46	6.33	1.71	0.93

Churches 1929			Sittings
Anglican	6		5,620
Catholic	0		0
Nonconformist	10	(Welsh) 2	9,074 (1,420)

School rolls 1923	
Anglican	1,091
Catholic	0
Board	0
Wesleyan	497

Trades Council delegates 1905		WMCA branch
Cabinet-makers		1920 ✓
Glassworkers		1931 ✓
Hammermen	(total 4)	1939 ✓
Shipwrights		

Summary of municipal election results

Years	Lab. wins	Tory wins	Av. Lab. vote (%)	Av. Tory vote (%)	Av. turnout	NC	Nats. (wins)	Prots. (wins)
1905–9	0	4	—	55	65	0	0	0
1910–13	0	4	—	61	53	3	0	0
1905–13	0	8	—	56	63	3	0	0
1919–23	0	5	—	58	40	4	0	0
1924–28	0	5	39	61	40	3	0	0
1929–33	0	5	36	63	35	0	0	0
1934–38	2	3	51	49	44	0	0	0
1919–38	2	18	44	58	40	7	0	0

Full list of municipal election results

Year	Candidates	Votes	%	Voters	Turnout (%)
1905	A. Black (L)	850	51	2,647	63
	W. Phillips (C)	827	49		
1906	E. Lawrence (C)	879	54	2,580	63
	Col. Whitney (L)	756	46		
1907	J. T. Smith jun. (C)	973	59	2,514	66
	Dr Permewan (L)	676	41		
1908	H. H. Clarke (C)	873	56	2,417	64
	A. Black (L)	677	44		
1909	E. Lawrence (C)	882	56	2,369	67
	P. D. Holt (L)	700	44		
1910	T. J. Smith jun. (C)	761	61	2,344	53
	Miss H. M. Johnson (L)	487	39		
1911	C. H. Hayhurst (C)	NC	—	2,510	—
1912	E. Lawrence (C)	NC	—	2,355	—
1913[1] (Mar)	F. J. S. Heaney (C)	NC	—	2,355	—
1913	J. W. Smith (C)	NC	—	2,412	—
1914	C. H. Hayhurst (C)	NC	—	2,401	—
1919	E. Thompson (C)	1,439	58	6,251	40
	J. B. Baillie (Soldiers)	1,038	42		
1920	F. W. Bailey (C)	NC	—	6,828	—
1921	W. T. Roberts (C)	NC	—	6,916	—
1922[2] (Sep)	C. F. Francis (C)	1,741	66	6,916	38
	A. Robinson (L)	897	34		
1922	E. Thompson (C)	NC	—	7,524	—
1923	C. F. Francis (C)	NC	—	7,504	—
1924	W. T. Roberts (C)	NC	—	8,187	—
1925	E. Thompson (C)	NC	—	8,077	—
1926	C. F. Francis (C)	1,899	60	8,221	38
	S. S. Silverman(Lab)	1,263	40		
1927	W. T. Roberts (C)	2,077	62	8,218	41
	S. S. Silverman (Lab)	1,274	38		
1928	E. Thompson (C)	NC	—	7,959	—
1929[3] (Apr)	G. C. Ollason (C)	1,507	56	7,959	34
	B. L. Myer (Lab)	1,187	44		
1929	C. F. Francis (C)	1,813	54	9,020	37
	B. L. Myer (Lab)	1,535	46		
1930	W. T. Roberts (C)	2,209	75	9,000	33
	P. Campbell (Lab)	723	25		
1931	A. M. Finlason (C)	2,447	74	9,493	35
	B. L. Myer (Lab)	851	26		
1932	C. W. Bailey (C)	1,821	57	9,444	34
	Mrs A. Milton (Co-op. Lab)	1,231	39		
	L. J. P. McAdam (Youth)	139	4		

1933	W. T. Roberts (C)	1,896	56	9,619	35
	R. Tissyman (Lab)	1,513	44		
1934	A. Lumb (Lab)	1,535	51	9,633	31
	A. M. Finlason (C)	1,496	49		
1935	C. W. Bailey (C)	2,118	50	9,574	44
	J. R. Bevins (Lab)	2,081	50		
1935[4]	J. R. Bevins (Lab)	1,991	53	9,574	39
(Dec)	A. M. Finlason (C)	1,756	47		
1936	W. T. Roberts (C)	2,383	51	9,829	47
	Mrs A. E. Elliott (Lab)	2,245	49		
1937	J. R. Bevins (Lab)	2,803	55	9,647	53
	R. Clitherow (C)	2,291	45		
1938[5]	J. J. E. Sloan (C)	1,978	50	9,647	41
(Apr)	A. Campbell (Lab)	1,972	49		
	T. L. Hurst (Ind)	27	1		
1938	C. W. Bailey (C)	2,239	51	9,676	45
	J. H. Sayle (Lab)	2,154	49		

[1] Death of T. J. Smith jun.
[2] Death of F. W. Bailey.
[3] Election of E. Thompson as alderman.
[4] Resignation of A. Lumb.
[5] Election of W. T. Roberts as alderman.

AIGBURTH (2)

	Population	Electorate	Acreage	Persons/Acre
1911	9,493	1,819	1,101	8.6
1921	11,331	4,612		10.3
1931	16,122	8,493		14.6

1931	Av. family size	Rooms per dwelling	Families per dwelling	Persons per room
	3.64	5.81	1.03	0.65

Churches 1929			Sittings
Anglican	2		1,732
Catholic	1		224
Nonconformist	2	(Welsh) 0	1,020

School rolls 1923	
Anglican	176
Catholic	133
Board	1,009

Trades Council delegates 1905	WMCA branch
Nil	None

Summary of municipal election results

Years	Lab. wins	Tory wins	Av. Lab. vote (%)	Av. Tory vote (%)	Av. turnout	NC	Nats. (wins)	Prots. (wins)
1905–9	0	3	—	51	75	1	0	0
1910–13	0	4	—	54	74	3	0	0
1905–13	0	7	—	52	75	4	0	0
1919–23	0	5	—	67	64	4	0	0
1924–28	0	3	—	—	—	5	0	0
1929–33	0	4	25	69	41	1	0	0
1934–38	0	5	—	60	43	1	0	0
1919–38	0	17	25	65	44	11	0	0

Full list of municipal election results

Year	Candidates	Votes	%	Voters	Turnout (%)
1905	H. Wilson (C)	469	50	1,319	71
	A. E. Jacob (L)	466	50		
1906	A. E. Jacob (L)	559	52	1,405	77
	W. P. Wethered (C)	520	48		
1907	W. P. Wethered (C)	696	64	1,450	75
	A. Bathgate (L)	389	36		
1908	H. Wilson (C)	NC	—	1,593	—
1909	A. E. Jacob (L)	760	58	1,691	77
	D. Jackson (C)	542	42		
1910	W. P. Wethered (C)	704	54	1,754	74
	W. Abercromby (L)	591	46		
1911	H. Wilson (C)	NC	—	1,819	—
1912	H. M. Miller (C)	NC	—	1,858	—
1913	W. P. Wethered (C)	NC	—	1,937	—
1914	W. J. Burgess (C)	NC	—	2,079	—
1919	H. M. Miller (C)	NC	—	4,422	—
1920	A. E. Jacob (C)	NC	—	4,476	—
1921	J. Ritchie (C)	1,955	67	4,612	64
	W. J. Austin (MCU)	974	33		
1922	H. M. Miller (C)	NC	—	4,960	—
1923	A. E. Jacob (C)	NC	—	5,085	—
1924[1] (Jan)	E. J. Deane (C)	1,407	52	5,085	54
	Col. A. Melly (L)	1,319	48		
1924	E. J. Deane (C)	NC	—	5,237	—
1924[2] (Nov)	W. B. Stoddart (L)	NC	—	5,237	—
1925[3] (Jun)	W. S. Mitcalfe (C)	NC	—	5,237	—

1925	W. B. Stoddart (L)	NC	—	5,507	—
1926	A. Layfield (C)	NC	—	5,831	—
1927	E. J. Deane (C)	NC	—	6,489	—
1928	W. B. Stoddart (L)	NC	—	6,899	—
1929	F. C. Wilson (C)	2,549	69	7,561	49
	Revd J. H. Howard (Lab)	1,147	31		
1930	E. J. Deane (C)	2,743	82	8,187	41
	W. E. Lloyd (Lab)	582	18		
1931[4] (May)	V. E. Cotton (C)	NC	—	8,187	—
1931	W. B. Stoddart (L)	NC	—	8,493	—
1932	V. E. Cotton (C)	1,974	60	8,819	37
	A. D. Dennis (L)	1,293	40		
1933	E. J. Deane (C)	2,132	63	9,165	37
	A. D. Dennis (L)	1,272	37		
1934	E. Errington (C)	2,001	59	9,653	35
	A. D. Dennis (L)	1,418	41		
1935	V. E. Cotton (C)	2,699	60	10,095	44
	A. D. Dennis (L)	1,780	40		
1936[5] (Mar)	A. D. Dennis (L)	2,415	66	10,095	36
	H. D. Arrowsmith (C)	1,267	34		
1936[6] (Sep)	J. R. Jones (L)	NC	—	10,095	—
1936	E. J. Deane (C)	2,777	60	10,421	44
	P. Binnes (L)	1,853	40		
1937	W. E. S. Napier (C)	3,121	59	10,569	50
	J. R. Jones (L)	2,151	41		
1938	V. E. Cotton (C)	NC	—	10,993	—

[1] Death of J. Ritchie.
[2] Election of H. M. Miller as alderman.
[3] Election of A. E. Jacob as alderman.
[4] Election of F. C. Wilson as alderman.
[5] Resignation of E. Errington.
[6] Resignation of A. D. Dennis.

ALLERTON (3) [created 1913, first contested 1920]

	Population	Electorate	Acreage	Persons/Acre
1911	—	—	—	—
1921	2,072	803	1,589	1.3
1931	9,068	4,379		5.7

1931	Av. family size	Rooms per dwelling	Families per dwelling	Persons per room
	3.91	5.41	1.04	0.75

Churches 1929		*Sittings*
Anglican	2	1,250
Catholic	1	200
Nonconformist	0	0

School rolls 1923
Anglican —
Catholic —
Board —

Trades Council delegates 1905	*WMCA branch*
Nil	None

Summary of municipal election results

Years	Lab. wins	Tory wins	Av. Lab. vote (%)	Av. Tory vote (%)	Av. turnout	NC	Nats. (wins)	Prots. (wins)
1919–23	0	2	—	32	54	1	0	0
1924–28	0	3	24	65	50	0	0	0
1929–33	0	5	23	66	48	2	0	0
1934–38	0	5	25	75	46	0	0	0
1919–38	0	15	24	67	48	3	0	0

Full list of municipal election results

Year	Candidates		Votes	%	Voters	Turnout (%)
1920	Dr P. Nelson (C)		NC	—	787	—
1923	Mrs G. E. Wilson (Nat. L)		518	35	1,385	54
	W. J. Austin (C)	(2 elected)	475	32		
	F. Williams (Ind L)		388	26		
	J. H. Naylor (Ind)		116	7		
1924	G. A. Strong (C)		803	66	2,277	53
	F. Williams (L)		406	34		
1925	Mrs G. E. Wilson (Ind)		1,041	78	2,487	54
	G. F. Dutton (Lab)		298	22		
1926	W. J. Austin (C)		674	63	2,619	41
	W. Murphy (Lab)		395	37		
1927	G. A. Strong (C)		837	65	2,277	56
	G. McKinnon (L)		362	28		
	T. Crossland (Lab)		84	7		
1928	Mrs G. E. Wilson (Ind)		1,130	72	3,359	47
	T. Crossland (Lab)		445	28		
1929	H. J. Davis (C)		950	50	3,903	49
	H. N. Whittall (Lab)		626	33		

	W. J. Tristram (L)	317	17		
1930	G. A. Strong (C)	1,351	66	4,115	50
	Mrs A. E. Elliott (Lab)	380	19		
	H. Banks (L)	315	15		
1931[1] (Oct)	W. G. Heath (C)	NC	—	4115	—
1931	G. E. Wilson (C)	1,624	83	4,379	45
	Miss Hickling (Lab)	337	17		
1932	J. W. Jones (C)	NC	—	4,572	—
1933	G. A. Strong (C)	NC	—	4,802	—
1934	G. E. Wilson (C)	1,181	66	4,969	36
	C. E. Hargreaves (Lab)	612	34		
1935	J. W. Jones (C)	1,968	71	5,250	53
	C. E. Hargreaves (Lab)	790	29		
1936	G. A. Strong (C)	2,091	80	5,428	48
	C. W. Baker (Lab)	517	20		
1937	G. E. Wilson (C)	2,453	79	6,074	51
	J. A. Riddell (Lab)	635	21		
1938	J. McMillan (C)	2,061	79	6,459	40
	C. E. Hargreaves (Lab)	537	21		

[1] Election of H. J. Davis as alderman.

ANFIELD (4)

	Population	Electorate	Acreage	Persons/Acre
1911	20,303	3,578	536	37.9
1921	20,731	9,246		38.7
1931	24,261	10,867		45.3

1931	Av. family size	Rooms per dwelling	Families per dwelling	Persons per room
	3.87	5.35	1.05	0.76

Churches 1929			Sittings
Anglican	5		3,375
Catholic	2		1,100
Nonconformist	11	(Welsh) 6	5,494 (2,544)

School rolls 1923
Anglican	1,532
Catholic	1,373
Board	243

Trades Council delegates 1905	WMCA branch
NAUL (2)	None

Summary of municipal election results

Years	Lab. wins	Tory wins	Av. Lab. vote (%)	Av. Tory vote (%)	Av. turnout	NC	Nats. (wins)	Prots. (wins)
1905–9	0	1	—	83	42	3	0	0
1910–13	0	2	—	80	25	3	0	0
1905–13	0	3	—	82	36	6	0	0
1919–23	1	1	23	41	51	0	0	0
1924–28	0	3	22	41	52	0	0	0
1929–33	0	1	24	34	37	2	0	0
1934–38	0	3	31	69	35	2	0	0
1919–38	1	8	24	45	46	4	0	0

Full list of municipal election results

Year	Candidates	Votes	%	Voters	Turnout (%)
1905	W. Evans (L)	NC	—	2,570	—
1906	H. Jones (L)	1,030	86	2,737	44
	J. Bowers (Ind)	174	14		
1907	E. Russell Taylor (C)	930	83	2,830	40
	W. R. Roberts (Ind)	190	17		
1908	W. Evans (L)	NC	—	2,848	—
1909	H. Jones (L)	NC	—	2,957	—
1910	E. Russell Taylor (C)	628	80	3,170	25
	W. R. Roberts (Ind)	154	20		
1911	W. Evans (L)	NC	—	3,578	—
1912	H. Jones (L)	NC	—	3,628	—
1913	E. Russell Taylor (C)	NC	—	3,735	—
1914	W. Evans (L)	NC	—	3,930	—
1919	G. T. Holliday (Lab)	1,294	36	8,706	41
	J. E. Richardson (C)	1,276	35		
	W. O Thomas (L)	1,030	29		
1920	W. O. Thomas (L)	3,445	75	8,707	53
	J. P. Redish (Lab)	1,149	25		
1921	W. B. Stoddart (L)	1,950	41	9,246	51
	A. Morrow (C)	1,927	41		
	M. H. Taylor (Lab)	870	18		
1922	G. Y. Williamson (C)	2,602	50	9,243	57
	A. Gates (L)	1,510	29		
	F. Robinson (Lab)	1,124	21		
1923[1]	A. Gates (L)	1,524	53	9,243	31
(Jan)	A. Venmore (Nat. L)	1,336	47		
1923	A. Gates (L)	2,400	47	9,448	54

	J. P. Thomas (C)	1,866	36		
	W. J. Daniel (Lab)	855	17		
1924	C. G. S. Gordon (C)	2,268	43	9,500	55
	W. B. Stoddart (L)	2,060	40		
	J. Badlay (Lab)	897	17		
1925	G. Y. Williamson (C)	2,633	49	9,493	57
	J. J. Cleary (Lab)	1,416	26		
	W. H. Cartwright (L)	1,342	25		
1926	A. Gates (L)	2,036	42	9,663	50
	A. Morrow (C)	1,620	34		
	J. J. Cleary (Lab)	1,167	24		
1927	A. R. Price (L)	1,952	44	10,061	44
	C. G. S. Gordon (C)	1,639	37		
	R. J. McDonnell (Lab)	845	19		
1928	G. Y. Williamson (C)	2,233	42	10,088	53
	C. Baxter (L)	1,863	35		
	J. Sheehan (Lab)	1,206	23		
1929	A. Gates (L)	2,231	43	10,873	47
	L. S. Holmes (C)	1,723	34		
	W. A. Robinson jun. (Lab)	1,164	23		
1930	A. R. Price (L)	2,364	78	10,924	28
	A. Rainford (Lab)	682	22		
1931	G. Y. Williamson (C)	NC	—	10,867	—
1932	A. Gates (L)	2,989	74	10,829	37
	J. Jones (Lab)	1,024	26		
1933	A. R. Price (L)	NC	—	10,703	—
1934	G. Y. Williamson (C)	2,244	65	10,696	32
	R. H. Williams (Lab)	1,227	35		
1935[2] (Mar)	A. R. Gates (L)	NC	—	10,696	—
1935	A. R. Gates (L)	NC	—	10,987	—
1936	A. O. Roberts (L)	2,257	85	11,285	23
	R. H. Williams (Ind)	389	15		
1937	G. Y. Williamson (C)	4,179	73	11,273	51
	J. F. Kenrick (Lab)	1,528	27		
1938[3] (Aug)	W. J. Harrop (C)	NC	—	11,273	—
1938	A. J. White (C)	NC	—	11,270	—

[1] Resignation of W. O. Thomas.
[2] Election of A. Gates as alderman.
[3] Election of G. Y. Williamson as alderman.

256

BRECKFIELD (5)

	Population	Electorate	Acreage	Persons/Acre
1911	24,481	4,225	175	139.9
1921	25,182	9,624		143.9
1931	22,273	10,369		127.3

1931	Av. family size	Rooms per dwelling	Families per dwelling	Persons per room
	3.93	5.44	1.15	0.83

Churches 1929		Sittings
Anglican	3	2,250
Catholic	0	0
Nonconformist	2 (Welsh) 0	1,200

School rolls 1923	
Anglican	0
Catholic	0
Board	2,489

Trades Council delegates 1905		WMCA branch
Engineers		1920 ✓
Saddlers	(total 4)	1931 ✓
Upholsterers		1939 ✓
Whitesmiths		

Summary of municipal election results

Years	Lab. wins	Tory wins	Av. Lab. vote (%)	Av. Tory vote (%)	Av. turnout	NC	Nats. (wins)	Prots. (wins)
1905–9	0	5	—	62	59	3	0	1 (0)
1910–13	0	4	42	59	47	1	0	0
1905–13	0	9	42	60	52	4	0	1 (0)
1919–23	1	4	34	65	53	1	0	1 (0)
1924–28	1	4	44	57	45	0	1 (0)	0
1929–33	1	4	41	55	41	0	0	0
1934–38	0	5	35	63	43	0	1 (0)	0
1919–38	3	17	39	60	45	1	2 (0)	1 (0)

Full list of municipal election results

Year	Candidates	Votes	%	Voters	Turnout (%)
1905	L. S. Cohen (C)	1,1612	62	4,190	62
	J. H. Taylor (P)	978	38		
1906	W. H. Priest (C)	NC	—	4,214	—
1907	L. S. Cohen (C)	1421	62	4,133	56
	J. Meek (L)	881	38		
1908	F. J. Leslie (C)	NC	—	4,132	—
1909	W. H. Priest (C)	NC	—	4,126	—
1910	W. Rudd (C)	1,109	59	4,040	47
	T. Williams (L)	781	41		
1911	F. J. Leslie (C)	966	53	4,225	43
	R. Donaldson (Lab)	867	47		
1912	A. Griffiths (C)	1,339	64	4,176	50
	R. Donaldson (Lab)	738	36		
1913	W. Rudd (C)	NC	—	4,212	—
1914	E. Powell (C)	NC	—	4,282	—
1919	H. A. Booth (Lab)	2,295	55	9,269	45
	A. Griffiths (C)	1,873	45		
1920	A. Griffiths (C)	3,859	73	9,427	56
	A. N. Denaro (Lab)	1,398	27		
1921	T. H. Burton (C)	3,811	75	9,624	53
	W. Smith (Lab)	1,281	25		
1922	E. J. Jones (C)	3,594	67	9,557	56
	H. A. Booth (Lab)	1,611	30		
	J. Gaffney (N)	121	3		
1923	A. Griffiths (C)	NC	—	9,637	—
1924	T. H. Burton (C)	3,000	68	9,708	46
	C. Wilson (Lab)	1,425	32		
1925	E. J. Jones (C)	2,822	58	9,957	48
	T. J. C. Rowan (Lab)	1,966	41		
1925[1] (Dec)	Revd H. D. Longbottom (C)	2,451	53	9,957	46
	W. A. Robinson (Lab)	2,175	47		
1926	H. E. Rose (Lab)	1,977	51	9,846	39
	H. D. Longbottom (Prot. Const)	1,883	49		
1927	T. H. Burton (C)	2,081	52	9,697	42
	W. J. Riddick (Lab)	1,947	48		
1928	E. J. Jones (C)	2,491	51	9,405	52
	W. J. Riddick (Lab)	2,368	49		
1929	H. E. Rose (Lab)	2,430	53	10,418	44
	C. H. Beatty (C)	2,119	47		
1930	T. H. Burton (C)	2,338	51	10, 398	44
	W. J. Riddick (Lab)	1,324	29		
	G. E. Lewis (L)	921	20		
1931[2]	Mrs A. M. Burton (C)	1,506	51	10,398	29

(Mar)	W. J. Riddick (Lab)	857	29		
	G. E. Lewis (P)	604	20		
1931	H. J. Pearson jun. (C)	3,066	71	10,369	42
	A. Hargreaves (Lab)	1,281	29		
1932	Mrs A. M. Burton (C)	2,134	53	10,450	39
	A. Hargreaves (Lab)	1,910	47		
1933	T. H. Burton (C)	2,054	52	10,547	38
	A. Hargreaves (Lab)	1,912	48		
1934	H. J. Pearson (C)	1,880	52	10,353	35
	A. W. Boothman (Lab)	1,365	38		
	G. E. Lewis (P)	389	10		
1935	Mrs A. M. Burton (C)	2,294	55	10,292	41
	A. W. Boothman (Lab)	1,895	45		
1936[3]	D. J. Lewis (C)	1,398	67	10,292	20
(Jan)	A. W. Boothman (Lab)	682	33		
1936	D. J. Lewis (C)	2,679	62	10,154	43
	J. L. Jones (Lab)	1,640	38		
1937	G. W. Prout (C)	4,546	77	9,955	59
	W. Tipping (Lab)	1,343	23		
1938	Mrs A. M. Burton (C)	2,642	70	9,948	38
	W. Tipping (Lab)	1,139	30		

[1] Death of A. Griffiths.
[2] Election of H. E. Rose as alderman.
[3] Election of T. H. Burton as alderman.

BRUNSWICK (6)

	Population	Electorate	Acreage	Persons/Acre
1911	21,994	2,661	238	92.4
1921	23,077	7,576		97.0
1931	22,016	9,088		92.5

1931	Av. family size	Rooms per dwelling	Families per dwelling	Persons per room
	4.19	4.86	1.46	1.26

Churches 1929			Sittings
Anglican	4		2,900
Catholic	2		2,074
Nonconformist	4	(Welsh) 0	1,510

School rolls 1923	
Anglican	336
Catholic	2,128
Board	1,174

Trades Council delegates 1905
NAUL (1)

WMCA branch
1920 ✓
1931 ✓
1939 ✓

Summary of municipal election results

Years	Lab. wins	Tory wins	Av. Lab. vote (%)	Av. Tory vote (%)	Av. turnout	NC	Nats. (wins)	Prots. (wins)
1905–9	0	0	—	—	—	5	2 (2)	0
1910–13	1	0	54	45	57	2	1 (1)	0
1905–13	1	0	54	45	54	7	3 (3)	0
1919–23	1	0	32	—	46	2	3 (3)	0
1924–28	3	0	76	26	51	2	3 (2)	0
1929–33	5	0	81	23	45	1	0	0
1934–38	5	0	—	—	—	5	0	0
1919–38	14	0	68	27	47	10	6 (5)	0

Full list of municipal election results

Year	Candidates	Votes	%	Voters	Turnout (%)
1905	T. Roberts (L)	NC	—	2,793	—
1906[1]	P. C. Kelly (L)	730	54	2,793	48
(May)	W. R. Gasking (C)	444	33		
	T. Byrne (Ind)	174	13		
1906	J. A. Kelly (N)	NC	—	2,827	—
1907	P. C. Kelly (L)	NC	—	2,758	—
1908	T. Roberts (L)	NC	—	2,605	—
1909	J. A. Kelly (N)	NC	—	2,571	—
1910	P. C. Kelly (L)	NC	—	2,575	—
1911	T. J. Hickling (Lab)	781	54	2,661	54
	T. Roberts (L)	667	46		
1912	J. A. Kelly (N)	NC	—	2,571	—
1913	P. C. Kelly (L)	861	55	2,640	59
	W. Fraser (C)	693	45		
1914	P. Kean (Lab)	NC	—	2,710	—
1919	J. A. Kelly (N)	2,493	74	7,251	46
	M. Mason (C)	857	26		
1920	L. King (Ind)	NC	—	7,484	—
1921	L. Hogan (Lab)	2,171	59	7,576	48
	E. E. Jacks (C)	1,503	41		

1922	J. A. Kelly (N)	NC	—	7,786	—
1923	L. King (IP)	3,433	96	8,197	44
1923	J. H. Dutton (Lab)	154	4		
1924	L. Hogan (Lab)	3,228	69	8,451	55
	B. Fisher (C)	1,456	31		
1925	J. A. Kelly (Cath)	NC	—	8,523	—
1926	L. King (Centre)	NC	—	8,570	—
1927	T. Hanley (Lab)	3,431	79	8,589	51
	T. H. Nabb (C)	930	21		
1928	P. Moorhead (Lab)	3,111	81	8,447	46
	J. A. Kelly (Centre)	740	19		
1929	L. King (Lab)	3,615	83	9,643	46
	T. H. Nabb (C)	606	14		
	J. F. Hughes (Ind)	145	3		
1930	T. Hanley (Lab)	2,382	72	9,058	37
	D. Jukes (C)	935	28		
1931	P. Moorhead (Lab)	3,422	74	9,088	51
	D. Jukes (C)	1,190	26		
1932	L. King (Lab)	3,912	95	8,843	47
	F. W. Gibson (Comm)	212	5		
1933	T. Hanley (Lab)	NC	—	8,746	—
1934	P. Moorhead (Lab)	NC	—	8,580	—
1935	L. King (Lab)	NC	—	8,356	—
1936	T. Hanley (Lab)	NC	—	8,169	—
1937[2] (Feb)	Mrs A. Cain (Lab)	NC	—	8,169	—
1937	P. Moorhead (Lab)	NC	—	7,993	—
1937[3] (Dec)	J. Whitehead (Lab)	NC	—	7,993	—
1938	Mrs A. Cain (Lab)	NC	—	7,815	—

[1] Resignation of T. Byrne (previously Liberal councillor).
[2] Election of L. King as alderman.
[3] Resignation of P. Moorhead.

CASTLE STREET (7)

	Population	Electorate	Acreage	Persons/Acre
1911	560	2,053	78	7.2
1921	512	2,678		6.6
1931	366	2,360		4.7

1931	Av. family size	Rooms per dwelling	Families per dwelling	Persons per room
	3.47	4.32	1.01	0.81

Churches 1929		Sittings
Anglican	0	—
Catholic	0	—
Nonconformist	0	—

School rolls 1923	
Anglican	0
Catholic	0
Board	0

Trades Council delegates 1905	WMCA branch
Nil	None

Summary of municipal election results

Years	Lab. wins	Tory wins	Av. Lab. vote (%)	Av. Tory vote (%)	Av. turnout	NC	Nats. (wins)	Prots. (wins)
1905–9	0	3	—	53	62	3	0	0
1910–13	0	3	—	—	—	4	0	0
1905–13	0	6	—	53	62	7	0	0
1919–23	0	4	—	65	46	4	0	0
1924–28	0	3	—	—	—	5	0	0
1929–33	0	3	—	—	—	5	0	0
1934–38	0	4	—	66	39	4	0	0
1919–38	0	14	—	66	43	18	0	0

Full list of municipal election results

Year	Candidates	Votes	%	Voters	Turnout (%)
1905	T. A. Patterson (L)	675	53	2,106	61
	A. Wilson (C)	600	47		
1905[1] (Dec)	J. W. Alsop (C)	NC	—	2,106	—
1906	J. W. Alsop (C)	NC	—	2,135	—
1907	C. F. Garner (C)	774	59	2,099	62
	F. C. Bowring (L)	533	41		
1908	R. G. Hough (L)	NC	—	2,076	—
1909	J. W. Alsop (C)	NC	—	2,034	—
1910	J. P. Reynolds (C)	NC	—	2,028	—
1911	R. G. Hough (L)	NC	—	2,053	—
1912	J. W. Alsop (C)	NC	—	1,975	—
1913	J. P. Rayner (C)	NC	—	1,982	—
1914	R. G. Hough (L)	NC	—	1,958	—

1919	F. A. Goodwin (C)	NC	—	2,409	—
1920	B. Cookson (C)	NC	—	2,557	—
1921[2]	J. S. Allen (C)	NC	—	2,557	—
(Sep)					
1921	R. G. Hough (L)	NC	—	2,678	—
1922	J. S. Allen (C)	NC	—	2,514	—
1923[3]	F. W. Frodsham (C)	NC	—	2,514	—
(Jun)					
1923	F. W. Frodsham (C)	793	65	2,643	46
	T. R. Little (L)	418	35		
1924	W. Denton (L)	NC	—	2,640	—
1925	J. S. Allen (C)	NC	—	2,586	—
1926	R. Rutherford (C)	NC	—	2,593	—
1927	W. Denton (L)	NC	—	2,606	—
1928	J. S. Allen (C)	NC	—	2,576	—
1928[4]	R. G. Sheldon (C)	NC	—	2,576	—
(Dec)					
1929	R. G. Sheldon (C)	NC	—	2,666	—
1929[5]	A. E. Shennan (C)	967	96	2,666	38
(Dec)	C. H. Taunton (Lab)	41	4		
1930	W. Denton (L)	NC	—	2,426	—
1931	A. E. Shennan (C)	NC	—	2,360	—
1932	R. G. Sheldon (C)	NC	—	2,340	—
1932[6]	J. Bennett (C)	NC	—	2,340	—
(Nov)					
1933	W. Denton (L)	NC	—	2,246	—
1934[7]	W. S. S. Hannay (L)	NC	—	2,249	—
(Sep)					
1934	H. N. Bewley (C)	565	66	2,203	39
	W. E. McLachlan (Ind. C)	295	34		
1935	J. Bennett (C)	NC	—	2,182	—
1936	W. S. S. Hannay (L)	NC	—	2,099	—
1937	H. N. Bewley (C)	NC	—	2,070	—
1938	J. Bennett (C)	NC	—	2,010	—

[1] Resignation of J. T. Wood.
[2] Death of F. A. Goodwin.
[3] Death of B. Cookson.
[4] Election of R. Rutherford as alderman.
[5] Resignation of J. S. Allen.
[6] Election of R. G. Sheldon as alderman.
[7] Election of W. Denton as alderman.

CHILDWALL (8) [created 1913, first contested 1920]

	Population	Electorate	Acreage	Persons/Acre
1911	—	—	—	—
1921	1,590	952	1,285	1.2
1931	5,986	3,105		4.7

1931	Av. family size	Rooms per dwelling	Families per dwelling	Persons per room
	3.45	6.04	1.01	0.58

Churches 1929		*Sittings*
Anglican	1	500
Catholic	1	300
Nonconformist	0	0

School rolls 1923	
Anglican	0
Catholic	0
Board	0

Trades Council delegates 1905	*WMCA branch*
Nil	None

Summary of municipal election results

Years	Lab. wins	Tory wins	Av. Lab. vote (%)	Av. Tory vote (%)	Av. turnout	NC	Nats. (wins)	Prots. (wins)
1919–23	0	1	33	69	73	1	0	0
1924–28	0	5	36	63	60	1	0	0
1929–33	0	3	14	49	60	1	0	0
1934–38	0	1	14	52	46	1	0	0
1919–38	0	10	24	56	57	4	0	0

Full list of municipal election results

Year	Candidates	Votes	%	Voters	Turnout (%)
1920	Mrs H. Muspratt (L)	491	66	1,016	73
	J. M. Robertson (Lab)	250	34		
1921	H. J. Davis (C)	479	69	952	73
	J. M. Robertson (Lab)	214	31		
1923	Mrs H. Muspratt (Nat. Lib)	NC	—	992	—
1924	H. J. Davis (C)	NC	—	1,242	—
1926	Mrs H. Muspratt (C)	674	59	1,795	63

	Miss L. M. Hamilton (Lab)	356	31		
	J. Whiteside (L)	104	10		
1927	H. J. Davis (C)	777	34	2,107	55
(2 elected)	E. N. Heath (C)	719	31		
	Mrs Hamilton (Lab)	438	19		
	C. M. Belk (Lab)	382	16		
1928	E. P. Johnson (C)	972	63	2,525	61
	Mrs Hamilton (Lab)	570	37		
1929[1]	A. A. Boyle (L)	621	45	2,525	54
(Apr)	G. H. Taylor (C)	523	38		
	F. Stapleton (Lab)	225	16		
1929	Mrs H. Muspratt (C)	893	52	2,941	58
	A. C. Williams (L)	435	25		
	G. T. Pollard (Lab)	391	23		
1930	A. A. Boyle (L)	936	53	3,076	57
	H. Beckett (C)	679	38		
	T. Crossland (Lab)	151	9		
1931	G. C. Ollason (C)	1,094	57	3,105	62
	A. C. Williams (L)	816	43		
1932	Mrs H. Muspratt (C)	978	48	3,299	61
	W. J. Tristram (L)	849	42		
	A. Donohue (Lab)	195	10		
1933	A. A. Boyle (L)	NC	—	3,557	—
1934[2]	W. J. Tristram (L)	1,033	53	3,557	55
(Jun)	J. D. R. Tilney (C)	929	47		
1934	Mrs C. M. Boyle (L)	907	51	3,854	46
	G. C. Ollason (C)	866	49		
1935	W. J. Tristram (L)	1,813	82	4,554	48
	A. A. Arnot (Lab)	385	18		
1936	A. A. Boyle (L)	NC	—	6,140	—
1937	S. Foster (C)	2,423	55	7,427	59
	W. M. Mirrless (L)	1,639	38		
	J. Wood (Lab)	319	7		
1938[3]	W. H. Moss (Ind. Ratep'rs)	2,142	56	7,427	52
(Feb)	E. T. White (C)	878	23		
	A. M. Morris (Ratep'rs)	581	15		
	A. Campbell (Lab)	226	6		
1938	W. J. Tristam (L)	2,017	83	8,252	29
	A. A. Arnot (Lab)	417	17		

[1] Election of H. J. Davis as alderman.
[2] Election of Mrs H. Muspratt as alderman.
[3] Resignation of A. A. Boyle.

CROXTETH (9) [created and first contested 1928]

	Population	Electorate	Acreage	Persons/Acre
1911	—	—	—	—
1921	—	—	—	—
1931	25,024	10,851	3,553	7.0

1931	Av. family size	Rooms per dwelling	Families per dwelling	Persons per room
	4.62	4.71	1.00	0.98

Churches 1929		Sittings
Anglican	0	
Catholic	1	
Nonconformist	0	

School rolls 1923
Anglican
Catholic
Board

Trades Council delegates 1905	WMCA branch
Nil	1920
	1931
	1939 ✓

Summary of municipal election results

Years	Lab. wins	Tory wins	Av. Lab. vote (%)	Av. Tory vote (%)	Av. turnout	NC	Nats. (wins)	Prots. (wins)
1924–28	1	0	63	37	53	0	0	0
1929–33	4	2	56	43	39	0	1 (0)	0
1934–38	5	0	62	34	33	2	0	1 (0)
1919–38	10	2	59	40	39	2	1 (0)	1 (0)

Full list of municipal election results

Year	Candidates	Votes	%	Voters	Turnout (%)
1928	A. Hargreaves (Lab)	1,935	63	5,886	53
	W. E. McLachlan (C)	1,157	37		
1929	G. H. Boothman (Lab)	2,014	31	8,125	40
(2 elected)	Miss L.M.Hamilton (Lab)	1,976	30		
	Miss G. E. Bartlett (C)	1,253	19		

266

	H. Beckett (C)	1,246	19		
1930	O. Wade (C)	1,853	55	9,541	35
	A. Hargreaves (Lab)	1,520	45		
1931	F. W. Anderson (C)	2,091	51	10,851	39
	Mrs M. L. Hamilton (Lab)	2,000	49		
1932	G. H. Boothman (Lab)	3,397	55	12,936	48
	J. Moores (C)	2,422	39		
	P. J. Haines (Dem. Lab)	221	4		
	C.W. Heaton (Comm)	118	2		
1932[1] (Nov)	Mrs M. L. Hamilton (Lab)	3,574	70	12,936	40
	D. Walker (C)	1,556	30		
1933	Mrs M. L. Hamilton (Lab)	2,896	64	15,544	35
	P. G. Moore (C)	1,658	36		
1934	A. Hargreaves (Lab)	3,617	64	17,330	32
	J. Loughlin (C)	1,602	29		
	F. Kenny (P)	392	7		
1935	G. H. Boothman (Lab)	NC	—	18,803	—
1936	Mrs M. L. Hamilton (Lab)	4,374	61	19,357	37
	Miss B. Whittingham-Jones (C)	2,833	39		
1937[2] (Jun)	J. L. Jones (Lab)	3,331	66	19,357	26
	Miss B. Whittingham-Jones (C)	1,727	34		
1937	A. Hargreaves (Lab)	3,570	62	19,973	29
	J. C. Pollard (Ind)	2,148	38		
1938	G. H. Boothman (Lab)	NC	—	20,489	—

[1] Resignation of O. Wade.
[2] Resignation of Mrs Hamilton.

DINGLE (10)

	Population	Electorate	Acreage	Persons/Acre
1911	35,757	5,785	376	95.1
1921	37,571	13,445		99.9
1931	35,235	15,469		93.7

	Av. family size	Rooms per dwelling	Families per dwelling	Persons per room
1931	4.2	4.56	1.16	1.07

Churches 1929   Sittings
Anglican   3   2,480
Catholic   1   800
Nonconformist   6   (Welsh) 0   2,700

School rolls 1923
Anglican   1,646
Catholic   925
Board   5,347

Trades Council delegates 1905   WMCA branch
Carpenters (2)   Railway servants   1920 ✓ (2)
Gasfitters   Engineers and cranemen   1939 ✓ (2)
Hammermen   Painters   1939 ✓ (2)
Loco engineers and firemen   (total 8)

Summary of municipal election results

Years	Lab. wins	Tory wins	Av. Lab. vote (%)	Av. Tory vote (%)	Av. turnout	NC	Nats. (wins)	Prots. (wins)
1905–9	0	5	—	69	42	3	0	0
1910–13	0	4	38	63	52	2	0	0
1905–13	0	9	38	66	47	5	0	0
1919–23	0	5	39	61	57	0	0	0
1924–28	0	5	45	55	60	0	0	0
1929–33	3	2	46	43	55	0	0	4 (0)
1934–38	2	3	50	50	55	0	0	0
1919–38	5	15	45	52	57	0	0	4 (0)

Full list of municipal election results

Year	Candidates	Votes	%	Voters	Turnout (%)
1905	R. Caton (C)	NC	—	5,168	—
1906	O. H. Williams (C)	1,499	72	5,131	41
	T. Byrne (Ind)	586	28		
1907	E. J. Chevalier (C)	1,487	66	5,268	43
	Miss Johnson (L)	765	34		
1908	R. Caton (C)	NC	—	5,502	—
1909	O. H. Williams (C)	NC	—	5,566	—
1910	A. C. F. Henderson (C)	NC	—	5,567	—
1911	R. Caton (C)	1,686	55	5,785	53

	J. F. Bower (Lab)	1,360	45		
1912	T. C. Huxley (C)	2,012	70	5,747	50
	J. F. Bower (Lab)	860	30		
1913	A. J. Branwood (C)	NC	—	5,728	
1914	J. C. Walker (C)	NC	—	5,919	—
1919	W. W. Kelly (C)	3,594	66	12,830	43
	W. J. Daniel (Lab)	1,869	34		
1920	J. D. Flood (C)	5,214	75	13,212	53
	W. M. Wright (Lab)	1,751	25		
1921	W. P. Coslett (C)	4,362	52	13,445	63
	H. G. Cole (Lab)	4,044	48		
1922	W. W. Kelly (C)	4,741	53	13,765	65
	H. G. Cole (Lab)	4,243	47		
1923	J. D. Flood (C)	4,803	58	13,968	60
	J. Gibbins (Lab)	3,482	42		
	D. Protheroe (Unemp)	56	1		
1924[1]	F. B. Brown (C)	3,769	52	13,968	51
(Jul)	H. G. Cole (Lab)	3,420	48		
1924	F. B. Brown (C)	5,619	62	14,408	63
	R. J. McDonnell (Lab)	3,512	38		
1925	W. W. Kelly (C)	5,314	56	14,446	66
	Mrs G. A. Cole (Lab)	4,252	44		
1926	J. D. Flood (C)	3,842	52	14,497	51
	J. H. R. Latham (Lab)	3,589	48		
1927	F. B. Brown (C)	4,092	52	14,428	55
	T. H. Jones (Lab)	3,811	48		
1928	W. W. Kelly (C)	4,696	51	14,084	66
	W. Jones (Lab)	4,560	49		
1929[2]	W. Jones (Lab)	NC	—	14,084	—
(Sep)					
1929	W. Jones (Lab)	4,385	51	15,671	54
	Mrs N. Proctor (C)	4,134	49		
1929[3]	Mrs N. Proctor (C)	4,291	50	15,671	54
(Nov)	A. Newman (Lab)	4,224	50		
1930	H. Bosworth (C)	4,088	51	15,516	51
	A. Demain (Lab)	3,061	39		
	A. H. Osborne (P)	789	10		
1931	Mrs Proctor (C)	4,108	48	15,469	56
	J. Lawrenson (Lab)	3,027	35		
	R. Bradley (P)	1,501	17		
1932	W. Jones (Lab)	4,478	50	15,518	58
	J. Bennett (C)	3,084	35		
	R. Bradley (P)	1,362	15		
1933	J. Gibbins (Lab)	4,750	57	15,543	54
	W. S. Finlason (C)	2,565	31		
	G. E. Lewis (P)	1,087	12		
1934[4]	C. M. Belk (Lab)	2,875	54	15,543	34
(Mar)	H. H. Nuttall (C)	2,479	46		
1934	J. D. Towers (Lab)	3,915	59	15,330	43

	Mrs N. Proctor (C)	2,691	41		
1935	C. M. Belk (Lab)	4,817	59	15,215	54
	Mrs N. Proctor (C)	3,365	41		
1936	G. H. Duckett (C)	4,480	50	14,930	59
	J. Gibbins (Lab)	4,393	50		
1937	G. W. N. Gillespie (C)	5,798	61	14,812	64
	J. D. Towers (Lab)	3,678	39		
1938	E. T. White (C)	4,645	58	14,990	53
	C. M. Belk (Lab)	3,306	42		

[1] Death of W. P. Coslett.
[2] Election of J. D. Flood as alderman.
[3] Election of W. W. Kelly as alderman.
[4] Resignation of W. Jones.

EDGE HILL (11)

	Population	Electorate	Acreage	Persons/Acre
1911	31,493	4,858	248	127.0
1921	34,449	11,652		138.9
1931	31,008	13,274		125.0

1931	Av. family size	Rooms per dwelling	Families per dwelling	Persons per room
	4.18	4.55	1.14	1.05

Churches 1929		Sittings
Anglican	2	1,656
Catholic	2	1,300
Nonconformist	4 (Welsh) 0	2,240

School rolls 1923	
Anglican	1,486
Catholic	1,141
Board	3,752

Trades Council delegates 1905		WMCA branch
Blind basketmakers	Plasterers	1920 ✓
Carpenters	Upholsterers	1931 ✓
Coachmakers		1939 ✓
Painters	(total 6)	

Summary of municipal election results

Years	Lab. wins	Tory wins	Av. Lab. vote (%)	Av. Tory vote (%)	Av. turnout	NC	Nats. (wins)	Prots. (wins)
1905–9	0	4	—	61	51	1	0	0
1910–13	2	2	49	50	53	0	0	0
1905–13	2	6	49	55	52	1	0	0
1919–23	1	4	42	53	51	0	1 (0)	0
1924–28	5	0	56	43	48	0	0	0
1929–33	3	2	48	46	40	0	0	0
1934–38	4	1	52	48	48	0	0	0
1919–38	13	7	50	47	47	0	1 (0)	0

Full list of municipal election results

Year	Candidates	Votes	%	Voters	Turnout (%)
1905	C. Freeman (L)	1,380	51	4,831	56
	J. Gordon (C)	1,341	49		
1906	W. E. Parry (C)	1,551	64	4,922	49
	G. Parker (L)	870	36		
1907	J. H. Harrison (C)	1,461	61	4,791	50
	T. Byrne (Ind)	589	25		
	C. Wilson (SDF)	341	14		
1908	W. W. Walker (C)	1,605	70	4,643	50
	C. Freeman (L)	701	30		
1909	R. J. Clarke (C)	NC	—	4,645	—
1910	E. Whitely (Lab)	1,001	49	4,525	45
	J. H. Harrison (C)	952	47		
	C. Wilson (SDF)	69	3		
	J. Murphy (Soc)	8	—		
1911[1] (Apr)	F. R. Brough (C)	1,017	55	4,525	41
	W. R. Blair (Soc)	848	45		
1911	W. R. Blair (Lab)	1,544	57	4,858	56
	A. J. Bramwood (C)	1,159	43		
1912	R. J. Clarke (C)	1,444	58	4,744	53
	A. Hawkes (Lab)	1,064	42		
1913	F. B. Brough (C)	1,323	51	4,714	56
	E. Whitely (Lab)	1,294	49		
1914	F. T. Richardson (Lab)	NC	—	4,838	—
1919	C. Burden (Lab)	2,527	53	11,068	43
	D. C. Williams (C)	2,240	47		
1919[2] (Nov)	S. Mason (Lab)	2,759	52	11,068	48
	D. C. Williams (C)	2,516	48		
1920	D. C. Williams (C)	4,333	67	11,416	57

	B. L. Myer (Lab)	2,153	33		
1921	J. Jude (C)	3,364	52	11,652	55
	R. Tissyman (Lab)	3,055	48		
1922	R. J. Hall (C)	3,206	49	11,955	54
	C. Burden (Lab)	2,438	38		
	W. H. McGuiness (N)	502	8		
	C. Stamper (Pat. Lab)	345	5		
1923	D. C. Williams (C)	2,920	50	12,228	48
	C. Burden (Lab)	2,690	46		
	W. H. McGuiness (IP)	182	3		
	C. Stamper (Pat. Lab)	52	1		
1924	R. Tissyman (Lab)	3,373	51	12,421	53
	J. Jude (C)	3,193	49		
1925	C. Wilson (Lab)	3,542	55	12,571	51
	R. J. Hall (C)	2,916	45		
1926[3]	W. Smith (Lab)	3,045	54	12,571	45
(Apr)	A. Layfield (C)	2,642	46		
1926	W. Smith (Lab)	3,315	59	12,679	45
	Miss E. R. Conway (C)	2,340	41		
1927	R. Tissyman (Lab)	3,230	58	12,616	44
	R. Roberts (C)	2,301	42		
1928[4]	A. Griffin (Lab)	3,144	55	12,616	45
(Sep)	H. G. Grace (C)	2,368	42		
	L McGree (Comm)	172	3		
1928	C. Wilson (Lab)	3,314	59	12,188	46
	E. Cheshire (C)	2,172	39		
	L. McGree (Comm)	155	2		
1929	A. Griffin (Lab)	3,143	63	13,310	37
	D. Jukes (C)	1,721	35		
	L. McGree (Comm)	110	2		
1929[5]	Mrs S. A. McArd (Lab)	NC	—	13,310	—
(Nov)					
1930[6]	R. Tissyman (Ind. Lab)	986	63	13,310	12
(Aug)	H. O. Pugh (Lab)	585	37		
1930	H. H. Nuttall (C)	2,508	52	13,336	36
	R. Tissyman (Ind. Lab)	1,241	26		
	H. O. Pugh (Lab)	1,050	22		
	D. Protheroe (Fasc)	36	—		
1931	S. R. Williams (C)	3,772	62	13,274	46
	Mrs S. A. McArd (Lab)	2,272	38		
1932	A. Griffin (Lab)	3,402	60	13,138	43
	W. Murphy (C)	2,018	36		
	J. F. Hughes (ILP)	246	4		
1933	J. Johnstone (Lab)	2,834	55	13,055	40
	H. H. Nuttall (C)	2,231	43		
	C. W. Heaton (Comm)	107	2		
1934	Mrs A. Mitton (Lab)	2,499	53	12,827	37
	S. A. Williams (C)	2,212	47		
1935	A. Griffin (Lab)	3,443	60	12,745	45
	B. S. Morgan (C)	2,325	40		

1936	J. Johnstone (Lab)	2,908	52	12,274	45
	B. S. Morgan (C)	2,675	48		
1937	B. S. Morgan (C)	3,518	56	11,591	55
	Mrs A. Mitton (Lab)	2,817	44		
1938	A. Griffin (Lab)	3,230	51	11,129	57
	S. Minion (C)	3,082	49		

[1] Resignation of E. Whitely.
[2] Election of F. T. Richardson as alderman.
[3] Death of D. C. Williams.
[4] Resignation of W. Smith.
[5] Election of C. Wilson as alderman.
[6] Resignation of R. Tissyman.

EVERTON (12)

	Population	Electorate	Acreage	Persons/Acre
1911	35.547	4,484	210	169.3
1921	35,966	11,768		171.3
1931	32,602	13,501		155.3

1931	Av. family size	Rooms per dwelling	Families per dwelling	Persons per room
	3.93	4.74	1.33	1.10

Churches 1929			Sittings
Anglican	4		4,870
Catholic	2		2,533
Nonconformist	7	(Welsh) (2)	3,926 (1,750)

School rolls 1923
Anglican	1,704
Catholic	3,101
Board	2,737
Wesleyan	574

Trades Council delegates 1905		WMCA branch
Brassfounders	Masons	
Brushmakers	Postmen	1920 ✓
Carpenters	Printers/cutters	1931
Coachmakers	Typo. printers	1939
Mill sawyers	(total 9)	

Summary of municipal election results

Years	Lab. wins	Tory wins	Av. Lab. vote (%)	Av. Tory vote (%)	Av. turnout	NC	Nats. (wins)	Prots. (wins)
1905–9	0	3	—	56	52	3	0	0
1910–13	1	3	46	67	41	2	0	0
1905–13	1	6	46	62	47	5	0	0
1919–23	2	2	48	50	51	0	1 (0)	0
1924–28	5	0	62	38	54	0	0	0
1929–33	4	1	58	36	43	0	0	1 (0)
1934–38	5	0	69	31	44	1	0	0
1919–38	16	3	59	39	48	1	1 (0)	1 (0)

Full list of municipal election results

Year	Candidates	Votes	%	Voters	Turnout (%)
1905	Capt. Denton (L)	1,319	53	4,631	54
	O. H. Williams (C)	1,163	47		
1906	E. L. Lloyd (C)	NC	—	4,501	—
1907	G. Kyffin-Taylor (C)	1,392	64	4,375	49
	C. Philips (L)	768	36		
1907[1] (Dec)	R. Rutherford (C)	NC	—	4,375	—
1908	W. Denton (L)	NC	—	4,252	—
1909	R. Rutherford (C)	NC	—	4,188	—
1910	G. Kyffin-Taylor(C)	NC	—	4,088	—
1911	J. H. Naylor (Lab)	983	58	4,484	38
	W. Denton (L)	718	42		
1912	R. Rutherford (C)	1,230	67	4,197	44
	R. Dixon (Lab)	616	33		
1913	G. Kyffin-Taylor (C)	NC	—	4,237	—
1914	J. H. Naylor (Lab)	NC	—	4,407	—
1919[2] (May)	Mrs M Bamber (Lab)	1,427	50	10,678	27
	Dr J. A. Manson (C)	1,407	50		
1919	H. Walker (Lab)	2,974	63	11,010	43
	C. E. Pugh (C)	1,784	37		
1920	J. Ellis (C)	3,736	56	11,672	57
	J. Whittaker (Lab)	2,931	44		
1921	T. Dugdale Stubbs (Co. L)	2,947	54	11,768	47
	J. H. Naylor (Lab)	2,535	46		
1922	H. Walker (Lab)	4,633	56	12,025	68
	A. M. Urding (C)	3,542	43		
	M. Grogan (N)	26	—		

	J. Linge (Ind)	11	—		
1923	J. Ellis (C)	3,177	65	12,350	40
	J. H. Naylor (Lab)	1,590	33		
	J. Young (Unemp)	115	2		
1924	B. V. Kirby (Lab)	3,790	54	12,526	57
	H. A. Proctor (C)	3,243	46		
	D. Dolovitz (Ind)	51	—		
1925	H. Walker (Lab)	4,732	59	12,768	63
	A. Hemmons (C)	3,329	41		
1926	F. T. Richardson (Lab)	4,028	63	12,782	50
	J. Ellis (C)	2,380	37		
1927	B. V. Kirkby (Lab)	3,809	68	12,647	45
	J. Gardner (C)	1,826	32		
1928	H. Walker (Lab)	4,278	67	12,194	53
	W. J. L. Croft (C)	2,153	33		
1929	F. T. Richardson (Lab)	3,787	67	13,731	41
	H. E. Davies (C)	1,824	33		
1929[3]	J. Braddock (Lab) (2 seats)	NC	—	13,731	—
(Dec)	A. Smitton (Lab)	NC	—	13,731	—
1930	B. V. Kirby (Lab)	2,680	47	13,549	42
	T. H. Nabb (C)	1,411	25		
	T. Conifer (Ind. Lab)	1,008	18		
	T. Dunne (P)	645	10		
1931	J. McKay (C)	3,128	53	13,501	43
	A. Smitton (Lab)	2,735	47		
1932	J. Braddock (Lab)	4,408	65	13,436	51
	J. H. Irwin (C)	2,383	35		
1933	B. V. Kirby (Lab)	3,547	65	13,243	40
	D. Rowan (C)	1,744	35		
1934	D. Nickson (Lab)	3,296	75	12,985	34
	M. R. F. Rogers (C)	1,372	25		
1935	J. Braddock (Lab)	3,936	74	12,831	41
	M. R. F. Rogers (C)	1,372	26		
1936	B. V. Kirby (Lab)	3,530	64	12,570	44
	G.G. Mulligan (C)	1,970	36		
1937	D. Nickson (Lab)	4,258	64	12,052	55
	J. Moore (C)	2,418	36		
1938	J. Braddock (Lab)	NC	—	11,583	—

[1] Election of E. L. Lloyd as alderman.
[2] Resignation of G. Kyffin-Taylor.
[3] Election of F. T. Richardson and H. Walker as aldermen.

EXCHANGE (13)

	Population	Electorate	Acreage	Persons/Acre
1911	3,928	1,792	82	47.9
1921	3,482	2,664		42.5
1931	3,091	2,492		37.7

1931	Av. family size	Rooms per dwelling	Families per dwelling	Persons per room
	4.04	3.82	1.19	1.26

Churches 1929		Sittings
Anglican	1	1,332
Catholic	1	900
Nonconformist	0	0

School rolls 1923

Anglican	487
Catholic	839
Board	0

Trades Council delegates 1905	WMCA branch
Nil	None

Summary of municipal election results

Years	Lab. wins	Tory wins	Av. Lab. vote (%)	Av. Tory vote (%)	Av. turnout	NC	Nats. (wins)	Prots. (wins)
1905–9	0	2	—	55	72	4	0	0
1910–13	0	1	—	—	—	4	0	0
1905–13	0	3	—	55	72	8	0	0
1919–23	0	0	—	34	61	1	5 (5)	0
1924–28	0	0	18	—	36	3	5 (5)	0
1929–33	0	0	21	—	45	1	3 (3)	0
1934–38	0	0	31	—	48	2	0	0
1919–38	0	0	24	34	49	7	13 (13)	0

Full list of municipal election results

Year	Candidates	Votes	%	Voters	Turnout (%)
1905	J. Bibby (L)	NC	—	1,735	—
1906	J. S. Harmood Banner (C)	NC	—	1,756	—

Year	Candidate	Votes	%		%
1907	R. D. Holt (L)	NC	—	1,643	—
1908	J. Bibby (L)	NC	—	1,625	—
1909[1] (Jan)	F. C. Bowring (L)	NC	—	1,625	—
1909	J. S. Harmood Banner (C)	683	55	1,705	72
	A. Gates (L)	549	45		
1910	F. C. Bowring (L)	NC	—	1,726	—
1911	J. Bibby (L)	NC	—	1,792	—
1912	J. S. Harmood Banner(C)	NC	—	1,625	—
1913	F. C. Bowring (L)	NC	—	1,634	—
1914	C. S. Jones (L)	NC	—	1,603	—
1919	P. Kavanagh (N)	935	66	2,549	56
	P. T. Stolterfoht (C)	486	34		
1920	H. Granby (N)	907	52	2,672	65
	F. C. Bowring (L)	829	48		
1921	J. Quinn (N)	948	53	2,664	67
	C. S. Jones (L)	840	47		
1922	P. Kavanagh (N)	NC	—	2,692	—
1923	Miss A. McCormick (IP)	904	59	2,747	56
	M. P. Rathbone (L)	575	37		
	J. Masterman (Ind)	50	3		
	J. Bingham (Unemp)	7	—		
1924	J. Quinn (N)	NC	—	2,768	—
1925	P. Kavanagh (Cath)	NC	—	2,805	—
1926	Miss A. M. McCormick (Centre)	709	77	2,758	33
	A. E. Price (Lab)	214	23		
1927	J. Quinn (Centre)	910	88	2,710	38
	J. Nugent (Lab)	123	12		
1928	P. Kavanagh (Centre)	NC	—	2,582	—
1929	Miss A. McCormick (Centre)	760	66	2,697	42
	Mrs M. McFarlane (Lab)	384	34		
1930	J. Farrell jun. (Centre)	NC	—	2,553	—
1931	P. Kavanagh (Ind)	1,228	91	2,492	54
	S. S. Silverman (Lab)	116	9		
1932	Miss A. McCormick (Centre)	717	68	2,465	43
	A. Smitton (Lab)	258	25		
	A. J. G. Smyth (Youth)	69	6		
	M. E. Boggin (ILP)	7	1		
1933	J. Farrell (Ind)	837	83	2,407	42
	A. Smitton (Lab)	166	17		
1934	P. Kavanagh (Ind)	NC	—	2,383	—
1935[2] (Feb)	T. P. Staunton (Ind)	640	61	2,383	44
	J. Gorman (Lab)	417	39		
1935	T. P. Staunton (Lab)	757	63	2,351	51
	A. Donohue (Lab)	438	37		
1936	J. Farrell (Ind)	731	71	2,332	44

	H. Carr (Lab)	304	29	
1937	P. Kavanagh (Ind)	NC	—	2,168	—
1938	H. Granby (Ind)	765	72	2,122	50
	J. G. Morgan (Lab)	300	28	

[1] Death of R. D. Holt.
[2] Death of Miss A. M. McCormick.

FAIRFIELD (14)

	Population	Electorate	Acreage	Persons/Acre
1911	22,740	3,991	506	44.9
1921	25,544	9,140		50.4
1931	22,630	10,220		44.7

1931	Av. family size	Rooms per dwelling	Families per dwelling	Persons per room
	3.83	6.03	1.16	0.74

Churches 1929			Sittings
Anglican	4		2,650
Catholic	1		200
Nonconformist	5	(Welsh) 2	3,303 (1,100)

School rolls 1923	
Anglican	0
Catholic	424
Board	3,896

Trades Council delegates 1905		WMCA branch
Painters (2)		None
Tailors	(total 3)	

Summary of municipal election results

Years	Lab. wins	Tory wins	Av. Lab. vote (%)	Av. Tory vote (%)	Av. turnout	NC	Nats. (wins)	Prots. (wins)
1905–9	0	2	—	63	50	2	1 (0)	0
1910–13	0	1	—	56	49	1	0	0
1905–13	0	3	—	60	50	3	1 (0)	0
1919–23	0	1	—	55	49	1	0	0
1924–28	0	3	34	52	47	1	0	0

Years	Lab. wins	Tory wins	Av. Lab. vote (%)	Av. Tory vote (%)	Av. turnout	NC	Nats. (wins)	Prots. (wins)
1929–33	0	3	32	67	40	1	0	0
1934–38	0	4	37	63	37	0	0	0
1919–38	0	11	34	60	43	3	0	0

Full list of municipal election results

Year	Candidates	Votes	%	Voters	Turnout (%)
1905	F. J. Leslie (C)	650	84	3,694	21
	J. McCormick (IP)	126	16		
1906[1]	A. Gates (L)	1,000	53	3,694	51
(Apr)	T. Dowd (C)	894	47		
1906	F. L. Joseph (L)	NC	—	3,855	—
1907	J. Hughes jun. (L)	1,141	50	3,845	59
	H. S. Badger (C)	1,124	50		
1908	T. Dowd (C)	1,477	56	3,816	69
	A. Gates (L)	1,156	44		
1909	F. L. Joseph (L)	NC	—	3,870	—
1910	J. Hughes jun. (L)	1,118	53	3,864	55
	Dr Bailey (C)	989	47		
1911	T. Dowd (C)	861	71	3,991	30
	A. E. Kennedy (Ind)	352	29		
1912	F. L. Joseph (L)	NC	—	3,957	—
1913[2]	J. Lucas (L)	956	53	3,957	46
(Oct)	J. Waterworth (C)	861	47		
1913	J. Hughes (L)	1,297	51	4,045	63
	K. Kusel (C)	1,238	49		
1914	T. Dowd (C)	NC	—	4,186	—
1919	J. Lucas (L)	NC	—	8,636	—
1920	J. Hughes (L)	3,455	75	8,949	52
	E. Rose (Co-op)	1,154	25		
1921	T. Dowd (C)	2,566	55	9,140	51
	G. F. Travis (L)	2,127	45		
1922	G. F. Travis (L)	2,809	61	9,061	51
	J. Lucas (Co. L)	1,821	39		
1923[3]	C. S. Jones (L)	NC	—	9,061	—
(Mar)					
1923	J. Hughes (Nat. L)	1,966	51	9,159	42
	W. H. Davies (L)	1,854	49		
1924	C. S. Jones (L)	NC	—	9,143	—
1924[4]	J. Barry (C)	1,842	56	9,143	36
(Dec)	J. R. Hobhouse (L)	1,432	44		
1925	A. J. Chapman-Durant (C)	2,813	57	9,445	53

	V. H. E. Baker (Lab)	1,346	27		
	E. D. Roberts (L)	814	16		
1926	J. Barry (C)	2,261	60	9,457	40
	V. H. E. Baker (Lab)	1,483	40		
1927	C. S. Jones (L)	2,475	64	9,478	41
	V. H. E Baker (Lab)	1,411	36		
1928	C. G. S. Gordon (C)	2,043	40	9,233	55
	V. H. E. Baker (Lab)	1,659	33		
	A. Boyle (L)	1,392	27		
1929	J. Barry (C)	2,653	59	10,252	44
	J. Braddock (Lab)	1,821	41		
1930	C. S. Jones (L)	2,361	72	10,272	32
	W. H. Baxter (Lab)	931	28		
1931	C. G. S. Gordon (C)	3,444	76	10,220	44
	R. J. Hughes (Lab)	1,085	24		
1932	J. Barry (C)	2,557	65	10,309	38
	R. T. Hughes (Lab)	1,350	35		
1933	C. S. Jones (L)	NC	—	10,487	—
1934	C. G. S. Gordon (C)	1,776	58	10,385	30
	R. T. Hughes (Lab)	1,292	42		
1935	J. Barry (C)	2,595	62	10,430	40
	R. T. Hughes (Lab)	1,573	38		
1936	C. M. Dolby (L)	2,239	65	10,470	33
	T. D. Vallance (Lab)	1,231	35		
1937	C. G. S. Gordon (C)	2,983	62	10,410	46
	H. S. Martin (Lab)	1,813	38		
1937[5]	R. Clitherow (C)	2,305	74	10,410	30
(Nov)	H. S. Martin (Lab)	831	26		
1938	R. Clitherow (C)	2,665	70	10,410	36
	Mrs I. Levin (Lab)	1,121	30		

[1] Resignation of F. J. Leslie.
[2] Resignation of F. L. Joseph.
[3] Election of T. Dowd as alderman.
[4] Death of J. Hughes.
[5] Death of J. Barry.

FAZAKERLEY (15)

	Population	Electorate	Acreage	Persons/Acre
1911	5,155	752	1,710	3.0
1921	6,054	2,411		3.5
1931	25,940	10,866		15.2

1931	Av. family size	Rooms per dwelling	Families per dwelling	Persons per room
	4.52	4.68	1.02	0.98

Churches 1929   *Sittings*

Anglican	2		1,200
Catholic	0		0
Nonconformist	1	(Welsh) 0	300

School rolls 1923

Anglican	120
Catholic	0
Board	346

Trades Council delegates 1905   *WMCA branch*
Nil

1920
1931
1939 ✓

Summary of municipal election results

Years	Lab. wins	Tory wins	Av. Lab. vote (%)	Av. Tory vote (%)	Av. turnout	NC	Nats. (wins)	Prots. (wins)
1905–9	0	2	—	65	79	1	0	0
1910–13	0	1	—	67	50	0	0	0
1905–13	0	3	—	66	65	1	0	0
1919–23	0	5	37	63	53	2	0	0
1924–28	1	4	36	62	48	0	0	1 (0)
1929–33	1	4	42	54	41	0	0	0
1934–38	1	4	42	57	44	0	0	1 (0)
1919–38	3	17	40	58	46	2	0	2 (0)

Full list of municipal election results

Year	Candidates	Votes	%	Voters	Turnout (%)
1905	H. S. Higginbottom (C)	290	65	560	79
	T. Hesketh (N)	154	35		
1908	H. S. Higginbottom (C)	NC	—	684	—
1911	Dr H. H. Clarke (C)	252	67	752	50
	G. Lovely (Ind)	123	33		
1914	G. B. S. Broderick (C)	NC	—	823	—
1919	F. Quayle (C)	701	58	2,421	50
	A. N. Denaro (Lab)	506	42		
1920	M. Leitch sen. (C)	870	66	2,577	51
	J. Williams (Lab)	452	34		
1921	G. H. Charters (C)	901	64	2,411	58

	R. Watson (Lab)	498	36		
1922	F. Quayle (C)	NC	—	2,630	—
1923	A. H. Letheren (C)	NC	—	2,707	—
1924	G. H. Charters (C)	1,055	66	2,775	57
	A. N. Denaro (Lab)	539	34		
1925	F. S. H. Ashcroft (C)	944	56	2,886	59
	A. F. Johnson (Lab)	410	24		
	Revd H. D. Longbottom (P)	341	20		
1926	A. H. Letheren (C)	868	67	3,070	42
	R. A. Rockcliff (Lab)	418	33		
1927	G. H. Charters (C)	1,053	70	4,366	35
	Mrs Davison (Co-op)	459	30		
1928	F. B. Fitzpatrick (Lab)	1,699	51	7,324	46
	F. Ashcroft (C)	1,659	49		
1929	R. Edwards (Lab)	2,287	58	9,145	43
	C. S. McNair (C)	1,686	42		
1930[1]	W. G. Gregson (C)	1,798	59	9,145	33
(Jun)	B. L. Myer (Lab)	1,245	41		
1930	W. G. Gregson (C)	2,347	58	10,374	39
	B. L. Myer (Lab)	1,727	42		
1931	E. Tyson (C)	3,125	66	10,866	43
	F. B. Fitzpatrick (Lab)	1,593	34		
1932	R. Disley (C)	2,413	52	11,026	42
	F. Lavery (Lab)	1,261	27		
	R. Edwards (ILP)	943	21		
1933	W. G. Gregson (C)	2,262	51	10,943	40
	F. Lavery (Lab)	2,161	49		
1934	F. Lavery (Lab)	2,203	50	11,422	38
	W. E. Backhouse (C)	1,898	43		
	R. F. Henderson (P)	271	7		
1935	F. Baxter (C)	2,505	52	11,367	42
	Mrs S. A. Demain (Lab)	2,286	48		
1936	W. G. Gregson (C)	3,077	62	11,992	42
	L Cunningham (Lab)	1,919	38		
1937	A. G. Meredith (C)	4,168	65	11,985	54
	F. Lavery (Lab)	2,278	35		
1938	K. P. Thompson (C)	3,477	62	13,039	43
	Mrs S. A. McArd (Lab)	2,100	38		

[1] Resignation of G. H. Charters.

GARSTON (16)

	Population	Electorate	Acreage	Persons/Acre
1911	14,359	2,258	573	25.1
1921	17,399	5,318		30.4
1931	17,262	7,131		30.1

1931	Av. family size	Rooms per dwelling	Families per dwelling	Persons per room
	4.51	4.89	1.12	1.03

Churches 1929			Sittings
Anglican	2		1,650
Catholic	1		320
Nonconformist	8	(Welsh) 3	2,297 (590)

School rolls 1923	
Anglican	1,391
Catholic	521
Board	1,544

Trades Council delegates 1905		WMCA branch
Painters		1920 ✓
Railway servants		1931 ✓
NAUL	(total 3)	1939 ✓

Summary of municipal election results

Years	Lab. wins	Tory wins	Av. Lab. vote (%)	Av. Tory vote (%)	Av. turnout	NC	Nats. (wins)	Prots. (wins)
1905–9	0	3	36	55	76	3	0	0
1910–13	1	3	46	54	80	1	0	0
1905–13	1	6	44	54	78	4	0	0
1919–23	1	4	42	55	64	0	0	0
1924–28	1	4	44	52	62	0	0	0
1929–33	3	2	53	47	58	0	0	0
1934–38	3	2	53	44	58	0	0	1 (0)
1919–38	8	12	48	49	61	0	0	1 (0)

Full list of municipal election results

Year	Candidates	Votes	%	Voters	Turnout (%)
1905	J. Pickthall (L)	832	54	2,016	76
	G. W. Hughes (C)	706	46		
1906	J. Burrow (C)	1,035	64	2,139	75
	W. G. Gerrard (Lab)	575	36		
1907	F. J. Rawlinson (C)	NC	—	2,185	—
1908	J. Pickthall (L)	NC	—	2,229	—
1909	J. Burrow (C)	NC	—	2,192	—
1910	F. J. Rawlinson (C)	NC	—	2,145	—
1911	W. A. Robinson (Lab)	1,035	62	2,258	73
	J. Pickthall (L)	624	38		
1912	J. Burrow (C)	1,127	60	2,270	83
	J. Cleary (Lab)	757	40		
1913	F. J. Rawlinson (C)	1,234	63	2,353	83
	G. Porter (Lab)	713	37		
1914	W. A. Robinson (Lab)	NC	—	2,489	—
1919	J. H. Dutton (Lab)	1,458	51	5,114	56
	T. Tushingham (C)	1,419	49		
1919[1]	A. E. Beavan (Lab)	1,977	51	5,114	75
(Nov)	T. Tushingham (C)	1,879	49		
1920	J. Burrow (C)	2,267	61	5,187	72
	W. H. Paulson (Lab)	1,468	39		
1921	G. Atkin (C)	2,082	58	5,318	68
	W. H. Paulson (Lab)	1,525	42		
1922	E. R. Thompson (C)	1,988	57	5,802	60
	J. H. Dutton (Lab)	1,496	43		
1923	J. Case (C)	1,841	49	5,897	64
	H. O. Pugh (Lab)	1,375	37		
	J. Scott (L)	530	14		
1924	G. Atkin (C)	2,137	52	6,040	68
	R. P. Edwards (Lab)	1,506	36		
	W. J. Ireland (L)	490	12		
1925	E. R. Thompson (C)	2,010	57	6,175	57
	J. Lawrenson (Lab)	1,521	43		
1926	J. Case (C)	1,776	52	6,287	54
	J. Lawrenson (Lab)	1,616	48		
1927[2]	J. Williams (C)	1,731	51	6,287	54
(May)	J. J. Cleary (Lab)	1,684	49		
1927[3]	E. W. Turner (C)	1,841	46	6,287	64
(Jun)	J. J. Cleary (Lab)	1,827	46		
	N. McKinnon (L)	335	8		
1927	J. J. Cleary (Lab)	2,011	50	6,400	63
	E. W. Turner (C)	1,993	50		
1928	J. Williams (C)	2,208	49	6,421	70
	W. S. Dytor (Lab)	2,038	45		
	J. Fry (L)	259	6		

1929	J. Case (C)	2,359	55	7,124	60
	W. S. Dytor (Lab)	1,937	45		
1930	J. J. Cleary (Lab)	2,218	53	7,042	59
	R. Abel (C)	1,953	47		
1931	J. Williams (C)	2,189	55	7,131	56
	W. S. Dytor (Lab)	1,813	45		
1932	W. S. Dytor (Lab)	2,658	60	7,695	58
	J. Case (C)	1,808	40		
1933	J. J. Cleary (Lab)	2,844	64	7,741	58
	J. Moore (C)	1,611	36		
1934	J. H. Webster (Lab)	2,436	57	7,395	58
	J. Williams (C)	1,302	31		
	J. Moore (P)	524	12		
1935	W. S. Dytor (Lab)	2,766	59	7,920	59
	A. M. Profitt (C)	1,939	41		
1936	J. J. Cleary (Lab)	2,963	60	7,960	62
	J. Williams (C)	1,973	40		
1937	A. M. Profitt (C)	2,857	56	8,205	62
	J. H. Webster (Lab)	2,201	44		
1938	J. Williams (C)	2,299	53	8,467	51
	W. S. Dytor (Lab)	2,044	47		

[1] Election of W. A. Robinson as alderman.
[2] Death of E. R. Thompson.
[3] Death of G. Atkin.

GRANBY (17)

	Population	Electorate	Acreage	Persons/Acre
1911	22,547	3,754	185	121.9
1921	20,791	8,890		112.4
1931	23,419	9,918		126.6

1931	Av. family size	Rooms per dwelling	Families per dwelling	Persons per room
	3.86	5.36	1.23	0.88

Churches 1929		Sittings
Anglican	3	2,050
Catholic	1	350
Nonconformist	3 (Welsh) 1	2,010 (800)

School rolls 1923	
Anglican	1,692
Catholic	487
Board	2,514

Trades Council delegates 1905	WMCA branch
Engineers	1929 ✓
Machine-workers (total 3)	1931 ✓
NAUL	1939 ✓

Summary of municipal election results

Years	Lab. wins	Tory wins	Av. Lab. vote (%)	Av. Tory vote (%)	Av. turnout	NC	Nats. (wins)	Prots. (wins)
1905–9	0	2	27	40	52	3	0	0
1910–13	0	1	—	39	56	3	0	0
1905–13	0	3	27	40	53	6	0	0
1919–23	0	1	—	—	40	3	0	0
1924–28	1	1	42	38	47	0	0	0
1929–33	0	2	39	54	36	2	0	0
1934–38	2	3	50	53	43	0	0	0
1919–38	3	7	45	48	43	5	0	0

Full list of municipal election results

Year	Candidates	Votes	%	Voters	Turnout (%)
1905	J. Lea (C)	NC	—	3,849	—
1906	J. H. Jones (L)	NC	—	3,797	—
1907	R. H. Bullen (L)	941	40	3,683	63
	H. J. Davis (C)	928	40		
	F. J. Welland (Soc)	463	20		
1908	J. Lea (C)	NC	—	3,659	—
1909	J. H. Jones (L)	962	66	3,600	41
	F. J. Welland (Soc)	497	34		
1910	Miss E. Rathbone (Ind)	1,211	61	3,556	56
	R. Richards (C)	769	39		
1911	J. Lea (C)	NC	—	3,754	—
1912	J. H. Jones (L)	NC	—	3,631	—
1913	Miss E Rathbone (Ind)	NC	—	3,645	—
1914	J. Waterworth (C)	NC	—	3,819	—
1919	J. H. Jones (L)	1,922	59	8,293	39
	F. J. Norris (Co-op)	1,353	41		
1920[1]	F. C. Wilson (L)	NC	—	8,293	—
1920	Miss E. Rathbone (Ind)	NC	—	8,623	—
1921	J. Waterworth (C)	NC	—	8,890	—
1922	F. C. Bowring (L)	2,283	65	8,847	40
	R. Tissyman (Ind)	1,225	35		

1923	Miss E. Rathbone (Ind)	NC	—	9,075	—
1924	Mrs R. Hoch (C)	2,096	45	9,425	47
	C. Burden (Lab)	1,937	43		
	S. Skelton (L)	490	12		
1925	F. C. Bowring (L)	2,851	62	9,450	49
	W. H. Barton (Lab)	1,734	38		
1926	Miss E. Rathbone (Ind)	2,581	62	9,360	45
	K. T. Graham (C)	1,587	38		
1927	J. Johnstone (Lab)	1,873	44	9,322	45
	Mrs R. Hoch (C)	1,361	32		
	A. D. Dennis (L)	986	24		
1928	F. C. Bowring (L)	2,743	59	9,132	51
	G. H. Boothman (Lab)	1,886	41		
1929	Miss E. Rathbone (Ind)	NC	—	9,932	—
1930	W. A. Edwards (C)	1,983	58	9,408	36
	J. Johnstone (Lab)	1,414	42		
1931	F. C. Bowring (L)	2,974	75	9,918	40
	J. Johnstone (Lab)	1,015	25		
1932	Miss E. Rathbone (Ind)	NC	—	9,858	—
1933	W. A. Edwards (C)	1,618	50	9,966	32
	D. Nickson (Lab)	1,617	50		
1934	Miss M. A. Cumella (Lab)	1,922	57	9,914	34
	H. H. Jones (L)	1,424	43		
1935	C. E. Burke (Lab)	2,191	53	9,760	42
	H. H. Jones (L)	1,949	47		
1936	W. A. Edwards (C)	2,201	53	9,774	43
	G. E. Humphrey (Lab)	1,953	47		
1937[2]	W. Clark (C)	1,630	52	9,774	32
(Jun)	J. Bagot (Lab)	1,479	48		
1937	E. Tyrer (C)	2,781	52	9,699	55
	Mrs M. Cumella (Lab)	2,554	48		
1938	J. E. Thompson (C)	2,203	54	9,422	43
	C. E. Burke (Lab)	1,888	46		

[1] Election of J. H. Jones as alderman.
[2] Death of W. A. Edwards.

GREAT GEORGE (18)

	Population	Electorate	Acreage	Persons/Acre
1911	14,307	1,662	236	60.6
1921	14,241	4,006		60.3
1931	12,995	5,043		55.1

	Av. family size	*Rooms per dwelling*	*Families per dwelling*	*Persons per room*
1931	3.92	5.49	1.57	1.12

Churches 1929   *Sittings*

Anglican	2		1,950
Catholic	3		2,740
Nonconformist	2	(Welsh) 0	1,850

School rolls 1923

Anglican	360
Catholic	2,333
Board	1,597

Trades Council delegates 1905   *WMCA branch*
Life assurance agents (total 1)   None

Summary of municipal election results

Years	Lab. wins	Tory wins	Av. Lab. vote (%)	Av. Tory vote (%)	Av. turnout	NC	Nats. (wins)	Prots. (wins)
1905–9	0	3	—	59	73	3	0	0
1910–13	0	1	—	52	73	2	1 (1)	0
1905–13	0	4	—	56	73	5	1 (1)	0
1919–23	0	0	17	—	57	2	5 (5)	0
1924–28	2	0	44	—	41	2	4 (3)	0
1929–33	3	0	44	—	33	0	5 (2)	0
1934–38	5	0	61	40	43	0	2 (0)	0
1919–38	10	0	51	40	42	4	16 (10)	0

Full list of municipal election results

Year	Candidates	Votes	%	Voters	Turnout (%)
1905	J. L. Eills (L)	NC	—	1,734	—
1906	W. Muirhead (C)	836	65	1,755	74
	H. Muspratt (L)	454	35		
1907	Dr A. E. Davies (C)	641	52	1,761	71
	B. W. Eills (L)	601	48		
1908	J. L. Eills (L)	NC	—	1,729	—
1909	W. Muirhead (C)	NC	—	1,663	—
1910	S. Skelton (C)	575	51	1,608	71
	A. E. Davies (C)	559	49		
1911	J. L Eills (L)	NC	—	1,662	—
1912	W. Muirhead (C)	656	55	1,607	74
	Dr W. H. Broad (L)	529	45		
1913	S. Skelton (L)	NC	—	1,608	—
1913[1]	T. P. .Maguire (N)	478	47	1,608	63

(Nov)	J. C. Walker (C)	468	46		
	J. Cleary (Lab)	72	7		
1914	J. L. Eills (L)	NC	—	1,571	—
1919	T. O. Ruddin (N)	NC	—	3,853	—
1920	W. Grogan (N)	1,766	65	3,875	70
	S. Skelton (L)	955	35		
1921	T. J. Marner (N)	1,299	57	4,006	57
	W. H. Broad (L)	703	31		
	J. Bennett (Ind)	283	12		
1922	T. O. Ruddin (N)	NC	—	4,267	—
1923	W. Grogan (IP)	1,587	83	4,461	43
	G. H. Bennett (Lab)	322	17		
1924	T. J. Marner (Ind)	NC	—	4,596	—
1925	T. O. Ruddin (Cath)	1,199	68	4,665	38
	A. J. Ward (Lab)	561	32		
1926	W. Grogan (Centre)	1,016	55	4,694	39
	J. Loughlin (Lab)	816	45		
1927	J. Loughlin (Lab)	1,265	56	4,840	47
	Dr Bligh (Centre)	810	36		
	T. J. Marner (Ind)	125	6		
	W. J. Doyle (People's)	67	3		
1928	H.L Gaffeney (Lab)	NC	—	4,820	—
1928[2]	M. Grogan (Ind)	945	56	4,820	35
(Dec)	J. Coburne (Lab)	756	44		
1929	M. Grogan (Lab)	1,546	76	5,299	39
	Miss L. M. Murray (Centre)	496	24		
1930	J. Loughlin (Ind. Lab)	814	68	5,042	24
	R. T. Hughes (Lab)	389	32		
1931	H. L. Gaffeney (Dem. Lab)	858	59	5,043	29
	P. Campbell (Lab)	594	41		
1932[3]	J. Hamilton (Lab)	NC	—	5,043	—
(Aug)					
1932	P. E. Sherwin (Lab)	951	49	5,048	39
	M. Grogan (Dem. Lab)	933	48		
	L. P. Taylor (Youth)	64	3		
1933	J. Campbell (Lab)	1,047	66	4,912	32
	J. Loughlin (Ind. N)	538	34		
1934	J. Hamilton (Lab)	1,121	66	4,916	34
	W. O Stein (C)	569	34		
1935	P. E. Sherwin (Lab)	1,403	59	4,771	50
	D. R. Jones (C)	964	41		
1936	J. Campbell (Lab)	1,220	56	4,563	48
	Dr W. H. Broad (C)	965	44		
1937	J. Hamilton (Lab)	1,310	67	4,346	45
	S. Botley (Ind. N)	631	33		
1938	P. E. Sherwin (Lab)	886	56	4,144	38
	M. J. Fanning (Ind. N)	690	44		

[1] Election of W. Muirhead as alderman.
[2] Death of W. Grogan.
[3] Resignation of H. L. Gaffeney.

KENSINGTON (19)

	Population	Electorate	Acreage	Persons/Acre
1911	26,823	4,718	252	106.4
1921	27,841	10,492		110.5
1931	25,588	11,351		97.6

1931	Av. family size	Rooms per dwelling	Families per dwelling	Persons per room
	3.86	5.09	1.09	0.82

Churches 1929			Sittings
Anglican	2		1,645
Catholic	0		0
Nonconformist	9	(Welsh) 4	4,166 (1,370)

School rolls 1923	
Anglican	483
Catholic	0
Board	2,840

Trades Council delegates 1905		WMCA branch
Carpenters (5)	Masons	1920 ✓
Farriers	Organ builders	1931 ✓
NAFTA	Painters	1939 ✓
Musicians	Litho printers	
Postmen	(total 13)	

Summary of municipal election results

Years	Lab. wins	Tory wins	Av. Lab. vote (%)	Av. Tory vote (%)	Av. turnout	NC	Nats. (wins)	Prots. (wins)
1905–9	1	4	38	59	56	0	0	0
1910–13	0	4	36	64	52	0	0	0
1905–13	1	8	37	61	54	0	0	0
1919–23	1	4	40	60	54	0	1 (0)	0
1924–28	0	5	45	55	52	0	0	0
1929–33	1	4	40	57	44	0	0	1 (0)
1934–38	0	5	36	64	43	0	0	0
1919–38	2	18	40	59	48	0	1 (0)	1 (0)

Full list of municipal election results

Year	Candidates	Votes	%	Voters	Turnout (%)
1905	J. W. T. Morrisey (Soc)	1,137	40	4,632	62
	C. A. Hill (C)	1,076	37		
	B. L. Wilson(L)	659	23		
1906	R. L. Burns (C)	1,784	69	4,725	54
	A. K. Bulley (Soc)	787	31		
1907	S. M. Hutchinson (C)	1,677	69	4,754	51
	N. Taylor (ILP)	767	31		
1908	J. Gordon (C)	1,641	58	4,639	61
	J. W. T. Morrisey (Soc)	1,203	42		
1909	R. L. Burns (C)	1,434	62	4,606	50
	J. W. T. Morrisey (Soc)	865	38		
1910	S. M. Hutchinson (C)	1,404	80	4,537	41
	A. K. Bulley (Soc)	470	20		
1911	J. Gordon (C)	1,260	51	4,718	53
	A. K. Bulley (Lab)	1,234	49		
1912	R. L. Burns (C)	1,718	61	4,712	60
	A. K. Bulley (Lab)	1,117	39		
1913	S. M. Hutchinson (C)	1,617	63	4,753	54
	P. M'Conville (Lab)	946	37		
1914	J. Gordon (C)	NC	—	4,876	—
1919	J. Badlay (Lab)	2,889	55	9,935	53
	R. L. Burns (C)	2,366	45		
1920	J. Ashworth (C)	4,174	65	10,212	63
	W. H. Smithwick (Lab)	2,286	35		
1921	J. Gordon (C)	3,512	64	10,492	52
	J. Mooney (Lab)	1,955	36		
1922[1] (May)	W. B. Lewis (C)	NC	—	10,492	—
1922	J. H. Rutherford (C)	3,755	67	10,548	53
	C. Wilson (Lab)	1,703	31		
	E. J. Delaney (N)	121	2		
1923	J. Ashworth (C)	2,970	59	10,677	47
	F. Jones (Lab)	2,098	41		
1924	H. Baxter (C)	3,204	55	10,724	54
	F. T. Richardson (Lab)	2,623	45		
1925	J. H. Rutherford (C)	3,403	60	10,874	53
	R. A. Rockcliff (Lab)	2,310	40		
1926	J. Ashworth (C)	2,308	50	10,874	42
	J. Kay (Lab)	2,268	50		
1926[2] (Dec)	A. Fry (C)	2,688	51	10,874	49
	J. Kay (Lab)	2,618	49		
1927	A. Fry (C)	3,202	55	10,846	54
	W. R. Blair (Lab)	2,634	45		
1928	Sir H. Rutherford (C)	3,347	55	10,641	57
	G. E. Swift (Lab)	2,697	45		

1929[3]	T. N. Jones (C)	2,259	53	10,641	40
(Apr)	G. E. Swift (Lab)	2,041	47		
1929	G. E. Swift (Lab)	2,575	49	11,485	46
	T. N. Jones (C)	2,313	44		
	A. D. Dennis (L)	347	7		
1930	T. N. Jones (C)	2,935	64	11,398	40
	G. Porter (Lab)	1,626	36		
1931	J. Gardner (C)	3,877	69	11,351	49
	J. Whitehead (Lab)	1,708	31		
1932	E. C. R. Littler-Jones (C)	2,479	52	11,270	42
	B. L. Myer (Lab)	1,944	41		
	W. H. Ledson (L)	323	7		
1933[4]	J. Case (C)	1,850	51	11,270	32
	G. Porter (Lab)	1,324	36		
	A. D. Adams (P)	299	8		
	W. H. Ledson (L)	183	5		
1933	J. Moores (C)	2,694	58	11,169	42
	A. Donohue (Lab)	1,990	42		
1934	J. Case (C)	2,233	58	11,041	35
	Mrs S. A. Demain (Lab)	1,587	42		
1935[5]	J. Cresswell (C)	2,018	57	11,041	32
(Feb)	Mrs S. A. Demain (Lab)	1,500	43		
1935	E. C. R. Littler-Jones (C)	2,753	60	11,030	42
	T. E. Martin (Lab)	1,844	40		
1936	J. Cresswell (C)	3,152	66	10,954	44
	C. G. Prest (Lab)	1,660	34		
1937[6]	F. H. Bailey (C)	2,093	67	10,954	28
(Jul)	G. Williams (Lab)	1,018	33		
1937	J. Case (C)	3,808	68	10,871	51
	L. P. Taylor (Lab)	1,780	32		
1938	F. H. Bailey (C)	2,961	67	10,824	41
	J. M. Campbell (Lab)	1,443	33		

[1] Election of J. Gordon as alderman.
[2] Death of H. Baxter.
[3] Election of J. Ashworth as alderman.
[4] Death of J. Gardner.
[5] Resignation of J. Moores.
[6] Death of E. C. R. Littler-Jones.

KIRKDALE (20)

	Population	Electorate	Acreage	Persons/Acre
1911	42,778	6,476	317	134.9
1921	43,210	14,363		136.3
1931	40,389	17,017		127.4

1931	Av. family size	Rooms per dwelling	Families per dwelling	Persons per room
	4.18	4.97	1.18	0.99

Churches 1929   *Sittings*
Anglican   6   4,695
Catholic   1   900
Nonconformist   10   (Welsh) 2   5,350 (1,120)

School rolls 1923
Anglican   2,592
Catholic   2,580
Board   5,884

Trades Council delegates 1905   *WMCA branch*
Coppersmiths   NAUL   1920 ✓
Engine and cranemen   Shipwrights   1931 ✓
Loco engineers and firemen   1939 ✓
Railway servants   (total 6)

Summary of municipal election results

Years	Lab. wins	Tory wins	Av. Lab. vote (%)	Av. Tory vote (%)	Av. turnout	NC	Nats. (wins)	Prots. (wins)
1905–9	0	4	31	58	45	1	0	2 (1)
1910–13	0	4	40	60	46	0	0	0
1905–13	0	8	36	59	45	1	0	2 (1)
1919–23	0	5	34	65	47	1	0	0
1924–28	2	3	45	59	41	0	0	0
1929–33	3	2	39	40	47	0	0	4 (0)
1934–38	2	3	47	50	49	0	0	1 (0)
1919–38	7	13	41	53	46	1	0	5 (0)

Full list of municipal election results

Year	Candidates	Votes	%	Voters	Turnout (%)
1905	J. Utting (C)	1,609	62	6,338	41
	J. S. Ratcliffe (Lab)	986	38		
1906	T. Lowey (C)	1,570	46	6,367	53
	W. Singleton (P)	1,200	35		
	F. Norris (Lab)	612	19		
1907	J. G. Paris (P)	1,584	65	6,396	38
	W. Brooks (Lab)	847	35		

Year	Candidate	Votes	%	Electorate	Turnout %
1908	J. Utting (C)	NC	—	6,342	—
1909	T. Lowey (C)	1,937	67	6,236	47
	W. White (Lab)	967	33		
1910	J. G. Paris (C)	1,620	63	6,314	41
	J. W. T. Morrisey (Lab)	948	37		
1911	J. Utting (C)	1,625	53	6,476	48
	W. McLean (Lab)	1,456	47		
1912	A. Buckley (C)	1,832	61	6,401	47
	J. Clayton (Lab)	1,151	39		
1913	J. G. Paris (C)	1,900	63	6,542	46
	J. Clayton (Lab)	1,120	37		
1914	J. L. Rankin (C)	NC	—	6,584	—
1919	R. G. Sheldon (C)	2,971	49	14,107	43
	S. Mason (Lab)	2,813	46		
	J. G. Freeman (L)	340	5		
1920	J. G. Paris (C)	5,486	70	14,288	55
	F. Jones (Lab)	2,396	30		
1921[1]	A. G. Gullan (C)	3,839	73	14,288	37
(Aug)	F. Jones (Lab)	1,450	37		
1921	J. L. Rankin (C)	4,577	71	14,363	45
	F. Jones (Lab)	1,855	29		
1922	R. G. Sheldon (C)	4,629	70	14,890	45
	F. Jones (Lab)	1,903	30		
	A. Slater (Pat. Lab)	117			
1923	A. G. Gullan (C)	NC	—	15,211	—
1924	C. Porter (C)	4,794	67	15,312	47
	F. Jones (Lab)	2,328	33		
1925	R. G. Sheldon (C)	3,824	77	15,740	32
	J. Dodd (Ind)	1,165	23		
1926	A. G. Gullan (C)	2,889	51	15,874	36
	F. Jones (Lab)	2,481	44		
	F. T. J. Evans (Ind)	307	5		
1927	F. Jones (Lab)	2,874	50	15,680	37
	C. Porter (C)	2,868	50		
1928	R. J. McDonnell (Lab)	4,120	51	15,321	53
	R. G. Sheldon (C)	4,008	49		
1929	W. H. Barton (Lab)	4,099	51	16,959	47
	A. G. Gullan (C)	3,914	49		
1930	C. Porter (C)	3,283	37	17,015	51
	F. Jones (Lab)	3,160	36		
	Mrs M. J. Longbottom (P)	2,316	26		
1931	F. S. H. Ashcroft (C)	3,801	44	17,017	51
	R. J. McDonnell (Lab)	2,708	31		
	Mrs M. J. Longbottom (P)	2,217	25		
1932	W. H. Barton (Lab)	2,546	34	17,097	44
	E. Tyrer (C)	2,471	33		
	W. R. Price (P)	1,771	24		
	C. H. Cund (ILP)	536	7		
	A. E. Cole (Comm)	125	2		

1933	F. Jones (Lab)	3,167	45	17,149	41
	E. Tyrer (C)	2,562	36		
	W. R. Price (P)	1,301	19		
1934	W. J. Riddick (Lab)	3,204	42	16,985	45
	F. S. H. Ashcroft (C)	3,171	42		
	G. H. Dunbar (P)	1,222	16		
1935	W. H. Barton (Lab)	4,259	55	16,787	46
	A. M. Brown (C)	3,494	45		
1936	A. M. Brown (C)	3,844	53	16,419	44
	F. Jones (Lab)	3,383	47		
1937	J. A. Reston (C)	5,420	56	16,128	60
	W. J. Riddick (Lab)	4,209	44		
1938[2]	W. E. McLachlan (C)	3,226	55	16,128	36
(Jul)	J. H. Sayle (Lab)	2,644	45		
1938	H. H. Nuttall (C)	4,376	54	16,007	51
	W. H. Barton (Lab)	3,699	46		

[1] Election of J. G. Paris as alderman.
[2] Resignation of A. M. Brown.

LITTLE WOOLTON (21) [created 1913, first contested 1922]

	Population	Electorate	Acreage	Persons/Acre
1911	—	—	—	—
1921	1,319	427	1,389	0.9
1931	1,470	592		1.1

1931	Av. family size	Rooms per dwelling	Families per dwelling	Persons per room
	3.85	5.96	1.03	0.66

Churches 1929		Sittings
Anglican	0	—
Catholic	0	—
Nonconformist	0	—

School rolls 1923	
Anglican	309
Catholic	0
Board	0

Trades Council delegates 1905	WMCA branch
Nil	None

Summary of municipal election results

Years	Lab. wins	Tory wins	Av. Lab. vote (%)	Av. Tory vote (%)	Av. turnout	NC	Nats. (wins)	Prots. (wins)
1919–23	0	1	—	—	—	1	0	0
1924–28	0	2	6	94	64	1	0	0
1929–33	0	1	—	—	—	1	0	0
1934–38	0	2	12	88	65	1	0	0
1919–38	0	6	9	91	65	4	0	0

Full list of municipal election results

Year	Candidates	Votes	%	Voters	Turnout (%)
1922	R. H. Bremner (C)	NC	—	433	—
1925	R. H. Bremner (C)	267	94	443	64
	J. H. Naylor jun. (Lab)	16	6		
1928	R. H. Bremner (C)	NC	—	444	—
1931	R. H. Bremner (C)	NC	—	592	—
1934	R. H. Bremner (C)	NC	—	744	—
1937	R. H. Bremner (C)	496	88	874	65
	G. T. Wood (Lab)	69	12		

LOW HILL (22)

	Population	Electorate	Acreage	Persons/Acre
1911	27,167	3,909	175	155.2
1921	29,255	9,695		167.2
1931	26,345	11,271		150.5

1931	Av. family size	Rooms per dwelling	Families per dwelling	Persons per room
	3.97	4.91	1.21	0.97

Churches 1929			Sittings
Anglican	2		1,600
Catholic	1		700
Nonconformist	3	(Welsh) 0	1,800

School rolls 1923	
Anglican	695
Catholic	990
Board	2,178

		WMCA branch
Carpenters	Painters	1920 ✓
Litho printers	Postmen (total 8)	1931
Masons	Slaters	1939✓
Packing-case makers	Clothier operatives	

Summary of municipal election results

Years	Lab. wins	Tory wins	Av. Lab. vote (%)	Av. Tory vote (%)	Av. turnout	NC	Nats. (wins)	Prots. (wins)
1905–9	0	4	36	61	48	1	0	0
1910–13	1	3	45	56	49	0	0	0
1905–13	1	7	42	58	48	1	0	0
1919–23	1	4	38	52	53	0	2 (0)	0
1924–28	4	1	55	45	49	0	0	0
1929–33	3	2	53	47	39	0	0	0
1934–38	2	3	49	51	49	0	0	0
1919–38	10	10	49	49	48	0	2 (0)	0

Full list of municipal election results

Year	Candidates	Votes	%	Voters	Turnout (%)
1905	J. M'Evoy (L)	1,013	51	3,977	50
	J. Roby (C)	972	49		
1906	A. Shelmerdine (C)	1,277	64	3,938	50
	E. A. Davies (L)	703	36		
1907	W. Boote (C)	1,265	65	3,874	50
	D. Little (Lab)	686	35		
1908[1] (Apr)	D. Pearson (C)	1,013	60	3,874	44
	W. Nash (L)	689	40		
1908	D. Pearson (C)	NC	—	3,777	—
1909	A. Shelmerdine (C)	1,039	64	3,803	43
	G. J. Jones (Lab)	591	36		
1910	W. Boote (C)	893	60	3,624	41
	G. Nelson (Lab)	602	40		
1910[2] (Dec)	F. W. Bailey (C)	999	52	3,624	53
	G. Nelson (Lab)	909	48		
1911	G. Nelson (Lab)	993	51	3,909	50
	D. Pearson (C)	955	49		
1912	F. W. Bailey (C)	1,129	59	3,729	51
	A. Broom (Lab)	769	41		

1913	W. Boote (C)	1,084	54	3,845	52
	J. P. Cotter (Lab)	918	46		
1914	G. Nelson (Lab)	NC	—	3,978	—
1919	T. J. Rowan (Lab)	1,872	44	8,947	48
	F. W. Bailey (C)	1,729	40		
	J. Masterson (L)	672	16		
1920	R. H. Ritchell (C)	3,309	61	9,454	57
	J. H. Johnston (Lab)	2,086	39		
1921	A. G. Alsop (C)	2,876	57	9,695	52
	G. Nelson (Lab)	2,126	43		
1922	E. K. Yates (C)	2,978	53	9,851	57
	T. J. Rowan (Lab)	1,530	27		
	J. Loughran (N)	1,112	20		
1923	R. H. Mitchell (C)	2,432	49	10,128	49
	T. J. Rowan (Lab)	1,170	36		
	J. Loughran (IP)	708	14		
	P. Maguire (Unemp)	33	1		
1924	A. G. Alsop (C)	2,684	52	10,268	50
	T. J. Rowan (Lab)	2,484	48		
1925[3] (Feb)	R. E. B. Trevor (C)	1,948	51	10, 268	43
	F. Robinson (Lab)	1,886	49		
1925	F. Robinson (Lab)	2,880	51	10,392	55
	R. E. B. Trevor (C)	2,818	49		
1926	M. J. McEntegart (Lab)	2,782	56	10,351	48
	W. J. Acheson (C)	2,228	44		
1927	E. G. Deery (Lab)	2,835	56	10,305	49
	A. G. Alsop (C)	2,229	44		
1928	F. Robinson (Lab)	2,926	64	10,095	
	F. J. Gearing (C)	1,617	36		
1929	M. J. McEntegart (Lab)	2,562	71	11,215	32
	S. Smart (C)	1,024	29		
1929[4] (Nov)	J. Whitehead (Lab)	2,624	62	11,215	38
	T. Broster (C)	1,615	38		
1930	C. E. Pugh (C)	2,049	54	11,186	34
	J. Whitehead (Lab)	1,744	46		
1931	G. R. Kitchen (C)	3,334	59	11,271	50
	F. Robinson (Lab)	2,273	41		
1932	F. Robinson (Lab)	2,520	54	11,316	41
	G. E. Mills (C)	2,053	44		
	J. F. Hedley (Comm)	103	2		
1933	A. Kay (Lab)	2,213	51	11,213	38
	C. E. Pugh (C)	2,096	49		
1934	F. C. Pasco (Lab)	2,235	54	11,171	37
	G. W. Prout (C)	1,934	46		
1935	F. Robinson (Lab)	2,783	53	11,056	47
	D. Rowan (C)	2,422	47		
1936	S. C. Saltmarsh (C)	3,055	57	10,780	49
	A. Kay (Lab)	2,265	43		
1937	K. H. Steel (C)	3,271	53	10,319	60

	F. C. Pasco (Lab)	2,932	47		
1938	J. N. M. Entwhistle (C)	2,840	51	10,007	52
	F. Robinson (Lab)	2,686	49		

[1] J. M'Evoy resigned.
[2] Election of A. Shelmerdine as alderman.
[3] Death of E. K. Yates.
[4] Resignation of E. G. Deery.

MUCH WOOLTON (23) [created 1913, first contested 1920]

	Population	Electorate	Acreage	Persons/Acre
1911	—	—	—	—
1921	4,416	1,600	792	5.6
1931	5,200	2,299		6.6

1931	Av. family size	Rooms per dwelling	Families per dwelling	Persons per room
	4.01	4.92	1.04	0.85

Churches 1929			Sittings
Anglican	2		750
Catholic	1		200
Nonconformist	3	(Welsh) 0	730

School rolls 1923	
Anglican	579
Catholic	399
Board	0

Trades Council delegates 1905	WMCA branch
Nil	None

Summary of municipal election results

Years	Lab. wins	Tory wins	Av. Lab. vote (%)	Av. Tory vote (%)	Av. turnout	NC	Nats. (wins)	Prots. (wins)
1919–23	0	2	38	63	77	1	0	0
1924–28	0	2	30	71	56	0	0	0
1929–33	0	5	23	55	64	0	0	0
1934–38	0	4	21	63	63	0	0	0
1919–38	0	13	26	61	64	1	0	0

Full list of municipal election results

Year	Candidates	Votes	%	Voters	Turnout (%)
1920	T. Harrison (C)	756	63	1,586	75
	C. J. Edwards (Lab)	438	37		
1921	R. Gladstone (Co. L)	776	62	1,600	78
	C. J. Edwards (Lab)	475	38		
1923	J. F. R. Reynolds (C)	NC	—	1,647	—
1924	R. Gladstone (Ind)	785	69	1,691	67
	C. J. Edwards (Lab)	346	31		
1926	J. F. R. Reynolds (C)	600	69	1,755	50
	W. H. Paulson (Lab)	271	31		
1927	W. E. S. Napier (C)	683	72	1,801	52
	F. Stapleton (Lab)	262	28		
1929	C. S. Pethick (C) (2 elected)	773	57	2,046	64
	J. F. R. Reynolds (C)	736			
	J. R. Bevins (Lab)	513	38		
	R. E. Cottier (Lab)	495			
	E. A. Ferguson (L)	108	5		
1930	W. E. S. Napier (C)	753	74	2,186	46
	W. R. Snell (Lab)	258	26		
1931	H. N. Bewley (C)	885	52	2,299	74
	E. Whitely (Ind)	821	48		
1932	Mrs C. Whitely (Ind)	850	52	2,371	70
	E. P. Thompson (C)	740	45		
	A. Lumb (Lab)	52	3		
	P. O. Hendley (Ind. Lab)	7	—		
1933	J. Butterfield (C)	759	46	2,558	65
	E. Whitely (Ind)	745	44		
	J. R. Bevins (Lab)	163	10		
1934	E. Whitely (Ind)	731	40	2,591	70
	I. Robinson (C)	724	40		
	C. F. Hind (Ratep'rs)	227	12		
	A. J. Holman (Lab)	140	8		
1935	I. Robinson (C)	1,013	51	2,747	72
	Mrs C. Whitely (Ind)	853	43		
	J. R. Jones (L)	123	6		
1935[1]	V. F. Crosthwaite (C)	804	54	2,747	55
(Dec)	Mrs C. Whitely (Ind)	611	41		
	C. E. Haig (Lab)	87	5		
1936	J. Butterfield (C)	1,104	77	2,828	51
	W. S. Fraser (Lab)	331	23		
1937	V. F. Crosthwaite (C)	1,453	71	2,911	70
	A. Campbell (Lab)	586	29		
1938	I. Robinson (C)	1,144	76	2,975	51
	D. Whelan (Lab)	359	24		

[1] Resignation of E. Whitely.

NETHERFIELD (24)

	Population	Electorate	Acreage	Persons/Acre
1911	32,023	4,015	129	248.2
1921	32,835	10,615		254.5
1931	29,257	12,090		226.8

1931	Av. family size	Rooms per dwelling	Families per dwelling	Persons per room
	4.50	4.28	1.23	1.3

Churches 1929			Sittings
Anglican	6		4,752
Catholic	0		0
Nonconformist	5	(Welsh) 0	2,350

School rolls 1923	
Anglican	1,600
Catholic	0
Board	4,398

Trades Council delegates 1905		WMCA branch
Iron and steel dressers		1920 ✓
French polishers	(total 4)	1931 ✓
Scientific instruments makers		1939 ✓
Carpenters		

Summary of municipal election results

Years	Lab. wins	Tory wins	Av. Lab. vote (%)	Av. Tory vote (%)	Av. turnout	NC	Nats. (wins)	Prots. (wins)
1905–9	0	4	—	60	46	0	0	4 (1)
1910–13	0	3	39	54	44	0	0	1 (1)
1905–13	0	7	39	57	45	0	0	5 (2)
1919–23	0	3	19	74	43	0	1 (0)	3 (2)
1924–28	2	2	46	55	50	0	0	2 (1)
1929–33	3	2	41	43	56	0	0	3 (0)
1934–38	1	3	37	57	54	0	0	3 (1)
1919–38	6	10	36	55	51	0	1 (0)	11 (4)

Full list of municipal election results

Year	Candidates	Votes	%	Voters	Turnout (%)
1905	W. W. Rutherford (C)	1,244	78	4,144	38
	J. Carr (Ind)	342	22		
1906[1]	J. Tomkinson (C)	797	56	4,144	34
(Jul)	J. Walker (P)	619	44		
1906	C. H. Rutherford (C)	1,057	57	4,151	45
	J. Walker (P)	807	43		
1907	G. Sturla (C)	1,400	65	4,093	53
	J. Walker (P)	764	35		
1907[2]	W. Waugh (C)	879	60	4,093	36
(Nov)	J. Walker (P)	585	40		
1908	W. Waugh (C)	996	57	4,007	43
	J. Walker (P)	740	43		
1908[3]	J. A. Irving (C)	1,008	58	4,007	43
(Nov)	J. Walker (P)	721	42		
1909	J. Walker (P)	1,064	56	3,711	51
	C. H. Rutherford (C)	831	44		
1910	W. Ball (C)	792	72	3,514	31
	W. H. Archer (Ind)	310	28		
1911	H. E. Davies (C)	855	46	4,015	46
	J. Challinor (Lab)	722	39		
	J. Carr (Ind)	268	15		
1912	J. Walker (P)	1,230	63	3,841	51
	W. E. MacLachlan (C)	717	37		
1913	W. Ball (C)	1,116	60	3,975	47
	C. Rolls (Ind)	759	40		
1914	H. E. Davies (C)	NC	—	4,060	—
1919	J. Walker (P)	2,109	76	10,152	27
	W. E. MacLachlan (C-Lab)	649	24		
1920	W. Ball (C)	4,042	73	10,349	53
	J. A. Metcalf (Lab)	1,481	27		
1921	H. E. Davies (C)	3,696	86	10,615	40
	V. Lloyd (Lab)	598	14		
1922	J. Walker (Pat. Lab)	2,654	42	10,745	58
	W. E. MacLachlan (Ind. C)	2,219	35		
	C. Chadwick (Lab)	1,350	22		
	P. C. Roche (N)	55	1		
1923[4]	W. E. MacLachlan (C)	2,437	68	10,745	33
(Jul)	C. Stamper (Ind. P)	717	20		
	G. Chadwick (Lab)	406	12		
1923	W. E. MacLachlan (C)	2,665	62	11,291	38
	C. Haigh (Pat. P)	1,155	27		
	G. Chadwick (Lab)	470	11		
1924[5]	A. M. Urding (C)	2,134	76	11,291	25
(Apr)	C. Haigh (Pat. Lab)	673	24		

Year	Candidate	Votes	%	Total	%
1924	A. M. Urding (C)	4,358	73	11,548	52
	G. Chadwick (Lab)	1,617	27		
1925	J. Walker (P)	2,844	58	11,763	41
	G. Chadwick (Lab)	2,023	42		
1926	G. Chadwick (Lab)	3,341	59	11,808	48
	W. E. MacLachlan (C)	2,280	41		
1927	A. M. Urding (C)	3,164	50	11,590	54
	J. Bagot (Lab)	3,102	50		
1928	J. Bagot (Lab)	3,150	52	11,178	54
	J. Walker (P)	2,864	48		
1929	G. Chadwick (Lab)	3,199	50	12,438	51
	J. Walker (C)	3,165	50		
1930	A. M. Urding (C)	3,770	52	12,178	60
	A. Kay (Lab)	1,721	24		
	A. Clayton (P)	1,518	21		
	W. E. MacLachlan (Ind)	276	3		
1931	W. J. M. Clark (C)	3,632	55	12,090	55
	J. Bagot (Lab)	2,984	45		
1932	G. Chadwick (Lab)	3,079	47	12,078	54
	A. Barkby (C)	1,980	30		
	A. Clayton (P)	1,490	23		
1933	J. Bagot (Lab)	2,823	40	11,895	59
	R. Bradley (P)	2,384	34		
	A. M. Urding (C)	1,815	26		
1934	Dr J. Sytner (Lab)	2,344	38	11,544	53
	R. Bradley (P)	1,912	32		
	W. J. M. Clark (C)	1,855	30		
1935	W. J. M. Clark (C)	3,451	57	11,301	53
	G. Chadwick (Lab)	2,505	42		
	J. G. Perkins (Ind. P)	68	1		
1936	R. Bradley (P)	3,497	57	11,023	56
	J. Bagot (Lab)	2,692	43		
1937	E. T. Edwards (C)	4,436	68	10,638	61
	J. Bagot (Lab)	2,073	32		
1938	W. J. M. Clark (C)	3,571	72	10,299	48
	W. J. Riddick (Lab)	1,379	28		

[1] Election of S. Jude as alderman.
[2] Election of W. Rutherford as alderman.
[3] Resignation of G. Sturla.
[4] Death of W. Ball.
[5] Election of H. E. Davies as alderman.

OLD SWAN (25)

	Population	Electorate	Acreage	Persons/Acre
1911	21,307	3,641	1,140	18.7
1921	29,788	10,866		26.1
1931	35,706	15,881		31.3

1931	Av. family size	Rooms per dwelling	Families per dwelling	Persons per room
	4.12	5.12	1.06	0.85

Churches 1929   *Sittings*

Anglican	3			1,414
Catholic	2			900
Nonconformist	4	(Welsh) 0		1,790

School rolls 1923

Anglican	1,296
Catholic	1,128
Board	2,879

Trades Council delegates 1905   *WMCA branch*

Carpenters   None
Painters   (total 3)
Railway servants

Summary of municipal election results

Years	Lab. wins	Tory wins	Av. Lab. vote (%)	Av. Tory vote (%)	Av. turnout	NC	Nats. (wins)	Prots. (wins)
1905–9	0	5	26	69	54	1	0	0
1910–13	0	4	36	65	45	2	0	0
1905–13	0	9	31	67	51	3	0	0
1919–23	1	4	36	61	49	0	2 (0)	0
1924–28	0	5	40	60	39	0	0	0
1929–33	2	3	43	57	40	0	0	0
1934–38	0	5	42	58	40	0	0	0
1919–38	3	17	40	59	42	0	2 (0)	0

Full list of municipal election results

Year	Candidates	Votes	%	Voters	Turnout (%)
1905	J. Hunter (C)	849	58	2,473	59
	J. Hoult (L)	609	42		
1906	J. W. Walker (C)	1,044	68	2,731	56
	J. Harrison (L)	498	32		
1907	J. Lister (C)	1,042	74	2,984	47
	A. Tracy (Soc)	364	26		
1908	J. Edwards (C)	1,265	75	3,173	53
	A. Tracy (Soc)	431	25		
1908[1] (Nov)	C. Burchall (C)	NC	—	3,173	—
1909	J. W. Walker (C)	NC	—	3,227	—
1910	C. Burchall (C)	NC	—	3,430	—
1911	J. Edwards (C)	NC	—	3,641	—
1912	J. Walker (C)	1,116	65	3,696	46
	J. Mooney (Lab)	588	35		
1913	C. Burchall (C)	1,056	64	3,909	43
	J. Mooney (Lab)	606	36		
1914	J. Edwards (C)	NC	—	4,163	—
1919	H. E. Rose (Lab)	2,161	50	9,548	45
	T. H. Burton (C)	2,126	50		
1920	A. E. Shennan (C)	3,617	69	9,945	52
	J. E. Summers (Lab)	1,599	31		
1921	J. Edwards (C)	3,598	69	10,866	48
	W. J. Daniel (Lab)	1,619	31		
1922	J. Waterworth (C)	3,485	56	11,263	55
	H. E. Rose (Lab)	1,893	31		
	J. Farrell jun. (N)	813	13		
1923[2] (Feb)	G. Whittle (C)	2,060	55	11,263	33
	H. E. Rose (Lab)	1,664	45		
1923	A. E. Shennan (C)	3,011	60	11,474	44
	H. E. Rose (Lab)	1,965	39		
	W. O'Neill (IP)	67	1		
1924	J. P. Thomas (P)	3,394	68	11,733	43
	J. E. Summers (Lab)	1,616	32		
1925	J. Waterworth (C)	3,193	66	11,996	40
	R. J. McDonnell (Lab)	1,648	34		
1926	A. E. Shennan (C)	2,196	61	12,279	30
	Mrs S. A. McArd (Lab)	1,430	39		
1927	J. P. Thomas (C)	2,520	55	12,949	35
	Mrs S. A. McArd (Lab)	2,072	45		
1928	J. Waterworth (C)	3,112	51	13,273	46
	Mrs S. A. McArd (Lab)	3,023	49		
1929	T. Williamson (Lab)	3,280	48	14,824	46
	A. E. Shennan (C)	3,237	48		
	W. H. Ledson (L)	273	4		

1930	M. Greenberg (C)	3,571	62	15,247	38
	W. S. Dytor (Lab)	2,219	38		
1931	J. Waterworth (C)	4,495	72	15,881	40
	A. Demain (Lab)	1,780	28		
1932	T. Williamson (Lab)	3,659	52	16,181	44
	G. C. E. Simpson (C)	3,440	48		
1933	M. Greenberg (C)	2,916	53	16,465	34
	C. M. Belk (Lab)	2,607	47		
1934	J. Waterworth (C)	3,145	53	17,065	35
	T. E. Martin (Lab)	2,792	47		
1935	C. H. Leftwich (C)	3,913	51	18,115	42
	T. Williamson (Lab)	3,784	49		
1936	M. Greenberg (C)	4,428	59	18,486	41
	J. Strathdene (Lab)	3,118	41		
1937	J. Waterworth (C)	5,770	63	18,227	50
	J. G. Houston (Lab)	3,370	37		
1938[3]	A. Haswell (C)	2,223	65	18,227	19
(Jun)	J. G. Houston (Lab)	1,212	35		
1938	Mrs J. Waterworth (C)	3,573	63	18,159	31
	Mrs J. Riddell (Lab)	2,070	37		

[1] Election of J. Lister as alderman.
[2] Election of J. Edwards as alderman.
[3] Death of J. Waterworth.

PRINCE'S PARK (26)

	Population	Electorate	Acreage	Persons/Acre
1911	21,344	3,614	259	82.4
1921	23,017	8,437		88.9
1931	21,570	9,913		83.3

1931	Av. family size	Rooms per dwelling	Families per dwelling	Persons per room
	3.8	5.15	1.19	0.88

Churches 1929			Sittings
Anglican	4		4,070
Catholic	0		0
Nonconformist	11	(Welsh) 3	7,650 (2,350)

School rolls 1923	
Anglican	1,519
Catholic	0
Board	662

Trades Council delegates 1905

			WMCA branch
Bricklayers	Brassfounders		1920 ✓
Engineers			1931 ✓
Engine and cranemen	(total 4)		1939 ✓

Summary of municipal election results

Years	Lab. wins	Tory wins	Av. Lab. vote (%)	Av. Tory vote (%)	Av. turnout	NC	Nats. (wins)	Prots. (wins)
1905–9	0	3	—	56	60	2	0	0
1910–13	0	3	—	—	—	4	0	0
1905–13	0	6	—	56	60	6	0	0
1919–23	0	4	30	70	52	3	0	0
1924–28	0	5	40	60	51	1	0	0
1929–33	0	5	39	61	44	0	0	0
1934–38	1	4	43	57	50	0	0	0
1919–38	1	18	39	61	48	4	0	0

Full list of municipal election results

Year	Candidates	Votes	%	Voters	Turnout (%)
1905	A. L. R. Rathbone (L)	1,098	51	3,686	59
	F. W. Frodsham (C)	1,069	49		
1906	H. C. Dowdall (C)	1,297	61	3,617	59
	W. E. Woodhall (L)	838	39		
1907	F. W. Frodsham (C)	1,331	59	3,600	63
	M. Muspratt (L)	927	41		
1908	A. L. R. Rathbone (L)	NC	—	3,590	—
1909	H. C. Dowdall (C)	NC	—	3,546	—
1910[1] (Aug)	D. Jackson (C)	NC	—	3,546	—
1910	C. H. Rutherford (C)	NC	—	3,394	—
1911	A. L. R. Rathbone (L)	NC	—	3,614	—
1912	D. Jacksonn (C)	NC	—	3,523	—
1913	C. H. Rutherford (C)	NC	—	3,589	—
1914	A. L. R. Rathbone (L)	NC	—	3,612	—
1919	D. Jackson (C)	2,365	64	7,765	48
	J. Hayes (Lab)	1,330	36		
1920	C. H. Rutherford (C)	3,461	76	8,211	56
	T. Griffiths (Lab)	1,116	24		
1920[2] (Dec)	R. L. Burns (C)	NC	—	8,211	—

1921[3]	Miss M. Beavan (L)	1,883	79	8,211	29
(Mar)	T. Griffiths (Lab)	489	21		
1921	Miss M. Beavan (L)	NC	—	8,437	—
1922	D. Jackson (C)	NC	—	8,477	—
1923	A. Wood (C)	NC	—	8,853	—
1924[4]	D. M. Ritchie (C)	2,686	70	8,853	43
	Mrs L. Hughes (Lab)	1,128	30		
1924	Miss M. Beavan (C)	NC	—	9,130	—
1925	D. M. Ritchie (C)	3,259	64	9,344	54
	R. Dixon-Smith (Lab)	1,815	36		
1926	A. Wood (C)	2,431	58	9,410	45
	W. Jones (Lab)	1,757	42		
1927	Miss M. Beavan (C)	2,919	64	9,256	49
	R. Edwards (Lab)	1,621	36		
1928	J. D. Griffiths (C)	2,671	55	9,094	54
	R. Edwards (Lab)	2,198	45		
1929	A. Wood (C)	2,325	55	9,982	43
	F. Lavery (Lab)	1,921	45		
1930	Miss M. Beavan (C)	3,077	70	9,857	44
	R. E. Cottier (Lab)	1,298	30		
1931	J. D. Griffiths (C)	3,122	72	9,913	44
	J. Hamilton (Lab)	1,213	28		
1932[5]	C. R. Clare (C)	1,794	57	9,913	32
(Sep)	A. Demain (Lab)	1,331	43		
1932	C. R. Clare (C)	2,448	55	9,905	45
	A. Demain (Lab)	2,029	45		
1933	W. T. Thomas (C)	2,155	51	9,968	42
	A. Demain (Lab)	2,058	49		
1934	A. Demain (Lab)	1,985	51	9,860	40
	J. B. Noble (C)	1,912	49		
1935	C. R. Clare (C)	2,746	53	9,850	52
	J. S. Ogden (Lab)	2,406	47		
1936	D. Rowan (C)	2,896	58	9,811	51
	Mrs S. A. Demain (Lab)	2,079	42		
1937	A. P. Bevan (C)	3,484	63	9,664	57
	A. Demain (Lab)	2,050	37		
1938	C. R. Clare (C)	2,849	64	9,239	48
	A. Demain (Lab)	1,607	36		

[1] Resignation of H. C. Dowdall.
[2] Election of C. H. Rutherford as alderman.
[3] Resignation of A. L. R. Rathbone.
[4] Resignation of D. Jackson.
[5] Death of A. Wood.

ST ANNE'S (27)

	Population	Electorate	Acreage	Persons/Acre
1911	24,651	2,735	213	115.7
1921	23,129	7,013		108.6
1931	20,944	9,253		98.3

1931	Av. family size	Rooms per dwelling	Families per dwelling	Persons per room
	3.84	4.06	1.6	1.51

Churches 1929			Sittings
Anglican	5		4,034
Catholic	1		500
Nonconformist	1	(Welsh) 0	700

School rolls 1923
Anglican	650
Catholic	310
Board	0

Trades Council delegates 1905		WMCA branch
Bootmakers		1920 ✓
Brassfounders	(total 4)	1931 ✓
Carvers		1939
Engineers		

Summary of municipal election results

Years	Lab. wins	Tory wins	Av. Lab. vote (%)	Av. Tory vote (%)	Av. turnout	NC	Nats. (wins)	Prots. (wins)
1905–9	2	0	55	44	42	2	1 (0)	0
1910–13	1	0	51	48	62	2	0	0
1905–13	3	0	53	46	50	4	1 (0)	0
1919–23	1	0	42	—	46	1	2 (2)	0
1924–28	4	0	54	—	44	1	4 (1)	0
1929–33	5	0	76	—	37	2	3 (0)	0
1934–38	5	0	79	21	40	4	0	0
1919–38	15	0	61	21	42	8	9 (3)	0

Full list of municipal election results

Year	Candidates	Votes	%	Voters	Turnout (%)
1905	J. Sexton (Lab)	884	55	2,903	55
	H. Fineberg (C)	709	44		
	J. Murphy (Ind)	2	—		
1906[1]	Dr J. C. Baxter (L)	710	55	2,903	44
(Mar)	Dr Maguire (N)	574	45		
1906	G. King (L)	NC	—	2,883	—
1907	Dr J. C. Baxter (L)	984	57	2,806	61
	D. Pearson (C)	929	43		
1908	J. Sexton (Lab)	NC	—	2,788	—
1909	G. King (L)	209	86	2,703	9
	G. Gretton (Ind)	34	14		
1910[2]	P. D. Holt (L)	NC	—	2,703	—
(Jun)					
1910	Dr J. C. Baxter (L)	NC	—	2,692	—
1911	J. Sexton (Lab)	913	51	2,735	65
	R. J. Ward (C)	870	49		
1912	P. D. Holt (L)	NC	—	2,578	—
1913	Dr J. C. Baxter (L)	813	53	2,665	58
	R. J. Ward (C)	735	47		
1914	J. Sexton (Lab)	NC	—	2,701	—
1919	P. D. Holt (L)	NC	—	7,087	—
1920	P. A. Durkin (N)	2,563	74	6,977	50
	Dr J. C. Baxter (L)	918	26		
1921	J. Sexton (Lab)	1,685	57	7,013	42
	J. Nield (Comm)	1,274	43		
1922	J. Nield (Comm)	2,181	57	7,745	49
	P. D. Holt (L)	1,642	43		
1923	P. A. Durkin (IP)	2,155	62	8,412	41
	R. McCann (Lab)	903	26		
	A. Phillips (Unemp)	432	12		
1924	J. Sexton (Lab)	1,567	53	8,556	34
	J. Farrell (IP)	1,322	45		
	J. Young (Comm)	25	1		
	J. Corcoran (Ind)	21	1		
1925	J. Farrell (Cath)	2,093	48	8,639	51
	M. Eschwege (Lab)	1,545	35		
	J. Nield (Comm)	706	16		
	J. Corcoran (Ind)	27	1		
1926	M. Eschwege (Lab)	2,932	73	8,591	47
	P. A. Durkin (Centre)	1,051	26		
	J. Nield (Comm)	32	1		
1927	J. Sexton (Lab)	2,152	56	8,525	45
	C. Devlin (Centre)	1,666	44		
1928	J. D. Mack (Lab)	NC	—	8,473	—
1929	M. Eschwege (Lab)	3,468	81	9,751	44

	H. Granby (Centre)	838	19		
1929[3]	Mrs L. F. Hughes (Lab)	NC	—	9,751	—
(Nov)					
1930	Mrs M. E. Braddock (Lab)	1,392	60	9,436	25
	Mrs L. F. Hughes (Ind. Lab)	935	40		
1931	J. D. Mack (Lab)	NC	—	9,253	—
1932	S. S. Silverman (Lab)	3,227	86	9,108	41
	T. Conifer (Dem. Lab)	505	14		
1933	Mrs E. Braddock (Lab)	NC	—	8,983	—
1934	J. D. Mack (Lab)	NC	—	8,228	—
1935	S. S. Silverman (Lab)	2,425	79	7,725	40
	T. H. Nabb (C)	650	21		
1936	Mrs E. Braddock (Lab)	NC	—	7,182	—
1937	J. D. Mack (Lab)	NC	—	6,919	—
1938	H. Livermore (Lab)	NC	—	6,612	—

[1] Reason for by-election unstated.
[2] Resignation of G. King.
[3] Election of J. Sexton as alderman.

ST DOMINGO (28)

	Population	Electorate	Acreage	Persons/Acre
1911	28,814	4,547	179	161.0
1921	30,520	10,431		170.5
1931	27,182	11,734		151.9

1931	Av. family size	Rooms per dwelling	Families per dwelling	Persons per room
	4.27	4.56	1.14	1.06

Churches 1929			*Sittings*
Anglican	3		2,130
Catholic	1		575
Nonconformist	7	(Welsh) 0	3,938

School rolls 1923	
Anglican	746
Catholic	1,188
Board	3,189

Trades Council delegates 1905		*WMCA branch*	
Enginemen and cranemen		1920 ✓	
Painters		1931 ✓	
Stereotypers	(total 3)	1939 ✓	

Summary of municipal election results

Years	Lab. wins	Tory wins	Av. Lab. vote (%)	Av. Tory vote (%)	Av. turnout	NC	Nats. (wins)	Prots. (wins)
1905–9	0	4	—	65	46	1	0	4 (0)
1910–13	1	3	33	53	49	2	0	0
1905–13	1	7	33	60	47	3	0	4 (0)
1919–23	0	4	39	68	41	2	0	1 (1)
1924–28	1	3	44	57	43	0	0	2 (1)
1929–33	0	2	28	37	48	0	0	4 (3)
1934–38	0	0	33	32	42	0	0	5 (5)
1919–38	1	9	36	48	44	2	0	12 (10)

Full list of municipal election results

Year	Candidates	Votes	%	Voters	Turnout (%)
1905	G. W. Whittaker (Ind. C)	1,406	57	4,553	55
	W. Ellis Jones (P)	1,059	43		
1906	J. Roby (C)	1,155	54	4,587	47
	S. G. Thomas (P)	984	46		
1907	Dr C. A. Hill (C)	1,214	56	4,522	48
	H. Porter (P)	946	44		
1908	G. W. Whittaker (C)	1,345	85	4,447	35
	J. Adams (P)	232	15		
1909	J. Roby (C)	NC	—	4,365	—
1910	Dr C. A. Hill (C)	NC	—	4,284	—
1911	J. Stephenson (Lab)	939	38	4,547	54
	D. J. Williams (C)	798	33		
	G. W. Whittaker (Ind. C)	715	29		
1912	W. H. Moore (C)	1,382	72	4,394	44
	J. Murphy (Lab)	535	28		
1913	C. A. Hill (C)	NC	—	4,539	—
1914	C. Wilson (Lab)	NC	—	4,639	—
1919	T. White (C)	1,991	52	9,920	39
	W. S. Shaw (Lab)	1,831	48		
1920	W. E. Backhouse (C)	NC	—	10,179	—
1921	A. Clayton (P)	3,008	70	10,431	41
	C. Wilson (Lab)	1,277	30		
1922	T. White (C)	3,917	84	10,545	44
	C. H. Allam (Pat. Lab)	721	16		
1923	W. E. Backhouse (C)	NC	—	10,762	—
1924	A. Clayton (P)	2,542	61	10,926	38

Year	Candidate	Votes	%		
	G. Williams (Lab)	1,597	39		
1925	T. White (C)	3,565	68	11,130	47
	Mrs S. A. McArd (Lab)	1,648	32		
1926	W. E. Backhouse (C)	2,128	50	11,188	38
	J. Hamilton (Lab)	2,087	50		
1927	J. Hamilton (Lab)	2,243	54	11,101	38
	A. Clayton (P)	1,948	46		
1928	Sir T. White (C)	3,044	53	10,805	53
	W. H. Barton (Lab)	2,699	47		
1929	W. E. Backhouse (C)	2,882	54	12,053	44
	W. J. Daniel (Lab)	2,473	46		
1930	Revd H. D. Longbottom (P)	2,862	46	11,737	52
	W. T. Thomas (C)	1,682	28		
	J. Hamilton (Lab)	1,570	26		
1931	C. H. Leftwich (C)	2,292	41	11,734	48
	A. Clayton (P)	1,848	33		
	F. Jones (Lab)	1,489	26		
1932	Mrs M. J. Longbottom (P)	1,784	35	11,712	44
	W. E. Backhouse (C)	1,566	30		
	R. J. McDonnell (Lab)	1,370	27		
	G. E. Humphreys (ILP)	432	8		
1933	Revd H. D. Longbottom (P)	3,101	52	11,669	51
	W. E. Backhouse (C)	1,907	32		
	R. J. McDonnell (Lab)	922	16		
1934	W. R. Price (P)	1,452	33	11,365	39
	C. H. Leftwich (C)	1,411	32		
	F. Stapleton (Lab)	1,379	31		
	H. S. Revill (Ind. P)	193	4		
1935	Mrs M. J. Longbottom (P)	2,506	55	11,382	40
	G. T. Holliday (Lab)	2,024	45		
1935 [1] (Dec)	G. H. Dunbar (P)	2,024	57	11,382	31
	G. T. Holliday (Lab)	1,482	43		
1936	G. H. Dunbar (P)	2,836	63	11,166	40
	Mrs S. A. McArd (Lab)	1,686	37		
1937	W. R. Price (P)	4,559	77	10,968	54
	J. V. Shortt (Lab)	1,350	23		
1938	Mrs M. J. Longbottom (P)	2,828	70	10,957	37
	J. Cullen (Lab)	1,189	30		

[1] Election of Revd H. D. Longbottom as alderman.

ST PETER'S (29)

	Population	Electorate	Acreage	Persons/Acre
1911	6,624	1,711	225	29.4
1921	5,669	2,632		25.2
1931	5,567	2,779		24.7

1931	Av. family size	Rooms per dwelling	Families per dwelling	Persons per room
	3.99	4.96	1.46	1.17

Churches 1929		Sittings
Anglican	1	900
Catholic	1	1,300
Nonconformist	0	0

School rolls 1923	
Anglican	387
Catholic	1,600
Board	0

Trades Council delegates 1905	WMCA branch
Nil	None

Summary of municipal election results

Years	Lab. wins	Tory wins	Av. Lab. vote (%)	Av. Tory vote (%)	Av. turnout	NC	Nats. (wins)	Prots. (wins)
1905–9	0	1	—	50	61	2	0	0
1910–13	0	1	—	47	69	2	0	0
1905–13	0	2	—	49	64	4	0	0
1919–23	0	2	38	64	46	1	2 (0)	0
1924–28	0	2	39	54	42	1	0	0
1929–33	0	1	29	81	43	0	0	0
1934–38	1	1	43	53	42	0	0	0
1919–38	1	6	37	60	43	2	2 (0)	0

Full list of municipal election results

Year	Candidates	Votes	%	Voters	Turnout (%)
1905	A. Armour (L)	NC	—	1,805	—
1906	G. F. Clarke (C)	629	59	1,809	59
	W. Crosfield (L)	430	41		

Year	Candidate	Votes	%		%
1907	H. Miles (Ind)	NC	—	1,791	—
1908[1] (Apr)	H. K. Muspratt (L)	NC	—	1,791	—
1908	B. W. Eills (L)	617	54	1,744	65
	H. Lyons (C)	516	46		
1909[2] (Jun)	J Byrne (L)	NC	—	1,744	—
1909	T. Shaw (L)	562	55	1,715	59
	H. Toner (C)	456	45		
1910	J. Byrne (L)	NC	—	1,687	—
1911	B. W. Eills (L)	NC	—	1,711	—
1912	H. A. Cole (C)	596	53	1,650	68
	T. Shaw (L)	533	47		
1913	L. D. Holt (L)	655	59	1,591	70
	J. C. Walker (C)	454	41		
1914	B. W. Eills (L)	NC	—	1,535	—
1919	H. A. Cole (C)	743	62	2,520	47
	E. Fergus (Lab)	451	38		
1920	L. D. Holt (L)	991	91	2,697	40
	J. Friery (N)	101	9		
1921	B. W. Eills (L)	NC	—	2,632	—
1922	H. A. Cole (C)	732	65	2,564	44
	F. Bowman (Ind)	402	35		
1923	L. D. Holt (L)	946	65	2,729	53
	F. Bowman (Ind)	333	23		
	O. Gerachty (IP)	155	11		
	J. E. Ashton (Unemp)	16	1		
1924	B. W. Eills (L)	846	68	2,882	43
	F. Bowman (Ind)	399	32		
1924[1] (Nov)	H. W. Levy (C)	695	51	2,882	47
	F. Bowman (Ind)	369	27		
	C. Wilson (Lab)	286	21		
1925	H. W. Levy (C)	766	57	2,947	46
	J. Loughlin (Lab)	369	27		
	F. Bowman (Ind)	207	16		
1926	L. D. Holt (L)	NC	—	2,931	—
1927	B. W. Eills (L)	806	80	2,885	35
	F. Bowman (Ind)	198	20		
1928	H. W. Levy (C)	631	50	2,778	45
	G. W. Hincks (Lab)	628	50		
1929	L. D. Holt (L)	1,130	71	3,070	52
	F. W. Tucker (Lab)	472	29		
1930	Miss M. M. Eills (L)	850	74	3,054	38
	Miss E. E. L. Hickling (Lab)	304	26		
1931	H. W. Levy (C)	973	81	2,779	43
	J. Nugent (Lab)	232	19		
1932	A. Robinson (L)	671	52	2,853	45
	R. E. Cottier (Lab)	488	38		

	W. E. MacLachlan (Ind)	130	10		
1933[4]	S. J. Hill (C)	485	54	2,853	31
(May)	J. Whitehead (Lab)	340	38		
	F. Bowman (Ind)	72	8		
1933	Miss M. M. Eills (L)	666	68	2,778	35
	P. Campbell (Lab)	309	32		
1934	S. J. Hill (C)	623	58	2,761	39
	S. Part (Lab)	445	42		
1935	J. Bennion (L)	630	57	2,504	44
	L. W. Kennan (Lab)	482	43		
1936	Miss M. M. Eills (L)	647	62	2,455	42
	L. W. Kennan (Lab)	393	38		
1937	H. Carr (Lab)	551	52	2,353	45
	S. J. Hill (C)	512	48		
1938	J. Bennion (L)	545	59	2,214	42
	R. E. Cottier (Lab)	374	41		

[1] Death of H. Miles.
[2] Resignation of H. K. Muspratt.
[3] Election of H. A. Cole as alderman.
[4] Resignation of H. W. Levy.

SANDHILLS (30)

	Population	Electorate	Acreage	Persons/Acre
1911	24,685	3,539	611	40.4
1921	26,647	8,603		43.6
1931	24,031	9,499		39.3

1931	Av. family size	Rooms per dwelling	Families per dwelling	Persons per room
	4.46	4.63	1.20	1.16

Churches 1929			Sittings
Anglican	0		0
Catholic	2		1,330
Nonconformist	1	(Welsh) 0	500

School rolls 1923	
Anglican	837
Catholic	1,926
Board	1,248

Trades Council delegates 1905		WMCA branch	
Engineers		1920	✓
Sailors		1931	✓
NAUL	(total 3)	1939	

Summary of municipal election results

Years	Lab. wins	Tory wins	Av. Lab. vote (%)	Av. Tory vote (%)	Av. turnout	NC	Nats. (wins)	Prots. (wins)
1905–9	0	0	—	50	54	3	4 (4)	0
1910–13	0	0	—	43	52	1	3 (3)	0
1905–13	0	0	—	45	53	4	7 (7)	0
1919–23	0	0	11	—	43	2	5 (5)	0
1924–28	4	0	57	—	45	1	4 (1)	0
1929–33	5	0	88	18	37	2	0	0
1934–38	5	0	—	—	—	5	0	0
1919–38	14	0	63	18	42	10	9 (6)	0

Full list of municipal election results

Year	Candidates	Votes	%	Voters	Turnout (%)
1905	P. J. Deery (L and N)	1,002	51	3,332	59
	W. Singleton (P)	978	49		
1906	M. Kearny (N)	NC	—	3,340	—
1907	J. A. Appleton (L)	938	50	3,353	56
	J. L. Rankin (C)	932	50		
1908	P. J. Deery (N)	928	61	3,303	46
	J. Carr (Ind. C)	459	39		
	J. Maher (Ind)	134	10		
1909	M. Kearney (N)	NC	—	3,196	—
1910	A. Gates (L)	1,085	60	3,199	57
	J. L. Rankin (C)	736	40		
1911	J. Cunningham (N)	806	64	3,539	36
	P. J. Deery (Ind. N)	456			
1912[1] (May)	T. W. Byrne (N)	NC	—	3,539	—
1912	T. W. Byrne (N)	NC	—	3,294	—
1913	A. Gates (L)	1,207	55	3,423	64
	W. B. Anderson (C)	994	45		
1914	J. Cunningham (N)	NC	—	3,586	—
1919	T. W. Byrne (N)	NC	—	8,268	—
1920	J. W. Baker (N)	2,780	55	8,321	60
	A. Gates (L)	2,243	45		
1921	J. Cunningham (N)	2,181	78	8,603	32
	J. Freeman (L)	600	22		
1922[2] (Jul)	J. Hanratty (N)	1,852	73	8,603	29
	J. Freeman (L)	669	27		
1922	T. W. Byrne (N)	NC	—	8,678	—

1923	J. W. Baker (IP)	2,680	84	8,711	37
	P. Roy (Lab)	353	11		
	D. Williams (Unemp.)	161	5		
1924	T. Dakin (Lab)	2,120	53	8,808	45
	W. H. McGuiness (IP)	1,855	47		
1925	T. W. Byrne (Lab)	2,829	63	8,995	50
	W. H. McGuiness (Cath)	1,696	37		
1926	J. W. Baker (Centre)	1,790	51	8,996	39
	T. H. Dunford (Lab)	1,737	49		
1927	J. W. T. Morrisey (Lab)	2,638	64	8,841	47
	C. Maguire (Centre)	1,492	36		
1928	T. W. Byrne (Lab)	NC	—	8,656	—
1929	J. W. Baker (Lab)	3,905	82	9,535	50
	J. E. Freeman (C)	868	18		
1929[3] (Dec)	T. H. Dunford (Lab)	NC	—	9,535	—
1930	J. W. T. Morrisey (Lab)	NC	—	9,495	—
1931	T. H. Dunford (Lab)	2,355	88	9,499	28
	Mrs Bruce (Comm)	314	12		
1932	J. W. Baker (Lab)	2,904	94	9,396	33
	I. P. Hughes (Comm)	198	6		
1933	J. W. T. Morrisey (Lab)	NC	—	9,308	—
1934	T. H. Dunford (Lab)	NC	—	9,194	—
1934[4] (Nov)	S. Part (Lab)	NC	—	9,194	—
1935	S. Part (Lab)	NC	—	9,153	—
1936	J. W. T. Morissey (Lab)	NC	—	8,920	—
1937	T. H. Dunford (Lab)	NC	—	8,722	—
1937[5]	H. Alldritt (Lab)	3,085	67	8,722	53
	W. E. MacLachlan (C)	1,548	33		
1938	S. Part (Lab)	NC	—	8,490	—

[1] Death of M. Kearney.
[2] Death of J. Cunningham.
[3] Election of T. W. Byrne as alderman.
[4] Death of J. W. Baker.
[5] Election of J. W. T. Morrisey as alderman.

SCOTLAND NORTH (31)

	Population	Electorate	Acreage	Persons/Acre
1911	23,922	2,938	282	84.8
1921	22,205	7,379		78.7
1931	21,381	8,758		75.8

1931	Av. family size	Rooms per dwelling	Families per dwelling	Persons per room
	4.43	3.87	1.28	1.46

Churches 1929			Sittings
Anglican	1		800
Catholic	3		3,000
Nonconformist	1	(Welsh) 0	700

School rolls 1923	
Anglican	229
Catholic	4,664
Board	0

Trades Council delegates 1905	WMCA branch
Nil	None

Summary of municipal election results

Years	Lab. wins	Tory wins	Av. Lab. vote (%)	Av. Tory vote (%)	Av. turnout	NC	Nats. (wins)	Prots. (wins)
1905–9	0	0	—	—	49	4	5 (5)	0
1910–13	0	0	—	—	—	4	4 (4)	0
1905–13	0	0	—	—	49	8	9 (9)	0
1919–23	0	0	47	—	56	2	5 (5)	0
1924–28	4	0	53	—	54	1	4 (1)	0
1929–33	5	0	89	—	34	0	0	0
1934–38	5	0	86	—	40	4	0	0
1919–38	14	0	70	—	46	7	9 (6)	0

Full list of municipal election results

Year	Candidates	Votes	%	Voters	Turnout (%)
1905	M. Phelan (N)	809	53	3,123	49
	J. Bolger (Ind. N)	713	47		
1906	T. Kelly (N)	NC	—	3,154	—
1907	G. J. Lynskey (N)	NC	—	3,174	—
1908	J. Bolger (N)	NC	—	3,120	—
1909	Dr Maguire (N)	NC	—	2,963	—
1910	G. J. Lynskey (N)	NC	—	2,848	—
1911[1] (Sep)	J. Clancy (N)	NC	—	2,848	—
1911	J. Bolger (N)	NC	—	2,938	—

1912	J. Clancy (N)	NC	—	2,822	—
1913[2]	W. J. Loughrey (N)	NC	—	2,822	—
1913	W. J. Loughrey (N)	NC	—	2,868	—
1914	J. Bolger (N)	NC	—	2,900	—
1919	J. Clancy (N)	NC	—	7,233	—
1920	W. J. Loughrey (N)	NC	—	7,584	—
1921	J. Bolger (N)	3,634	98	7,379	50
	W. H. Davies (L)	85	2		
1922	J. Clancy (N)	2,499	55	7,649	59
	E. Campbell (Lab)	2,011	45		
1923	J. P. Farrelly (IP)	2,412	51	8,075	58
	E. Campbell (Lab)	2,283	49		
1924[3]	D. G. Logan (Lab)	3,272	79	8,075	51
(Jul)	T. J. Hennessey (IP)	881	21		
1924	D. G. Logan (Lab)	3,403	82	8,178	51
	E. Gerachty (IP)	734	18		
1925[4]	R. McCann (Lab)	1,850	66	8,178	34
(Aug)	F. W. Tucker (IP)	935	34		
1925	Revd T. George (Cath)	3,465	80	8,121	53
	R. McCann (Lab)	617	14		
	J. Kearney (Ind)	256	6		
1926	W. A. Robinson (Lab)	2,328	57	8,182	50
	Revd T. J. Rigby (Centre)	1,780	43		
1927	D. G. Logan (Lab)	3,059	60	8,214	63
	J. O'Hare (Centre)	2,048	39		
	E. Campbell (Ind)	30	1		
1928	P. Fay (Lab)	NC	—	8,025	—
1929	W. A. Robinson (Lab)	3,055	86	8,931	40
	W. H. Hill (Ind)	477	14		
1929[5]	P. Duffy (Lab) (2 elected)	NC	—	8,931	—
(Dec)	Mrs M. McFarlane (Lab)	NC	—	8,931	—
1930	F. W. Tucker (Lab)	1,985	82	8,695	28
	L. McGree (Comm)	428	18		
1931	P. Fay (Lab)	2,966	88	8,758	39
	L. J. McGree (Comm)	412	12		
1932	Mrs M. McFarlane (Lab)	2,429	92	8,684	30
	L. J. McGree (Comm)	206	8		
1933	F. W. Tucker (Lab)	2,715	97	8,703	32
	W. F. Fielding (Comm)	88	3		
1934	P. Fay (Lab)	NC	—	8,561	—
1935	H. Gaskin (Lab)	2,870	86	8,360	40
	Mrs M. McFarlane (Ind)	465	14		
1936	F. W. Tucker (Lab)	NC	—	8,019	—
1937	P. Fay (Lab)	NC	—	7,860	—
1937[6]	P. O'Brien (Lab)	NC	—	7,860	—
(Dec)					
1938	P. O'Brien (Lab)	NC	—	7,547	—

[1] Resignation of Dr Maguire.
[2] Election of G. J. Lynskey as alderman.
[3] Election of J. Bolger as alderman.
[4] Election of J. Clancy as alderman.
[5] Election of W. A. Robinson and D. G. Logan as aldermen.
[6] Death of H. Gaskin.

SCOTLAND SOUTH (32)

	Population	Electorate	Acreage	Persons/Acre
1911	22,654	2,944	238	95.2
1921	22,937	8,053		96.4
1931	21,372	8,789		89.8

1931	Av. family size	Rooms per dwelling	Families per dwelling	Persons per room
	4.34	3.51	1.24	1.54

Churches 1929		Sittings
Anglican	5	4,760
Catholic	5	4,220
Nonconformist	0	0

School rolls 1923	
Anglican	846
Catholic	5,145
Board	1,008

Trades Council delegates 1905
Nil

WMCA branch
1920 ✓
1931
1939

Summary of municipal election results

Years	Lab. wins	Tory wins	Av. Lab. vote (%)	Av. Tory vote (%)	Av. turnout	NC	Nats. (wins)	Prots. (wins)
1905–9	0	0	—	—	—	5	5 (5)	0
1910–13	0	0	—	—	—	4	4 (4)	0
1905–13	0	0	—	—	—	9	9 (9)	0
1919–23	0	0	46	—	61	2	5 (5)	0

Years	Lab. wins	Tory wins	Av. Lab. vote (%)	Av. Tory vote (%)	Av. turnout	NC	Nats. (wins)	Prots. (wins)
1924–28	2	0	45	—	50	1	4 (3)	0
1929–33	5	0	71	—	40	3	2 (0)	0
1934–38	5	0	95	—	41	3	2 (0)	0
1919–38	12	0	59	—	49	9	13 (8)	0

Full list of municipal election results

Year	Candidates	Votes	%	Voters	Turnout (%)
1905	A. Harford (N)	NC	—	3,166	—
1906	J. O'Shea (N)	NC	—	3,152	—
1907	F. J. Harford (N)	NC	—	3,021	—
1908	A. Harford (N)	NC	—	3,025	—
1909	J. O'Shea (N)	NC	—	2,963	—
1910	F. J. Harford (N)	NC	—	2,902	—
1911	A. Harford (N)	NC	—	2,944	—
1912	J. O'Shea (N)	NC	—	2,840	—
1913	F. J. Harford (N)	NC	—	2,989	—
1914[1] (Jul)	P. J. Kelly (N)	NC	—	2,989	—
1914	P. J. Kelly (N)	NC	—	3,133	—
1919	J. O'Shea (N)	NC	—	7,864	—
1920	D. G. Logan (N)	2,611	54	8,036	61
	H. Gaskin (Lab)	2,252	46		
1921	P. J. Kelly (N)	NC	—	8,053	—
1922	M. O'Mahoney (N)	2,540	50	8,036	63
	H. Gaskin (Lab)	2,499	50		
1923	J. G. Murphy (IP)	2,841	59	8,289	59
	D. G. Logan (Lab)	2,014	41		
1924	J. O'Donoghue (Lab)	2,419	57	8,121	52
	P. J. Kelly (IP)	1,832	43		
1925	M. O'Mahoney (Cath)	3,013	65	8,468	55
	E. Campbell (Lab)	1,646	35		
1926	J. G. Murphy (Centre)	1,673	52	8,544	37
	J. Harrington (Lab)	1,523	48		
1927	Miss M. O'Shea (Centre)	2,767	59	8,437	56
	J. Harrington (Lab)	1,927	41		
1928	J. Harrington (Lab)	NC	—	8,298	—
1929[2] (Feb)	M. J. Reppion (Lab)	NC	—	8,298	—
1929	J. Sheehan (Lab)	2,604	59	9,235	48
	J. G. Murphy (Centre)	1,793	41		
1930	M. J. Reppion (Lab)	2,310	82	8,839	32

	J. Loughran (Ind. Lab)	524	18		
1931	J. Harrington (Lab)	NC	—	8,789	—
1932	J. Sheehan (Lab)	NC	—	8,712	—
1933	M. J. Reppion (Lab)	NC	—	8,602	—
1934	J. Harrington (Lab)	NC	—	8,428	—
1935	J. Sheehan (Lab)	2,625	93	8,308	34
	T. P. Sheehan (Ind. Lab)	187	7		
1936	M. J. Reppion (Lab)	NC	—	8,193	—
1937	J. Harrington (Lab)	3,619	97	7,964	47
	C. M. Williams (Ind. Lab)	113	3		
1938	J. Sheehan (Lab)	NC	—	7,477	—

[1] Election of A. Harford as alderman.
[2] Death of Miss M. O'Shea.

SEFTON PARK EAST (33)

	Population	Electorate	Acreage	Persons/Acre
1911	21,256	3,846	490	43.4
1921	20,788	8,569		42.4
1931	19,885	8,969		40.6

1931	Av. family size	Rooms per dwelling	Families per dwelling	Persons per room
	3.68	6.15	1.11	0.66

Churches 1929			Sittings
Anglican	3		1,260
Catholic	1		450
Nonconformist	6	(Welsh) 1	3,610 (200)

School rolls 1923	
Anglican	1,239
Catholic	0
Board	1,946

Trades Council delegates 1905		WMCA branch
Postmen	(total 1)	1920 ✓
		1931 ✓
		1939 ✓

Summary of municipal election results

Years	Lab. wins	Tory wins	Av. Lab. vote (%)	Av. Tory vote (%)	Av. turnout	NC	Nats. (wins)	Prots. (wins)
1905–9	0	1	—	49	64	2	0	0
1910–13	0	3	18	69	53	2	0	0

Years	Lab. wins	Tory wins	Av. Lab. vote (%)	Av. Tory vote (%)	Av. turnout	NC	Nats. (wins)	Prots. (wins)
1905–13	0	4	18	57	60	4	0	0
1919–23	0	5	—	51	53	3	0	0
1924–28	0	5	—	60	44	3	0	0
1929–33	0	5	29	71	37	4	0	0
1934–38	0	5	23	69	39	2	0	0
1919–38	0	20	25	62	44	12	0	0

Full list of municipal election results

Year	Candidates	Votes	%	Voters	Turnout (%)
1905	W. B. Stoddart (L)	1,137	54	3,484	61
	W. P. Wethred (C)	983	46		
1906	J. Japp (L)	NC	—	3,556	—
1907	J. Morris (L)	1,122	50	3,643	61
	R. G. Layton (C)	1,100	50		
1908	R. G. Layton (C)	1,318	52	3,634	70
	W. B. Stoddart (L)	1,239	48		
1909	J. Japp (L)	NC	—	3,668	—
1910	J. S. Rankin (C)	1,238	55	3,729	61
	J. Morris (L)	1,033	45		
1911[1] (Apr)	A. A. Paton (L)	NC	—	3,729	—
1911	R. G. Layton (C)	1,405	82	3,846	45
	G. Porter (Lab)	312	18		
1912	A. A. Paton (L)	NC	—	3,840	—
1913	J. S. Rankin (C)	NC	—	3,871	—
1914	A. B. Holmes (C)	NC	—	3,933	—
1919	A. Rushton (C)	2,261	53	8,104	53
	J. P. Edwards (L)	1,302	31		
	Mrs A. Billinge (Co-op)	695	16		
1920	M. C. Dixon (C)	NC	—	8,346	—
1921	G. E. Holme (C)	2,170	48	8,569	53
	Mrs J. J. Beavan (L)	1,671	37		
	W. T. Oversby (MCU)	696	15		
1922	A. Rushton (C)	NC	—	8,505	—
1923	M. C. Dixon (C)	NC	—	8,667	—
1924	G. E. Holme (C)	2,662	67	8,905	45
	A. M. Finlason (L)	1,312	33		
1925	A. Rushton (C)	NC	—	8,899	—
1926	M. C. Dixon (C)	NC	—	8,727	—
1927	G. E. Holme (C)	1,941	53	8,688	42

	A. O. Roberts (L)	1,735	47		
1928	A. Rushton (C)	NC	—	8,629	—
1929	M. C. Dixon (C)	2,382	71	9,138	37
	P. L. Duncan (Lab)	967	29		
1930[2]	G. Robertson (C)	1,815	58	9,138	34
(Mar)	A. O. Roberts (L)	934	30		
	F. Stapleton (Lab)	359	12		
1930	G. E. Holme (C)	NC	—	8,946	—
1931	G. Robertson (C)	NC	—	8,969	—
1932	M. C. Dixon (C)	NC	—	8,993	—
1933	G. E. Holme (C)	NC	—	8,917	—
1934	G. W. G. Armour (C)	NC	—	8,892	—
1935	M. C. Dixon (C)	NC	—	8,871	—
1936	E. D. M. Heriot-Hill (C)	2,104	56	8,782	43
	G. E. Holme (Dem. C)	860	23		
	G. Porter (Lab)	793	21		
1937[3]	J. Moores (C)	1,494	85	8,782	20
(Mar)	J. Murphy (Ratep'rs)	274	15		
1937	G. W. G. Armour (C)	2,710	76	8,752	41
	J. H. Higgins (Lab)	848	24		
1938[4]	D. Walker (C)	1,344	76	8,752	20
(May)	Miss M. E. Mee (Lab)	418	24		
1938	J. Moores (C)	2,249	75	8,809	34
	A. Leadbetter (Lab)	761	25		

[1] Death of J. Japp.
[2] Death of A. Rushton.
[3] Election of M. C. Dixon as alderman.
[4] Resignation of E. D. M. Heriot-Hill.

SEFTON PARK WEST (34)

	Population	Electorate	Acreage	Persons/Acre
1911	13,242	2,531	828	16.0
1921	13,326	5,809		16.1
1931	13,226	6,438		16.0

1931	Av. family size	Rooms per dwelling	Families per dwelling	Persons per room
	3.67	6.03	1.08	0.65

Churches 1929			Sittings
Anglican	3		2,030
Catholic	1		470
Nonconformist	1	(Welsh) 0	900

School rolls 1923
Anglican   447
Catholic   141
Board   926

Trades Council delegates 1905   *WMCA branch*
Nil   None

Summary of municipal election results

Years	Lab. wins	Tory wins	Av. Lab. vote (%)	Av. Tory vote (%)	Av. turnout	NC	Nats. (wins)	Prots. (wins)
1905–9	0	3	—	58	66	3	0	0
1910–13	0	1	—	46	68	2	0	0
1905–13	0	4	—	52	67	5	0	0
1919–23	0	1	14	64	55	3	0	0
1924–28	0	5	25	69	53	2	0	0
1929–33	0	5	29	77	44	3	0	0
1934–38	0	5	24	76	48	2	0	0
1919–38	0	16	23	73	50	10	0	0

Full list of municipal election results

Year	Candidates	Votes	%	Voters	Turnout (%)
1905	R. Dart (C)	780	56	2,092	67
	H. G. Crossfield (L)	618	44		
1906	H. R. Rathbone (L)	NC	—	2,307	—
1907	F. Pritchard (C)	949	60	2,467	64
	J. Wilson (L)	630	40		
1908	R. Dart (C)	NC	—	2,520	—
1909[1]	E. C. Given (C)	NC	—	2,520	—
1909	H. R. Rathbone (L)	NC	—	2,481	—
1910	F. Wilson (L)	875	52	2,491	67
	F. Pritchard (C)	800	48		
1911	E. C. Given (C)	NC	—	2,531	—
1912	H. R. Rathbone (L)	NC	—	2,540	—
1913	F. C. Wilson (L)	989	56	2,566	69
	J. D. Flood (C)	774	44		
1914	E. C. Given (C)	NC	—	2,618	—
1919[2] (May)	Miss M. Fletcher (C)	NC	—	5,251	—

1919	H. R. Rathbone (L)	NC	—	5,484	—
1920	F. C. Wilson (L)	2,944	86	5,607	61
	Mrs J. Taylor (Lab)	460	14		
1921	Miss M. Fletcher (C)	1,825	64	5,809	49
	Mrs L. Scaiff (Anti-waste)	518	18		
	A. B. Harper (MCU)	498	18		
1922	H. R. Rathbone (L)	NC	—	5,768	—
1923	F. C. Wilson (Nat. L)	NC	—	5,836	—
1924	Miss M. Fletcher (C)	NC	—	5,944	—
1925	J. G. Reece (C)	2,051	56	6,047	60
	H. R. Rathbone (L)	1,580	44		
1926	F. C. Wilson (C)	NC	—	5,944	—
1927	Miss M. Fletcher (C)	2,093	75	6,025	46
	Mrs G. A. Cole (Lab)	690	25		
1927[3]	R. Clayton (C)	1,955	74	6,025	44
(Dec)	Mrs G. A. Cole (Lab)	675	26		
1928	J. G. Reece (C)	2,375	75	5,948	53
	Mrs G. A. Cole (Lab)	784	25		
1929	R. P. Clayton (C)	2,057	71	6,341	46
	Mrs G. A. Cole (Lab)	830	29		
1930	W. T. Lancashire (C)	2,160	83	6,328	42
	Mrs J. G. Taylor (Co-op)	446	17		
1931	J. G. Reece (C)	NC	—	6,438	—
1932	R. P. Clayton (C)	NC	—	6,435	—
1933	W. T. Lancashire (C)	NC	—	6,453	—
1934	J. G. Reece (C)	NC	—	6,575	—
1935	W. J. Austin (C)	NC	—	6,547	—
1936	W. T. Lancashire (C)	2,426	76	6,713	48
	G. Thompson (Lab)	782	24		
1937	J. G. Reece (C)	2,785	76	6,718	54
	Mrs W. M. Wallbank (Lab)	876	24		
1938	A. M. Finlason (C)	2,255	77	6,839	43
	Miss M. E. Mee (Lab)	684	23		

[1] Election of R. Dart as alderman.
[2] Resignation of E. Given.
[3] Election of F. C. Wilson as alderman.

VAUXHALL (35)

	Population	Electorate	Acreage	Persons/Acre
1911	8,691	1,749	244	35.6
1921	8,247	3,530		33.8
1931	8,635	3,783		35.4

1931	Av. family size	Rooms per dwelling	Families per dwelling	Persons per room
	4.36	4.30	1.24	1.25

Churches 1929		Sittings
Anglican	0	0
Catholic	1	1,500
Nonconformist	1	0

School rolls 1923	
Anglican	408
Catholic	785
Board	0

Trades Council delegates 1905	WMCA branch
Nil	1920 ✓
	1931
	1939

Summary of municipal election results

Years	Lab. wins	Tory wins	Av. Lab. vote (%)	Av. Tory vote (%)	Av. turnout	NC	Nats. (wins)	Prots. (wins)
1905–9	0	0	—	45	66	4	3 (3)	0
1910–13	0	0	—	—	—	4	3 (3)	0
1905–13	0	0	—	45	66	8	6 (6)	0
1919–23	0	0	24	—	43	1	5 (5)	0
1924–28	1	0	26	—	40	2	4 (4)	0
1929–33	2	0	48	—	45	1	5 (3)	0
1934–38	5	0	75	36	37	2	2 (0)	0
1919–38	8	0	45	36	41	6	16 (12)	0

Full list of municipal election results

Year	Candidates	Votes	%	Voters	Turnout (%)
1905	R. R. Meade-King (L)	NC	—	1,797	—
1906	T. Burke (N)	NC	—	1,789	—
1907	J. G. Taggart (N)	NC	—	1,789	—
1908[1]	J. Hughes (N)	574	58	1,789	55
(Sept)	G. M. Davey (C)	413	42		
1908	M. Muspratt (L)	651	55	1,779	66
	G. M. Davey (C)	530	45		
1909	T. Burke (N)	NC	—	1,754	—
1910	J. Hughes (N)	NC	—	1,671	—

Year	Candidate	Votes	%	Total	%
1911	M. Muspratt (L)	NC	—	1,749	—
1912	T. Burke (N)	NC	—	1,630	—
1913	J. Hughes (N)	NC	—	1,662	—
1914	M. Muspratt (L)	NC	—	1,654	—
1919	T. Burke (N)	NC	—	3,484	—
1920	J. O'Hare (N)	1,234	69	3.494	51
	J. Bennion (L)	542	31		
1921	J. Belger (N)	1,313	92	3,530	40
	A. McCabe (L)	115	8		
1922	T. A. Murphy (N)	1,068	73	3,572	41
	M. J. Mulvihill (Lab)	389	27		
1923	Dr P. Hayes (IP)	1,167	79	3,720	40
	J. McChrystal (Lab)	294	20		
	J. W. Veidman (Unemp)	15	1		
1924	J. Belger (IP)	1,200	74	3,821	42
	R. McCann (Lab)	422	26		
1925	T. A. Murphy (Cath)	NC	—	3,848	—
1926	Dr P. H. Hayes (Centre)	949	71	3,756	36
	H. Hayes (Lab)	386	29		
1927	J. Belger (Centre)	1,171	77	3723	41
	P. Duffy (Lab)	349	23		
1928	A. B. Hoer (Lab)	NC	—	3,565	—
1929	Dr P. H. Hayes (Lab)	1,016	57	3,979	45
	J. O' Hare (Centre)	782	43		
1930	J. Belger (Centre)	NC	—	3,816	—
1931	T. A. Murphy (Dem. Lab)	849	57	3,783	39
	A. B. Hoer (Lab)	644	43		
1931[2] (Nov)	S. McBride (Dem. Lab)	771	61	3,783	33
	S. Part (Lab)	486	39		
1932[3] (Jun)	J. O'Hare (Dem. Lab)	801	55	3,783	38
	A. B. Hoer (Lab)	651	45		
1932	A. B. Hoer (Lab)	953	55	3,704	47
	S. McBride (Dem. Lab)	779	45		
1933	J. O'Hare (Ind)	1,044	63	3,581	47
	J. E. Orford (Lab)	622	37		
1934	J. L. Carney (Lab)	1,010	81	3,715	34
	Mrs M. V. Fernie (Ind)	236	19		
1935	A. B. Hoer (Lab)	877	80	3,604	30
	Mrs M. V. Fernie (Ind)	220	20		
1936	T. Hogan (Lab)	1,057	64	3,556	46
	J. A. Bryning (C)	588	36		
1937	J. L. Carney (Lab)	NC	—	3,324	—
1938	A. B. Hoer (Lab)	NC	—	3,123	—

[1] Election of J. G. Taggart as alderman.
[2] Resignation of Dr P. H. Hayes.
[3] Election of J. Belger as alderman.

WALTON (36)

	Population	Electorate	Acreage	Persons/Acre
1911	28,559	5,079	679	42.1
1921	30,785	11,761		45.3
1931	36,510	16,395		53.8

1931	Av. family size	Rooms per dwelling	Families per dwelling	Persons per room
	4.14	4.96	1.07	0.85

Churches 1929			*Sittings*
Anglican	3		2,700
Catholic	3		800
Nonconformist	10	(Welsh) 2	3,505

School rolls 1923	
Anglican	952
Catholic	336
Board	7,151

Trades Council delegates 1905   *WMCA branch*
Nil   None

Summary of municipal election results

Years	Lab. wins	Tory wins	Av. Lab. vote (%)	Av. Tory vote (%)	Av. turnout	NC	Nats. (wins)	Prots. (wins)
1905–9	0	4	—	58	55	3	0	0
1910–13	0	4	30	71	43	0	0	0
1905–13	0	8	30	66	47	3	0	0
1919–23	0	5	36	69	44	2	0	0
1924–28	0	5	44	56	37	2	0	0
1929–33	0	5	39	61	40	0	0	0
1934–38	0	5	33	65	43	0	0	1 (0)
1919–38	0	20	37	63	41	4	0	1 (0)

Full list of municipal election results

Year	Candidates	Votes	%	Voters	Turnout (%)
1905	G. B. Smith-Broderick (C)	1,079	50	4,062	53
	G. Mitchell (L)	1,059	50		

1906	R. Pritchard (C)	1,583	65	4,318	56
	T. Uttley (L)	835	35		
1907	Dr. J. G. Moyles (C)	NC	—	4,449	—
1908	J. McDermott (L)	NC	—	4,499	—
1909	R. Pritchard (C)	NC	—	4,618	—
1910	Dr. J. G. Moyles (C)	1,627	76	4,715	46
	H. D. Large (Soc)	520	24		
1911	S. Gannon (C)	1,089	56	5,079	38
	H. D. Large (Lab)	840	44		
1912	R. Pritchard (C)	1,694	71	5,181	47
	H. D. Large (Lab)	692	29		
1913	J. G. Moyles (C)	1,780	79	5,349	42
	W. Cruickshanks (Lab)	460	21		
1914	J. C. Cross (C)	NC	—	5,537	—
1919	S. A. Kelly (C)	3,177	55	11,292	52
	M. Curtis (Lab)	2,642	45		
1920[1] (Jul)	G. M. Platt (C)	2,504	57	11,292	39
	R. J. McDonnell (Lab)	1,890	43		
1920	G. M. Platt (C)	4,298	74	11,661	50
	R. J. McDonnell (Lab)	1,502	26		
1921	J. C. Cross (C)	NC	—	11,761	—
1922	C. R. Clare (C)	NC	—	12,124	—
1923	G. M. Platt (C)	3,029	78	·12,471	31
	J. E. Freeman (L)	842	22		
1924	J. C. Cross (C)	NC	—	12,734	—
1925	W. Swift (C)	NC	—	13,042	—
1926[2] (Feb)	R. J. Hall (C)	2,223	59	13,042	29
	R. A. Rockliff (Lab)	1,575	41		
1926	G. M. Platt (C)	2,596	56	13,819	33
	T. H. Pye (Lab)	2,009	44		
1927	R. J. Hall (C)	2,868	56	15,312	34
	T. H. Pye (Lab)	2,284	44		
1928	W. Swift (C)	3,845	56	15,283	45
	R. T. Hughes (Lab)	2,977	44		
1929	G. M. Platt (C)	3,638	52	14,437	49
	R. T. Hughes (Lab)	3,411	48		
1930	R. J. Hall (C)	3,776	65	16,119	36
	J. R. Bevins (Lab)	2,026	35		
1931	R. R. Bailey (C)	5,530	75	16,395	45
	W. J. Riddick (Lab)	1,888	25		
1932[3] (Feb)	J. H. Irwin (C)	2,558	62	16,395	25
	W. J. Riddick (Lab)	1,564	38		
1932	G. M. Platt (C)	3,581	58	16,370	38
	W. J. Riddick (Lab)	2,614	42		
1933	R. J. Hall (C)	3,169	57	16,251	34
	J. T. Kenny (Lab)	2,436	43		
1934	R. R. Bailey (C)	3,080	51	16,305	37
	J. T. Kenny (Lab)	2,527	42		
	R. Bradley (P)	431	7		

1935	J H. Irwin (C)	4,374	61	16,460	44
	M. F. Hudson (Lab)	2,852	39		
1936	R. J. Hall (C)	4,581	70	16,541	39
	A. W. Boothman (Lab)	1,946	30		
1937	R. R. Bailey (C)	6,289	72	16,609	53
	R. A. Rockcliff (Lab)	2,442	28		
1938	J. H. Irwin (C)	4,844	73	16,501	40
	C. W. Baker (Lab)	1,786	27		

[1] Election of J. G. Moyles as alderman.
[2] Election of J. C. Cross as alderman.
[3] Election of G. M. Platt as alderman.

WARBRECK (37)

	Population	Electorate	Acreage	Persons/Acre
1911	26,320	4,160	691	38.1
1921	29,522	10,746		42.7
1931	28,267	12,376		40.9

1931	Av. family size	Rooms per dwelling	Families per dwelling	Persons per room
	3.85	5.39	1.08	0.77

Churches 1929			Sittings
Anglican	1		800
Catholic	1		650
Nonconformist	3	(Welsh) 1	1,370 (300)

School rolls 1923	
Anglican	419
Catholic	501
Board	2,640

Trades Council delegates 1905	WMCA branch
Nil	1920 ✓
	1931
	1939

Summary of municipal election results

Years	Lab. wins	Tory wins	Av. Lab. vote (%)	Av. Tory vote (%)	Av. turnout	NC	Nats. (wins)	Prots. (wins)
1905–9	0	3	—	65	53	2	0	0
1910–13	0	2	28	57	48	1	0	0
1905–13	0	5	28	61	51	3	0	0

Years	Lab. wins	Tory wins	Av. Lab. vote (%)	Av. Tory vote (%)	Av. turnout	NC	Nats. (wins)	Prots. (wins)
1919–23	0	4	22	70	39	0	0	0
1924–28	0	4	34	66	37	2	0	0
1929–33	0	5	30	68	38	0	0	0
1934–38	0	5	28	70	35	0	0	0
1919–38	0	18	29	69	37	2	0	0

Full list of municipal election results

Year	Candidates	Votes	%	Voters	Turnout (%)
1905	E. West (L)	957	59	2,828	57
	T. A. Bell (C)	663	41		
1906	R. C. Herman (C)	1,194	65	2,998	62
	R. M. Owen (L)	651	35		
1907	R. Kelly (C)	1,157	89	3,190	41
	J. S. Smith (Ind)	141	11		
1907[1] (Nov)	S. E. Davies (C)	1,103	67	3,190	52
	W. Holgate (L)	553	33		
1908	E. West (L)	NC	—	3,332	—
1909	R. C. Herman (C)	NC	—	3,559	—
1910	T. Fleming (L)	978	54	3,792	48
	S. E. Davies (C)	850	46		
1911	E. West (L)	NC	—	4,160	—
1912	R. C. Herman (C)	1,436	72	4,183	47
	J. Lowry (Lab)	549	28		
1913	J. A. Thompson (C)	1,114	52	4,327	50
	T. Fleming (L)	1,029	48		
1914	E. West (L)	NC	—	4,631	—
1919	R. C. Herman (C)	2,588	61	10,391	41
	Mrs A. Blair (Co-op)	1,674	39		
1920	J. A. Thompson (C)	3,540	78	10,521	43
	Mrs Daniels (Co-op)	982	22		
1921	E. West (Co. L)	3,811	78	10,746	46
	J. H. Mawdsley (Lab)	1,082	22		
1922	J. B. Herman (C)	2,856	79	10,902	33
	F. Fitzpatrick (Lab)	745	21		
1923	J. A. Thompson (C)	2,287	61	10,965	34
	W. Pritchard (L)	1,467	39		
1924	E. West (L)	NC	—	11,152	—
1925	A. Critchley (C)	3,515	68	11,430	45
	F. Lavery (Lab)	1,673	32		
1926[2] (Feb)	J. Jude (C)	2,019	59	11,430	30
	F. Lavery (Lab)	1,394	41		

1926	J. Jude (C)	2,348	60	11,450	34
	F. Lavery (Lab)	1,567	40		
1927[3]	J. Hill (C)	2,165	68	11,450	28
(Mar)	F. Lavery (Lab)	1,023	32		
1927	J. Hill (C)	2,494	70	11,572	31
	J. Fraser (Lab)	1,094	30		
1928	A. Critchley (C)	NC	—	11,543	—
1929	J. Jude (C)	2,536	49	12,425	41
	J. C. Branson (Lab)	2,139	42		
	S. F. Heape (L)	454	9		
1930	J. Hill (C)	3,299	70	12,415	38
	J. F. Kitchen (Co-op)	1,392	30		
1931	A. Critchley (C)	4,504	84	12,376	44
	E. A. Rockliff (Lab)	883	16		
1932	J. Jude (C)	2,847	66	12,409	35
	W. Bent (Lab)	1,460	34		
1933	H. Wagstaff (C)	2,706	71	12,527	30
	E. J. McCartney (Lab)	1,083	29		
1934	A. Critchley (C)	2,585	69	12,539	30
	A. Mutton (Lab)	1,140	31		
1935	J. Jude (C)	3,003	63	13,188	36
	A. Smitton (Lab)	1,470	31		
	W. Fry (Ind)	264	6		
1936	H. Wagstaff (C)	3,350	74	13,219	34
	A. Rainford (Lab)	956	21		
	W. Fry (Ind)	213	5		
1937	A. Critchley (C)	4,251	71	13,336	45
	W. Bent (Lab)	1,778	29		
1938	J. Jude (C)	2,986	73	13,363	31
	C. McDonald (Lab)	1,128	27		

[1] Election of R. Kelly as alderman.
[2] Death of J. A. Thompson.
[3] Election of E. West as alderman.

WAVERTREE (38)

	Population	Electorate	Acreage	Persons/Acre
1911	23,750	3,966	1,076	22.1
1921	23,927	9,456		22.2
1931	30,702	14,576		28.5

1931	Av. family size	Rooms per dwelling	Families per dwelling	Persons per room
	3.86	5.60	1.04	0.71

Churches 1929		Sittings
Anglican	3	2,100
Catholic	2	850
Nonconformist	7 (Welsh) 1	4,605 (750)

School rolls 1923	
Anglican	1,318
Catholic	371
Board	2,054

Trades Council delegates 1905	WMCA branch
Nil	1920 ✓
	1931
	1939

Summary of municipal election results

Years	Lab. wins	Tory wins	Av. Lab. vote (%)	Av. Tory vote (%)	Av. turnout	NC	Nats. (wins)	Prots. (wins)
1905–9	0	3	—	50	61	0	0	0
1910–13	0	3	—	55	53	3	0	0
1905–13	0	6	—	51	60	3	0	0
1919–23	0	4	29	53	51	0	0	0
1924–28	0	4	33	55	40	0	0	0
1929–33	0	5	33	67	39	1	0	0
1934–38	0	5	29	72	37	1	0	0
1919–38	0	18	31	62	42	2	0	0

Full list of municipal election results

Year	Candidates	Votes	%	Voters	Turnout (%)
1905	C. C. Morrison (L)	907	63	2,323	62
	J. Sewart (C)	543	37		
1906	A. Crosthwaite (C)	805	58	2,479	56
	T. P. Maguire (L)	586	42		
1907	R. S. Porter (C)	884	54	2,629	62
	J. Kellitt (L)	752	46		
1908	C. C. Morrison (L)	960	53	2,958	62
	G. B. Smith-Broderick (C)	864	47		
1909	G. Bowler (C)	1,117	54	3,313	63
	W. B. Stoddart (L)	959	46		
1910	R. S. Porter (C)	1,040	55	3,593	53
	H. T. Ellis (L)	865	45		

1911	C. C. Morrison (L)	NC	—	3,966	—
1912	G. Bowler (C)	NC	—	4,214	—
1913	R. S. Porter (C)	NC	—	4,162	—
1914	C. C. Morrison (L)	NC	—	4,328	—
1919	P. Gill (C)	2,305	54	9,065	47
	A. E. Johns (Lab)	1,955	46		
1920	H. L. Beckwith (C)	3,793	68	9,456	59
	R. Tissyman (Lab)	1,795	32		
1921	J. M. Griffith (Co. L)	2,073	43	9,456	51
	H. Frame (L)	1,491	31		
	G. H. Boothman (Lab)	1,265	26		
1922[1]	A. Angers (C)	1,785	68	9,456	28
(Apr)	G. H. Boothman (Lab)	846	32		
1922	A. Angers (C)	2,228	43	9,707	53
	C. S. Jones (L)	2,070	40		
	G. Boothman (Lab)	885	17		
1923	H. L. Beckwith (C)	2,184	47	10,314	45
	H. Frame (L)	1,318	29		
	R. Tissyman (Lab)	1,110	24		
1924	J. M. Griffith (L)	2,556	67	11,070	35
	A. C. Crosby (Lab)	1,287	33		
1925	A. Angers (C)	2,860	50	11,603	50
	W. S. Dytor (Lab)	1,598	28		
	E. E. Edwards (L)	1,318	22		
1926	H. L. Beckwith (C)	2,495	63	12,100	33
	W. S. Dytor (Lab)	1,466	37		
1927	J. M. Griffith (C)	2,728	62	12,737	35
	W. S. Dytor (Lab)	1,700	38		
1928	H. Shuttleworth (C)	2,852	44	13,247	48
	P. L. Duncan (Lab)	1,823	28		
	J. R. Jones (L)	1,737	27		
1929[2]	J. G. Elliott (Lab)	1,655	34	13,247	36
(Apr)	H. G. Nash (C)	1,607	33		
	J. R. Hobhouse (L)	1,537	32		
1929	A. E. Martin (C)	3,248	54	14,314	42
	J. G. Elliott (Lab)	2,717	46		
1930	J. M. Griffith (C)	3,525	69	14,333	36
	J. G. Elliott (Lab)	1,582	31		
1931	J. Village (C)	4,767	77	14,576	42
	J. R. Bevins (Lab)	1,396	23		
1931[3]	F. Redmond (C)	NC	—	14,576	—
(Dec)					
1932	F. Redmond (C)	3,583	68	14,857	36
	J. R. Bevins (Lab)	1,701	32		
1933	J. M. Griffith (C)	NC	—	15,080	—
1934	J. Village (C)	3,232	73	15,209	29
	D. H. James (ILP)	1,184	27		
1935	S. R. Williams (C)	4,337	64	15,480	44
	J. G. Elliott (Lab)	2,445	36		

1936	J. M. Griffith (C)	4,184	75	15,498	36
	D. Whelan (Lab)	1,421	25		
1937	J. Village (C)	NC	—	16,252	—
1938 [4]	H. T. Wilson (C)	2,969	96	16,252	19
(Jan)	E. Edwards (Fasc)	132	4		
1938	S. R. Williams (C)	4,243	74	15,491	37
	D. Mackay (Lab)	1,475	26		

[1] Death of P. Gill.
[2] Election H. L. Beckwith as alderman.
[3] Death of A. E. Martin.
[4] Election of J. M. Griffith as alderman.

WAVERTREE WEST (39)

	Population	Electorate	Acreage	Persons/Acre
1911	18,852	3,673	308	61.2
1921	20,618	8,213		66.9
1931	18,881	8,906		61.3

1931	Av. family size	Rooms per dwelling	Families per dwelling	Persons per room
	3.84	5.31	1.07	0.78

Churches 1929			Sittings
Anglican	1		850
Catholic	0		0
Nonconformist	3	(Welsh) 0	1,450

School rolls 1923	
Anglican	515
Catholic	856
Board	1,734

Trades Council delegates 1905		WMCA branch
Bricklayers		1920 ✓
Carpenters (2)		1931 ✓
Coachmakers	(total 5)	1939 ✓
Shipwrights		

Summary of municipal election results

Years	Lab. wins	Tory wins	Av. Lab. vote (%)	Av. Tory vote (%)	Av. turnout	NC	Nats. (wins)	Prots. (wins)
1905–9	0	4	—	52	59	0	0	0
1910–13	0	3	37	51	58	0	0	0

Years	Lab. wins	Tory wins	Av. Lab. vote (%)	Av. Tory vote (%)	Av. turnout	NC	Nats. (wins)	Prots. (wins)
1905–13	0	7	37	51	58	0	0	0
1919–23	1	4	34	55	52	0	1 (0)	0
1924–28	2	3	37	43	53	0	0	0
1929–33	1	4	40	53	48	0	0	0
1934–38	0	5	37	62	44	0	0	0
1919–38	4	16	37	53	49	0	1 (0)	0

Full list of municipal election results

Year	Candidates	Votes	%	Voters	Turnout (%)
1905	W. B. Jones (L)	1,167	55	3,496	60
	J. W. Alsop (C)	938	45		
1906	H. P. Reynolds (C)	1,065	54	3,558	55
	G. R. Searle (L)	890	46		
1907	J. M. Hargreaves (C)	1,188	55	3,552	61
	C. H. Brunner (L)	971	45		
1908	E. G. Jackson (C)	1,175	55	3,475	62
	W. B. Jones (L)	971	45		
1909	H. P. Reynolds (C)	987	51	3,465	56
	C. H. Brunner (L)	960	49		
1910	C. H. Brunner (L)	1,119	55	3,503	58
	H. Davies (C)	909	45		
1911	E. G. Jackson (C)	1,214	56	3,673	60
	W. A. Colcutt (Lab)	972	44		
1912	A. Parsons (C)	1,136	57	3,673	54
	W. A. Colcutt (Lab)	854	43		
1913	E. Haigh (C)	988	44	3,726	60
	C. Brunner (L)	726	33		
	J. Cleary (Lab)	513	23		
1914	D. B. Seaman (C)	NC	—	3,847	—
1919	W. A. Colcutt (Lab)	1,856	50	7,633	48
	J. Glynn (C)	1,837	50		
1920	E. Haigh (C)	3,303	67	8,040	61
	A. E. Johns (Lab)	1,612	33		
1921	S. S. Dawson (C)	2,967	67	8,213	54
	C. M. Belk (Lab)	1,470	33		
1922	J. G. Legge (C)	2,067	46	9,239	49
	W. A. Colcutt (Lab)	1,170	26		
	J. R. Hobhouse (L)	1,149	25		
	B. McGinnity (N)	134	3		
1923[1] (May)	J. R. Hobhouse (L)	1,490	40	9,239	40
	E. P. Parker (C)	1,270	34		
	W. A. Colcutt (Lab)	934	26		

Year	Candidate				
1923	E. Haigh (C)	1,915	45	8,396	50
	A. M. Finlason (L)	1,193	28		
	C. M. Belk (Lab)	1,129	27		
1924	C. H. Barker (C)	2,095	47	8,525	52
	H. E. Rose (Lab)	1,365	31		
	J. R. Hobhouse (L)	1,009	22		
1925	W. M. Paul (C)	2,414	57	8,555	49
	H. E. Rose (Lab)	1,794	43		
1926	E. Haigh (C)	1,697	44	8,499	45
	F. Stapleton (Lab)	1,085	28		
	J. R. Hobhouse (L)	1,043	28		
1927	E. Whiteley (Lab)	1,856	40	8,402	56
	C. H. Barker (C)	1,509	32		
	J. R. Hobhouse (L)	1,313	28		
1928	C. M. Belk (Lab)	2,097	42	8,235	61
	W. A. Edwards (C)	1,782	36		
	W. J. Tristram (L)	1,136	22		
1928[2] (Dec)	Mrs C. Whiteley (Lab)	1,571	43	8,235	44
	W. A. Edwards (C)	1,395	39		
	W. J. Tristram (L)	647	18		
1929	Mrs C. Whiteley (Lab)	2,389	52	8,901	51
	Miss M. J. Haigh (C)	2,186	48		
1930	A. Levy (C)	2,243	47	8,973	53
	E. Whiteley (Lab)	1,970	41		
	W. H. Shepherd (L)	580	12		
1931	N. J. Price (C)	2,936	67	8,906	49
	C. M. Belk (Lab)	1,444	33		
1932	C. Thompson (C)	2,141	53	8,898	46
	C. M. Belk (Lab)	1,000	25		
	Mrs C. Whiteley (Ind)	929	22		
1933	A. Levy (C)	1,787	52	8,786	39
	W. J. Riddick (Lab)	1,647	48		
1934	N. J. Price (C)	1,766	56	8,813	36
	Mrs S. A. McArd (Lab)	1,376	44		
1935	C. Thompson (C)	2,152	59	8,833	41
	D. Whelan (Lab)	1,508	41		
1936	A. Levy (C)	2,433	61	8,788	45
	T. Williamson (Lab)	1,548	39		
1937[3] (Jan)	D. Walker (C)	1,598	58	8,788	31
	R. E. Cottier (Lab)	783	29		
	T. J. A. Duggan (L)	363	13		
1937	M. Voss (C)	3,129	67	8,681	54
	D. Whelan (Lab)	1,436	31		
	W. Edwards (Fasc)	129	2		
1938	H. Lees (C)	2,485	68	8,624	43
	F. Stapleton (Lab)	1,195	32		

[1] Resignation S. S. Dawson.
[2] Election of E. Haigh as alderman.
[3] Resignation of C. Thompson.

WEST DERBY (40)

	Population	Electorate	Acreage	Persons/Acre
1911	19,571	3,512	1,329	14.7
1921	24,188	9,282		18.2
1931	41,855	18,498		31.5

1931	Av. family size	Rooms per dwelling	Families per dwelling	Persons per room
	4.20	5.39	1.07	0.83

Churches 1929			Sittings
Anglican	1		1,000
Catholic	0		0
Nonconformist	2	(Welsh) 0	880

School rolls 1923
Anglican	1,325
Catholic	559
Board	2,628

Trades Council delegates 1905   WMCA branch
Nil   None

Summary of municipal election results

Years	Lab. wins	Tory wins	Av. Lab. vote (%)	Av. Tory vote (%)	Av. turnout	NC	Nats. (wins)	Prots. (wins)
1905–9	0	4	—	58	64	1	0	0
1910–13	0	4	23	69	48	1	0	0
1905–13	0	8	23	62	57	2	0	0
1919–23	1	4	29	62	51	0	1 (0)	0
1924–28	0	5	32	62	42	0	0	0
1929–33	0	5	37	63	35	2	0	0
1934–38	0	5	31	69	38	1	0	0
1919–38	1	19	32	64	42	3	1 (0)	0

Full list of municipal election results

Year	Candidates	Votes	%	Voters	Turnout (%)
1905	S. Skelton (L)	966	57	2,742	62
	S. S. Dawson (C)	741	43		
1906	W. H. Parkinson (C)	1,208	66	2,847	64

	T. Shaw (L)	624	34		
1907	R. E. W. Stephenson (C)	1,182	66	2,917	62
	Miss E. Robinson (L)	620	34		
1908	W. J. Bailes (C)	1,103	56	3,029	66
	S. Skelton (L)	882	44		
1909	W. H. Parkinson (C)	NC	—	3,149	—
1910	R. E. W. Stephenson (C)	1,066	63	3,295	51
	C. Freeman (L)	616	37		
1911[1] (May)	T. Ithell (C)	600	56	3,295	32
	T. Utley (Ind)	463	44		
1911	W. J. Bailes (C)	1,114	77	3,512	41
	J. Murphy (Lab)	327	23		
1912	W. H. Parkinson (C)	NC	—	3,571	—
1913	E. H. Cooke (C)	1,310	66	3,758	53
	A. E. Faulkner (L)	673	34		
1914	W. J. Bailes (C)	NC	—	3,937	—
1919	W. P. Helm (Lab)	1,542	41	8,376	45
	A. J. Muskett (C)	1,294	34		
	T. Utley (Ind)	959	25		
1920	F. W. Riley (C)	3,755	71	8,928	59
	J. Smith (Lab)	1,550	29		
1921	W. J. Bailes (C)	3,468	72	9,282	52
	C. H. Taunton (Lab)	1,327	28		
1922[2] (Apr)	W. J. L. Croft (C)	2,185	70	9,282	34
	C. H. Taunton (Lab)	952	30		
1922	R. D. French (C)	3,950	72	10,754	51
	W. P. Helm (Lab)	1,489	27		
	J. P. Farrelly (N)	77	1		
1923	F. W. Riley (C)	3,953	63	12,909	49
	H. A. Crick (Lab)	1,270	20		
	S. Skelton (L)	1,078	17		
1924	J. H. Dovener (C)	4,079	64	13,800	46
	G. H. Boothman (Lab)	1,285	20		
	S. Skelton (L)	1,015	16		
1925	R. D. French (C)	4,451	60	14,321	52
	G. H. Boothman (Lab)	1,964	26		
	S. Skelton (L)	1,015	14		
1926	W. H. Young (C)	3,165	62	14,607	35
	G. H. Boothman (Lab)	1,904	38		
1927	J. H. Dovener (C)	3,304	61	15,837	34
	G. H. Boothman (Lab)	2,094	39		
1928	R. D. French (C)	4,182	61	16,297	42
	J. Blundell (Lab)	2,646	39		
1929[3] (Jan)	J. R. Dovener (C)	2,229	58	16,297	24
	J. Sheehan (Lab)	1,605	42		
1929	A. Morrow (C)	3,504	54	17,673	36
	F. J. Colson (Lab)	2,928	46		
1930	E. A. Cookson (C)	4,339	71	18,299	33
	W. D. Jones (Lab)	1,747	29		

1931	R. D. French (C)	NC	—	18,498	—
1932	A. Morrow (C)	4,176	64	18,628	35
	J. Hamilton (Lab)	2,322	36		
1933	E. A. Cookson (C)	NC	—	18,853	—
1934	R. D. French (C)	3,853	66	18,854	31
	L. W. Kennan (Lab)	2,006	34		
1935	A. Morrow (C)	4,777	64	19,521	38
	Miss M. Kennedy (Lab)	2,671	36		
1936	E. A. Cookson (C)	5,360	75	20,446	35
	Miss M. Kennedy (Lab)	1,782	25		
1937	R. D. French (C)	6,869	71	20,686	47
	J. H. Sayle (Lab)	2,810	29		
1938[4] (Jul)	C. M. Wingrove (C)	NC	—	20,686	—
1938	A. Morrow (C)	NC	—	20,742	—

[1] Election of R. E. W. Stephenson as alderman.
[2] Death of W. J. Bailes.
[3] Death of J. H. Dovener.
[4] Election of R. D. French as alderman.

APPENDIX V Estimated votes in uncontested seats, 1919–1938

The following formula has been applied to the raw voting figures. In each case where the Labour or Tory candidate was unopposed, a hypothetical vote for the winner has been calculated based on (i) the average of the share of the vote won by the winners on the last previous, and the next subsequent, occasion when the seat was contested; (ii) the average of the turnout in the last and next contested elections; (iii) the size of the electorate in the ward in the uncontested year. That hypothetical vote has then been added to the total votes won by each party in the relevant year. A similar formula based on the previous and next contested elections has been used to estimate the total vote expected in each uncontested election, and these estimates have been added to the total votes cast in the relevant year. New, hypothetical, estimates of the proportion of the total vote won by each of the two main parties can then be calculated which compensate each party for its uncontested winners.

An example will suffice to illustrate the formula more clearly. For Prince's Park in 1922, an estimated 3,263 votes would have been cast for the Conservative Party out of a total poll of 4,662 votes, calculated in the following way:

a)   Last previous election (1920) – Conservative vote 76%
b)   Next subsequent election (1925) – Conservative vote 64%
c)   Average of (a) and (b) = 70%
d)   1920 – turnout 56%
e)   1925 – turnout 54%
f)   Average of (d) and (e) = 55%
g)   Voters on electoral register in 1922 – 8,477
h)   Total estimated vote in 1922 – 55% of 8,477 = 4,662
i)   Total estimated Conservative vote in 1922 – 70% of 4,662 = 3,263

The only exceptions to this formula were where uncontested elections took place near the beginning or end of the inter-war period, and therefore the last previous election was before 1914 or the next subsequent one after 1945. In these cases only the nearest inter-war election was used to calculate the hypothetical votes, as the dislocation of war would clearly make comparisons dubious.

The effect of applying this formula is shown in the following table:

Labour and Conservative share of votes won, adjusted for non-contests, 1919–1938

Year	Actual Lab votes won	%	Actual Con votes won	%	Total votes cast	No contests Lab Con	Added Lab votes	Added Con votes	Added total votes	Adjusted Lab votes won	%	Adjusted Con votes won	%
1919	34,265	36	43,422	46	94,858	0 2	—	2,616	3,938	34,265	35	46,038	47
1920	32,125	25	63,813	50	126,849	0 6	—	9,434	15,827	32,125	23	73,247	51
1921	32,927	27	54,586	45	120,381	0 3	—	7,136	11,697	32,927	25	61,722	47
1922	33,112	29	50,270	43	115,609	0 8	—	15,114	22,519	33,112	24	65,384	47
1923	26,127	25	40,321	39	102,774	0 9	—	23,207	34,412	26,127	19	63,528	46
1924	46,686	39	52,070	43	119,706	0 6	—	12,662	19,389	46,686	34	64,732	47
1925	48,153	36	62,018	46	134,293	0 4	—	7,777	12,429	48,153	33	69,795	48
1926	53,991	45	49,282	41	120,227	0 4	—	7,754	12,067	53,991	41	57,036	43
1927	63,420	44	56,208	44	142,948	0 1	—	2,515	3,699	63,420	43	58,723	40
1928	60,837	47	57,993	45	130,106	6 5	12,476	7,466	31,703	73,313	45	65,459	40
1929	85,206	52	68,317	42	164,219	0 1	—	797	1,226	85,206	52	69,114	42
1930	48,126	35	66,860	48	138,543	1 1	3,148	2,290	7,281	51,274	35	69,150	47
1931	48,104	35	75,426	55	137,368	2 6	4,781	12,120	24,545	52,885	33	87,546	54
1932	66,732	46	57,097	39	144,830	1 4	2,530	6,725	12,319	69,262	44	63,822	41
1933	50,903	47	44,976	41	109,049	4 5	12,347	13,660	37,453	63,250	43	58,636	40
1934	51,210	43	54,893	46	119,311	5 3	14,765	5,083	23,303	65,975	46	59,976	42
1935	67,834	48	63,229	44	142,678	3 3	10,716	5,280	21,026	78,550	48	68,509	42
1936	57,089	39	73,609	50	146,220	5 0	14,634	—	16,223	71,723	44	73,609	45
1937	63,886	37	98,219	57	173,475	5 2	12,106	5,129	21,041	75,992	39	103,348	53
1938	40,957	36	65,689	58	113,491	8 4	22,353	14,962	50,799	63,310	39	80,651	49

APPENDIX VI Strength of Labour support in wards, by quinquennium, 1919–1938 (ranked in descending order)

	1919–1923				1924–1928		
Ward	Lab Votes	Total Votes*	Lab %	Ward	Lab Votes	Total Votes*	Lab %
1. Everton	14,663	30,001	48.9	1. Brunswick	9,770	12,896	75.8
2. Scotland N	4,294	9,205	46.6	2. Croxteth	1,935	3,092	62.6
3. Scotland S	6,765	14,757	45.8	3. Everton	20,637	33,619	61.4
4. Edge Hill	12,863	30,007	42.9	4. Sandhills	9,324	16,157	57.7
5. Garston	7,322	17,449	42.0	5. Edge Hill	16,774	29,851	56.2
6. Dingle	15,389	38,159	40.3	6. Low Hill	13,907	25,483	54.6
7. St Anne's	2,588	6,449	40.1	7. St Anne's	8,196	15,139	54.1
8. Kensington	10,931	27,829	39.3	8. Scotland N	9,407	17,720	53.1
9 St Domingo	3,108	8,107	38.3	9. Netherfield	13,233	28,743	46.0
10. St Peter's	451	1,194	37.8	10. Dingle	19,724	43,287	45.6
11. Much Woolton	913	2,445	37.3	11. Gt George	2,642	5,859	45.1
12. Low Hill	9,384	25,233	37.2	12. Kensington	12,532	27,996	44.8
13. Fazakerley	1,456	3,928	37.1	13. Scotland S	7,515	16,800	44.7
14. Walton	4,144	11,619	35.7	14. Garston	8,692	19,565	44.4
15. Old Swan	9,237	25,954	35.6	15. Kirkdale	11,803	26,669	44.3
16. Wavertree W	7,237	21,802	33.2	16. Breckfield	9,683	21,960	44.1
17. Breckfield	6,585	19,843	33.2	17. Walton	7,270	16,579	43.9
18. Kirkdale	8,967	27,087	33.1	18. St Domingo	10,274	23,501	43.7
19. Childwall	464	1,434	32.4	19. Granby	7,430	17,887	41.5
20. Brunswick	2,325	7,261	32.0	20. Old Swan	9,789	24,204	40.4
21. Prince's Park	2,446	8,272	29.6	21. Prince's Park	7,391	18,671	39.6
22. Wavertree	7,010	24,472	28.6	22. Abercromby	2,537	6,513	39.0
23. West Derby	7,178	25,712	27.9	23. Fazakerley	3,066	7,933	38.6
24. Vauxhall	683	2,933	23.3	24. St Peter's	997	2,601	38.3
25. Anfield	5,292	23,298	22.7	25. Wavertree W	8,197	22,195	36.9
26. Warbreck	1,827	8,494	21.5	26. Childwall	1,746	4,992	35.0
27. Netherfield	3,899	20,385	19.1	27. Warbreck	4,334	12,691	34.2
28. Gt George	322	1,909	16.9	28. Fairfield	5,899	17,697	33.3
29. Sefton Park W	460	3,404	13.5	29. Wavertree	7,874	24,420	32.2
30. Sandhills	353	3,194	11.1	30. West Derby	9,893	31,104	31.8
31. Abercromby	No candidates			31. Much Woolton	879	2,947	29.8
Aigburth	No candidates			32. Vauxhall	1,157	4,477	25.8
Allerton	No candidates			33. Sefton Park W	1,474	5,942	24.8
Castle St	No candidates			34. Allerton	1,222	5,266	23.2
Exchange	No candidates			35. Anfield	5,531	25,177	22.0
Fairfield	No candidates			36. Exchange	337	1,956	17.2
Granby	No candidates			37. Little Woolton	16	267	6.0
Little Woolton	No candidates			38. Aigburth	No candidates		
Sefton Park E	No candidates			Castle St	No candidates		
				Sefton Park E	No candidates		
Total	158,556	451,836	35.1	Total	273,087	621,856	43.9

*   These columns include all votes cast in contests where Labour stood candidates, but excludes contests where Labour did not stand.

	1929–1933				1934–1938		
Ward	Lab Votes	Total Votes*	Lab %	Ward	Lab Votes	Total Votes*	Lab %
1. Scotland N	13,150	14,761	89.1	1. Brunswick		No opponents	
2. Sandhills	9,164	10,544	86.9	2. Sandhills		No opponents	
3. Brunswick	13,331	16,419	81.2	3. Scotland S	6,244	6,544	95.4
4. St Anne's	8,087	10,365	78.0	4. Scotland N	2,870	3,335	86.1
5. Scotland S	4,914	7,231	68.0	5. St Anne's	2,425	3,075	78.9
6. Everton	17,157	29,300	58.6	6. Vauxhall	2,944	3,988	73.8
7. Croxteth	13,803	24,665	56.0	7. Everton	15,020	21,866	68.7
8. Gt George	4,527	8,230	55.0	8. Croxteth	11,561	18,536	62.4
9. Garston	11,470	21,390	53.6	9. Gt George	5,940	9,759	60.9
10. Low Hill	11,312	21,971	51.5	10. Garston	12,410	23,304	53.3
11. Vauxhall	3,235	6,689	48.4	11. Edge Hill	14,897	28,709	51.9
12. Edge Hill	12,701	26,691	47.6	12. Abercromby	10,818	21,345	50.7
13. Dingle	19,701	42,419	46.4	13. Granby	10,508	21,066	49.9
14. Old Swan	13,545	31,477	43.0	14. Dingle	20,109	41,088	48.9
15. Fazakerley	9,029	21,805	41.4	15. Low Hill	12,901	26,423	48.8
16. Breckfield	8,857	21,489	41.2	16. Kirkdale	18,754	40,281	46.6
17. Netherfield	13,806	33,836	40.8	17. St Peter's	2,245	5,202	43.2
18. Wavertree W	8,450	21,252	39.8	18. Prince's Park	10,127	24,014	42.2
19. Kensington	9,843	24,811	39.7	19. Old Swan	15,134	35,963	42.1
20. Prince's Park	8,519	21,646	39.4	20. Fazakerley	10,786	26,182	41.2
21. Kirkdale	15,680	39,977	39.2	21. Netherfield	10,993	29,783	36.9
22. Walton	12,375	32,069	38.6	22. Wavertree W	7,063	19,157	36.9
23. Granby	4,046	10,621	38.1	23. Fairfield	7,030	19,288	36.4
24. West Derby	6,997	19,016	36.8	24. Kensington	8,314	23,221	35.8
25. Abercromby	5,853	16,178	36.2	25. Breckfield	7,382	21,812	33.8
26. Wavertree	7,396	22,519	32.8	26. Walton	11,553	35,152	32.9
27. Fairfield	5,187	16,202	32.0	27. St Domingo	7,628	23,413	32.6
28. Warbreck	5,565	18,612	29.9	28. Exchange	1,042	3,295	31.6
29. St Peter's	1,805	6,225	29.0	29. West Derby	9,269	30,128	30.8
30. Sefton Park E	967	3,349	28.9	30. Anfield	2,755	9,178	30.0
31. Sefton Park W	830	2,887	28.7	31. Wavertree	5,341	18,105	29.5
32. St Domingo	7,824	28,180	27.8	32. Warbreck	6,472	23,124	28.0
33. Aigburth	1,729	7,021	24.6	33. Allerton	3,091	12,845	24.1
34. Anfield	2,870	12,177	23.6	34. Sefton Park W	2,342	9,808	23.9
35. Allerton	1,343	5,900	22.8	35. Sefton Park E	2,402	10,325	23.3
36. Much Woolton	1,481	6,952	21.3	36. Much Woolton	1,416	6,799	20.8
37. Exchange	924	4,542	20.3	37. Childwall	1,121	9,013	12.4
38. Childwall	737	5,507	13.4	38. Little Woolton	69	565	12.2
39. Castle St.		No candidates		39. Aigburth		No candidates	
Little Woolton		No candidates		Castle St.		No candidates	
Total	298,210	674,925	44.2	Total	280,976	665,691	42.2

(a) Chronological list of aldermanic elections 1919–1938

Approx. date	New alderman	Year of election	Old alderman	Ward
Nov 1919	F. T. Richardson (Lab)	1914	?	Everton
	W. A. Robinson (Lab)	1911	?	Fazakerley
Nov 1920	J. H. Jones (L)	1903	W. Evans (L)	Exchange
Jul 1920	J. G. Moyles (C)	1902	R. S. Porter (C)	Wavertree
Dec 1920	C. H. Rutherford (C)	1910	W. Roberts (C)	Walton
Aug 1921	J. G. Paris (C)	1904	J. W. Alsop (C)	Sefton Park E
Nov 1921	T. Burke (N)	1899	G. J. Lynskey (N)	Vauxhall
	M. Muspratt (C)	1908	Heald (C)	Much Woolton
Feb 1922	R. C. Herman (C)	1906	S. Jude (C)	Wavertree W
May 1922	J. Gordon (C)	1908	E. H. Cookson (C)	Dingle
Nov 1922	R. R. Burns (C)	1920	F. J. Rawlinson (C)	Old Swan
Feb 1923	J. Edwards (C)	1908	R. Dart (C)	Fairfield
Mar 1923	T. Dowd (C)	1908	J. R. Grant (C)	Warbreck
Apr 1924	H. E. Davies (C)	1911	F. T. Richardson (Lab)	Everton
	J. R. Grant (C)	1890	L. S. Cohen (C)	Kensington
Jul 1924	J. Bolger (IP)	1908	W. H. Watts (L)	St Anne's
Nov 1924	H. M. Miller (C)	1912	A. S. Mather (C)	Allerton
	H. A. Cole (C)	1912	W. Boote (C)	Prince's Park
Jun 1925	A. E. Jacob (C)	1920	J. H. Jones (L)	Exchange
Aug 1925	J. Clancy (IP)	1911 (Sep)	J. G. Taggart (N)	Gt George
Aug 1925	H. Rathbone (L)	1900	E. J. Chevalier (C)	Aigburth
Nov 1925	P. J. Kelly (Cath)	1914 (Jul)	W. A. Robinson (Lab)	Fazakerley
Feb. 1926	J. C. Cross (C)	1914	A. Crosthwaite (C)	Anfield
Mar 1927	E. West (L)	1905	H. Banner (C)	Breckfield
Oct 1927	L. Hogan (Lab)	1921	J. Lea (L)	St Domingo
	F. C. Wilson (C)	1910	J. Utting (C)	Granby
Nov 1928	R. Rutherford (C)	1926	H. E. Davies (C)	Everton
Nov 1928	E. Haigh (C)	1913	W. B. Forwood (C)	St Peter's
	H. E. Davies (C)	1911	J. R. Grant (C)	Kensington
? 1929	E. Thompson (C)	1919	A. Salvidge (C)	Abercromby
	J. Ashworth (C)	1920	J. Edwards (C)	Fairfield
	H. L. Beckwith (C)	1920	W. J. Burgess (C)	Garston
Sep 1929	J. D. Flood (C)	1920	A. E. Jacob (C)	Exchange
Oct 1929	W. W. Kelly (C)	1919	E. West (C)	Breckfield
Nov 1929	C. Wilson (Lab)	1925	J. W. Walker (C)	Edge Hill
	J. Sexton (Lab)	1905	F. C. Wilson (C)	Granby
	W. A. Robinson (Lab)	1926	R. Rutherford (C)	Everton
	R. Rutherford (C)	1926	H. Wilson (C)	Low Hill
Dec 1929	F. T. Richardson (Lab)	1926	A. S. Mather (C)	Childwall
	H. Walker (Lab)	1919	R. C. Herman (C)	Wavertree W
	T. W. Byrne (Lab)	1912 (May)	Hutchinson (C)	Kirkdale
	D. G. Logan (Lab)	1924 (Jul)	None	Croxteth
Apr 1930	Miss M. Fletcher (C)	1919	C. H. Rutherford (C)	Walton
Oct 1930	M. Muspratt (C)	1908	H. R. Rathbone (C)	Aigburth
	B. W. Eills (L)	1901	M. Muspratt (C)	Much Woolton
Jan 1931	H. E. Rose (Lab)	1926	T. W. Byrne (Lab)	Kirkdale

Apr 1931	F. C. Wilson (C)	1929	J. Gordon (C)	Dingle
May 1931	H. J. Davis (C)	1929	J. G. Moyles (C)	Wavertree
Oct 1931	T. White (C)	1919	R. Rutherford (C)	Low Hill
Jun 1932	J. Belger (Centre)	1921	C. Wilson (Lab)	Edge Hill
Jul 1932	R. Rutherford (C)	1932	H. J. Davis (C)	Wavertree
Nov 1932	R. G. Sheldon (C)	1928 (Dec)	J. D. Flood (C)	Exchange
Feb 1933	G. M. Platt (C)	1920 (Jul)	J. Ashworth (C)	Fairfield
May 1934	A. E. Shennan (C)	1929 (Dec)	W. W. Kelly (C)	Breckfield
June 1934	Mrs H. Muspratt (C)	1920	M. Muspratt (C)	Aigburth
Jul 1934	W. Denton (L)	1924	J. L. Eills (L)	Scotland S
Sep 1934	W. B. Stoddart (L)	1921	R. Meade-King (L)	Sandhills
Feb 1935	A. Gates (L)	1923 (Jan)	W. B. Stoddart (L)	Sandhills
Mar 1935	J. Bennett (C)	1932 (Nov)	J. Clancy (Centre)	Gt George
Dec 1935	H. D. Longbottom (P)	1930	J. Bennett (C)	Gt George
	T. H. Burton (C)	1921	H. Beckwith (C)	Garston
Jun 1936	C. S. Jones (L)	1923 (Mar)	B. W. Eills (L)	Much Woolton
	A. R. Price (L)	1927	F. Smith (Ind)	Castle St
Jan 1937	L. King (Lab)	1920	P. J. Kelly (Lab)	Fazakerley
Feb 1937	M. C. Dixon (C)	1920	A. Shelmerdine (C)	Sefton Park W
Oct 1937	J. W. T. Morrisey (Lab)	1927	H. Walker (Lab)	Wavertree W
Dec 1937	J. M. Griffith (C)	1921	M. H. Maxwell (C)	West Derby
Mar 1938	W. T. Roberts (C)	1921	T. White (C)	Low Hill
Jul 1938	R. D. French (C)	1922	E. Haigh (C)	St Peter's
	G. Y. Williamson (C)	1922	J. Bolger (Centre)	St Anne's

(b) Aldermen by ward, 1918-1938

Year	Name	Party	Year	Name	Party
Abercromby			*Brunswick*		
1918	A. T. Salvidge	C	1918	E. Russel-Taylor	C
1929	E. Thompson	C			
			Castle St		
Aigburth			1918	F. Smith	Ind
1918	E. J. Chevalier	C	1936	A. R. Price	L
1925	H. R. Rathbone	L			
1930	M. Muspratt	C	*Childwall*		
1934	Mrs H. Muspratt	C	1920	A. S. Mather	C
			1929	F. T. Richardson	Lab
Allerton					
1918	A. S. Mather	C	*Croxteth*		
1924	H. M. Miller	C	1929	D. G. Logan	Lab
Anfield			*Dingle*		
1918	A. Crosthwaite	C	1918	E. H. Cookson	C
1926	J. C. Cross	C	1922	J. Gordon	C
			1931	F. C. Wilson	C
Breckfield					
1918	H. Banner	C	*Edge Hill*		
1927	E. West	C	1918	J. W. Walker	C
1929	W. W. Kelly	C	1929	C. Wilson	Lab
1934	A. E. Shennan	C	1932	J. Belger	Centre

Year	Name	Party	Year	Name	Party
Everton			*Low Hill*		
1918	F. T. Richardson	Lab	1918	H. Wilson	C
1924	H. E. Davies	C	1929	R. Rutherford	C
1928	R. Rutherford	C	1931	T. White	C
1929	W. A. Robinson	Lab	1938	W. T. Roberts	C
Exchange			*Much Woolton*		
1918	W. Evans	L	1918	Heald	C
1920	J. H. Jones	L	1921	M. Muspratt	C
1925	A. E. Jacob	C	1930	B. W. Eills	L
1929	J. D. Flood	C	1936	C. S. Jones	L
1932	R. G. Sheldon	C			
			Netherfield		
Fairfield			1918	W. Muirhead	C
1918	R. Dart	C			
1923	J. Edwards	C	*Old Swan*		
1929	J. Ashworth	C	1918	F. J. Rawlinson	C
1933	G. M. Platt	C	1922	R. L. Burns	L
Fazakerley			*Prince's Park*		
1918	W. A. Robinson	Lab	1918	W. Boote	C
1925	P. J. Kelly	Lab	1924	H. A. Cole	C
1937	L. King	Lab			
			St Anne's		
Garston			1918	W. H. Watts	L
1918	W. J. Burgess	C	1924	J. Bolger	IP
1929	H. L. Beckwith	C	1938	G. Y. Williamson	C
1935	T. H. Burton	C			
			St Domingo		
Granby			1918	J. Lea	L
1918	J. Utting	C	1927	L. Hogan	Lab
1927	F. C. Wilson	C			
1929	J. Sexton	Lab	*St Peter's*		
			1918	W. B. Forwood	C
Gt George			1928	E. Haigh	C
1918	J. G. Taggart	N	1938	R. D. French	C
1925	J. Clancy	IP	1935	A. Gates	L
1935	J. Bennett	C			
1935	H. D. Longbottom	P	*Sandhills*		
			1918	R. R. Meade-King	L
Kensington			1934	W. Stoddart	L
1918	L. S. Cohen	C			
1924	J. R. Grant	C	*Scotland N*		
1928	H. E. Davies	C	1918	A. Harford	N
Kirkdale			*Scotland S*		
1918	S. M. Hutchinson	C	1918	J. L. Eills	L
1929	T. W. Byrne	Lab	1934	W. Denton	L
1931	H. E. Rose	Lab			
			Sefton Park E		
Little Woolton			1918	J. W. Alsop	C
None			1921	J. G. Paris	C

Year	Name	Party	Year	Name	Party
Sefton Park W			*Wavertree*		
1918	A. Shelmerdine	C	1918	R. S. Porter	C
1937	M. C. Dixon	C	1920	J. G. Moyles	C
			1931	H. J. Davis	C
			1932	R. Rutherford	C
Vauxhall					
1918	G. J. Lynskey	N	*Wavertree W*		
1921	T. Burke	N	1918	S. Jude	C
			1922	R. C. Herman	C
Walton			1929	H. Walker	Lab
1918	W. Roberts	C	1937	J. W. T. Morrisey	Lab
1920	C. Rutherford	C			
1930	M. Fletcher	C	*West Derby*		
			1918	M. H. Maxwell	C
Warbreck			1937	J. M. Griffith	C
1918	J. R. Grant	C			
1923	T. Dowd	C			

Key to parties:

C	=	Conservative	Lab	=	Labour
Ind	=	Independent	N	=	Nationalist
IP	=	Irish Party	P	=	Protestant
L	=	Liberal			

APPENDIX VIII Parliamentary and municipal electorates in Liverpool, 1919–1938 (by constituency)[1]

Year	Scotland/Exchange			West Toxteth			East Toxteth		
	Parl.	Mun.	Diff. (%)	Parl.	Mun.	Diff. (%)	Parl.	Mun.	Diff. (%)
1919	69,126	51,788	25.1	35,739	27,856	22.1	33,381	26,303	21.2
1920	68,702	53,041	22.8	36,483	28,907	20.8	33,959	27,054	20.3
1921	67,014	53,474	20.2	36,512	29,458	19.3	34,228	27,871	18.6
1922	69,158	55,239	20.1	36,500	30,028	17.7	33,877	28,080	17.1
1923	72,598	57,291	21.1	37,462	31,018	17.2	34,466	28,663	16.8
1924	74,075	58,795	20.6	38,546	31,989	17.0	35,238	29,511	16.3
1925	74,958	59,131	21.1	39,028	32,313	17.2	35,781	29,903	16.4
1926	75,064	59,266	21.0	38,954	32,477	16.6	35,803	29,862	16.6
1927	74,641	58,909	21.1	38,561	32,273	16.3	36,385	30,524	16.1
1928	72,884	57,732	20.8	37,775	31,625	16.3	36,388	30,608	15.9
1929	92,306	64,153	30.5	47,608	35,116	26.2	48,812	32,972	32.5
1930	90,622	62,356	31.2	46,840	34,431	26.5	49,518	33,279	32.8
1931	90,613	62,449	31.1	46,766	34,470	26.3	50,357	33,818	32.8
1932	89,709	61,754	31.2	46,309	34,266	26.0	50,898	34,105	33.0
1933	88,402	61,136	30.8	46,057	34,257	25.6	51,503	34,501	33.0
1934	86,870	60,039	30.9	45,373	33,770	25.6	52,182	35,034	32.9
1935	84,456	58,533	30.7	44,634	33,421	25.1	52,543	35,273	32.9
1936	81,493	57,150	29.9	43,558	32,910	24.4	52,963	35,690	32.6
1937	78,250	55,373	29.2	42,559	32,469	23.7	52,556	35,828	31.8
1938	74,954	53,615	28.5	41,580	32,044	22.9	52,432	36,063	31.2

Year	Edge Hill/Fairfield			Everton			Kirkdale		
	Parl.	Mun.	Diff. (%)	Parl.	Mun.	Diff. (%)	Parl.	Mun.	Diff. (%)
1919	62,109	48,134	22.5	27,019	21,162	21.7	31,148	24,027	22.9
1920	63,139	49,976	20.8	27,420	22,021	19.7	30,989	24,467	21.0
1921	64,419	51,845	19.5	27,362	22,383	18.2	30,862	24,794	19.7
1922	64,572	52,678	18.4	27,423	22,770	17.0	31,312	25,345	19.1
1923	65,212	53,767	17.6	28,193	23,641	16.1	31,955	25,973	18.7
1924	65,684	54,289	17.3	28,725	24,074	16.2	32,262	26,228	18.7
1925	67,224	55,278	17.8	29,402	24,521	16.6	33,076	26,870	18.8
1926	67,663	55,680	17.7	29,532	24,590	16.7	33,139	27,062	18.3
1927	67,598	56,094	17.0	28,982	24,237	16.4	32,804	26,781	18.4
1928	66,495	55,430	16.6	28,093	23,372	16.8	31,919	26,126	18.1
1929	85,699	61,086	28.7	35,430	26,169	26.1	40,646	29,012	28.6
1930	86,228	61,439	28.7	35,082	25,727	26.7	40,825	28,752	29.6
1931	87,373	61,997	29.0	34,969	25,591	26.8	40,862	28,751	29.6
1932	87,533	62,214	28.9	34,815	25,514	26.7	40,892	28,809	29.5
1933	87,752	62,427	28.9	34,166	25,138	26.4	40,833	28,818	29.4
1934	87,974	62,489	29.0	33,192	24,529	26.1	40,068	28,350	29.2

	Edge Hill/Fairfield			Everton			Kirkdale		
Year	Parl.	Mun.	Diff. (%)	Parl.	Mun.	Diff. (%)	Parl.	Mun.	Diff. (%)
1935	88,569	63,376	28.4	32,275	24,132	25.2	39,150	28,169	28.0
1936	87,793	62,964	28.3	31,383	23,593	24.8	38,189	27,585	27.8
1937	85,181	61,418	27.9	29,600	22,690	23.3	36,980	27,096	26.7
1938	83,629	60,529	27.6	28,454	21,882	23.1	36,321	26,964	25.8

	Walton			West Derby			Wavertree		
Year	Parl.	Mun.	Diff. (%)	Parl.	Mun.	Diff. (%)	Parl.	Mun.	Diff. (%)
1919	29,326	24,104	17.8	32,907	26,351	19.9	31,652	25,595	19.1
1920	29,629	24,759	16.4	32,989	27,062	18.0	32,475	26,475	18.5
1921	29,086	24,918	14.3	34,045	28,152	17.3	32,726	26,913	17.8
1922	30,478	25,656	15.8	35,330	29,554	16.3	33,558	27,744	17.3
1923	30,910	26,143	15.4	37,618	31,994	15.0	34,869	29,025	16.8
1924	31,482	26,661	15.3	38,579	33,008	14.4	36,936	31,294	15.3
1925	32,293	27,358	15.3	39,730	33,771	15.0	38,077	32,495	14.7
1926	33,088	28,339	14.4	40,230	34,116	15.2	39,167	33,521	14.4
1927	35,766	31,150	12.9	41,844	35,595	14.9	40,379	34,782	13.9
1928	39,131	34,150	12.7	41,791	35,790	14.4	41,795	36,182	13.4
1929	51,175	38,007	25.7	54,745	38,964	28.8	53,989	39,729	26.4
1930	53,170	38,908	26.8	55,192	39,621	28.2	55,622	40,268	27.6
1931	54,605	39,637	27.4	55,752	39,736	28.7	57,171	40,987	28.3
1932	55,238	39,855	27.8	56,367	39,907	29.2	58,341	42,344	27.4
1933	55,295	39,718	28.2	56,674	40,103	29.2	59,584	43,022	27.8
1934	56,164	40,266	28.3	56,892	39,903	29.9	61,053	44,165	27.7
1935	57,136	41,285	27.7	58,031	40,802	29.7	62.840	45,577	27.5
1936	57,404	41,662	27.4	59,457	41,885	29.6	65,375	47,494	27.4
1937	57,781	41,930	27.4	59,163	41,914	29.2	67,397	50,224	25.5
1938	58,807	42,903	27.0	59,061	41,960	29.0	68,803	51,189	25.6

	All Liverpool divisions				All Liverpool divisions		
Year	Parl.	Mun.[2]	Diff. (%)	Year	Parl.	Mun.[2]	Diff. (%)
1919	352,407	275,320	21.9	1929	510,410	365,208	28.4
1920	355,755	283,762	20.2	1930	513,099	364,781	28.9
1921	357,034	289,817	18.8	1931	518,468	367,436	29.1
1922	362,208	297,164	18.0	1932	520,102	368,768	29.1
1923	373,283	307,514	17.6	1933	520,316	369,320	29.0
1924	381,527	315,859	17.2	1934	519,718	368,545	29.1
1925	389,569	321,660	17.4	1935	519,634	370,568	28.7
1926	392,640	324,913	17.2	1936	517,695	370,933	28.3
1927	396,960	330,345	16.8	1937	509,466	368,942	27.6
1928	396,271	331,015	16.5	1938	504,041	366,980	27.2

[1] Where wards were divided between divisions, the totals for the combined divisions have had to be compared. This applies to the Scotland and Exchange divisions, which shared Vauxhall ward, and the Edge Hill and Fairfield divisions, which shared Kensington ward.

[2] From 1928, the municipal electorate of Croxteth ward has not been included, as it was not incorporated into any of the Liverpool parliamentary divisions. The total for municipal voters here, then, is not the same as the full municipal electorate.

APPENDIX IX   Estimates of population aged 21 or over in Liverpool wards, 1931

To calculate these estimates, it has been necessary to combine the figures provided in the 1931 census for:

        (i) the total population for each ward;
        (ii) the number of private families in each ward;
        (iii) the total population in private families in each ward;
  and (iv) the total population aged 21 or over for the whole county borough of Liverpool (which was not broken down by ward).

These figures were combined in the following way:

(A) The total population in private families in each ward was divided by the total number of private families in each ward, to obtain an average family size in each ward. These figures varied between a maximum of 4.62 per family in Croxteth ward, and a minimum of 3.45 per family in Childwall ward.

(B) The total population in private families for the whole county borough was divided by the total number of private families in the whole borough, to obtain an average family size for the borough as a whole. This figure was 4.06 per family.

(C) The degree to which average family size in each ward diverged from the average for the borough as a whole was then calculated as a percentage, either negative or positive. As an example, Croxteth ward was .56 over the average of 4.06, which in percentage terms is 13.79% above average. Conversely, Childwall was .61 below the average, which in percentage terms is 15.02% below average.

(D) The proportion of the population aged 21 or over for the borough as a whole was then calculated. There were 517,645 people aged 21 or over out of a total of 855,688, which gives a figure of 60.49% aged 21 or over for the borough as a whole.

(E) For each ward, therefore, 60.49% of the total population is then calculated, but this figure is then either reduced or increased in inverse proportion to the degree to which they diverged from the average family size, as calculated in (C) above. This is on the assumption that the larger the average family size in a ward, the more members of each family were likely to be under 21. This assumption cannot be guaranteed to be absolutely accurate, as the proportion of children over 21 still living in the family cannot be calculated, and may have varied between wards. However, most children still living in the home were probably below 21, and therefore these estimates are probably not too far away from the real figures for each ward.

As an example, Croxteth ward had a total population of 25,024. 60.49% of this total gives a figure of 15,137, but as Croxteth was 13.79% above average for family size, this figure must be reduced by 13.79%, giving a final aggregate of 13,050. Conversely, Childwall's population of 5,986 reduced by 60.49% is 3,621, but as its family size was 15.01% below average, this total has to be increased by 15.01%, giving a final aggregate of 4,165. [N.B. There may be slight discrepancies between these final figures and those quoted in Table 4.10, as figures have been rounded here to two decimal points, whereas the full table was constructed by computer with much greater precision]

The full list of these estimated figures of population aged 21 or over is given in Table 4.10 on page 128.

APPENDIX X Parliamentary election results in Liverpool, by division, 1918–1935

The results of by-elections are printed in italics.

The abbreviations of party names are the same as those used in Appendix IV, with the exception of the following:

> Ind. Irish = Independent Irish
> Nat. C = National Conservative
> Nat. Lab = National Labour
> NFDSS = National Federation of Discharged Soldiers and Sailors

N.B. Of the Liverpool municipal wards, all were part of Liverpool divisions, with the exception of Croxteth ward (from its formation in 1928) in the Ormskirk division, and the Speke part (from its inclusion in 1932) of Garston ward, in Widnes division.

East Toxteth (1)   Wards: Aigburth, Granby, Sefton Park E, Sefton Park W

Year	Candidates	Votes	%	Voters	Turnout (%)
1918 (Dec)	J. S. Rankin (C)	NC	—	33,067	—
1922 (Nov)	J. S. Rankin (C)	15,149	60	33,877	74
	Miss E. Rathbone (Ind)	9,984	40		
1923 (Dec)	J. S. Rankin (C)	NC	—	34,466	—
1924 (Oct)	A. E. Jacob (C)	16,139	60	35,238	76
	C. Burden (Lab)	6,620	25		
	F. C. Bowring (L)	4,163	15		
1929 (May)	H. L. Mond (C)	17,678	48	48,812	76
	J. J. Cleary (Lab)	9,904	27		
	A. O. Roberts (L)	9,287	25		
1931 (Feb)	*P. G. T. Buchan Hepburn (C)*	*17,040*	*75*	*49,518*	*46*
	C. Burden (Lab)	*5,550*	*25*		
1931 (Oct)	P. G. T. Buchan Hepburn (C)	28,817	76	50,357	74
	A. S. Doran (Nat. L)	9,093	24		
1935 (Nov)	P. G. T. Buchan Hepburn (C)	20,638	60	52,543	65
	A. D. Dennis (L)	13,622	40		

Edge Hill (2) Wards: Edge Hill, Kensington (part), Low Hill

Year	Candidates	Votes	%	Voters	Turnout (%)
1918	W. W. Rutherford (C)	9,832	64	30,558	50
(Dec)	P. J. Tevenan (Lab)	5,587	36		
1922	W. W. Rutherford (C)	14,186	60	33,634	70
(Nov)	J. H. Hayes (Lab)	9,520	40		
1923	*J. H. Hayes (Lab)*	*10,300*	*53*	*33,634*	*58*
(Mar)	*J. W. Hills (C)*	*9,250*	*47*		
1923	J. H. Hayes (Lab)	13,538	57	34,021	70
(Dec)	O. Stanley (C)	10,249	43		
1924	J. H. Hayes (Lab)	14,168	53	34,254	78
(Oct)	D. C. Williams (C)	12,587	47		
1929	J. H. Hayes (Lab)	17,650	55	42,516	75
(May)	H. Rutherford (C)	11,622	36		
	A. D. Dennis (L)	2,581	8		
1931	H. Rutherford (C)	19,901	63	42,394	75
(Oct)	J. H. Hayes (Lab)	11,772	37		
1935	A. Critchley (C)	13,882	51	40,328	68
(Nov)	J. H. Hayes (Lab)	13,581	49		

Everton (3) Wards: Everton, Netherfield

Year	Candidates	Votes	%	Voters	Turnout (%)
1918	J. S. Harmood-Banner (C)	6,370	52	25,606	48
(Dec)	A. W. Brooksbank (NFDSS)	5,799	48		
1922	J. S. Harmood-Banner (C)	11,667	61	27,423	70
(Nov)	J. Toole (Lab)	7,600	39		
1923	J. S. Harmood-Banner (C)	9,183	54	28,193	60
(Dec)	H. Walker (Lab)	7,693	46		
1924	H. C. Woodcock (C)	10,705	58	28,725	72
(Oct)	H. Walker (Lab)	10,075	48		
1929	D. H. Caine (Lab)	14,234	53	35,430	76
(May)	Miss M. Beavan (C)	12,667	47		
1931	F. Hornby (C)	12,186	49	34,969	71
(Oct)	S. L. Treleavan (Lab)	7,786	31		
	D. H. Caine (Nat. Lab)	4,950	20		
1935	B. V. Kirby (Lab)	10,962	50	32,275	67
(Nov)	R. Etherton (C)	10,785	50		

Exchange (4)   Wards: Abercromby, Castle Street, Exchange, Gt George, St Anne's, St Peter's, Vauxhall (part)

Year	Candidates	Votes	%	Voters	Turnout (%)
1918	L. F. Scott (C)	10,286	56	35,614	52
(Dec)	A. Harford (N)	8,225	44		
1922	L. F. Scott (C)	15,650	55	37,797	75
(Nov)	J. Devlin (N)	12,614	45		
1923	L. F. Scott (C)	10,551	51	40,221	52
(Dec)	W. Grogan (Ind. Irish)	10,322	49		
1924	L. F. Scott (C)	NC	—	41,178	—
(Oct)					
1929	J. P. Reynolds (C)	17,169	50	51,820	66
(May)	W. A. Robinson (Lab)	16,970	50		
1931	J. P. Reynolds (C)	24,038	69	50,638	69
(Oct)	T. McLean (Lab)	10,894	31		
1933	*J. J. Shute (C)*	*15,198*	*55*	*50,060*	*55*
(Jan)	*S. S. Silverman (Lab)*	*12,412*	*45*		
1935	J. J. Shute (C)	17,439	57	46,404	66
(Nov)	S. Mahon (Lab)	13,027	43		

Fairfield (5)   Wards: Fairfield, Kensington (part), Old Swan

Year	Candidates	Votes	%	Voters	Turnout (%)
1918	J. B. Brunel Cohen (C)	7,698	51	27,727	55
(Dec)	F. L. Joseph (L)	4,188	28		
	G. Porter (Lab)	3,337	21		
1922	J. B. Brunel Cohen (C)	14,316	72	30,938	64
(Nov)	G. Porter (Lab)	5,478	28		
1923	J. B. Brunel Cohen (C)	NC	—	31,191	—
(Dec)					
1924	J. B. Brunel Cohen (C)	14,277	63	31,430	72
(Oct)	Mrs M. E. Mercer (Lab)	8,412	37		
1929	J. B. Brunel Cohen (C)	16,436	53	43,183	72
(May)	J. H. Sutcliffe (Lab)	14,614	47		
1931	C. E. R. Brocklebank (C)	24,639	76	44,979	72
(Oct)	A. Dodd (Lab)	7,960	24		
1935	C. E. R. Brocklebank (C)	18,596	63	48,241	62
(Nov)	A. S. Moody (Lab)	11,155	37		

Kirkdale (6)   Wards: Kirkdale, St Domingo

Year	Candidates	Votes	%	Voters	Turnout (%)
1918	J. De F. Pennefather (C)	10,380	67	30,760	50
(Dec)	S. Mason (Lab)	5,012	33		
1922	J. De F. Pennefather (C)	NC	—	31,312	—
(Nov)					
1923	J. De F. Pennefather (C)	NC	—	31,955	—
(Dec)					
1924	J. De F. Pennefather (C)	14,392	61	32,262	74
(Oct)	E. Sandham (Lab)	9,369	39		
1929	E. Sandham (Lab)	15,222	51	40,646	73
(May)	R. Rankin (C)	14,429	49		
1931	R. Rankin (C)	14,303	45	40,862	77
(Oct)	E. Sandham (Lab)	9,531	30		
	H. D. Longbottom (P)	7,834	25		
1935	R. Rankin (C)	10,540	39	39,150	69
(Nov)	J. Hamilton (Lab)	9,984	37		
	H. D. Longbottom (P)	6,677	24		

Scotland (7)   Wards: Sandhills, Scotland N, Scotland S, Vauxhall (part)

Year	Candidates	Votes	%	Voters	Turnout (%)
1918	T. P. O'Connor (N)	NC	—	33,098	—
(Dec)					
1922	T. P. O'Connor (N)	NC	—	31,361	—
(Nov)					
1923	T. P. O'Connor (N)	NC	—	32,377	—
(Dec)					
1924	T. P. O'Connor (N)	NC	—	32,897	—
(Oct)					
1929	T. P. O'Connor (N)	NC	—	40,486	—
(May)					
1929	*D. G. Logan (Lab)*	*NC*	*—*	*40,486*	*—*
(Dec)					
1931	D. G. Logan (Lab)	15,521	57	39,975	69
(Oct)	E. Errington (C)	10,280	37		
	L. J. McGree (Comm)	1,544	6		
	F. Abraham (Ind)	99	—		
1935	D. G. Logan (Lab)	16,036	66	38,052	64
(Nov)	L. H. Wright (C)	8,372	34		

Walton (8)   Wards: Fazakerley, Walton, Warbreck

Year	Candidates	Votes	%	Voters	Turnout (%)
1918	H. W. Chilcott (C)	11,457	71	28,916	55
(Dec)	R. Dixon Smith (Lab)	4,580	29		
1922	H. W. S. Chilcott (C)	NC	—	30,478	—
(Nov)					
1923	H. W. S. Chilcott (C)	NC	—	30,910	—
(Dec)					
1924	H. W. S. Chilcott (C)	13,387	55	31,482	77
(Oct)	T. Gillinder (Lab)	8,924	37		
	S. Skelton (L)	1,910	8		
1929	R. Purbrick (C)	16,623	43	51,175	76
(May)	F. A. P. Rowe (Lab)	16,395	42		
	G. H. Jones (L)	5,857	15		
1931	R. Purbrick (C)	31,135	74	54,605	77
(Oct)	F. A .P. Rowe (Lab)	11,183	26		
1935	R. Purbrick (C)	22,623	62	57,136	64
(Nov)	F. L. McGhee (Lab)	14,079	38		

Wavertree (9)   Wards: Allerton, Childwall, Garston, (excluding Speke part which was in Widnes division), Little Woolton, Much Woolton, Wavertree, Wavertree W

Year	Candidates	Votes	%	Voters	Turnout (%)
1918	D. N. Raw (C)	11,326	60	31,287	60
(Dec)	C. Wilson (Lab)	5,103	27		
	A. Booth (L)	2,484	13		
1922	H. Smith (C)	14,372	62	33,558	69
(Nov)	Revd J. Vint-Laughland (Lab)	8,941	38		
1923	H. R. Rathbone (L)	9,349	37	34,869	72
(Dec)	H. Smith (C)	8,700	35		
	Revd J. Vint-Laughland (Lab)	7,025	28		
1924	J. A. Tinne (C)	14,063	47	36,936	80
(Oct)	W. A. Robinson (Lab)	10,383	35		
	H. R. Rathbone (L)	5,206	18		
1929	J. A. Tinne (C)	16,880	40	53,989	78
(May)	S. T. Treleavan (Lab)	13,585	32		
	H. R. Rathbone (L)	11,723	28		
1931	*A. R. Nall-Cain (C)*	*18,687*	*65*	*57,171*	*50*
(Jun)	*S. T. Treleavan (Lab)*	*10,042*	*35*		
1931	A. R. Nall-Cain (C)	33,476	78	57,171	75
(Oct)	C. G. Clark (Lab)	9,503	22		
1935	*J. J. Cleary (Lab)*	*15,611*	*35*	*61,053*	*72*
(Feb)	*J. Platt (Nat. C)*	*13,771*	*31*		
	R. Churchill (Ind. C)	*10,575*	*24*		
	W. A. Morris (L)	*4,208*	*10*		
1935	P. S. Shaw (C)	26, 915	59	62,840	73
(Nov)	J. J. Cleary (Lab)	19,068	41		

West Derby (10)   Wards: Anfield, Breckfield, West Derby

Year	Candidates	Votes	%	Voters	Turnout (%)
1918	F. E. Smith (C)	11,622	67	31,310	55
(Dec)	G. Nelson (Lab)	5,618	33		
1919	*R. Hall (C)*	*6,062*	*56*	*31,310*	*34*
(Feb)	*G. Nelson (Lab)*	*4,670*	*44*		
1922	R. Hall (C)	16,179	70	35,330	65
(Nov)	D. R. Williams (Lab)	6,785	30		
1923	C. S. Jones (L)	12,942	54	37,618	64
(Dec)	R. Hall (C)	10,952	46		
1924	J. S. Allen (C)	15,667	53	38,579	77
(Oct)	T. G. Adams (Lab)	8,807	30		
	C. S. Jones (L)	5,321	18		
1929	J. S. Allen (C)	16,794	43	54,745	72
(May)	W. H. Moore (Lab)	14,124	36		
	A. P. Jones (L)	8,368	21		
1931	J. S. Allen (C)	32,202	78	55,762	74
(Oct)	J. J. Cleary (Lab)	9,077	22		
1935	*D. P. Maxwell-Fyfe (C)*	*NC*	—	*58,031*	—
(Jul)					
1935	D. P. Maxwell-Fyfe (C)	21,196	58	58,031	63
(Nov)	J. Haworth (Lab)	10,218	28		
	D. K. Mitchell (L)	4,911	14		

West Toxteth (11)   Wards: Brunswick, Dingle, Prince's Park

Year	Candidates	Votes	%	Voters	Turnout (%)
1918	R. P. Houston (C)	13,083	66	35,806	56
(Dec)	W. A. Robinson (Lab)	6,850	34		
1922	R. P. Houston (C)	15,030	60	36,500	69
(Nov)	J. Gibbins (Lab)	10,209	40		
1923	R. P. Houston (C)	12,457	50	37,462	66
(Dec)	J. Gibbins (Lab)	12,318	50		
1924	*J. Gibbins (Lab)*	*15,505*	*54*	*37,462*	*76*
(May)	*T. White (C)*	*13,034*	*46*		
1924	J. Gibbins (Lab)	15,542	51	38,546	80
(Oct)	T. White (C)	15,163	49		
1929	J. Gibbins (Lab)	19,988	55	47,608	76
(May)	G. Watson (C)	16,309	45		
1931	C. T. Wilson (C)	20,613	58	46,766	76
(Oct)	J. Gibbins (Lab)	14,978	42		
1935	*J. Gibbins (Lab)*	*14,908*	*61*	*44,634*	*52*
(Jul)	*J. W. J. Cremlyn (C)*	*9,565*	*39*		
1935	J. Gibbins (Lab)	18,543	53	44,634	79
(Nov)	R. Churchill (C)	16,539	47		

APPENDIX XI Parliamentary and municipal election results compared, 1918–1935

These tables show the votes cast in general elections for parliamentary divisions, compared with the votes cast in the nearest municipal elections for the combined wards that made up those divisions. In many cases this direct comparison was not possible, for two main reasons.

First, some divisions did not correspond exactly with ward boundaries. Edge Hill and Fairfield divisions cut through the middle of Kensington ward, and Scotland and Exchange divisions cut through Vauxhall ward. These four divisions have been excluded throughout, therefore. After 1932, the new Speke portion of Garston ward lay within the Widnes division, and so the Wavertree division is automatically excluded for the 1935 general election.

Second, where wards and/or divisions were uncontested, direct comparison could also not be made.

Most of the general elections between the wars coincided fairly closely with the November municipal elections, and therefore the choice of years to compare with was fairly obvious. The only exceptions were:

(a) The December 1918 general election, which was held immediately after the end of the war and before municipal elections could be organized for that year. The first post-war municipal elections did not take place until November 1919, and it is with these that the comparison has to be made.

(b) The May 1929 general election, which fell almost equidistant between the 1928 and 1929 municipal elections. Both the general election and local elections of 1929 were the first to be fought with the new franchise including women voters between the ages of 21 and 30. It is not appropriate, therefore, to make the comparison with the smaller electorate which pertained in the 1928 elections, and the November 1929 local elections are the ones compared.

The abbreviations for party names are as those used in Appendices IV and X (% figure shown in brackets).

1918 general election

Parliamentary election (December 1918)			Municipal election (November 1919)		
Kirkdale			*Kirkdale and St Domingo*		
Con	10,380	(67)	Con	4,962	(50)
Lab	5,012	(33)	Lab	4,644	(47)
			L	340	(3)[1]
Voters	30,760		Voters	24,027	
Turnout (%)	50		Turnout (%)	41	
Walton			*Fazakerley, Walton and Warbreck*		
Con	11,457	(71)	Con	6,466	(58)
Lab	4,580	(29)	Lab	4,822	(42)
Voters	28,916		Voters	24,104	
Turnout (%)	55		Turnout (%)	47	

Parliamentary election (December 1918)			Municipal election (November 1919)		
West Derby			**Anfield, Breckfield and West Derby**		
Con	11,622	(67)	Con	4,443	(38)
Lab	5,618	(33)	Lab	5,131	(44)
			L	1,030	(9)[2]
			Ind	959	(8)[3]
Voters	31,310		Voters	26,351	
Turnout (%)	55		Turnout (%)	44	

[1] Liberal candidate in Kirkdale ward only.
[2] Liberal candidate in Anfield ward only.
[3] Independent candidate in West Derby ward only.

1922 general election

Parliamentary election (November 1922)			Municipal election (November 1922)		
Everton			**Everton and Netherfield**		
Con	11,667	(61)	Con	5,761	(40)[1]
Lab	7,600	(39)	Lab	5,983	(41)
			N	81	(—)
			Ind	11	(—)[2]
			Pat. Lab	2,654	(18)[3]
Voters	27,423		Voters	22,770	
Turnout (%)	70		Turnout (%)	64	
West Derby			**Anfield, Breckfield and West Derby**		
Con	16,179	(70)	Con	10,146	(63)
Lab	6,785	(30)	Lab	4,224	(26)
			L	1,510	(9)[4]
			N	198	(1)[5]
Voters	35,330		Voters	29,554	
Turnout (%)	65		Turnout (%)	54	

[1] Independent Conservative candidate in Netherfield ward, unopposed by official Conservative, and standing again as official candidate six months later in by-election, counted as a Conservative.
[2] Independent candidate in Everton ward only.
[3] Patriotic Labour candidate in Netherfield ward only.
[4] Liberal candidate in Anfield ward only.
[5] Nationalist candidates in Breckfield and West Derby wards only.

1923 general election

Parliamentary election (December 1923)			Municipal election (November 1923)		
Everton			*Everton and Netherfield*		
Con	9,183	(54)	Con	5,842	(64)
Lab	7,673	(46)	Lab	2,060	(22)
			Pat. P	1,155	(13)[1]
			Unemp	155	(1)[2]
Voters	28,193		Voters	23,641	
Turnout (%)	60		Turnout (%)	39	
West Toxteth			*Brunswick, Dingle and Prince's Park*[3]		
Con	12,457	(50)	Con	7,489	(48)
Lab	12,318	(50)	Lab	4,764	(30)
			IP	3,433	(22)[4]
			Unemp	56	(—)[5]
Voters	37,462		Voters	31,018	
Turnout (%)	66		Turnout (%)	51	

[1] Patriotic Protestant candidate in Netherfield ward only.
[2] Unemployed candidate in Everton ward only.
[3] Prince's Park ward was uncontested in the 1923 municipal elections, but was contested in a by-election later in the same month, and the figures for the by-election are used here.
[4] Irish Party candidate in Brunswick ward only.
[5] Unemployed candidate in Dingle ward only.

1924 general election

Parliamentary election (October 1924)			Municipal election (November 1924)		
Everton			*Everton and Netherfield*		
Con	10,705	(52)	Con	7,601	(41)
Lab	10,075	(48)	Lab	5,407	(58)
			Ind	51	(—)[1]
Voters	28,725		Voters	24,074	
Turnout (%)	73		Turnout (%)	54	
Kirkdale			*Kirkdale and St Domingo*		
Con	14,392	(61)	Con	4,794	(43)[2]
Lab	9,369	(39)	Lab	3,925	(35)
			P	2,542	(23)[3]
Voters	32,262		Voters	26,238	
Turnout (%)	74		Turnout (%)	43	

Parliamentary election (October 1924)			Municipal election (November 1924)		
West Derby			*Anfield, Breckfield and West Derby*		
Con	15,667	(53)	Con	9,347	(58)
Lab	8,807	(30)	Lab	3,607	(23)
L	5,321	(18)	L	3,075	(19)[4]
Voters	38,579		Voters	33,008	
Turnout (%)	77		Turnout (%)	49	

[1] Independent candidate in Everton ward only.
[2] No conservative candidate in St Domingo ward.
[3] Protestant candidate in St Domingo ward only.
[4] Liberal candidates in Anfield and West Derby wards only.

1929 general election

Parliamentary election (May 1929)			Municipal election (November 1929)		
Everton			*Everton and Netherfield*		
Con	12,667	(47)	Con	4,989	(42)
Lab	14,234	(53)	Lab	6,986	(58)
Voters	35,430		Voters	26,169	
Turnout (%)	76		Turnout (%)	46	
Kirkdale			*Kirkdale and St Domingo*		
Con	14,429	(49)	Con	6,796	(51)
Lab	15,222	(51)	Lab	6,572	(49)
Voters	40,646		Voters	29,012	
Turnout (%)	73		Turnout (%)	46	
Walton			*Fazakerley, Walton and Warbreck*		
Con	16,623	(43)	Con	7,860	(49)
Lab	16,395	(42)	Lab	7,837	(49)
L	5,857	(15)	L	454	(3)[1]
Voters	51,175		Voters	36,007	
Turnout (%)	76		Turnout (%)	45	
Wavertree			*Allerton, Childwall, Garston, Little and Much Woolton, Wavertree, Wavertree West*[2]		
Con	16,880	(40)	Con	10,390	(52)
Lab	13,585	(32)	Lab	8,564	(43)
L	11,723	(28)	L	860	(4)[3]
Voters	53,989		Voters	39,229	
Turnout (%)	78		Turnout (%)	51	

Parliamentary election (May 1929)			Municipal election (November 1929)		
West Derby			Anfield, Breckfield and West Derby		
Con	16,794	(43)	Con	7,346	(46)
Lab	14,124	(36)	Lab	6,522	(41)
L	8,368	(21)	L	2,231	(14)[4]
Voters	54,745		Voters	38,964	
Turnout (%)	72		Turnout (%)	41	
West Toxteth			Brunswick, Dingle and Prince's Park		
Con	16,309	(45)	Con	7,065	(41)
Lab	19,988	(55)	Lab	9,921	(58)
			Ind	145	(1)[5]
Voters	47,608		Voters	35,296	
Turnout (%)	76		Turnout (%)	49	

[1] Liberal candidate in Warbreck ward only.
[2] No election held in Little Woolton ward (electorate 444) in 1929.
[3] Liberal candidates in Allerton, Childwall and Much Woolton wards only.
[4] Liberal candidate in Anfield ward only.
[5] Independent candidate in Brunswick ward only.

1931 general election

Parliamentary election (October 1931)			Municipal elections (November 1931)		
Everton			Everton and Netherfield		
Con	12,186	(49)	Con	6,760	(54)
Lab	7,786	(31)	Lab	5,719	(46)
Nat. Lab	4,950	(20)			
Voters	34,969		Voters	25,591	
Turnout (%)	71		Turnout (%)	49	
Kirkdale			Kirkdale and St Domingo		
Con	14,303	(45)	Con	6,093	(42)
Lab	9,531	(30)	Lab	4,197	(29)
P	7,834	(25)	P	4,065	(28)
Voters	40,862		Voters	28,751	
Turnout (%)	77		Turnout (%)	50	
Walton			Fazakerley, Walton and Warbreck		
Con	31,135	(74)	Con	13,159	(75)
Lab	11,183	(26)	Lab	4,364	(25)
Voters	54,605		Voters	39,637	
Turnout (%)	77		Turnout (%)	44	

Parliamentary election (October 1931)			Municipal elections (November 1931)		
West Toxteth			Brunswick, Dingle and Prince's Park		
Con	20,613	(58)	Con	8,420	(48)
Lab	14,978	(42)	Lab	7,662	(44)
			P	1,501	(9)[1]
Voters	46,766		Voters	34,470	
Turnout (%)	76		Turnout (%)	51	

[1] Protestant candidate in Dingle ward only.

1935 general election

Parliamentary election (November 1935)			Municipal elections (November 1935)		
Everton			Everton and Netherfield		
Con	10,785	(50)	Con	4,823	(43)
Lab	10,962	(50)	Lab	6,441	(57)
			Ind. P	68	(1)[1]
Voters	32,275		Voters	24,132	
Turnout (%)	67		Turnout (%)	47	
Kirkdale			Kirkdale and St Domingo		
Con	10,540	(39)	Con	3,494	(28)
Lab	9,984	(37)	Lab	6,283	(51)
P	6,677	(24)	P	2,506	(20)[2]
Voters	39,150		Voters	28,169	
Turnout (%)	69		Turnout (%)	44	
Walton			Fazakerley, Walton and Warbreck		
Con	22,623	(62)	Con	9,882	(59)
Lab	14,079	(38)	Lab	6,608	(39)
			Ind	264	(2)[3]
Voters	57,136		Voters	41,015	
Turnout (%)	64		Turnout (%)	41	

[1] Independent Protestant candidate in Netherfield ward only.
[2] Protestant candidate in St Domingo ward only.
[3] Independent candidate in Warbreck ward only.

Women's sections in wards, August 1923–June 1930

	Aug 1923*	Jul 1925*	Nov 1926	Aug 1927	Nov 1928	Nov 1929	Jun 1930
Abercromby							
Aigburth							
Allerton							
Anfield		✓					
Breckfield							✓
Brunswick							
Castle Street							
Childwall		✓	✓	✓	✓	✓	✓
Croxteth+			✓				
Dingle			✓	✓	✓	✓	✓
Edge Hill		✓	✓	✓	✓	✓	✓
Everton	✓	✓		✓	✓	✓	✓
Exchange		✓	✓	✓	✓	✓	✓
Fairfield		✓	✓		✓		✓
Fazakerley		✓	✓				
Garston		✓	✓	✓	✓	✓	✓
Granby		✓	✓				
Gt George		✓					
Kensington				✓	✓	✓	✓
Kirkdale							
Little Woolton		✓	✓	✓	✓	✓	✓
Low Hill							
Much Woolton							

	Aug 1923*	Jul 1925*	Nov 1926	Aug 1927	Nov 1928	Nov 1929	Jun 1930
Netherfield	✓				✓	✓	✓
Old Swan	✓	✓					
Prince's Park			✓	✓	✓	✓	✓
St Anne's							
St Domingo		✓	✓	✓	✓	✓	✓
St Peter's							
Sandhills							
Scotland N							
Scotland S							
Sefton Park E							
Sefton Park W					✓	✓	✓
Vauxhall							
Walton		✓	✓		✓	✓	✓
Warbreck		✓	✓				
Wavertree	✓			✓	✓	✓	✓
Wavertree W	✓			✓	✓	✓	✓
West Derby	✓	✓				✓	✓
Total	6	16	14	12	16	18	18

* In August 1923 and July 1925 a women's section was also listed for the combined constituency parties of East and West Toxteth
+ Croxteth ward existed only from 1928.

Source: LTCLP, *Minutes*, various dates, 1923–30.

APPENDIX XII B Women's sections in wards, January 1931–June 1939

Ward	Jan 1931	Feb 1932*	Mar 1933*	Jan 1935*	May 1937	Sep 1938	Jun 1939
Abercromby							
Aigburth			✓	✓	✓	✓	✓
Allerton							
Anfield		✓	✓	✓		✓	✓
Breckfield	✓						
Brunswick							
Castle Street							
Childwall							
Croxteth	✓	✓	✓	✓	✓	✓	✓
Dingle	✓	✓	✓	✓	✓	✓	✓
Edge Hill	✓	✓	✓	✓	✓	✓	✓
Everton	✓			✓			
Exchange	✓	✓	✓	✓	✓	✓	✓
Fairfield	✓		✓	✓			
Fazakerley			✓	✓			
Garston			✓	✓			
Granby	✓	✓	✓	✓	✓	✓	✓
Gt George							
Kensington	✓	✓	✓			✓	
Kirkdale							
Little Woolton						✓	
Low Hill							
Much Woolton	✓						

	Jan 1931	Feb 1932*	Mar 1933*	Jan 1935*	May 1937	Sep 1938	Jun 1939
Netherfield		✓	✓				
Old Swan	✓	✓	✓				
Prince's Park	✓			✓			
St Anne's	✓	✓	✓			✓	✓
St Domingo		✓	✓				
St Peter's							
Sandhills							
Scotland N							
Scotland S							
Sefton Park E	✓	✓	✓	✓	✓		
Sefton Park W	✓	✓	✓	✓	✓	✓	
Vauxhall							
Walton						✓	
Warbreck							
Wavertree	✓	✓	✓	✓	✓	✓	✓
Wavertree W		✓	✓	✓		✓	✓
West Derby	✓	✓	✓			✓	✓
Total	17	18	20	17	10	14	11

* In February 1932, March 1933 and January 1935 a women's section is also listed for West Toxteth constituency.

Source: LTCLP, *Minutes*, various dates, 1931–3, 1937–9; *The Liverpool Official Red Book* (1935), p. 328.

Survey of male occupations in ten Liverpool wards, 1900, 1911 and 1940.

A survey of nine working-class wards was carried out using *Gore's Street Directory* of 1900 and 1911. The wards were selected in order to cover both Catholic and non-Catholic areas, and also the various geographical parts of the city where working-class neighbourhoods were located. The 1911 directory would have been most appropriate, coinciding with a census year, but in some wards very few streets were listed for that year, and it was necessary to go back to 1900 in some cases. In all cases, the figures found in the directories were supplemented by information on occupations of heads of households given in lists of tenants of corporation tenements for 1907 (Report of MOH, 1907), in order to reflect the occupations of the poorest streets excluded from the street directories.

The data for these nine wards was compiled as follows. An alphabetical list of all streets in the wards was taken from electoral registers. A 50 per cent sample of streets was then drawn by taking the names of alternate streets. The directory was then consulted, and, where the streets were listed, occupations were counted. The data is not perfect, since not all names appearing against a particular address had occupations attached to them. Also, where streets were not listed it was assumed that the distribution of occupations of corporation tenants would be similar to that in the population of unlisted streets. There is ample justification for this, as most corporation tenants at this time were people rehoused from slum clearance (i.e. from the poorest streets most likely to be unlisted in the directories). Therefore, the proportions of occupations listed among corporation tenants in 1907 were incorporated into the raw figures for each ward, in proportions according to the number of unlisted streets in each ward. This also requires the further assumption that, on average, unlisted streets contained as many addresses as those listed. An example will illustrate this procedure more clearly.

In Everton ward, there were 144 streets listed in the electoral register. Of the 72 streets in the 50 per cent sample, 50 were listed in the directory and 22 were unlisted. In total, there were 948 people with occupations stated listed in the directory for those 50 streets. It was assumed that there were another 417 people (i.e. $948/50 \times 22$) to be added to this total, representing the missing streets. These extra 417 people were then allocated to the various occupational categories in the proportions found in the list of corporation tenants. Thus, for instance, labourers made up 20 per cent of the corporation tenants, so 20 per cent of 417 (83) was added to the raw figure of 85, giving a total of 168 for labourers in Everton. By the same process, 33 carters (8 per cent of 417) were added to 70 in the raw figures, giving a total of 103, and so on.

The figures for the tenth ward, Croxteth, were simply taken from the 1940 directory, as nearly all streets were listed. Due to the large size of this ward, not all streets were sampled, but only those that made up the central section of the Norris Green estate. New job classifications that only apply to the Croxteth survey are indicated in brackets. The full results of these surveys are listed in the following tables.

(NB: The compilation of the data was carried out by the following people: Dingle, Garston, Everton, St Anne's, Scotland South and Croxteth, by the author; Edge Hill and Kirkdale, by Tony Lane; Brunswick, by Ron Noon; and St Domingo, by Andrew Shallice.)

	Edge Hill 1900	Dingle 1900	Scotland South 1900	Kirkdale 1900	Brunswick 1911	Garston 1911	Everton 1911	St Anne's 1911	St Domingo 1911	Croxteth 1940
Building trades										
(Asphalters)	—	—	—	—	—	—	—	—	—	3
Bricklayers	28	14	3	19	5	4	6	2	17	9
(Decorators)	—	—	1	—	—	—	—	—	—	3
Flaggers and paviors (and floorlayers)	3	1	1	3	—	2	—	—	6	4
(Demolition workers)	—	—	—	—	—	—	—	—	—	1
Glaziers (and leadlighters)	1	1	—	—	1	—	1	2	1	2
Jobbers	3	3	—	2	2	3	9	5	4	1
Joiners and carpenters	101	42	11	99	30	21	29	17	94	27
(Mosaic-makers)	—	—	—	—	—	—	—	—	—	1
Painters and paperhangers	90	46	3	29	29	20	59	20	126	20
Plasterers	11	10	5	4	13	4	10	2	9	7
Plumbers	30	14	2	27	16	11	11	8	28	6
Scaffolders and erectors	2	—	—	—	—	—	1	—	—	3
Signwriters	4	—	—	—	—	—	1	—	—	2
Slaters (and tilers)	4	—	—	—	—	—	3	—	4	1
Steeplejacks	—	—	—	—	—	—	—	—	1	1
Stonemasons	29	10	4	15	3	—	7	—	14	1
Totals	306	141	29	198	99	65	137	56	304	92

	Edge Hill 1900	Dingle 1900	Scotland South 1900	Kirkdale 1900	Brunswick 1911	Garston 1911	Everton 1911	St Anne's 1911	St Domingo 1911	Croxteth 1940
Furnishing trades										
Cabinetmakers	32	4	5	2	2	—	10	45	13	2
Chairmakers	1	—	—	—	1	—	4	5	—	—
French polishers	11	2	1	2	3	—	6	11	8	2
Upholsterers	8	3	1	3	4	3	3	4	11	4
Totals	52	9	7	7	10	3	23	65	32	8
Railwaymen										
Brakesmen	—	—	—	—	—	25	1	—	—	—
Clerks, ticket inspectors	20	11	1	20	—	5	2	3	4	9
Engine drivers and guards	43	30	7	60	12	50	7	4	12	6
(Loco firemen)	—	—	—	—	—	—	—	—	—	1
Managers, stationmasters	1	—	—	—	1	2	—	—	—	—
Foremen	—	—	—	—	3	8	—	—	—	—
Pointsmen, shunters and engine cleaners	24	5	1	7	—	33	4	—	6	2
Railway porters, platelayers and railway carters	25	24	4	22	6	28	7	4	9	4
Railwaymen	—	—	—	—	5	—	—	—	—	7
Signalmen	4	—	—	1	—	15	—	—	2	1
Totals	117	70	13	110	27	166	21	11	33	30

	Edge Hill 1900	Dingle 1900	Scotland South 1900	Kirkdale 1900	Brunswick 1911	Garston 1911	Everton 1911	St Anne's 1911	St Domingo 1911	Croxteth 1940
Engineering and metal trades										
Boilermakers	7	31	13	68	27	10	5	6	34	2
Copper/tin/blacksmiths/ moulders, iron and brass workers (sheet metal workers)	68	56	29	94	29	58	40	29	81	19
(Die setters, tool grinders/ setters, coremakers)	—	—	—	—	—	—	—	—	—	5
Electricians (and electrical engineers)	11	5	—	5	—	—	2	—	7	24
Fitters, engineers, mechanics, etc.	72	65	16	147	20	37	24	8	59	50
Patternmakers	3	—	—	13	4	—	—	—	6	1
Safemakers	15	—	—	—	—	—	—	—	—	—
Scalers	4	5	7	3	8	5	3	4	6	—
Shipwrights, (ships' rivetters/ fendermakers/riggers)	10	56	1	44	14	7	2	—	4	10
(Welders)	—	—	—	—	—	—	—	—	—	1
Totals	190	218	66	374	102	117	76	47	197	112

	Edge Hill 1900	Dingle 1900	Scotland South 1900	Kirkdale 1900	Brunswick 1911	Garston 1911	Everton 1911	St Anne's 1911	St Domingo 1911	Croxteth 1940
Workshop trades										
Basketmakers	1	—	2	—	—	—	3	—	—	—
Brushmakers	1	1	3	—	2	—	2	2	2	—
Coachbuilders (and motor body builders)	26	2	—	6	—	—	7	2	6	2
(Coffin-makers)	—	—	—	—	—	—	—	—	—	1
Coopers	12	12	18	20	12	3	12	10	22	3
Cutlers	2	—	—	1	—	—	—	3	1	—
Cycle-makers	4	—	—	1	—	—	1	—	2	—
Dyers	—	1	—	1	—	—	1	—	1	—
(Frame-makers)	—	—	—	—	—	—	—	—	—	2
Instrument makers	2	—	—	1	—	—	3	—	—	5
Leather workers	1	1	3	11	—	4	2	—	5	2
Locksmiths	2	2	5	3	3	3	3	2	7	2
Packing-case makers	2	1	3	2	—	—	3	—	4	—
Saddlers	9	9	2	8	9	—	2	1	16	1
Sail, canvas and rope makers	1	2	—	3	—	—	1	—	1	—
Spar and block makers	1	—	—	—	—	—	—	—	1	—
Umbrella makers	1	—	—	—	—	—	—	—	1	—
Watch and clock makers (and jewellers)	23	1	1	4	8	3	3	4	6	1
Wheelwrights	—	3	6	17	2	2	3	6	9	1
(Window–blind makers)	—	—	—	—	—	—	—	—	—	1
Totals	88	35	43	78	36	15	46	28	83	21

	Edge Hill 1900	Dingle 1900	Scotland South 1900	Kirkdale 1900	Brunswick 1911	Garston 1911	Everton 1911	St Anne's 1911	St Domingo 1911	Croxteth 1940
Printing trades										
Printers, compositors, lithographers	29	11	3	10	8	13	29	13	32	14
(Bookbinders)	—	—	—	—	—	—	—	—	—	1
(Stereotypers)	—	—	—	—	—	—	—	—	—	1
Totals	29	11	3	10	8	13	29	13	32	16
Clothing trades										
Boot- and shoe-makers	21	11	15	13	19	17	17	32	20	—
Hatters	1	—	—	—	—	—	—	—	—	—
Tailors, dressmakers	38	6	2	8	12	13	27	65	18	1
Totals	60	17	17	21	31	30	44	97	38	1

	Edge Hill 1900	Dingle 1900	Scotland South 1900	Kirkdale 1900	Brunswick 1911	Garston 1911	Everton 1911	St Anne's 1911	St Domingo 1911	Croxteth 1940
Retail and services										
Artists	—	1	—	1	—	—	—	—	2	—
Bakers	27	16	3	21	25	11	27	12	37	3
Bottlers	2	3	3	2	7	2	5	1	12	—
Butchers	17	6	3	18	20	13	24	24	2	7
Carpet planners	4	—	—	—	2	5	2	—	—	—
Cooks	7	3	2	4	3	3	7	3	8	1
(Footballers)	—	—	—	—	—	—	—	—	—	1
(Furniture porters)	—	—	—	—	—	—	—	—	—	1
Gardeners	4	6	—	4	—	9	—	—	2	5
Hairdressers	5	1	2	8	11	9	10	17	6	4
Lamplighters	—	—	—	1	—	2	2	—	6	—
Laundry workers	—	—	—	—	—	6	—	—	—	—
(Lift attendants)	—	—	—	—	—	—	—	—	—	5
Musicians	6	1	1	1	—	3	5	1	8	4
(Pawnbrokers)	—	—	—	—	—	—	—	—	—	1
Piano tuners	5	1	—	1	1	2	1	—	—	1
Shop assistants	31	10	2	25	2	5	11	4	35	17
Waiters, barmen, stewards, etc.	11	12	1	18	4	4	29	3	42	11
Window cleaners, sweeps	—	—	—	—	—	6	1	4	—	4
Totals	119	60	17	104	75	80	124	69	160	65

Transport and associated

	Edge Hill 1900	Dingle 1900	Scotland South 1900	Kirkdale 1900	Brunswick 1911	Garston 1911	Everton 1911	St Anne's 1911	St Domingo 1911	Croxteth 1940
Carters, coachmen, drivers (bus drivers and conductors, chauffeurs)	164	107	149	174	75	46	103	69	290	58
Checkers	10	17	—	21	4	12	10	10	32	7
Crane drivers	—	—	—	—	—	3	—	—	—	5
Dock labourers	—	136	217	108	177	102	105	151	270	15
(Ferrymen)	—	—	—	—	—	—	—	—	—	1
Grooms, ostlers	7	—	—	5	—	—	2	1	5	—
Labourers	268	108	200	91	306	117	168	155	459	149
Mariners	121	145	147	180	142	59	67	71	185	20
Packers	14	4	2	4	—	2	14	2	15	—
Porters	67	53	58	58	27	19	52	36	119	16
Portworkers: dockgatemen boatmen, stevedores, wharfingers, flatmen	19	46	7	91	15	36	12	8	46	3
Ships' stewards	2	1	—	35	4	—	9	—	19	16
Storekeepers	9	2	—	8	4	2	2	1	8	7
Tramwaymen	2	12	1	10	—	—	3	—	8	21
Warehousemen	60	19	21	46	5	1	28	9	65	16
Watchmen	20	7	9	15	3	7	14	10	15	10
Weighmen	4	—	—	3	—	2	—	—	—	—
Totals	767	657	811	849	762	408	589	523	1,536	344

White-collar and supervisory	Edge Hill 1900	Dingle 1900	Scotland South 1900	Kirkdale 1900	Brunswick 1911	Garston 1911	Everton 1911	St Anne's 1911	St Domingo 1911	Croxteth 1940
Army officers	—	—	—	—	—	—	2	—	—	—
Bookkeepers	86	22	1	54	8	19	14	2	24	4
(Chemists, laboratory assistants)	—	—	—	—	—	—	—	—	—	4
Clerks	55	20	2	42	4	26	25	3	70	59
Commercial travellers	28	1	—	13	—	2	14	—	13	22
Customs	—	—	—	14	—	2	2	1	9	4
(Draughtsmen)	—	—	—	—	—	—	—	—	—	3
Foremen	21	12	7	45	19	45	8	4	28	14
Insurance and commission agents	19	3	1	14	8	10	9	—	17	10
Managers	11	3	—	17	7	15	24	4	19	21
(Meat inspectors)	—	—	—	—	—	—	—	—	—	1
(Office workers, secretaries, cashiers, civil servants)	—	—	—	—	—	—	—	—	—	11
(Piermasters)	—	—	—	—	—	—	—	—	1	1
Police	58	45	—	51	4	10	21	—	92	38
Post office	32	10	—	8	5	4	10	2	17	11
(Ships' officers, naval instructors)	—	—	—	—	—	—	—	—	—	2
Teachers (school and music)	5	1	—	14	4	4	14	5	8	1
Timekeepers	—	2	1	11	2	5	4	2	11	3
(Vicars, priests)	—	—	—	—	—	—	—	—	—	8
Totals	315	119	12	283	61	142	147	23	308	217

Miscellaneous

	Edge Hill 1900	Dingle 1900	Scotland South 1900	Kirkdale 1900	Brunswick 1911	Garston 1911	Everton 1911	St Anne's 1911	St Domingo 1911	Croxteth 1940
Brewery workers	—	1	—	—	—	—	6	—	—	2
Cable-makers	—	—	1	—	—	—	1	—	—	3
(Cinema operators)	—	—	—	—	—	—	—	—	—	2
Collectors	—	—	—	4	—	—	2	2	2	—
(Corporation workers)	—	—	—	—	—	—	—	—	—	6
Firemen and stokers	2	20	27	28	36	17	12	10	11	8
Food-process workers	—	—	1	7	—	—	7	2	3	14
(Factory hands, process workers)	—	—	—	—	—	—	—	—	—	8
Gas fitters	10	—	—	3	5	—	6	—	1	1
Gas stokers (and gas workers)	8	4	—	1	—	—	1	—	—	4
Glass workers	7	—	—	—	—	—	4	5	—	—
Hawkers	—	—	29	—	23	15	16	20	12	4
(Hospital workers)	—	—	—	—	—	—	—	—	—	—
Meter readers	—	1	—	—	—	—	—	—	1	—
Millers	1	4	5	18	14	4	7	4	10	—
Oil refiners	—	—	—	1	1	—	1	—	—	1
Others	75	69	24	55	26	55	51	69	8	15
Paint workers	—	—	—	—	—	—	—	—	2	1
Rubber workers	—	—	1	—	—	—	—	—	—	2
Soap workers	—	—	1	—	—	—	—	—	—	1

	Edge Hill 1900	Dingle 1900	Scotland South 1900	Kirkdale 1900	Brunswick 1911	Garston 1911	Everton 1911	St Anne's 1911	St Domingo 1911	Croxteth 1940
(Spinners, silk spinners)	—	—	—	—	—	—	—	—	—	5
(Timber labourers)	—	—	—	—	—	—	—	—	—	1
Tobacco workers	3	1	12	1	—	4	6	4	4	2
Woodworkers, turners, sawyers	11	—	3	4	2	19	9	3	3	3
Totals	117	100	104	122	107	114	130	119	45	83
Grand total	2,160	1,437	1,122	2,156	1,318	1,153	1,365	1,051	2,768	989

APPENDIX XIV   Branches of the Liverpool Working Men's Conservative Association, 1920–1939

	1920	1931	1939		1920	1931	1939
Abercromby	✓	✓	✓	Little Woolton			
Aigburth				Low Hill	✓		✓
Allerton				Much Woolton			
Anfield				Netherfield	✓	✓	✓
Breckfield	✓	✓	✓	Old Swan			
Brunswick	✓	✓	✓	Prince's Park	✓	✓	✓
Castle Street				St Anne's	✓	✓	
Childwall				St Domingo	✓	✓	✓
Croxteth			✓	St Peter's			
Dingle	✓✓	✓✓	✓✓	Sandhills	✓	✓	
Edge Hill	✓	✓	✓	Scotland N			
Everton	✓			Scotland S	✓		
Exchange				Sefton Park E	✓	✓	✓
Fairfield				Sefton Park W			
Fazakerley			✓	Vauxhall	✓		
Garston	✓	✓	✓	Walton			
Granby	✓	✓	✓	Warbreck	✓		
Gt George				Wavertree	✓		
Kensington	✓	✓	✓	Wavertree W	✓	✓	✓
Kirkdale	✓	✓	✓	West Derby			

Source: *Liverpool Official Red Book* (1920, 1931, 1939).

APPENDIX XV   Turnout in municipal elections, 1919–1938

Year	Votes	Total electorate	Voters in uncontested seats	Contested electorate[1]	Turnout[2] (%)
1919	94,858	275,320	66,552	208,768	45.44
1920	126,849	283,762	57,284	226,478	56.01
1921	120,381	289,817	50,597	239,220	50.32
1922	115,609	297,164	71,369	225,795	51.20
1923	102,774	307,514	86,400	221,114	46.48
1924	119,706	315,859	73,070	242,789	49.30
1925	134,293	321,660	56,519	265,141	50.65
1926	120,227	324,913	35,062	289,851	41.48
1927	142,948	330,345	9,558	320,787	44.56
1928	130,106	336,901	84,330	252,571	51.51
1929	164,219	373,333	13,098	360,235	45.59
1930	138,543	374,322	27,779	346,543	39.98
1931	137,368	378,287	74,259	304,028	45.18
1932	144,830	381,704	41,410	340,294	42.56
1933	107,549	384,864	117,280	267,584	40.19
1934	119,311	385,875	61,585	324,290	36.79
1935	142,678	389,371	65,872	323,499	44.10
1936	146,220	390,290	49,574	340,716	42.92
1937	173,475	388,915	55,308	333,607	52.00
1938	113,491	387,469	119,076	268,393	42.29
Total	2,595,435			5,701,703	45.52

[1] Total electorate minus those in uncontested seats.
[2] Votes cast divided by contested electorate, multiplied by 100.

APPENDIX XVI Occupational structure of Liverpool and four other cities, 1911, 1921 and 1931

1911	Liverpool	Manchester	London	Preston	Hull
Total male workforce (10+ yrs)	*224,584*	*231,204*	*1,404,262*	*36,753*	*87,714*
Proportion of male workers (%)					
Conveyance in docks	10	—	2	2	9
Conveyance on sea	6	—	1	1	7
Carters, etc.	5	4	4	3	3
Storage, porters, messengers	6	4	5	2	4
General labourers	3	3	3	3	4
Fishing	—	—	—	—	2
Sub-total	30	11	15	11	29
Metals, machines, etc.	10	18	8	14	13
Textiles	—	4	—	26	—
Clerical workers	6	6	6	2	4
Total female workforce (10+ yrs)	*95,563*	*116,583*	*769,552*	*27,716*	*29,070*
Females as proportion of total workforce (%)	30	34	35	43	25
Proportion of all females (10+ yrs) recorded as working (%)	32	39	40	54	26
Proportion of female workers (%)					
Domestic service	22	12	26	5	24
Textiles	2	14	1	69	2
Clerical workers	3	3	4	—	2

1921	Liverpool	Manchester	London	Preston	Hull
Total male workforce (12+ yrs)	*247,249*	*237,951*	*1,385,701*	*37,925*	*93,546*
Proportion of male workers (%)					
Conveyance in docks and on sea	15	1	3	2	16
Carters, etc.	5	4	5	3	2
Storage, porters, messengers	7	8	7	4	4
General labourers	9	7	6	9	9
Fishing	—	—	—	—	2
Sub-total	36	20	21	18	33
Metals, machines, etc.	9	18	8	14	12
Textiles	—	2	—	17	—
Clerical workers	7	7	7	4	5

Total female workforce (12+ yrs)	108,080	126,001	780,511	26,669	31,387
Females as proportion of total workforce (%)	30	35	36	41	25
Proportion of all females (12+ yrs) recorded as working (%)	34	41	40	52	28
Proportion of female workers (%)					
Domestic service	15	10	22	4	18
Textiles	1	12	1	64	1
Clerical workers	10	10	13	2	9

1931

1931	Liverpool	Manchester	London	Preston	Hull
Total male workforce (14+ yrs)	267,670	257,368	1,461,041	39,271	104,626
Proportion of male workers (%)					
Conveyance in docks and on sea	13	1	2	3	16
Carters, etc.	4	4	4	3	3
Storage, porters, messengers	7	8	8	4	4
General labourers	12	11	9	15	14
Fishing	—	—	—	—	3
Sub-total	37	24	23	25	40
Metals, machines, etc.	7	13	7	11	9
Textiles	—	2	—	10	—
Clerical workers	7	8	9	5	6
Total female workforce (14+ yrs)	122,075	146,215	850,667	26,844	36,766
Females as proportion of total workforce (%)	31	36	37	41	26
Proportion of all females (14+ yrs) recorded as working (%)	36	45	44	53	30
Proportion of female workers (%)					
Domestic service	16	10	22	6	23
Textiles	1	8	—	54	1
Clerical workers	11	11	15	4	10

Bibliography

1) Manuscripts and records
(In Local History Section, Liverpool Central Library, unless otherwise stated)

Liverpool City Council
Liverpool Co-operative Society
Liverpool Electoral Registers, 1918–1939
Liverpool Labour Party:
    Liverpool Labour Representation Committee (to 1918)
    Liverpool Trades Council (to 1921)
    Liverpool Labour Party (1918–21)
    Liverpool Trades Council and Labour Party (from 1921)
National Unemployed Workers' Movement
    (Marx Memorial Library, London, and University of Hull Library)
Protestant Reformers' Memorial Church, Liverpool
Women's Citizens' Association, Liverpool
Women's Co-operative Guild (University of Hull Library)

2) Works of reference and official publications

Census Reports, 1891, 1901, 1911, 1921, 1931.
C. Cook and J.Stevenson, *The Longman Handbook of Modern British History, 1714–1980* (London, 1983).
F. W. S. Craig, *British Parliamentary Election Results, 1918–49* (London, 1969).
F. W. S. Craig, *British Parliamentary Election Results, 1885–1918* (London, 1974).
F. W. S. Craig, *British Electoral Facts, 1885–1975* (London, 1976).
J. Eaton and C.Gill, *The Trade Union Directory: A Guide to All TUC Unions*, (London, 1981).
Gore's (later *Kelly's*) *Directory of Liverpool* (Annual).
Liverpool Official Red Books (Annual).
Manchester Official Red Books (Annual).
A. Marsh and V. Ryan, *Historical Directory of Trade Unions, Vol.3*, (Aldershot, 1987).
Parliamentary Debates.

3) Contemporary newspapers and periodicals

Daily Worker
Labour's Northern Voice

Liverpool Daily Courier
Liverpool Daily Post

Liverpool Catholic Herald
Evening Express (Liverpool)
Liverpool Labour Chronicle
Liverpool Mercury
Liverpool Review
Liverpool Trade Review
North-Western Daily Mail
Porcupine

Liverpool Echo
Protestant Reformers' Monthly Magazine
Protestant Standard
Southern Daily Echo
The Times
Western Daily Press and Bristol Mirror
Yorkshire Post

4) Unpublished theses

R. Baxter, 'The Liverpool Labour Party, 1918–1963', D.Phil. thesis, University of Oxford (1969).

L. W. Brady, 'T. P. O'Connor and Liverpool Politics, 1880–1929', Ph.D. thesis, University of Liverpool (1968).

R. S. W. Davies, 'Differentiation in the Working Class, Class Consciousness, and the Development of the Labour Party in Liverpool up to 1939', Ph.D. thesis, Liverpool John Moores University (1993).

T. L. Drinkwater, 'A History of the Trade Unions and Labour Party in Liverpool, 1911 to the General Strike', BA thesis, University of Liverpool (1940).

S. Elliott, 'The Electoral System in Northern Ireland since 1920', Ph.D. thesis, Queen's University, Belfast (1971).

L. Feehan, 'Liverpool Corporation and Municipal Housing for the Working Classes', MA thesis, University of Liverpool (1974).

S. Fielding, 'The Irish Catholics of Manchester and Salford: Aspects of their Religious and Political History, 1890–1939', Ph.D. thesis, University of Warwick (1988).

R. S. Gibson, 'Influences on Labour Party Thinking on Educational Issues in Liverpool, 1916–1931', M.Ed. thesis, University of Liverpool (1982).

J. A. Gillespie, 'Economic and Political Change in the East End of London during the 1920s', D.Phil. thesis, University of Cambridge (1984).

L. Grant, 'Women Workers and the Sexual Division of Labour: Liverpool 1890–1939', Ph. D. thesis, University of Liverpool (1987).

M. McKenna, 'The Development of Suburban Council Housing Estates in Liverpool between the Wars', Ph.D. thesis, University of Liverpool (1986).

S. Maddock, 'The Liverpool Trades Council and Politics, 1878–1918', MA thesis, University of Liverpool (1959).

B. O'Connell, 'The Irish Nationalist Party in Liverpool, 1873–1922' MA thesis, University of Liverpool (1971).

J. D. Papworth, 'The Irish in Liverpool, 1835–71: Segregation and Dispersal', Ph.D. thesis, University of Liverpool (1981).

D. A. Roberts, 'Religion and Politics in Liverpool since 1900', M.Sc. thesis, University of London (1965).

J. S. Rowett, 'The Labour Party and Local Government: Theory and Practice in the Inter-War Years', D.Phil. thesis, University of Oxford (1979).

J. Smith, 'Commonsense Thought and Working Class Consciousness: Some Aspects of the Liverpool and Glasgow Labour Movement in the Early Years of the Twentieth Century', Ph.D. thesis, University of Edingburgh (1981).

G. Trodd, 'Political Change and the Working Class in Blackburn and Burnley, 1880–1914', D.Phil. thesis, University of Lancaster (1978).

J. D. Walsh, 'Aspects of Labour and Industrial Relations in Liverpool, 1891–1932', MA thesis, University of Liverpool (1976).

D. C. Wright, 'Socialist Municipal Politics in Twentieth Century Limoges, France', unpublished Ph.D. thesis, University of Wisconsin-Madison (1991).

5) Books

a) Relating to the economy, society and politics of Liverpool

G. C. Allen, F. E. Hyde, D. J. Morgan and W.J.Corlett, *The Import Trade of the Port of Liverpool: Future Prospects* (Liverpool, 1946).

G. Anderson, *Victorian Clerks* (Manchester, 1976).

J. Arnison, *Leo McGree: What a Man ... What a Fighter!* (London, 1980).

P. Ayers, *The Liverpool Docklands: Life and Work in Athol Street* (Liverpool, n.d.).

J. Belchem (ed.), *Popular Politics, Riot and Labour: Essays in Liverpool History, 1780–1940* (Liverpool, 1992).

J. and E. Braddock, *The Braddocks* (London, 1963).

L. W. Brady, *T. P. O'Connor and the Liverpool Irish* (London, 1983).

D. Caradog Jones (ed.), *Social Survey of Merseyside* (3 Vols.) (Liverpool, 1934).

S. Davies *et al.*, *Genuinely Seeking Work: Mass Unemployment on Merseyside in the 1930s* (Liverpool, 1992).

F. Deegan, *There's No Other Way* (Liverpool, 1980).

W. Hamling, *A Short History of the Liverpool Trades Council, 1848–1948* (Liverpool, 1948).

J. R. Harris (ed.), *Liverpool and Merseyside: Essays in the Economic and Social History of the Port and its Hinterland* (London, 1969).

H. R. Hikins (ed.), *Building the Union: Studies on the Growth of the Workers' Movement: Merseyside, 1756–1967* (Liverpool, 1973).

A. Johnson, *Working the Tides: Gatemen and Masters on the River Mersey* (Liverpool, 1988).

T. Lane, *Liverpool: Gateway of Empire* (London, 1987).

F. Neal, *Sectarian Violence: The Liverpool Experience, 1819–1914* (Manchester, 1988).

M. Nightingale (ed.), *Merseyside in Crisis* (Manchester, 1980).

C. G. Pooley and S. Irish, *The Development of Corporation Housing in Liverpool, 1869-1945* (Lancaster, 1984).

A. Salvidge, *Salvidge of Liverpool* (London, 1934).

J. Sexton, *Sir James Sexton, Agitator. The Life Story of the Dockers' M.P.* (London, 1936).

E. L. Taplin, *Liverpool Dockers and Seamen, 1870–1890* (Hull, 1974).

E. L. Taplin, *The Dockers' Union: A Study of the National Union of Dock Labourers, 1889–1922* (Leicester, 1986).

M. Toole, *Mrs. Bessie Braddock MP* (London, 1957).

P. J. Waller, *Democracy and Sectarianism: A Political and Social History of Liverpool 1868–1939* (Liverpool, 1981).

b) Relating to the Labour Party and the British working class

A. Briggs (ed.), *Chartist Studies* (London, 1959).

A. Briggs and J. Saville (eds.), *Essays in Labour History, 1918–39* (London, 1977).

D. Coates, *The Labour Party and the Struggle for Socialism* (Cambridge, 1975).

G. D. H. Cole, *A History of the Labour Party from 1914* (London, 1948).

J. E. Cronin, *Labour and Society in Britain, 1918–1979* (London, 1984).

J. Epstein and D. Thompson (eds), *The Chartist Experience: Studies in Working-Class Radicalism and Culture, 1830–1860* (London, 1982).

T. Forester, *The Labour Party and the Working Class* (London, 1976).

B. Hindess, *The Decline of Working Class Politics* (London, 1971).

J. Hinton, *Labour and Socialism: A History of the British Labour Movement, 1867–1974* (Brighton, 1983).

D. Howell, *British Social Democracy: A Study of Development and Decay* (2nd edn, London, 1980).

D. Howell, *British Workers and the Independent Labour Party, 1888–1906* (Manchester, 1983).

D. Howell, *A Lost Left: Three Studies in Socialism and Nationalism* (Manchester, 1986).

D. James, T. Jowitt and K. Laybourn (eds), *The Centennial History of the ILP* (Halifax, 1992).

H. Jones, *Health and Society in Twentieth-Century Britain* (London, 1994).

P. Joyce, *Visions of the People: Industrial England and the Question of Class, 1849–1914* (Cambridge, 1991).

N. Kirk, *Labour and Society in Britain and the USA, Vol. 1: Capitalism, Custom and Protest, 1780–1850; Vol. 2: Challenge and Accommodation, 1850–1939* (Aldershot, 1994).

M. Langan and B. Schwartz (eds.), *Crises in the British State, 1880–1930* (London, 1985).

K. Laybourn, *The Rise of Labour: The British Labour Party, 1890–1979* (London, 1988).

R. McKibbin, *The Evolution of the Labour Party, 1910–1924* (London, 1974).

R. McKibbin, *The Ideologies of Class: Social Relations in Britain 1880–1950* (Oxford, 1990).

R. Miliband, *Parliamentary Socialism: A Study in the Politics of Labour* (2nd edn, London, 1972).

A. L. Morton and G. Tate, *The British Labour Movement, 1770–1920* (London, 1956).

L. Panitch (ed.), *Working Class Politics in Crisis* (London, 1986).

H. Pelling, *A History of British Trade Unionism* (3rd. edn, Harmondsworth, 1976).

H. Pelling, *A Short History of the Labour Party* (2nd edn, London, 1965).

H. Pelling, *Origins of the Labour Party* (2nd edn, London, 1965).

B. Pimlott, *Labour and the Left in the 1930s* (Cambridge, 1977).

G. Stedman Jones, *Languages of Class: Studies in English Working-Class History, 1832–1982* (Cambridge, 1983).

D. Tanner, *Political Change and the Labour Party, 1900–18* (Cambridge, 1990).

E. P. Thompson, *The Making of the English Working Class* (Harmondsworth, 1968).

J. Vernon, *Politics and the People: A Study in English Political Culture, c.1815–1867* (Cambridge, 1993).

H. Wainwright, *Labour: A Tale of Two Parties* (London, 1987).

J. Winter (ed.), *The Working Class in Modern British History: Essays in Honour of Henry Pelling* (Cambridge, 1983).

J. D. Young, *Socialism and the English Working Class: A History of English Labour, 1883–1939* (London, 1989).

c) Local studies of working-class politics in Britain

F. Bealey, J. Blondel and W. P. McCann, *Constituency Politics: A Study of Newcastle-under-Lyme* (London, 1965).

D. Clark, *Colne Valley: Radicalism to Socialism. The Portrait of a Northern Constituency in the Formative Years of the Labour Party, 1890–1910* (London, 1981).

G. Crossick, *An Artisan Elite in Victorian Society: Kentish London, 1840–1880* (London, 1978).

J. Foster, *Class Struggle and the Industrial Revolution: Early Industrial Capitalism in Three English Towns* (London, 1974).

S. Goss, *Local Labour and Local Government: A Study of Changing Interests, Politics and Policy in Southwark from 1919 to 1982* (Edinburgh, 1988).

R. Q. Gray, *The Labour Aristocracy in Victorian Edinburgh* (Oxford, 1976).

W. Hampton, *Democracy and Community: A Study of Politics in Sheffield* (London, 1970).

J. Holford, *Reshaping Labour: Organisation, Work and Politics in Edinburgh in the Great War and After* (London, 1988).

G. W. Jones, *Borough Politics: A Study of the Wolverhampton Borough Council, 1888–1964* (London, 1969).

P. Joyce, *Work, Society and Politics: The Culture of the Factory in Later Victorian England* (London, 1980).

N. Kirk, *The Growth of Working Class Reformism in Mid-Victorian England* (London, 1985).

B. Lancaster, *Radicalism, Cooperation and Socialism: Leicester Working Class Politics 1860–1906* (Leicester, 1987).

B. Lancaster and T. Mason (eds), *Life and Labour in a Twentieth Century City: The Experience of Coventry* (Coventry, 1986).

J. Marriott, *The Culture of Labourism: The East End between the Wars* (Edinburgh, 1991).

L. Murgatroyd *et al.*, *Localities, Class and Gender* (London: 1985).

J. Reynolds and K. Laybourn, *Labour Heartland: A History of the Labour Party in W. Yorkshire during the Inter-War Years, 1918–1939* (Bradford, 1987).

M. Savage, *The Dynamics of Working-Class Politics: The Labour Movement in Preston, 1880–1940* (Cambridge, 1987).

G. Stedman Jones, *Outcast London: A Study in the Relationship between Classes in Victorian Society* (London, 1971).

d) Relating to local government and electoral politics

G. Alderman, *British Elections: Myth and Reality* (London, 1978).

V. Bogdanor, *The People and the Party System: The Referendum and Electoral Reform in British Politics* (Cambridge, 1981).

C. Cook, *The Age of Alignment: Electoral Politics in Britain, 1922–1929* (London, 1975).

S. R. Daniels, *The Case for Electoral Reform* (London, 1938).

H. Finer, *English Local Government* (London: 1933).

S. E. Finer (ed.), *Adversary Politics and Electoral Reform* (London, 1975).

J. Hart, *Proportional Representation: Critics of the British Electoral System, 1820–1945* (Oxford, 1992).

E. L. Hasluck, *Local Government in England* (Cambridge, 1936).

B. Keith-Lucas, *The English Local Government Franchise: A Short History* (Oxford, 1952).

B. Keith-Lucas and P. G. Richards, *A History of Local Government in the Twentieth Century* (London, 1978).

V. D. Lipman, *Local Government Areas, 1834–1945* (Oxford, 1949).

J. D. Marshall (ed.), *The History of Lancashire County Council, 1889 to 1974* (London, 1977).

R. Miliband, *Capitalist Democracy in Britain* (Oxford, 1982).

H. Pelling, *Social Geography of British Elections 1885–1910* (London, 1967).

R. Simon, *Local Councils and the Citizen* (London, 1948).

J. Stevenson, *British Society, 1914–1945* (Harmondsworth, 1984).

J. Stevenson and C. Cook, *The Slump: Society and Politics during the Depression* (London, 1977).

e) Relating to women and the Labour Party

J. Alberti, *Beyond Suffrage: Feminists in War and Peace, 1914–28* (London, 1989).

O. Banks, *The Politics of British Feminism, 1918–1970* (Aldershot, 1993).

A. Baron (ed.), *Work Engendered: Toward a New History of American Labor* (Ithaca, 1991).

D. Beddoe, *Back to Home and Duty: Women between the Wars, 1918–1939* (London, 1989).

B. Campbell, *The Iron Ladies: Why do Women Vote Tory?* (London, 1987).

C. Collette, *For Labour and for Women: The Women's Labour League, 1906–14* (Manchester, 1989).

P. M. Graves, *Labour Women: Women in British Working-Class Politics, 1918–1939* (Cambridge, 1994)

B. Harrison, *Separate Spheres: The Opposition to Women's Suffrage in Britain* (London, 1978).

B. Harrison, *Prudent Revolutionaries: Portraits of British Feminists between the Wars* (Oxford, 1987).

P. Hollis, *Ladies Elect: Women in English Local Government, 1865–1914* (Oxford, 1987).

J. Lewis, *The Politics of Motherhood: Child and Maternal Welfare in England, 1900–1939* (London, 1980).

L. Middleton (ed.), *Women in the Labour Movement* (London, 1977).

M. Pugh, *Women and the Women's Movement in Britain, 1914–1959* (London, 1992).

V. Randall, *Women and Politics: An International Perspective* (2nd edn, London, 1987).

E. Roberts, *Women's Work, 1840–1940* (London, 1988).

S. Rowbotham, *A New World for Women. Stella Browne: Socialist Feminist* (London, 1977).

S. Rowbotham, *Hidden from History: 300 Years of Women's Oppression and the Fight Against It* (London, 1973).

J. Siltanen and M. Stanworth (eds.), *Women and the Public Sphere: A Critique of Sociology and Politics* (London, 1984).

H. Smith (ed.), *British Feminism in the Twentieth Century* (Aldershot, 1990).

M. Stacey and M. Price, *Women, Power and Politics* (London, 1981).

f) Local studies of working-class politics from other countries

R. Aminzade, *Class, Politics and Early Industrial Capitalism: A Study of Mid-Nineteenth Century Toulouse, France* (Albany, 1981).

J. E. Argersinger, *Toward a New Deal in Baltimore: People and Government in the Great Depression* (Chapel Hill, 1988).

J. R. Barrett, *Work and Community in the Jungle: Chicago's Packinghouse Workers, 1894–1922* (Urbana, 1987).

L. R. Berlanstein, *The Working People of Paris, 1871–1914* (Baltimore, 1984).

A. Bridges, *A City in the Republic: Antebellum New York and the Origins of Machine Politics* (Cambridge, 1984).

W. J. Chase, *Workers, Society and the Soviet State: Labor and Life in Moscow, 1918–1929* (Urbana, 1990).

L. Cohen, *Making a New Deal: Industrial Workers in Chicago, 1919–1939* (Cambridge, 1990).

R. A. Comfort, *Revolutionary Hamburg: Labor Politics in the Early Weimar Republic* (Stanford, 1966).

A. Dawley, *Class and Community: The Industrial Revolution in Lynn* (Cambridge, Mass., 1986).

E. Faue, *Community of Suffering and Struggle: Women, Men and the Labor Movement in Minneapolis, 1915–1945* (Chapel Hill, 1991).

D. Frank, *Purchasing Power: Consumer Organizing, Gender, and the Seattle Labor Movement, 1919–1929* (Cambridge, 1994).

G. Gerstle, *Working-Class Americanism: The Politics of Labor in a Textile City, 1914–1960* (Cambridge, 1989).

B. Greenberg, *Worker and Community: Response to Industrialization in a Nineteenth Century American City, Albany, New York, 1850–1884* (Albany, 1985).

S. E. Hirsch, *Roots of the American Working Class: The Industrialization of Crafts in Newark, 1800–1860* (Philadelphia, 1978).

I. Katznelson and A. R. Zolberg (eds), *Working-Class Formation: Nineteenth-Century Patterns in Western Europe and the United States* (Princeton, 1986).

S. J. Kleinberg, *The Shadow of the Mills: Working-Class Families in Pittsburgh, 1870–1907* (Pittsburgh, 1989).

B. Laurie, *Working People of Philadelphia, 1800–1850* (Philadelphia, 1980).

C. Lis, *Social Change and the Laboring Poor: Antwerp, 1770–1860* (New Haven, 1986).

B. Nelson, *Workers on the Waterfront: Seamen, Longshoremen and Unionism in the 1930s* (Urbana and Chicago, 1988).

S. J. Ross, *Workers on the Edge: Work, Leisure and Politics in Industrializing Cincinnati, 1788–1890* (New York, 1985).

R. A. Slayton, *Back of the Yards: The Making of a Local Democracy* (Chicago, 1986).

S. A. Smith, *Red Petrograd: Revolution in the Factories, 1917–1918* (Cambridge, 1983).

C. G. Steffen, *The Mechanics of Baltimore: Workers and Politics in the Age of Revolution, 1763–1812* (Chicago, 1984).

S. Wilentz, *Chants Democratic: New York City and the Rise of the American Working Class, 1788–1850* (Oxford, 1984).

6) Articles

a) Relating to the economy, society and politics of Liverpool

G. Anderson, 'A private welfare agency for white-collar workers between the wars: a study of the Liverpool Clerks' Association, 1918–39', *International Review of Social History* 21, pt. 1 (1986).

G. Anderson, 'Inequalities in the workplace: the gap between manual and white-collar workers in the port of Liverpool from the 1850s to the 1930s', *Labour History Review* 56, pt. 1 (1991).

P. Ayers and J. Lambertz, 'Marriage relations, money and domestic violence in working-class Liverpool, 1919–39', in J. Lewis (ed.), *Labour and Love: Women's Experience of Home and Family, 1850–1940* (Oxford, 1986).

R. Baxter, 'The working class and Labour politics', *Political Studies* 20, no. 1 (1972).

R. Bean, 'A note on the Knights of Labour in Liverpool, 1889–90', *Labor History* 13, no. 1 (1972).

R. Bean, 'Custom, job regulation and dock labour in Liverpool, 1911–39', *International Review of Social History* 37, pt. 3 (1982).

J. Bohstedt, 'More than one working class: Protestant and Catholic riots in Edwardian Liverpool', in J. Belchem (ed.), *Popular Politics, Riot and Labour: Essays in Liverpool History, 1790–1940* (Liverpool, 1982).

S. Davies, 'The Liverpool Labour Party and the Liverpool working class, 1900–1939', *Bulletin of the North West Labour History Society* 6 (1979–80).

S. Davies, 'Class, religion and gender: Liverpool Labour Party and women, 1918–39', in Belchem (ed.), *Popular Politics, Riot and Labour*.

J. Dawson, 'George Garrett: man and writer', *Bulletin of the North West Labour History Society* 14 (1990).

J. Des Forges, 'Co–operation, labour and consumption in Liverpool, c.1890–1914', in B. Lancaster and P. Maguire (eds), *Towards the Co-operative Commonwealth: Essays in the History of the Co-operative Movement* (Keele, forthcoming).

J. Des Forges, '"We make millions of pairs of boots, but not one pair of millionaires": co-operation and the working class in Liverpool and the Rhondda', *North West Labour History* 19 (1994/5).

D. Foy, 'He delivered the goods: a brief history of the Liverpool carter', *North West Labour History* 15 (1990/91).

W. Hamling, *A Short History of the Liverpool Trades Council, 1848–1948* (Liverpool, 1948).

R. J. Holton, 'Syndicalism and labour on Merseyside, 1906–14', in H. R. Hikins (ed.), *Building the Union: Studies on the Growth of the Workers' Movement: Merseyside 1756–1967* (Liverpool, 1973).

T. Lane, 'Proletarians and politics in Liverpool, c.1900–1911', unpublished paper (Liverpool, 1979).

T. Lane, 'A Merseysider in Detroit', *History Workshop* 11 (Spring 1981).

M. McKenna, 'The suburbanization of the working-class population of Liverpool between the wars', *Social History* 16, no. 2 (May 1991).

C. G. Pooley, 'The residential segregation of migrant communities in mid-Victorian Liverpool', *Transactions of the Institute of British Geographers*, new series, Vol. 2, no. 3 (1977).

I. Sellers, 'Nonconformist attitudes in later nineteenth-century Liverpool', *Transactions of the Historic Society of Lancashire and Cheshire*, Vol. 114 (1962).

A. Shallice, 'Orange and green and militancy: sectarianism and working class politics in Liverpool, 1900–1914', *Bulletin of the North West Labour History Society* 6 (1979–80).

A. Shallice, 'Liverpool Labourism and Irish Nationalism in the 1920s and 1930s', *Bulletin of the North West Labour History Society* 8 (1982–3).

J. Smith, 'Labour tradition in Glasgow and Liverpool', *History Workshop* 17 (Spring 1984).

J. Smith, 'Class, skill and sectarianism in Glasgow and Liverpool, 1880–1914', in R. J. Morris (ed.), *Class, Power and Social Structure in British Nineteenth-Century Towns* (Leicester, 1986).

E. L. Taplin, 'The Liverpool Trades Council, 1880–1914', *Bulletin of the North West Labour History Society* 3 (1976).

E. L. Taplin 'James Larkin, Liverpool and the National Union of Dock Labourers: the apprenticeship of a revolutionary', *Saothar* 4 (1978).

E. L. Taplin, 'Unionism among seamen and dockers, 1887–1914', *Bulletin of the North West Labour History Society* 14 (1990).

T. Wailey, 'The other stormy passage: Liverpool seamen and their union', *Bulletin of the North West Labour History Society* 14 (1990).

b) Relating to the Labour Party and the British working class

F. Bealey and M. Dyer, 'Size of place and the Labour vote in Britain, 1918–1966', *Western Political Quarterly* 24, no. 1 (March 1971).

C. Chamberlain, 'The growth of support for the Labour Party in Britain', *British Journal of Sociology* 24 (1973).

C. Cook, 'Liberals, Labour and local elections', in G. Peele and C. Cook (eds), *The Politics of Reappraisal, 1918–1939* (London, 1965).

E. J. Hobsbawm, 'The forward march of labour halted?', *Marxism Today* (September 1978).

D. Hopkin, 'The membership of the Independent Labour Party, 1904–1910: a spatial and occupational analysis', *International Review of Social History* 20, pt. 2 (1975).

C. Howard, 'Expectations born to death: local Labour Party expansion in the 1920s', in J. Winter (ed.), *The Working Class in Modern British History: Essays in Honour of Henry Pelling* (Cambridge, 1983).

P. Joyce, 'The end of social history?', *Social History* 20, no.1 (1995).

N. Kirk, 'History, language, ideas and post-modernism: a materialist view', *Social History* 19, no.2 (1994).

N. Kirk, 'Traditional working-class culture and the "rise of labour": some preliminary questions and observations', *Social History* 16, no. 2 (May 1991).

K. Laybourn, 'The rise of Labour and the decline of Liberalism: the state of the debate', *History*, 80, no. 259 (1995).

H. C. Mathews, R. I. McKibbin, and J. A. Kay, 'The franchise factor in the rise of the Labour Party', *English Historical Review* 91 (1976).

R. Miliband, 'Socialism and the myth of the golden past', *Socialist Register* (1964).

T. Nairn, 'The nature of the Labour Party', in P. Anderson and R. Blackburn (eds.), *Towards Socialism* (London, 1965).

B. D. Palmer, 'Critical theory, historical materialism, and the ostensible end of Marxism: the poverty of theory revisited', *International Review of Social History* 38, pt. 2 (1993).

L. Panitch, 'Ideology and integration: the case of the British Labour Party', in L. Panitch (ed.), *Working Class Politics in Crisis* (London, 1986).

M. Savage, 'The rise of the Labour Party in local perspective', *Journal of Regional and Local Studies* (Summer 1990).

J. Saville, 'The ideology of Labourism', in R. Benewick *et al.* (eds), *Knowledge and Belief in Politics* (1973).

J. Saville, 'May Day 1937', in A. Briggs and J. Saville (eds), *Essays in Labour History, 1918–39* (London, 1977).

M. G. Sheppard and J. L. Halstead, 'Labour municipal election performance in provincial England and Wales, 1901–1913', *Bulletin of the Society for the Study of Labour History* 39 (1979).

D. Tanner, 'Elections, statistics, and the rise of the Labour Party, 1906–1931', *Historical Journal* 34, no. 4 (1991).

E. P. Thompson, 'The moral economy of the English crowd in the eighteenth century', *Past and Present* 50 (1971).

E. P. Thompson, 'Patrician society, plebeian culture', *Journal of Social History* 7 (1974).

A. Thorpe, '"I am in the Cabinet": J. H. Thomas's decision to join the national government in 1931', *Historical Research* 64, no. 155 (October 1991).

J. M. Winter, 'Trade unions and the Labour Party in Britain', in W. J. Mommsen and H. G. Husung, *The Development of Trade Unionism in Britain and Germany, 1880–1914* (London, 1985).

c) Local studies of working-class politics in Britain

T. Adams, 'Labour and the First World War: economy, politics and the erosion of local peculiarity?', *Journal of Regional and Local Studies* (Summer 1990).

F. Carr, 'Municipal socialism: Labour's rise to power', in B. Lancaster and T. Mason (eds), *Life and Labour in a Twentieth Century City: The Experience of Coventry* (Coventry, 1986).

S. Fielding, 'Irish politics in Manchester, 1890–1914', *International Review of Social History* 33 (1988).

J. Foster, 'Strike action and working-class politics on Clydeside, 1914–1919', *International Review of Social History* 35 (1990).

B. Lancaster and T. Mason, 'Society and politics in Twentieth Century Coventry', in Lancaster and Mason, *Life and Labour in a Twentieth Century City*.

A. McKinlay, 'Labour and locality: Labour politics on Clydeside, 1900–39', *Journal of Regional and Local Studies* (Summer 1990).

J. Mark-Lawson, Michael Savage and Alan Warde, 'Gender and local politics: struggles over welfare policies, 1918–1939', in L. Murgatroyd *et al.* (eds), *Localities, Class and Gender* (London, 1985).

J. Melling, 'Whatever happened to red Clydeside? industrial conflict and the politics of skill in the First World War', *International Review of Social History* 35 (1990).

A. Warde, 'Conditions of dependence: working-class quiescence in Lancaster in the Twentieth Century', *International Review of Social History* 35 (1990).

d) Relating to local government and electoral politics

N. Blewett, 'The franchise in the United Kingdom, 1885–1918', *Past and Present* 32 (1965).

D. Butler, 'Electoral systems', in D.Butler, H.R.Penniman, and A. Ranney (eds), *Democracy at the Polls: A Comparative Study of Competitive National Elections* (Washington, 1981).

P. F. Clarke, 'Liberals, Labour and the franchise', *English Historical Review* 92 (July 1977).

J. Davis, 'Slums and the vote, 1867–90', *Historical Research* 64, no. 155 (October 1991).

J. D. Fair, 'The second Labour government and the politics of electoral reform, 1929–1931', *Albion* 13, no. 3 (1981).

W. P. Grant, 'Electoral reform and local government', in S. E. Finer (ed.), *Adversary Politics and Electoral Reform* (London, 1975).

M. Hart, 'The Liberals, the war and the franchise', *English Historical Review* 97 (October 1982).

J. C. Robertson, 'The British general election of 1935', *Journal of Contemporary History* (1974).

M. Steed, 'The evolution of the British electoral system', in Finer (ed.), *Adversary Politics and Electoral Reform*.

J. Turner, 'The Labour vote and the franchise after 1918: an investigation of the English evidence', in P. Denley and D. Hopkin (eds.), *History and Computing* (Manchester, 1987).

e) Relating to women and the Labour Party

M. J. Buhle, 'Gender and labor history', in J.Carroll Moody and A. Kessler-Harris (eds), *Perspectives on American Labor History: The Problem of Synthesis* (De Kalb, 1989).

M. Goot and E. Reid, 'Women: if not apolitical, then conservative', in J. Siltanen and M.Stanworth (eds), *Women and the Public Sphere: A Critique of Sociology and Politics* (London, 1984).

J. Hills, 'Women and voting in Britain', in Siltanen and Stanworth, *Women and the Public Sphere*.

Susan Kingsley Kent, 'Gender reconstruction after the First World War' in H. Smith (ed.), *British Feminism in the Twentieth Century* (Aldershot, 1990).

Susan Kingsley Kent, 'The politics of sexual difference: World War I and the demise of British feminism', *Journal of British Studies* 27, no. 3 (July, 1988).

Manchester Women's History Group, 'Ideology in bricks and mortar: women's housing in Manchester between the wars', *North West Labour History* 12 (1987).

A. Phillips and B. Taylor, 'Sex and skill: notes towards a feminist economics', *Feminist Review* 6 (1980).

M. Pugh, 'Domesticity and the decline of feminism, 1930–1950', in Smith (ed.), *British Feminism in the Twentieth Century*.

J. Rasmussen, 'Women in Labour: the flapper vote and party system transformation in Britain', *Electoral Studies* 3, no. 1 (1984).

M. Rendel, 'The contribution of the Women's Labour League to the winning of the franchise', in L. Middleton (ed.), *Women in the Labour Movement* (London, 1977).

H. Smith, 'Sex vs. class: British feminists and the labour movement, 1919–1929', *The Historian* 47 (1984).

P. Thane, 'The women of the British Labour Party and feminism, 1906–1945', in Smith (ed.), *British Feminism in the Twentieth Century*.

f) Local and comparative studies of working-class politics from other countries

A. Bridges, 'Becoming American: The working classes in the United States before the Civil War', in I. Katznelson and A. R. Zolberg, (eds.), *Working-Class Formation: Nineteenth Century Patterns in Western Europe and the United States* (Princeton, 1986).

I. Katznelson, 'Working-class formation: constructing cases and comparisons', in Katznelson and Zolberg (eds), *Working-Class Formation*.

B. Nelson, 'The uneven development of class and consciousness', *Labor History* 32 (1991).

M. Shefter, 'Trade unions and political machines: the organization and disorganization of the American working class in the late nineteenth century', in Katznelson and Zolberg (eds), *Working-Class Formation*.

S. Wilentz, 'Against exceptionalism: class consciousness and the American labor movement, 1790–1920', *International Labor and Working-Class History* 26 (1984).

A. R. Zolberg, 'How many exceptionalisms?', in Katznelson and Zolberg (eds), *Working-Class Formation*.

Summary of events, 1918–1939

1918

Dec.   General election, Dec. 14; results declared, Dec. 28; Tories won 10 out of 11 seats in Liverpool, Scotland division won unopposed by T. P. O'Connor for the Irish Nationalists; Labour put up 7 candidates; best result, 36% in Edge Hill.

1919

Jan.   Formby Lancs. and Yorks. Railway Co. electric powerhouse men on strike, disrupting suburban rail services, Jan. 2–8. Samuel Gompers, leader of the American Federation of Labor, arrived in Liverpool at start of tour, Jan. 17. Raid on suspected Sinn Fein base in Liverpool, Jan. 14; mass meeting held to demand release of Irish political prisoners, Jan. 19.

Apr.   Dock labourers in Liverpool and district on strike over starting-hours provisions of recent national settlement, Apr. 22–6. Demobbed unemployed soldiers staged protest march to Town Hall, Apr. 23.

May   Industrial dispute with workers at the Garston floating plant settled, important concessions won, May 23.

June   Race riots in Pitt St. area started, June 7; Charles Wooton drowned in Queen's Dock, 5 black people hospitalized; riots continued for over a week, with attacks on black houses, and 500 black people taken into police custody 'for their own safety'; 200 black people repatriated from Liverpool, 18 June. Ships' stewards' dispute, holding up Atlantic liners in the port, settled, June 12. Seven-week plumbers' strike in region, June–July. Strike of Mersey lightermen settled, with major concessions to the workers, June 19.

July   Strike over hours by floating plant workers employed by the Dock Board; spread to landing-stage hands and dockgatemen, leading to closure of the port on July 22; settled, 28 July, return to work the following day.

Aug.   Police strike began, Aug. 1; dreadnought and two destroyers stationed in the Mersey, Aug. 2; looting in London Road and Scotland Road and in Birkenhead, Aug. 2 and 3; rioter shot dead by soldier in Love Lane, Aug. 3; naval ratings used to guard docks, local railwaymen threatened sympathy strike, strike-breakers recruited after sacking of strikers, Aug. 4; trade-union delegates called for three-day local general strike in support of striking police, but threat never implemented, Aug. 14. Week-long strike by local bakers, Aug. 3–10.

Unofficial tram strike by Municipal Employees Assoc. over wages and hours; declared official by union, Aug. 6; settled, Aug. 8, services resumed following day. Protracted dispute over overtime working on the docks settled, Aug. 30, with victory for dockers in the form of a return to pre-war conditions.

Sept.   Four-month strike by moulders, Sept. 20–Jan. 22. Total railway strike, tunnel pumping staff called out; long-distance mail suspended; food-rationing introduced, dreadnought stationed in the Mersey, Sept. 29; university term postponed due to strike, Oct. 5; settled, Oct. 5, services resumed next day.

Oct.   British troops involved in Russian Civil War landed at Liverpool, Oct. 5. Frank Hodges, Secretary of the Miners' Federation of Great Britain, spoke at Sun Hall, and later addressed Liverpool Chamber of Commerce advocating nationalization of the mines, Oct. 27.

Nov.   First municipal elections after World War I, Nov. 1; Labour contested 18 seats, won 10; gained 36% of all votes cast, 47% in seats it contested; net gain of 10 seats. Labour gains also in Birkenhead, Bootle and Wallasey. Violent clashes at meeting of Middle Classes' Union in Picton Hall, Nov. 10. Joiners' union imposes embargo in protest against co-partnership scheme introduced at Lever Bros. Port Sunlight works.

1920

Jan.   Dockers' claim for 16*s.* per day minimum wage presented, Jan. 1; court of enquiry decided in workers' favour, Mar. 31; agreement signed, May 6. J. H. Thomas, MP and railwaymen's union leader, addressed local members defending settlement of previous year's strike, Jan. 18. Troopship 'Teutonic' held up in port by stoppage of crew over dissatisfaction with their accommodation, Jan. 21.

Mar.   Seafarers' Joint Council demanded 48-hour week for mariners and the abolition of Asiatic labour.

Apr.   Protest against holding of Irish political prisoners in Wormwood Scrubs led in Liverpool by P. J. Kelly; dock strike called in support of prisoners, Apr. 29, some ships held up, but strike petered out after three days.

May   Work-to-rule by Liverpool railwaymen adopted in early May to support claims over wages and hours; called off, June 3. Liverpool Master Builders' Association expelled from National Federation of Building Trades' Employers for granting unauthorized wage increase to local workers, May 7.

June   Strike of warehouse workers and clerks at Lever Bros. works, Port Sunlight; arbitration agreed, June 12; final settlement, June 18. Wireless operators' strike held up Atlantic liners in Liverpool, June 21–3.

July   Merseyside Council of Centre Liberals formed to act as representatives of coalition Liberalism. Black riot in Soho St. area, July 23, one man shot dead, three wounded, many arrested.

Aug.   Liverpool labour organizations declared opposition to war with Russian revolutionary government and supply of arms to Poland; local Council of Action formed, Aug. 17. Ten-week shipwrights' strike in Liverpool and district; started in Aug., settled, Nov. 6. Dr Mannix, radical Archbishop of Sydney and supporter of Irish independence, prohibited from landing at Liverpool by British government; violent clashes at the landing stage, Aug. 9. Liverpool and district printers' strike caused local newspapers to suspend publication from Aug. 28; TUC mediation resulted in settlement on Sept. 18, and return to work two days later.

Sept.   Summer time extended for one month owing to threatened coal strike.

Oct.   National coal strike from Oct. 18; restrictions on coal sales and use of gas and electricity introduced locally; liners held up in the Mersey, Oct. 22; normal conditions restored, Nov. 8. Threatened strike by Liverpool carters averted by last-minute negotiations, Oct. 25–30.

Nov.   Municipal elections, Nov. 1; Labour contested 21 seats, won none; gained 25% of all votes, 32% in seats it contested; no change in overall number of seats held by Labour; Irish Nationalists gained 4 seats; Labour gains in Bootle. Sinn Fein supporters caused 17 fires in Liverpool warehouses and timber yards, Nov. 27, man shot dead while helping police with their enquiries.

Dec.   Local shipyard joiners on strike for over eight months, with over 2,000 stopping work from Dec. 1, settled, Aug. 1921. Burton W. Eills appointed Chairman of Liverpool Liberal Federal Council, Dec. 3.

<h2 style="text-align:center">1921</h2>

Jan.   Sinn Fein explosives seized in raid on house in Edge Hill, Jan. 3. Ernest Bevin advocated unions merging to form the TGWU at meeting in Liverpool Stadium, Jan. 23. Riot outside council meeting in Birkenhead called to consider problem of unemployment, Jan. 31.

Feb.   Demonstration to demand action on unemployment, Feb. 15; mass meeting at Stadium demanded work or maintenance for the unemployed, Mar. 1. Home Secretary forbids reinstatement of 1919 police strikers by Liverpool Watch Committee, Feb. 24.

Mar.   Liverpool Trades Council and Liverpool Labour Party merged to form the Liverpool Trades Council and Labour Party (LTCLP). Farm fires at Roby and Crosby started by Sinn Fein activists, Mar. 9–10, several arrests.

Apr.   National coal strike from Apr. 1; local rail services reduced, Apr. 6; restrictions on use of electricity introduced locally, Apr. 15; local tram service reduced, Apr. 16; ferry services reduced, Apr. 27; further reductions up to May 9; services began to be reinstated from June 13. Liverpool trawler crews on strike over wage reductions, Apr. 19–20.

May   Ships' stewards on strike over wage reductions; liners held up in port from May 10; strike crumbled from May 18, when two vessels sailed with complement of stewards; return to work, June 3. Several houses in south end of the city set on fire by Sinn Fein supporters, May 15.

June   F. W. Keating appointed Catholic Archbishop of Liverpool, June 13. Conference of farmers and employees agreed wage reduction for agricultural labourers in Liverpool district, June 16. P. J. Kelly arrested in London after addressing meeting of the Irish Self-Determination League, June 25; Trafalgar Square demonstration of 15,000 demanded his release from Scotland Yard; released after two days.

Sept. Lord Mayor received unemployed delegation on Town Hall balcony, riotous scenes below, Sept. 7; Walker Art Gallery occupied by demonstration of 400 to protest against unemployment; police made baton charges, over 100 arrested, Sept. 12. Dispute over use of oxyacetylene burners being used to cut ships' plates; workers on strike, Sept. 29–Oct. 11.

Oct. Sinn Fein arms and ammunition seized in raid on house in Bootle, Oct. 15. Lightning strike overnight by bakers in Liverpool; settled in workers' favour same night, Oct. 31.

Nov. Municipal elections; Labour contested 21 seats, won 2; gained 27% of all votes, 35% in seats it contested; net loss of 4 seats. Unemployed staged demonstration during two minutes' silence at the Armistice Day celebrations, Nov. 11. Resolution by Sir Archibald Salvidge, Liverpool Tory leader, in support of Irish peace negotiations, carried at conference of National Unionist Association held in Liverpool, Nov. 17.

Dec. Liverpool supporters of Ulster Protestants at a meeting in Sun Hall denounced proposed settlement in Ireland, Dec. 8.

1922

Jan. Liverpool dockers agreed to merge with TGWU, Jan. 12. First meeting to consider construction of Catholic Cathedral in Liverpool, Jan. 17. AEU rejected agreement with employers over overtime and management procedures, Jan. 27; lock-out began, Mar. 10; other unions in engineering trade rejected same agreement; locked out, Apr. 25; over 10,000 workers idle on Merseyside; other unions settled on June 6, AEU accepted terms on June 13. Merseyside slaughtermen on strike from Jan. 29; transport workers asked to assist, Feb. 11.

Apr. Many arrests after police raids on Liverpool's Chinatown seeking opium-smokers, Apr. 17.

July Threatened carters' strike over wages in Liverpool averted by mediation of Lord Mayor. Printing trade dispute over wage reductions; Typographical Association rejected decision of Industrial Court in favour of employers' case, July 20; Liverpool printers on strike from July 24, but newspaper production not halted; strike crumbled through August, wage cuts eventually accepted. Protestant demonstration in St George's Hall, July 24.

Sept. Amalgamation of unions to form NUGMW advocated by J. R. Clynes at meeting in Picton Hall, Sept. 3. Wage cuts for dockers agreed after negotiations, Sept. 25; 1*s.* per day reduction from Oct. 1, and further 1*s.* from following June.

Oct. Mrs Snowden, wife of future Labour MP Philip Snowden, addressed Liverpool meeting of the Women's Citizen's Association, Oct. 3.

Nov. Municipal elections; Labour contested 18 seats, won 1; gained 29% of all votes, 34% in seats it contested; net loss of 9 seats. General election, Nov. 15; Tories won all seats in Liverpool apart from Scotland division, which was retained unopposed by T. P. O'Connor; Labour put up 6 candidates, best results in Edge Hill and W. Toxteth, with 40% of the vote.

Dec. Liverpool contingent of the NUWM set out to join the Hunger March to London, Dec. 2.

Jan. D. G. Logan, Irish Nationalist councillor for Scotland S. ward, defected to the Labour Party. Munitions seized in raid on house in Saltney St., three arrested, Jan. 9. Butchers at Liverpool abattoirs on strike, supported by Birkenhead carcass-men from Jan. 22, settled Jan. 27.

Mar. Labour won its first parliamentary seat in Liverpool in a by-election in Edge Hill division, Mar. 6; J. H. Hayes won, with 53% of the vote. Irish deportees, including 25 from Liverpool, sent to Ireland via Liverpool, Mar. 11; local deportees released and returned to Liverpool, May 18. Dock strike averted by decision of dockers to accept reduced wages for night work, Mar. 22. Boilermakers' lock-out began, Apr. 30, involving 600 in Liverpool district; some workers still idle at the end of the year.

June Carters accepted wage cuts, last-minute compromise offer averting strike, June 3. T. P. O'Connor, MP, addressed Liverpool meeting setting up Irish Democratic League to take the place of the United Irish League, June 17.

July Liverpool and Birkenhead dockers on unofficial strike against wage reduction from July 5; some strikers began to return to work from July 11; employers threatened import of strike-breakers from July 17; strike collapsed, July 19. Building and cabinet-making trade strike in Liverpool district averted by last-minute settlement, July 21. A. A. David appointed Anglican Bishop of Liverpool, July 26.

Nov. Municipal elections; Labour contested 19 seats, won none; gained 25% of all votes, 31% in seats it contested; no change in overall number of seats held.

Dec. General election, Dec. 6; Tories retained 7 seats in Liverpool, but lost Wavertree and West Derby to the Liberals; J. H. Hayes retained Edge Hill for Labour, with 57% of the vote, and T. P. O'Connor returned unopposed in Scotland division. L. D. Holt elected leader of Liberal group in council, Dec. 31.

1924

Jan. Railway strike by ASLEF members; Cheshire lines almost closed down, Mersey Tunnel services reduced, Wallasey ferry service reduced due to lack of coal, shortage of house coal across city. Austin Harford resigned as leader of Irish Party, Jan. 28; P. J. Kelly elected as his successor, Feb. 4.

Feb. National dock strike from Feb. 16, also supported by warehousemen in Liverpool; national officials accepted settlement, Feb. 21; warehousemen returned to work, Feb. 22, but Liverpool dockers stayed out; eventually accepted terms and returned to work, Feb. 26. Protestant demonstration in Picton Hall condemned alleged ritualistic innovations at Anglican Cathedral in Liverpool, Feb. 18.

Apr. Sack and bag workers in Liverpool on strike, Apr. 7–May 12. Shipyard lock-out on Merseyside, in support of unofficial strike at Southampton, Apr. 12–23. Coalheavers' dispute over night work settled, Apr. 14.

May Labour gained W. Toxteth division from the Tories in by-election, May 22; J. Gibbins won, with 54% of the vote. 2,000 local bricklayers and masons went on strike from May 31; became national strike, with 150,000 out, on July 7; government enquiry reported that attitude of Liverpool operatives was one barrier to peace in the industry; strike settled, Aug. 22, work resumed, Aug. 25.

July   P. J. Kelly called meeting of Irish Party and Labour Party to discuss electoral pact, July 5; eventually rejected by Labour, Aug. 24. Scalers' wage dispute settled by arbitration, July 25, narrowly averting dock strike in Liverpool.

Aug.   Liverpool dockers refused to handle fruit cargoes in support of fruit porters' dispute in Covent Garden, London, Aug. 18.

Sept.   Meeting at Stadium to protest Ulster boundary addressed by several Ulster MPs, Sept. 17.

Oct.   General election, Oct. 29; Tories regained Wavertree and West Derby from Liberals, but Labour retained Edge Hill and W. Toxteth, and T. P. O'Connor returned unopposed in Scotland division.

Nov.   Municipal elections; Labour contested 24 seats, won 7; gained 39% of all votes, 41% in seats it contested; net gain of 5 seats; Labour defeated Irish Party in 4 out of 5 direct confrontations, P. J. Kelly lost his seat in Scotland South ward. Protest against alleged ritualistic character of the service at St Stephen the Martyr led to riot and arrests, Nov. 15. Six-month boilermakers' strike ended with return to work in local shipyards, Nov. 26.

1925

Jan.   Mersey bargemen on strike over worsening work conditions; settled by compromise over manning levels, Jan. 31–Feb. 13.

Mar.   Harry Pollitt, leading member of the Communist Party and secretary of the National Minority Movement, kidnapped at Edge Hill station on his way to address meeting at the Stadium, Mar. 14; British Fascists denied involvement; 6 Liverpool men arrested, Mar. 19; Pollitt addressed meeting after his release, Mar. 22; all 6 accused acquitted, Apr. 23. J. H. Hayes, MP for Edge Hill division, appointed Labour whip in Parliament, Mar. 16. Liberal split in city council; Sir Max Muspratt and 5 other Coalition Liberals resigned whip and pledged general support to the Tories, Mar. 16. Co-op. employees in Garston and Birkenhead locked out over dispute with management, Mar. 30–Apr. 3.

June   7,500 carters on strike over 2s. per week wage cut, June 1–3.

Aug.   Council of Action set up in readiness for expected miners'/general strike, Aug. 8. Sailings from Liverpool to Dundalk and Newry suspended due to industrial disputes, Aug. 15–Sept. 3. Irish Party became the Catholic Party, encouraged by support of Archbishop Keating. Seamen in Liverpool belonging to the AMWU on strike over wage cut from Aug. 24; NSFU members forbidden by their officials to support strike; Emmanuel Shinwell came to Liverpool to organize strike, but Shipping Federation refused to negotiate and AMWU defeated, Sept. 21.

Sept.   Affray by Chinese seamen on board SS Cyclops in Queen's Dock, Sept. 7; numerous injuries and arrests. Labour meeting in Picton Hall, due to be addressed by MPs J. R. Clynes and Will Thorne, broken up by 'extremists', Sept. 28. New Trades and Labour Hall opened in Walton by Geo. Lansbury, MP, Sept. 29. Labour Party annual conference held in Liverpool; Communists banned from membership of the party, Sept. 29; Communism denounced by Ramsay Macdonald in speech, Sept. 30.

Oct.   Sir Archibald Salvidge presented with Freedom of the City, Oct. 12.

Nov. Dr Mannix, Archbishop of Melbourne, who had been barred from entering Liverpool in 1920, addressed Irish meeting at St Martin's Hall, Nov. 1. Municipal elections, Nov. 2; first time that ministers of religion could stand as candidates; Labour contested 27 seats, won 4; gained 36% of all votes, 38% in seats it contested; net gain of 4 seats, but lost 3 out of 4 direct confrontations with Catholic Party, including Scotland N. to a Catholic priest. Labour leader W. A. Robinson not re-elected as alderman, replaced by Catholic Party leader P. J. Kelly, who was not a member of the council, Nov. 9; Tories and Liberals abstained on vote.

Dec. Catholic Party changed name to Centre Party.

1926

Feb. Coalition Liberals who had left Liberal Party previous year formally joined Tory Party in the council.

Mar. Canal workers in Ellesmere Port on strike from Mar. 1. Liverpool women's suffrage meeting addressed by Viscountess Rhondda, Mar. 9.

Apr. Tory leaders Salvidge and White, and Protestant leader Longbottom, successfully sued Labour leader W. A. Robinson for libellous election leaflet, Apr. 27.

May General Strike; 100,000 workers called out locally on May 4; most local members supported strike, apart from tramwaymen and power workers and NUGMW members in Bootle; the NSFU refused to allow its members to join strike, taking out a court injunction to restrain them; strike run locally by Merseyside Council of Action; little sign of weakening by strikers before the TUC called it off on May 12, but some engineers and railway clerks were reported to be drifting back to work; many were still on strike up to May 18, and flour-millers only returned to work on May 25.

June Liverpool dockers rejected proposal to decasualize dock labour, June 26.

July Liverpool officials of the NSFU dismissed for supporting the General Strike, July 21.

Sept. J. Havelock Wilson, leader of the NSFU, entertained in Liverpool by the Lord Mayor in connection with the Industrial Peace Union, Sept. 3. Some building workers on strike over the use of building materials that they were boycotting, Sept. 14–28.

Oct. Miners' leader A. J. Cook addressed meetings in Liverpool and Bootle, appealing for support for striking miners.

Nov. Municipal elections; Labour contested 31 seats, won 7; gained 45% of all votes, 47% in seats it contested; net gain of 6 seats.

1927

Mar. Women's Conservative Club opened in Tuebrook, first outside London, Mar. 12.

May Liverpool Co-operative Society voted in favour of political alliance with Labour Party.

June   A. J. Cook addressed meeting in Liverpool opposing the Trade Disputes and Trade Union Bill, June 22.

Nov.   Municipal elections; Labour contested 34 seats, won 13; gained 44% of all votes, 46% in seats it contested; net gain of 6 seats.

1928

Jan.   Philip Snowden, former Labour Chancellor of the Exchequer, guest at Liverpool Chamber of Commerce lunch, Jan. 20.

Feb.   Tory Lord Mayor Margaret Beavan presided over conference of NW Maternity and Child Welfare Association in Liverpool.

Mar.   Liverpool Communist Jim Morton, who had accepted offer by Lady Astor to view conditions in Russia at her expense, died in Leningrad. First elections in newly incorporated Croxteth ward, Mar. 21.

May   Strike by hotting lads at Cammell Lairds shipyard in Birkenhead seriously curtailed rivetting work, May 1–8. Mayor Margaret Beavan denounced for giving Fascist salute and meeting Mussolini during official visit to Italy, May 30.

June   Mayor Beavan officially opened work on new Liverpool maternity hospital, June 21. Taxi drivers at Liverpool landing stage withdrew cabs in protest at competition from Corporation bus service, June 30.

July   Riot in Lime Street following Orange Order march, July 12.

Aug.   Dr Richard Downey succeeded Keating as Catholic Archbishop of Liverpool.

Oct.   Archbishop Downey called meeting to forge Catholic unity over municipal politics, Oct. 19; 5 Centre Party candidates for municipal elections withdrew their nominations, conceding to Labour Party candidates, Oct. 25.

Nov.   Municipal elections; Labour contested 32 seats, won 15; gained 47% of all votes, 47% in seats it contested; net gain of 11 seats.

Dec.   Tory leader Archibald Salvidge died, Dec. 11.

1929

Jan.–Oct.   Various meetings held to discuss possible amalgamation of Merseyside boroughs; opposed by Labour Party and eventually abandoned.

Jan.   Sir Thomas White elected leader of Tory Party in council, Jan. 7.

May   Building trades dispute settled with new three-year agreeement, averting all-out strike, May 24. General election, May 30, first since equalization of men and women's franchise; Tories retained 6 seats in Liverpool, but Labour won 4, gaining Everton and Kirkdale from the Tories and retaining Edge Hill and W. Toxteth; T. P. O'Connor again unopposed in Scotland division.

July   Inter-union disputes on Liverpool docks caused three-day stoppage, July 1–3. Strike by workers on New Brighton pier prevented opening in 1929. Margaret Bondfield, Minister of Labour in Labour government, paid visit to Liverpool, July 6.

Aug.–Nov.   4 Centre Party councillors converted to Labour, including Lawrence King and P. J. Kelly.

Oct.   Talking-film projectionists on strike, two cinemas closed, Oct. 25.

Nov.   Municipal elections, Nov. 1; Labour contested 38 seats, won 20; gained 52% of all votes, 52% in seats it contested; net gain of 13 seats. 7 new Labour aldermen elected on the council, Nov. 9. Death of T. P. O'Connor, Irish Nationalist MP for Scotland division since 1885.

Dec.   Liverpool Public Assistance Committee held first meeting, taking over duties previously administered by Poor Law Guardians. D. G. Logan returned unopposed for Labour in Scotland division by-election caused by the death of T. P. O'Connor.

1930

Feb.–May   Catholic Cathedral dispute; decision to sell Brownlow Hill workhouse site to Catholic Church split Labour Group, Feb. 5; Catholic councillors' refusal to sign new standing orders binding them to decisions of the LTCLP led to their expulsion, Mar. 24; Labour NEC enquiry instituted, effectively supported rebels, Apr. 18; Labour Group reunited May 2.

June   Catholic demonstration on St George's Plateau against Labour government's Education Bill, June 22; crowd of 150,000 claimed by organizers.

July   Elijah Sandham, Labour MP for Kirkdale, criticized sobriety and morality of MPs during speech to ILP conference in Manchester, July 26; censured by Commons' Committee of Privileges for 'gross libel'.

Oct.   ILP-dominated Edge Hill Divisional Party expelled from the LTCLP as a result of its criticism of the handling of the Cathedral dispute; reinstated, Apr. 1931.

Nov.   Municipal elections; Labour contested 33 seats, won 7; gained 35% of all votes, 37% in seats it contested; net loss of 7 seats.

1931

Feb.   Death of Margaret Beavan, Feb. 22.

Aug.   Meat porters at Liverpool abattoir staged unsuccessful strike over wage reductions, Aug. 13–21. Proposed cuts to overhead railwaymen's wages rejected by NUR, but members voted to reopen negotiations and settled for compromise, Aug. 19–28.

Oct.   General election, Oct. 27; Tories won 10 seats in Liverpool, gaining Edge Hill, Everton, Kirkdale and West Toxteth from Labour; only Scotland division retained by Labour.

Nov.   Municipal elections; Labour contested 31 seats, won 5; gained 35% of all votes, 36% in seats it contested; net loss of 10 seats.

1932

Jan.   Strike by Birkenhead dockers following nationally agreed wage reductions, Jan. 4; Ernest Bevin intervened to force acceptance, Jan. 10.

Sugar cargoes diverted from London due to lighterage dispute on Thames, loaded at Liverpool docks, Feb. 10. NUWM-led resistance to eviction of unemployed tenants in Bootle resulted in riot, Feb. 23; 21 arrested.

July   Sectarian disorder; St Bernard's RC church attacked, windows smashed at Liverpool Cathedral, July 14.

Sept.   Speke incorporated into City of Liverpool, added to Garston ward. Unemployed riots in Birkenhead, Sept. 15–18; further riots in Islington Square, Liverpool, Sept. 21.

Nov.   Municipal elections, Nov. 1; Labour contested 33 seats, won 16; gained 46% of all votes, 47% in seats it contested; net loss of 3 seats.

1933

May   Slaughterhouse workers at Stanley Cattle Market staged successful strike against wage cuts.

June   Dockers at Princes Dock held unofficial strike in support of Irish seamen on Liverpool/Ireland cargo routes, who were resisting wage cuts, June 28–July 5.

July   1,100 Garston dockers on strike, objecting to foremen being members of the union, July 17–Aug. 6.

Sept.   Local trade-union leaders entertained by Lord Mayor at luncheon in Town Hall, Sept. 22.

Nov.   Municipal elections; Labour contested 29 seats, won 14; gained 47% of all votes, 48% in seats it contested; net gain of 7 seats.

1934

Feb.   Workers at Walker's Dairies on strike over management attempts to restrict trade-union activities by NUDAW.

May   Sir Oswald Mosley addressed Fascist meeting in Liverpool Stadium, many clashes with anti-Fascist demonstrators on streets, May 6.

July   Workers at Donegal Tweed tailoring workshop in Fleet Street, Liverpool, on strike over victimization of union member; all strikers reinstated and Tailors' and Garment Workers' Union recognized officially by management, July 5–7.

Sept.   Clan Line sailings transferred from Birkenhead to Liverpool as a result of unofficial overtime ban on night shift at Birkenhead docks, Sept. 30.

Nov.   Municipal elections; Labour contested 32 seats, won 19; gained 43% of all votes, 47% in seats it contested; net gain of 14 seats; first elections since redistribution of wards in Birkenhead, Labour making 7 gains.

Dec.   Workers at British Enka artificial silk works in Aintree on strike against wage cuts; cuts withdrawn.

Feb.   Labour gained Wavertree division from the Tories at by-election, Feb. 6; Randolph Churchill standing as an Independent Conservative split the Tory vote, and J. J. Cleary won with 35% of the vote.

Mar.   Sir Oswald Mosley addressed Fascist meeting in city, riotous scenes on streets, Mar. 9.

July   Labour gained W. Toxteth division from the Tories at by-election, July 16; J. Gibbins regained his seat with 61% of the vote. Workers at Howard Ford and Co. hosiery works in Woolton on strike over management attempts to restrict trade-union activity by NUGMW.

Nov.   Municipal elections; Labour contested 33 seats, won 15; gained 48% of all votes, 50% in seats it contested; net loss of 1 seat. General election, Nov. 14; Labour gained Everton division from the Tories, retained Scotland and W. Toxteth, but lost Wavertree; all other seats retained by Tories.

1936

Jan.   Education Bill proposed grants of 50–75% for building or alteration of Church schools to facilitate development of secondary education; local Catholic church voiced opposition on the grounds that grants would be insufficient and would increase council control over Church schools; some Nonconformists also opposed, as subsidy to Church schools.

Mar.   Mosley addressed Fascist meeting, widespread protests, Mar. 2.

Apr.   Labour split in council over grant to Mothers' Welfare Clinic giving contraceptive advice, Apr. 1; Bessie Braddock supported grant, Luke Hogan opposed.

June   Bessie Braddock censured by the LTCLP for criticizing prominent right-wing Labour figures in a public speech.

July   Maternity and Child Welfare Conference held in Liverpool, Bessie Braddock being the main local organizer.

Aug.–Sept.   Series of Protestant attacks on Labour Party meetings in St Domingo Pit; meetings banned by Chief Constable, Aug. 26–8; culminated in riot, with 21 arrests, Sept. 23.

Aug.   A. Gates succeeded B. W. Eills as leader of Liberal Party in council.

Oct.   Fascist meeting in Stadium resulted in riots, Oct. 11.

Nov.   Municipal elections; Labour contested 35 seats, won 11; gained 39% of all votes, 41% in seats it contested; net loss of 3 seats.

Dec.   Death of P. J. Kelly, Dec. 1.

1937

Jan.   Lawrence King elected as alderman in place of the late P. J. Kelly, the first Labour alderman to be elected since 1931.

Feb.   Herr von Ribbentrop, German Ambassador, visited Knowsley as guest of Lord Derby, Feb. 18.

June–July Council discussion of grants for secondary schools under 1936 Education Act; Labour Party proposed maximum 75% grant for Catholic schools; precipitated Tory/Protestant election campaign against 'Rome on the rates' in 1937 and 1938.

June Basque children refugees from Spanish Civil War arrived in Liverpool and Birkenhead, June 18–25. Ribble motor services drivers and conductors in Liverpool area on strike over new working conditions, June 26–30.

Oct. Maternity and Child Welfare Centre opened in Walton, Oct. 5, Bessie Braddock centrally involved in project. Oswald Mosley struck on head by brick during Fascist demonstration at Queen's Drive, Walton, Oct. 10; held in Walton Hospital until Oct. 16.

Nov. Municipal elections; Labour contested 36 seats, won 12; gained 37% of all votes, 38% in seats it contested; net loss of 7 seats.

1938

Jan. Death of Sir Thomas White, Jan. 25. A. E. Shennan elected as leader of the Tory Party in the council, Feb. 4.

Feb. New Liverpool headquarters of NUS opened in Canning Place by Sir Walter Citrine, TUC secretary, Feb. 3.

Mar. Bessie Braddock censured by LTCLP for speaking on public platform with NUWM.

June Death of Mary Bamber, June 4.

Nov. Last municipal elections before World War II; Labour contested 35 seats, won 10; gained 36% of all votes, 36% in seats it contested; net loss of 5 seats.

Dec. Death of Sir James Sexton, Dec. 27.

1939

Jan. IRA explosion damaged electricity pylon in Crosby, Jan. 16; bomb exploded at Walton gaol, Feb. 6; various raids on houses for explosives, several arrests made, Jan. 23–Feb. 4. Meeting protesting Irish immigration to Liverpool organized by Tory councillors, Jan. 19; Revd H. D. Longbottom protested at Irish workers being employed in aircraft factory in Speke, claimed 'Rome behind it', Jan. 23; disturbance in Bootle at anti-Catholic street meeting, speaker arrested, Feb. 4. NUWM demonstration in Birkenhead led to clashes with police Jan. 20; NUWM held lie-down demonstrations in Lime Street and Rimrose Road, Bootle, Jan. 24.

May Dispute over grants for secondary schools finally resolved by compromise, whereby council agreed to build 15 schools and lease them to the churches.

Index

References to the appendices are indicated in bold type.

412

414